PELICAN BOOKS

A 763

THE PACIFIST CONSCIENCE

Peter Mayer was born in London in 1936. His family emigrated to the United States when he was three and he was naturalized an American citizen in 1947. He was educated at Columbia College and Christ Church, Oxford. In 1956 he went to sea and spent the following year in Spain. He returned to the States in 1958 and took up a Graduate Fellowship at Indiana University, moving to Germany in 1959 when he was awarded a Fulbright Fellowship to the Freie Universitat in West Berlin.

Peter Mayer is now Editor-in-Chief of a New York publishing company.

THE PACIFIST
CONSCIENCE

EDITED BY PETER MAYER

PENGUIN BOOKS

Penguin Books Ltd, Harmondsworth, Middlesex, England
Penguin Books Pty Ltd, Ringwood, Victoria, Australia

—

First published in the U.S.A. by Holt, Rinehart & Winston 1966
Published in Great Britain by Rupert Hart-Davis 1966
Published in Pelican Books 1966

—

Copyright © Peter Mayer, 1966

—

Made and printed in Great Britain by
Cox & Wyman Ltd,
London, Fakenham and Reading
Set in Monotype Bembo

This book is sold subject to the condition
that it shall not, by way of trade or otherwise,
be lent, re-sold, hired out, or otherwise circulated
without the publisher's prior consent in any form of
binding or cover other than that in which it is
published and without a similar condition
including this condition being imposed
on the subsequent purchaser

ACKNOWLEDGEMENTS

ALL possible care has been taken to obtain permission from the copyright holders to reprint selections protected by copyright; any errors or omissions are unintentional and will be corrected in any future printing upon notifying the editor, who wishes to express his gratitude for permission to reprint material from the following sources:

The Open Court Publishing Co., for selections from *The Canon of Reason and Virtue* by Paul Carus and 'The Sermon on Abuse' from *The Gospel of Buddha* by Paul Carus; Random House, Inc. and Michael Joseph Ltd, for selections from *The Wisdom of China and India*, edited by Lin Yutang, copyright 1942 by Random House, Inc.; Bayard Quincy Morgan, for his translation of selections from *The Adventurous Simplicissimus*; Paul R. Reynolds, Inc., for 'The Moral Equivalent of War' from *Memoirs and Studies* by William James, copyright 1911 by William James; Navajivan Trust, for portions of *Young India* Volume I, by M. K. Gandhi; Jonathan Cape Ltd, for selections from *Mars, Or The Truth About War* (1930) by Alain; Fellowship Publications, James Clark & Co. Ltd, Navajivan Trust, and Richard B. Gregg, for 'Moral Jiu-jitsu' from *The Power of Nonviolence,* copyright © 1935, 1939 by Richard B. Gregg; Otto Nathan, trustee, Estate of Albert Einstein, for Dr Einstein's letter to Sigmund Freud, 'Why War?', published by the International Institute of Intellectual Co-operation, Paris, 1933; Sigmund Freud Copyrights Ltd, for Dr Freud's letter to Albert Einstein, 'Why War?', published by the International Institute of Intellectual Cooperation, Paris, 1933; *The Christian Century*, for 'Why I Leave the F.O.R.' by Reinhold Niebuhr, copyright 1934 Christian Century Foundation, reprinted by permission from the 3 January 1934 issue of *The Christian Century*; E. P. Dutton & Co., Inc. and Curtis Brown Ltd, for 'Onward, Christian Soldiers' from *Peace With Honour* by A. A. Milne, copyright 1934 by A. A. Milne, renewal 1962 by Mrs Daphne Milne; Martin Buber and Harper and Row, Inc., for 'Letter to Mahatma Gandhi', parts of which appeared in *Pointing The Way*, edited and translated by Maurice Friedman, copyright © 1957 by Martin Buber; Vera Brittain for 'The Functions of a Minority' from *Humiliation with Honour* (1943); Dwight Macdonald, for 'The Iliad, a Poem of Force' by Simone Weil from *Politics* magazine, copyright 1945 by Politics Publishing Company; Simon & Schuster, Inc. and George Allen & Unwin Ltd, for 'Man's Peril' from *Portraits From Memory* by Bertrand Russell, copyright 1951, 1952, 1953, © 1956 by Bertrand Russell, and 'Inconsistency?' from *Common Sense and Nuclear Warfare* by Bertrand Russell, copyright © 1959 by George Allen & Unwin, Ltd; Pendle Hill Pamphlets and the author, for excerpts from 'Of Holy Disobedience' by A. J. Muste; *Peace News* and War

Resistors' International for 'Pacifism Under the Occupation' by Diderich Lund; Fellowship Publications, for 'We Challenged Jim Crow' by Bayard Rustin and George Houser; *The Catholic Worker,* for 'The Pope and Peace' by Dorothy Day; Orion Press, Inc., and Macgibbon & Kee Ltd, for excerpts from *Outlaws* by Danilo Dolci, © 1961, The Orion Press, Inc.; *The Christian Century,* for 'Pilgrimage to Nonviolence' by Martin Luther King, Jr., copyright 1960, Christian Century Foundation, reprinted by permission from the 13 April and 27 April 1960 issues of *The Christian Century*; Simon and Schuster, Inc., and Brandt & Brandt, for 'A Pagan Sermon to the Christian Clergy' by C. Wright Mills from *The Causes of World War Three,* © 1958, 1960 by C. Wright Mills; Dwight Macdonald, for 'Neither Victims Nor Executioners' by Albert Camus from *Politics* magazine, copyright 1947 by Politics Publishing Company; George Allen & Unwin Ltd, for portions from *Perpetual Peace* by Immanuel Kant, translated by M. Campbell Smith.

to my grandfather
OTTO GRUNDMANN
with love and
respect

CONTENTS

CONTENTS

CONSCIENTIOUS OBJECTION

CHRISTIAN PACIFISM
AND NONVIOLENCE TODAY

CONCLUSION

INTRODUCTION

W A R and violence, it has been said, are as old as mankind. The vision of
peace is perhaps as old as civilization. Since the most ancient times, as
techniques of mass killing have mounted from the sling and the spear to
the cannon, Gatling gun and the supersonic missiles outfitted to kill
whole cities, there have been voices counselling an alternative way.
These are the voices of the pacifist conscience – seldom heeded, yet
perennially posing a choice for each generation. Historically, it was
usually in turbulent times that men's thoughts turned most to peace,
and such a time is the present.

The terms in which the choice is set before us today are by no means
simple and easy. The use of violence in the resolution of differences has
implications which were never more frightening. Total destruction is
now a practical possibility. We have two objects: we must find adequate ways of making peace and we must learn to achieve social goals
without resorting to violence. The existence of aggressive states and
inflexibly undemocratic societies requires us to act, for we would not
have them persist by default. The purpose of this anthology, then, is
not merely to display the peace classics of the ages in a congratulatory
spirit, but to show something of the variety of viewpoints and approaches in which the pacifist conscience has manifested itself and
hopefully to indicate new approaches. This means, in part, featuring
both the visionary and the pragmatic, the noble and the delusive. Often
the boundary lines are not clearly demarcated, and this too is part of the
legacy.

Much peace literature is what Edmund Burke called 'a commonplace
against war; the easiest of all topics'. What does the pacifist tradition
have to offer in addition to the indictment of war we have heard so
often? Since World War II the public, with the general acquiescence of
pacifists themselves, has understood pacifism to mean the absolute
refusal to participate in, or support in any way, the waging of war. This
hard-core definition is not without semantic merit and it makes for an
identifying strand connecting the early Christian martyrs with the
conscientious objectors of today. It does not, however, exhaust the
peace tradition. Clearly within it, to mention only two examples, are

the non-violent struggles taking place for Negro rights in the United States (and in Africa as well, under Albert Luthuli's direction) and the Ban-the-Bomb and disarmament movements. We cannot ignore the many broadly conceived testimonies and plans for peace which happen to lack absolutist credentials and yet are far from being mere common-places. The distinction between the strict interpretation and the broad tradition emerges if we study the history of the peace proposition. Once largely inspired by religious principle, it is equally motivated by humanistic considerations today, while continuing to discover its sources largely in the religious texts of the past.

We find an early testimony of such ideas three to six centuries before the birth of Christ in the disorder of ancient China, in the writings of Lao-Tzu, Confucius, Mencius, and Motse. None have their pacifist credentials in what purists would call impeccable order, yet each questioned the need or validity of violence and warfare. Each moved beyond a simple acceptance of human conflict, and enunciated principles that are at least proto-pacifist in their direction and intent. One of the earliest of these writers is the Chinese Taoist philosopher Lao-Tzu (c. sixth century B.C.). In the quietism of this philosophy, as we understand its main current in Lao-Tzu's *Tao Teh Ching*, military institutions are recognized; the Tao, or Way, comprehends them, but it becomes quite clear that force is not the Tao. Lao-Tzu counsels restraint and acquiescence to the courses of nature. Water is his most frequently used metaphor – water, that most yielding of substances that can wear down the hardest. Confucius (551–479 B.C.) in his *Analects* taught that peace lay in social equilibrium, and his doctrine of *jen* (sympathy) was based on a hierarchic Golden Rule – treat your subordinates as you would be treated by your superiors. Mencius (371–288 B.C.), Confucius' interpreter, also believed in right conduct in a world of men and laws. He reasoned that selfishness was due to a lack of material security and misrule. Motse (468–401 B.C.) proposes a positive Love as a more radical position. In his writings, *Mo Tzu*, he argues against offensive war, while devoting considerable attention to defensive measures. A record of sorts is beginning to be written, a tradition established against the awful necessity of violence. In some instances, as with Motse, for example, the makers of this early record are of interest as unexpected precursors to better-known thinkers whose beliefs, often more clearly formulated, were to arise in different parts of the world. Motse's almost theistic teaching of all-embracing Love resembles that of Jesus, and it is augmented by a version of the Golden Rule that is much more utilitarian in tone:

> The world's leaders have no idea of what is for their own profit. . . . Those who love others will be loved in return. Do good to others and others will do good to you. Hate people and be hated by them. Hurt them and they will hurt you. What is hard about that?
>
> *Mo Tzu*, XV

It is also worth noting that Motse's advanced proposition proved too hard for ancient China. After two centuries it vanished, yielding to Confucian conservatism, and has only been exhumed in recent times.

The East of this early period offered the pacifist conscience example to support text. In the third century B.C., Asoka, the great Buddhist ruler, forswore conquest for proselytism. He sought to convert all those within his realm, but not by the sword. His actions are as much part of the heritage as such Buddhist texts as the *Dhammapada* and even the legends that sprang up around Gotama himself.

A work occupying the same exalted position in Hindu as the Gospels in Christian literature, and which has been influential in the thought of at least one great pacifist of our time is the *Bhagavad-Gita*. Part of the great epic the *Mahabharata*, its date of 'composition' has been usually set around 200 B.C. Mohandas K. Gandhi declared that it was one of the great spiritual influences in his life, but it has had various interpretations. The *Gita* recounts in dramatic dialogue the great fratricidal battle between the Kauravas and the Pandavas. Arjuna, the hero of the Pandavas, cannot bring himself to fight, but under the guidance of Krishna he succumbs. Krishna points out to him that it is his duty to fight but that he must do it not out of hatred nor in hope of any gain for himself. There is no such thing as death for one who has found his life in God. While Hindu orthodoxy may be correct in interpreting the *Gita* as a divine commandment to caste loyalty and killing, a sanctioning of warfare, Gandhi, who read the work in his maturity, saw in the *Gita*'s de-emphasis of self an allegory whose spirit suggested that of the Sermon on the Mount. Similar in so many ways to the *sense* of the *Tao Teh Ching*, the *Gita* led Gandhi in the direction of desirelessness; but the desirelessness Gandhi had in mind was not a state of indifference to evil in the world; it was action without regard to the fruits of action, conduct he felt must *succeed* in the world.

A century before Lao-Tzu and Confucius, the great Jewish prophet Isaiah, from strongly theistic and historical motives, depicted the reign of peace on earth in memorable terms and interpreted the evil of war in a didactic fashion as a chastisement for his people's moral failings. Despite such episodes of armed revolt as those led by the Maccabees and Bar Kokhba, and events of more recent times – the Warsaw Ghetto uprising and the war for Palestine in the forties – historic Judaism has been strongly marked by a tradition of peace and passivity under persecution, reflecting the impress of Isaiah and later prophets. Historical factors must certainly have contributed to this tradition. The Jewish historian Flavius Josephus in the first century A.D. recounts the non-violent resistance of the Jews to Roman defilation of the Temple. Here, as in other cases, we are sceptical as to whether non-violent principles informed their resistance or whether it was the requirements of the situation. But we do know of at least one Jewish group, the Essenes, who functioned in a strictly communitarian way, and whose nature was pacific on the basis of clearly articulated principles.

One of the strands of this tradition, breaking out of Judaism to form a new religion, was Christianity, whose scriptures abound in counsels of unselfish love, peace, non-resistance, and overcoming evil. The Sermon on the Mount has had a number of interpretations, but it is difficult to refute Jonathan Dymond, a Quaker writer of the eighteenth century, who, admitting to possible exceptions, insisted that whatever Christ spoke out against, he certainly never spoke out for force, and that therefore the sense of Christ's words was clear. Dymond wrote: '. . . for if we give to our objectors whatever license of interpretation they may desire, they cannot, without virtually rejecting the precepts, so interpret them as to make them allow War'.

The early Christian writers – Tertullian, Justin Martyr, Origen, Cyprian, Lactantius – insisted on the absolute incompatibility of Christ's teachings with warfare. It is hard to imagine a more blanket injunction on violence than the words of Lactantius who insisted it was un-Christian 'to accuse anyone of a capital charge, because it makes no difference whether you put a man to death by word, or rather by the sword, since it is the act of putting to death itself which is prohibited'. However, from the time of its *rapprochement* with the Emperor Constantine, the Church's attitude to war and peace became firmly established as that of the world. War was no longer inherently incompatible with the spirit of Christ, but it was sanctioned in circumstances which became more and more liberally interpreted. The story of the gradual accommodation of the Christian Church to the exigencies of power in the Roman Empire of Constantine, leading on to the Crusades against heretical Christians and men of other religions is too familiar to need retelling here.

The earliest Christians – pacifists by all accounts, who, as Jesus had done, would rather let themselves be killed than resort to arms – were part of a tradition now carried on by heretical sects like the Albigensians and in Catholic monastic orders like the Friars Minor, founded by Francis of Assisi. To these groups who at this time sustained the Christian witness against war, we add the Waldensians and the Bohemian (or Moravian) Brethren. The Waldensian Church is of some special interest, for it sprang from lay roots. Originally followers of Pierre Waldo, the humble 'poor men of Lyons' had as part of their discipline the refusal to bear arms. Although non-resistance was not consistently maintained by later generations, it has never ceased to be a factor giving a pacifist tinge to this group. But neither was it consistently maintained in any of these churches, for at different periods in the history of each, certain parties felt compelled to resist the civil power. Purity of intention did not, of course, exempt any group from the claims of this world; in a sense each was caught up in a dilemma as old as Christianity itself. The Bohemian Brethren arose out of a schism that took place in the ranks of Jan Hus' followers after his death in 1415. The most radical group recognized Peter Chelčický (Peter of Chelcic) as their leader. Much of their doctrine anticipated Tolstoy's later writings, and he refers to Chelčický in *The Kingdom of God is Within You*. The Brethren gave a literal interpretation to the Sermon on the Mount, called for a return to the simple teachings of Christ and his Apostles and denounced war.[1]

The background of the pacifist conscience was amplified in the fifteenth century by the humanism of Erasmus. He and other 'Catholic humanists' of the Renaissance argued for peace on largely secular rational grounds rather than on a strict interpretation of the Gospel. No pacifist in the absolute sense, Erasmus – particularly for his eloquent

1. A classic pacifist work, *The Angel of Peace*, was written by the bishop of the Brethren in a later period, John Amos Comenius (1592–1672), who held the Brethren together after their virtual extinction in the Thirty Years War. *The Angel of Peace* was written in 1667, in Holland where Comenius found refuge, and addressed to 'The Peace Ambassadors of England and the Netherlands in Breda'. It is an incredible document to us today, for in it Comenius speaks to the representatives of a diplomatic congress in theological language. And in fact the assembled peacemakers paid little attention to the work.

Complaint of Peace and *Antipolemus* – must be considered among the strong early influences on peace activity. In spite of his religious orientations his writings were the first great humanistic attacks in the West on the divine right of kings and nations to involve their subjects in bloodshed.

In the Reformation there are indications that the early writings of both Luther and Calvin leaned toward pacifism; *The Complaint of Peace* was published in the same year as the ninety-five theses. We are often apt to think of a clean break between periods and the connexion is only useful in establishing a frame of reference. Luther, Calvin and other leaders, in fact, soon yielded to the exigencies of the moment. Pacifism was only one aspect of the ferment of the times, and a clearer pacifist witness was left to Conrad Grebel and the Swiss Brethren, and scattered groups among the Anabaptists. But it has been suggested that Erasmus exercised a strong and direct influence on the Anabaptists (cf. George Williams, *The Radical Reformation*), and it is likely that Erasmus and Grebel met in Basle in 1522. Savagely persecuted by Reformed and Catholic forces alike, these groups were decimated in the sixteenth and seventeenth centuries. In 1536 in Friesland, Menno Simons, a hitherto undistinguished priest, formally renounced the Roman communion and was baptized and later ordained into the non-resistant branch of the Anabaptists. Their history was one of persecution, not only by the Roman Catholic Church, but also by the established Protestant bodies. The reasons lie in the special testimony Menno Simons's followers brought against any union of the Church and State; they understood the doctrine of 'two worlds' to mean that there was one 'world', Caesar's, from which the Christian ought to keep aloof. Not only was the State to keep itself separate from the Church, but Christians were to conduct their lives in a manner completely removed from all affairs of State. Calling themselves Mennonites after their leader, later generations of Swiss and German Anabaptists were among the first settlers of Pennsylvania, a haven in the New World for many other persecuted peace sects. Among these were the Moravians, the Schwenckfelders, and a century later the German Baptists who today are known in America as the Church of the Brethren. Later waves of emigrants included the 'inspirationists' and millennialists who founded religious utopias based on peace, love, sharing, such as Ephrata, Harmony, and Amana. But of all the pacifist groups that flocked to Pennsylvania the best known was the Society of Friends, or Quakers, founded by George Fox, which arose in the context of the English Civil War under the Cromwell commonwealth about 1650.

The history of these two important churches merges somewhat after the American settlement. While the Quakers and the Mennonites made common cause on many issues, important differences were immediately apparent. Most of the sects mentioned previously which had perpetuated the tradition of Christianity's incompatibility with war from the sixteenth century on were of German origin and were characterized by a non-political point of view. The Quakers were English, and England in this period was beginning to develop a broader parliamentary tradition. The Quakers had the unusual and fortunate experience of attracting in their earliest years the attention of such prominent Englishmen as William Penn. The Quakers, much like the German groups, found their strength in following a simpler Gospel and returning to a purer Christianity. Where the Mennonites based their non-resistance and opposition to bearing arms on what they considered a purified doctrinal understanding of the New Testament, rather a literalistic chapter-andverse interpretation (even today they stress theological training and a church headed by a pastor), the Quaker emphasis initiated by Fox might be traced to the mystical emphases of the *devotio moderna*. Although equally concerned with recapturing the essence of the early, pre-Constantian Church, Fox and his followers were of a more spiritual bent, claiming direct access to the Holy Spirit. They had no clergy, and the individual conscience was held supreme as illumined by an 'inner light' representing 'that of God' in every man. Thanks to a royal grant of land to Penn, the Friends were given an unprecedented opportunity to try their hand at government. The outcome of the experiment in all its ramifications – particularly as a pioneering step in freedom of religion, for nowhere else was toleration so broad – has yet to be fully assessed.

From generation to generation, however, the pacifism of all these groups has undergone attrition, with increasing numbers of young Quaker, Mennonite, Brethren and other men accepting military service rather than registering as conscientious objectors. Yet within each of these denominations there continue to be eloquent and vigorous spokesmen for peace. Probably a large share of the Quaker witness is due to the influx of pacifists from Baptist, Lutheran, Jewish, and other churches which have been less hospitable to them. It is not to minimize the very real Quaker contribution to the pacifist conscience that we must also note that 'Quaker' and 'pacifist' are often unjustifiably equated in the public eye, partly as a convenient way of disposing of the pacifist implications of Christianity itself. Pacifism is only one of several distinguishing elements in Quakerism; it is traditional but not binding and many Quakers have gone to war without leaving the Society. Equally, the public has for many years remained generally unaware of other peace churches. This is largely traceable to the prominence Quakers have had in our society in contrast to the roles played by other sects. Where the attitude to the State is essentially negative in the case of the German peace churches, the attitude is positive with Quakers. From the first, Quakers took part in State matters: they entered the courts in defence of their liberties, held public office whenever permitted, and performed public service. The Quaker testimony against war, therefore, has always been limited by their concept of the State.

Except for William Penn, the dominant motif in the religious quest for peace, dating from the days of the early Church, was the refusal to bear arms. Roughly parallel with this line of development was another motif, concerned less with personal commitment than with altering the existing modes of statecraft to reduce or eliminate warfare. Although not necessarily lacking in religious inspiration, the emphases here are manifestly secular. As early as 1310, Dante in his *De Monarchia* proposed a universal federation – actually an empire – the peace of which would be guaranteed by one ruler. Other plans were drawn up by Marsilius of Padua, Abbé Honoré Bonnor, King George Podiebad of Bohemia, Erasmus, Cardinal Wolsey, but until 1623 most of these plans were not truly 'international' since they were calculated to guarantee the peace through the dominance of one ruler or state. The seventeenth and eighteenth centuries, however, saw a proliferation of genuine international proposals, in particular the five great peace plans of Emeric Crucé (1623, *The New Cyneas*), William Penn (1693, *Essay Towards the Present and Future Peace of Europe*), Saint-Pierre (1713, *Projet pour rendre la Paix perpetuelle*), Jeremy Bentham (1789, *Plan for an Universal and Perpetual Peace*), and Immanuel Kant (1795, *Perpetual Peace*).

The world was paying more attention in the eighteenth century to those internationalist proposals. Leibnitz had written to Saint-Pierre: 'I have read your work with close attention and cherish the conviction that such a project is not only possible of execution, but that its accomplishment would be of the most incalculable benefit to Humanity'.

A version of the *Projet* as edited by the better-known Rousseau soon became more famous than Saint-Pierre's original text.

Elements of the Enlightenment could be seen in Bentham's plan with its optimistic emphasis on public opinion as a guarantor of international law, and in Kant's great plan. In earlier works Kant had already pointed out the necessity for some sort of a general league, an organization of all nations which would guarantee perpetual peace. The logic of history would provide the impetus for such an organization. In *Perpetual Peace* Kant declared war to be mankind's natural state and peace the institution men must establish. He laid great stress on the constitution of this organization: it was to be republican in structure; international law was to be based on a federation of free states; and the organization was to bring about a condition of international citizenship for mankind as the inevitable result of mankind's adopting the principle of universal hospitality. Reason and logic were thus to bring about this league of nations; reason and logic were to implement it; reason and logic would guarantee its success.

The direction in which these plans were heading was what we call today internationalism. Proposals were being made for governments to concern themselves with peace-making machinery. Two years before Kant's *Perpetual Peace* appeared, the Negro astronomer Benjamin Banneker had suggested that the administration of George Washington establish a federal Peace Office, and in 1798 a Philadelphia practitioner, Dr Benjamin Rush, was more specific, proposing the appointment of a Secretary of Peace who would propagandize for war's abolition. Hymns and odes to peace were to be sung and recited throughout the country; exhibits clearly depicting the horrors of war were to tour the major cities; museums with similar displays were to be established. These proposals did not get very far in the Congress.

When David Low Dodge, a wealthy New York merchant, wrote and had printed in 1808 *The Mediator's Kingdom Not of This World*, he was actually only continuing the work of clergymen like William Ellery Channing and Noah Worcester who had for years previously been preaching sermons condemning war as un-Christian. Dodge's writings are remembered today for two reasons: they ushered in an era of intense peace pamphleteering and they coincided – not fortuitously, to be sure – with the establishment of the first peace societies. Pamphlets had been printed condemning war before, but Dodge's writing seems to have struck the right note; hundreds of pamphlets and tracts appeared, sermons and lectures were given in support of Dodge, in attack on his position, in amendment to it.

To Dodge, as well, goes the distinction of founding the first peace society, although the original idea was not his. Dr David Brogue, an English preacher, in 1813 was the first man to propose a peace society, and William Allen, a prominent English Quaker, in 1814 actually set about organizing one. The most famous of the early peace societies, the Massachusetts Peace Society of Channing and Worcester, was founded later, in 1815.

Merle Curti in *Peace and War* writes movingly of the pioneers in what was to become an international movement of impressive scope: of Dodge tucking 'peace tracts into the boxes of goods sent out from his storerooms'; of William Ladd who 'on the last lecture tour he made into the West in 1841, his legs . . . badly ulcerated . . . was forced to deliver his message sitting on stools in church pulpits . . .'; of Elihu Burrit organizing women and workmen on both sides of the Atlantic in the first peace demonstrations and international conferences, travelling 10,000 miles each winter speaking, writing, editing, exhausting himself for the young movement.

The peace activity of these formative years was amazing. In 1816 in England, William Allen finally founded his postponed Society for Permanent and Universal Peace, and, in the same year in America, Noah Worcester founded, edited, and published *The Friend of Peace*, the young movement's first periodical. In 1821 an organization which planned to work specifically 'for international peace' was established in France, and in 1830 another peace society was founded in Geneva. By 1825, on Devere Allen's count, there were twenty-five peace societies in the British Isles, by 1828, thirty-six in the United States, most of which merged on 8 May 1828 into the American Peace Society.

A major strength and weakness of the American peace movement throughout its history can be traced to this period. The different 'societies' within the larger national organization continued to speak out separately, even after the merger. In 1837, for example, it was the New York Peace Society, not the national organization, which petitioned the federal government to take the first steps towards calling a 'Congress of Nations'.

The first efforts of peace groups in any country to prevent a conflict took place between 1837 and 1846, prior to the United States war with Mexico. These efforts failed, although attempts to get both sides to arbitrate questions of claims and damages were more successful. A pacifist point of view had made itself felt in national politics. Pacifists filled mail sacks with protest letters to their representatives, and Senator Charles Sumner of Massachusetts, a pacifist himself, spoke long and passionately in Washington on the need to avoid armed conflict with Mexico.

In these years internationalism was hopefully equated by many pacifists with 'Christian non-resistance', a term which Adin Ballou for the first time systematically defined in 1846, the year in which war broke out, signalling the failure of pacifist efforts. It was in this period, too, that Emerson and Thoreau, both familiar with Eastern texts, spoke out and wrote against war. Emerson had delivered his famous lecture 'War' in 1838, and Thoreau, by the example he set, and in the writing of his *Essay on Civil Disobedience,* suggested a political instrument which might reconcile the desire for justice with the demands of conscience. The essay (given first as a lecture in 1848 and then entitled 'On Resistance to Civil Government') dealt with Thoreau's refusal to pay a poll tax which, he felt, indirectly supported the imperialist war in Mexico. Its importance was not fully appreciated until much later, but it is today in all likelihood the most influential text for the pacifist conscience after the Sermon on the Mount. Antigone, of course, had been civilly disobedient earlier, but less was made of her example.

The efforts of the peace societies in England and America, formed out of a religious awareness, directed their energies and funds largely towards liaison with peace societies in other countries. The first peace congress was the London Peace Conference of 1843, but there were many others in the next hundred years, and for all the efforts and failures of internationalism in this period, it was the internationalist point of view that captured the public's imagination – so much so that in 1945, after the greatest desolation any war has ever produced, the nations put their hopes once more in an international order.

Perhaps this great hope was attached to internationalism because it seemed an easier road to peace: government would legislate, international agreements would be made and ratified, and citizens would easily follow in the footsteps of their leaders; the virtues of peace were no longer being debated for war had become too terrible. Tolstoy in *The Kingdom of God Is Within You* had commented sarcastically on the results of the Congress of Peace in London in 1891. 'To preach the evil of war and the good of peace are so well known to men that, so long as we have known man, the best greeting has been, "Peace be with you." What need is there, then, in preaching?' But there was no peace. Post-war periods became pre-war periods.

The problems of international organization became increasingly complex in the late nineteenth and early twentieth century; the negotia-tions of governments could no longer be followed by the public; internationalism became the legitimate activity of the State and with that international meetings became an arena for the extension of nationalistic politics. Absolute pacifists objected to the principle of *international* force which ultimately would guarantee the peace; other critics of internationalism claimed it had failed to guarantee the peace *because* there was no international force. And in the midst of these controversies, internationalism became not an aspect of the pacifist attitude, but an entirely separate aspect in the public's mind.

That the peace movement permitted this erosion of its foundation did it no good; for internationalism (that aspect of peace activity which put its trust in agreements between nations) and absolute pacifism (that aspect which relied on a personal testimony against violence – individual *acts* of conscience) were the extremities of the peace proposition and should not have excluded each other. Adherents of each position came to distrust each other in the midst of virulent nationalism. Working to-gether, their peace activity might have borne more fruit, but such cooperation did not come about.

Control of the American Peace Society had by now gradually shifted to wealthy men like Andrew Carnegie, and this change did not en-courage a large or very vital membership. Another peace group, the Universal Peace Society, founded in 1866 by Arthur Love, came to an end in 1913 with the death of its founder. Although hardly a rival organization, it had moved boldly in such areas as disarmament and women's suffrage. The breach was partially filled by the founding in 1914 in England and in 1915 in America of the Fellowship of Reconcilia-tion (F.O.R.), a broadly Christian pacifist organization whose activities continue to this day. Co-equal and directly related to its pacifist principles, the F.O.R. stressed the social gospel in the early years; the managing editor of *The World Tomorrow*, the first F.O.R. publication, was Norman Thomas. In the thirties, however, a split took place in F.O.R. ranks when influential members like Reinhold Niebuhr left the organization maintaining that, while they would continue strenuously to oppose *war*, pacifism as the F.O.R. understood it could not be squared with a class struggle in which the use of violence might be justified. The broad spectrum of pacifist thought became particularly evident in this period and the years that followed. While some pacifists maintained that nothing new had changed the equation, others felt that genocide and the development of weapons of mass destruction had altered the whole meaning of war and violence.

The strict interpretation by the public – and later by pacifists themselves – of pacifism as the absolute refusal to participate in any war dates back to World War I. This interpretation is associated with two events of that period: national conscription in the various countries and the refusal of significant numbers of men to be conscripted. It is in this light that we are best able to understand the delimitation of the public pacifist concept. Before World War I, for example, members of the American Peace Society called themselves pacifists, but with their commitment to Wilson's policy, they relinquished the term, henceforth calling themselves internationalists. The term pacifism became firmly associated in the public mind with the absolute position, implying a personal refusal to fight. It is one of the hopes of the writer to restore the earlier and broader understanding.

But while pacifism was being forced to comprehend an increasing number of distinctions, events in South Africa and India had revealed another approach. The example of Mohandas K. Gandhi (1869–1948), born in India and trained in England as a lawyer, more than any other enlarged the perspectives of the pacifist tradition in the twentieth century. Gandhi extended Thoreau's position on the moral rightness of an individual's nonviolent protest until civil disobedience had been elevated to the level of group relations. The activities of the Congress of Racial Equality, of Diderich Lund during the Nazi occupation of Norway, of Danilo Dolci in Sicily with his 'strike in reverse', of Martin Luther King's 'pilgrimage to nonviolence', and of Chief Albert Luthuli's struggle for African freedom should all be understood as outgrowths from and adaptations of principles of Gandhian non-violence. It was only after reading the later work of Tolstoy, in particular Tolstoy's interpretations of the Sermon on the Mount, and finding his own understanding confirmed in the *Gita*,[1] that Gandhi came to the decision after years of reflection to use passive resistance, the term Gandhi first used in his work. (He later went to considerable trouble to

1. Gandhi found further confirmation of his ideas in the works of Ruskin and Thoreau.

dissociate the traditional meaning of passive resistance from *satyagraha*, his own word.)

Satyagraha is the term most closely connected with Gandhi's work, and has been generally translated as truth or soul force. Gandhi explained it in this way: 'Truth (*satya*) implies love, and firmness (*agraha*) engenders and therefore serves as a synonym for force. I thus began to call the Indian movement "satyagraha", that is to say, the Force which is born of Truth and Love or non-violence. . . .' It was a rigorous discipline, involving training of both body and mind. It was manifest in general strikes, fasts, boycotts, and civil disobedience, although Gandhi always maintained that numbers were not crucial; truth and strength of purpose were. Gandhi did not clearly examine the implications of *ahimsa*, or non-injury, the guiding principle of Gandhian protest movements. He understood it essentially in a physical sense. But the implications of a strike or a boycott can also be physical: the nonviolent refusal of farmers to bring their goods to market, or even to plant crops, would be an extreme provocation and would cause widespread misery. The emergence of Gandhi as a leader in South Africa and India, as a leader who could realize the programme of a people, and as a rallying symbol to people all over the world who were not 'non-resistants' but who refused to resist violently, indicated another heritage besides the Judaeo–Christian one known in the West. The importance of Richard Gregg's classic work, *The Power of Nonviolence* (1934), was Gregg's conviction that Gandhi's method had applicability in the West and that points of tangency could be indicated and a programme marked out which might work in other situations.

c.o.r.e. (the Congress of Racial Equality) was founded by a group of young people in Chicago in 1942, not as a pacifist organization, although its earliest organizational connexion was with the f.o.r., which is avowedly pacifist. The directorships of both organizations overlapped for a period. c.o.r.e. originated in 1941 in two memoranda which James Farmer, then an f.o.r. worker and now National Director of c.o.r.e., sent to A. J. Muste, then Executive Secretary of the f.o.r., proposing plans for 'Brotherhood Mobilization'. They stressed that, while the membership should be open to anyone interested in improving race relations, all members would be obliged to make a commitment to nonviolence. He correctly predicted that the role of pacifists (using the word in an absolute sense) in such an organization would necessarily be great from the outset. c.o.r.e. did not want to be dragged into an extended argument over the 'larger' issues when its own goals were so clear; its commitment to non-violence was and remains essentially one of method, in spite of the religious orientation of many of its founding members. The influence of Gandhi remains very great in the work of C.O.R.E. Its leaders have familiarized themselves with *satyagraha*-like techniques, but the influence of Gandhi became even stronger in the fifties with the rise to prominence of Dr Martin Luther King, Jr. Where C.O.R.E. consciously dissociated itself from the religious orientation of the F.O.R. – C.O.R.E.'s early and continuing effectiveness may possibly be traced to this – King and other Negro ministers accepted the religious commitment to nonviolence. Gandhi's words, 'the conquest of the adversary by suffering in one's own person', suddenly had enormous relevance in the United States, as Gregg had earlier understood that it could have. The Southern Christian Leadership Conference and other organizations initiated a disciplined training for thousands of young Negroes and whites of every background. These young people accepted foul jails when arrested on trumped-up charges; when beaten they sang 'We Shall Overcome'; and they spoke and acted Love. The training, while not ascetic in the Gandhian sense, was thorough in its emphasis on the *techniques* of nonviolence. The 1955–6 bus boycott in Montgomery, Alabama, attracted and held world-wide attention. Sit-ins, freedom rides, swim-ins . . . all of these activities were planned in detail and in most of them the participants remained strictly disciplined. In the few cases where violence did break out, it was often the result of inadequate planning.

It is well to remember here that the pacifist tradition, even when broadly interpreted, is full of contradictions. In this collection the editor has also selected those statements which do not precisely fit the tradition, and some that appear inconsistent viewed in an historical light. Martin Buber, for example, generally considered a Hebrew pacifist, replied in 1939 to Gandhi's suggestion to the German Jews – that they practise nonviolence to demonstrate their moral superiority over the Nazis – that in certain situations resistance with violence was inevitable and necessary, but that 'No one who counts himself in the ranks of Israel can desire to use force'. On the issue of a Jewish homeland and the probable necessity of fighting for it, Buber confronted Gandhi with his own words: 'Have I not repeatedly said that I would have India become free even by violence than that she would remain in bondage?'

Randolph Bourne in 'The War and the Intellectuals' bitterly complains in 1919 of the intellectuals who professed peace in time of peace but who supported war when it came; and in 1946 Albert Camus, who had fought in the war, wrote what is certainly one of the most stirring appeals to mankind to give up violence and to seek communication through a 'dialogue' – a Buberian concept – with other men. Albert Einstein, our century's most prominent pacifist, wrote in the summer of 1929: 'I believe in taking a holy oath never to participate in any act of violence.' In the late thirties, however, he was able to maintain his pacifism by stating that his early absolutism was an absolutism within a specific context, the conditions of which no longer obtained. Deluged by letters from unbelieving former admirers, he did not seem overly embarrassed. He took care to state his position, declaring always that he had never ceased to consider himself a pacifist. He continued to make his signature available to a great number of causes, now insisting that only in strong international organization could the peace be preserved. He had come very far from his emphasis on the personal act. And Freud, in his too little known exchange of letters with Einstein, could write of war in 1932: 'We cannot do otherwise than hate it. Pacifists we are, since our organic nature wills us thus to be.' Only a few lines above he had written: '. . . all forms of war cannot be indiscriminately condemned; so long as there are nations and empires, each prepared callously to exterminate its rival, all alike must be equipped for war.'

Randolph Bourne might rail with great justice at the faint-hearted pacifists of his time, as he would have done again during World War II; but absolute pacifism is hardly the attitude of the large number of people active in peace work, all those who are *actively* opposed to war as an instrument of national (but usually not international) policy and to violence as a means to an end.

We said at first that unclear boundary lines are part of the legacy. We know that there are and always have been more pacifists of expedience than of faith, people like Bertrand Russell who proclaim that they never were and are not now absolute pacifists, but who advocate or support a politics of peace because it is the only prudent politics in an age of potential total destruction. When Günther Anders wrote that the atom bomb cannot be considered a weapon since a weapon is a means to an end which ought to dissolve in that end, the end then surviving the means (obviously not the case with atomic weapons since the ends can no longer survive the means nor are there any ends that can justify the cost of the means), he presented in terms of logic the terrifying actualities of today and the necessity for new approaches. The old approaches, the conventional policies of nations over thousands of years – the policies of deterrent armaments – stand nakedly revealed as ineffectual, and the hope of their *ever* becoming effectual must be an even greater illusion in the nuclear age. The scientists inform us that the warning time in the event of a nuclear attack is less than thirty minutes. There is very little to be lost then by non-provocative approaches, and certainly not time. Those who reject the tradition of pacifism because it has deterred few wars should consider that deterrent armaments have also failed. Since might cannot in logic or morality establish right, we ought to look back over the pacifist tradition and search within it for new beginnings, no matter whether it is principle or expedience that recommend them. If others in our century have found new points to depart from, we may too.

The editor wishes particularly to thank, among those who helped him, A. J. Muste, Professor Roy Finch, and Richard Gregg for the many suggestions they made. A special note of thanks to Howard Greenfeld, who made it possible for this work to begin and to William Robert Miller, whose continued interest, encouragement, and advice have seen the book through to its conclusion.

N.Y. 1965

BACKGROUND

LAO-TZU

c. SIXTH CENTURY B.C.

THE history of 'The Old Philosopher' is clouded in mystery. It is thought he was a contemporary of Confucius; according to some records, they had a meeting. The *Tao Teh Ching*, which Lao-Tzu is reputed to have written, is, together with the *Book of Lieh-Tzu* and the writings of Chuang-Tzu, one of the three great classics of Taoism. New Testament associations have often been made with such lines as 'Requite hatred [*injury*: Waley] with virtue' (Carus). Whether the meaning is identical with Christ's injunction to 'turn the other cheek' is problematical, but many translators have felt this to be the case: Holmes Welch in *The Parting of the Way* lists at least fifteen parallels between the texts of the *Tao Teh Ching* and the New Testament.

There have been over forty translations of the work into English and there are over eighty different editions of the work in the 'original' Chinese. The Chinese scholar, H. A. Giles, has written that 'The Chinese themselves ... are almost unanimous in denying its authenticity'. But other scholars have felt that if there is one thing that is not ambiguous about the work, it is its authenticity.

The text invariably teaches inactivity, which seems to mean effortless action, an inactivity suggesting the patience of the ages as a concomitant to the achievement of an end. Non-assertiveness or non-contentiousness are helpful interpretations. While there are certain affinities in the text of the *Tao Teh Ching* with the Gandhian concept of non-violence, there can be no great textual reconciliation between Gandhi's views and such lines as 'He that works through violence may get his way; but only what stays in its place can endure' (Waley; Waley suggests mountains). Other parts of the text can be easily reconciled with Gandhian non-violence.

It is the whole spirit of contentiousness which is opposed by the *Tao* ('The good are not contentious; the contentious are not good': Carus). Achievement must be through effortless action based on the way of Nature: 'The Heavenly Reason strives not, but it is sure to conquer. It speaks not, but it is sure to respond [*none the less to get an answer*: Waley]. It summons not, but it comes of itself. It works patiently, but is sure in its designs' (Carus).

The twisting, paradoxical nature of the work may also be seen in such lines confuting Confucianism as: 'Thus one loses Reason and then virtue appears. One loses virtue and then benevolence appears. One loses benevolence and then justice appears. One loses justice and then propriety appears. The rules of propriety are the semblance of loyalty and faith, and the beginning of disorder' (Carus). Or 'It is by not believing in people that you turn them into liars' (Waley).

These selections from the *Tao Teh Ching* are taken from *The Canon of Reason and Virtue* (1913) by Paul Carus. The lines quoted from Arthur Waley's translation are from *The Way and Its Power* (1958).

Taoist Non-Contentiousness

HUMILITY'S INCREASE

1. 'The crooked shall be straight,
   Crushed ones recuperate,
   The empty find their fill.
   The worn with strength shall thrill;
   Who little have receive,
   And who have much will grieve.'
2. Therefore
   The holy man embraces unity and becomes for all the world a model.
   Not self-displaying he is enlightened;
   Not self-approving he is distinguished;
   Not self-asserting he acquires merit;
   Not self-seeking he gaineth life.
   Since he does not quarrel, therefore no one in the world can quarrel with him.

NON-ASSERTION

1. When one desires to take in hand the empire and make it, I see him not succeed. The empire is a divine vessel which cannot be made. One who makes it, mars it. One who takes it, loses it.
2. And it is said of beings:
   'Some are obsequious, others move boldly,

Some breathe warmly, others coldly,
Some are strong and others weak,
Some rise proudly, others sneak.'

3. Therefore the holy man abandons excess, he abandons extravagance, he abandons indulgence.

BE CHARY OF WAR

1. He who with Reason assists the master of mankind will not with arms strengthen the empire. His methods invite requital.
2. Where armies are quartered briars and thorns grow. Great wars unfailingly are followed by famines. A good man acts resolutely and then stops. He ventures not to take by force.
3. Be resolute but not boastful; resolute but not haughty; resolute but not arrogant; resolute because you cannot avoid it; resolute but not violent.
4. Things thrive and then grow old. This is called un-Reason. Un-Reason soon ceases.

THE VIRTUE OF DISCRIMINATION

1. One who knows others is clever, but one who knows himself is enlightened.
2. One who conquers others is powerful, but one who conquers himself is mighty.
3. One who knows contentment is rich and one who pushes with vigour has will.
4. But only what stays in its place can endure.[1]
5. One who may die but will not perish has life everlasting.

FORGETTING KNOWLEDGE

1. He who seeks learnedness will daily increase. He who seeks Reason will daily diminish. He will diminish and continue to diminish until he arrives at non-assertion.
2. With non-assertion there is nothing that he cannot achieve. When he takes the empire, it is always because he uses no diplomacy. He who uses diplomacy is not fit to take the empire.

1. I have preferred Waley's translation of this line [P.M.].

CONSIDER BEGINNINGS

1. Assert non-assertion.
   Practise non-practice.
   Taste the tasteless.
   Make great the small.
   Make much the little.
2. Requite hatred [*injury* : Waley] with virtue.
3. Contemplate a difficulty when it is easy. Manage a great thing when it is small.
4. The world's most difficult undertakings necessarily originate while easy, and the world's greatest undertakings necessarily originate while small.
5. Therefore the holy man to the end does not venture to play the great, and thus he can accomplish his greatness.
6. Rash promises surely lack faith, and many easy things surely involve in many difficulties.
7. Therefore, the holy man regards everything as difficult, and thus to the end encounters no difficulties.

MIND THE INSIGNIFICANT

5. Therefore the holy man desires to be desireless, and does not prize articles difficult to obtain. He learns, not to be learned, and seeks a home where multitudes of people pass by.
6. He assists the ten thousand things in their natural development, but he does not venture to interfere.

PUTTING ONESELF BEHIND

1. That rivers and oceans can of the hundred valleys be kings is due to their excelling in lowliness. Thus they can of the hundred valleys be the kings.
2. Therefore the holy man, when anxious to be above the people, must in his words keep underneath them. When anxious to lead the people, he must with his person keep behind them.
3. Therefore the holy man dwells above, but the people are not burdened. He is ahead, but the people suffer no harm.
4. Therefore the world rejoices in exalting him and does not tire. Because he strives not, no one in the world will strive with him.

TRUST IN FAITH

1. In the world nothing is tenderer and more delicate than water. In attacking the hard and the strong nothing will surpass it. There is nothing that herein takes its place.
2. The weak conquer the strong, the tender conquer the rigid. In the world there is no one who does not know it, but no one will practise it.

MOTSE (or MO TI)

468–401 B.C.

THE ethical teachings of Motse are among the many teachings which for a time held considerable sway in China but did not survive the institutionalization of Confucianism under the Han emperors. Of all Chinese texts, those attributed to Motse (or his followers) most nearly approximate the teachings of Christianity. Although there is a clear distinction between offensive and defensive wars in Motse, which many pacifists do not recognize in the Christian canon, the emphasis everywhere in Motse's works is on peace, universal love, and the equality of all men before a Supreme Being.

While believing in a 'spirit world' he did not de-emphasize humanism, for he thought all institutions should be viewed in the light of their ability to promote the welfare of mankind. He was against the excesses of ritualism or ostentation, much as the Buddha had been in India somewhat earlier. There is an authoritarian strain in Motse as well, a sense of the crusading teacher, the evangelist. For a time the influence of Motse rivalled that of the Confucianists, and while it is not known exactly why Motse's teachings were almost totally neglected after the third century B.C., Lin Yutang has suggested that 'Quixotic heroism and extreme altruism did not appeal to the native Chinese common sense'.

The selections are taken from *The Works of Motse*, translated by Y. P. Mei, in the Modern Library edition, *The Wisdom of China and India* (1942), edited by Lin Yutang.

Universal Love

Motse said: The purpose of the magnanimous[1] is to be found in procuring benefits for the world and eliminating its calamities.

1. *Jen*, variously translated as 'benevolence', 'charity', 'love', 'kindness'. *Jenjen* philosophically means the 'true man' in Confucianism, and in general usage the 'good, kind man'. Throughout this translation the word 'magnanimous' refers to *jen*.

But what are the benefits of the world and what its calamities?

Motse said: Mutual attacks among states, mutual usurpation among houses, mutual injuries among individuals; the lack of grace and loyalty between ruler and ruled, the lack of affection and filial piety between father and son, the lack of harmony between elder and younger brothers – these are the major calamities in the world.

But whence did these calamities arise, out of mutual love?

Motse said: They arise out of want of mutual love. At present feudal lords have learned only to love their own states and not those of others. Therefore they do not scruple about attacking other states. The heads of houses have learned only to love their own houses and not those of others. Therefore they do not scruple about usurping other houses. And individuals have learned only to love themselves and not others. Therefore they do not scruple about injuring others. When feudal lords do not love one another there will be war on the fields. When heads of houses do not love one another they will usurp one another's power. When individuals do not love one another they will injure one another. When ruler and ruled do not love one another they will not be gracious and loyal. When father and son do not love each other they will not be affectionate and filial. When elder and younger brothers do not love each other they will not be harmonious. When nobody in the world loves any other, naturally the strong will overpower the weak, the many will oppress the few, the wealthy will mock the poor, the honoured will disdain the humble, the cunning will deceive the simple. Therefore all the calamities, strifes, complaints, and hatred in the world have arisen out of want of mutual love. Therefore the benevolent disapproved of this want.

Now that there is disapproval, how can we have the condition altered?

Motse said: It is to be altered by the way of universal love and mutual aid.

But what is the way of universal love and mutual aid?

Motse said: It is to regard the state of others as one's own, the houses of others as one's own, the persons of others as one's self. When feudal lords love one another there will be no more war; when heads of houses love one another there will be no more mutual usurpation; when individuals love one another there will be no more mutual injury. When ruler and ruled love each other they will be gracious and loyal; when father and son love each other they will be affectionate and filial; when elder and younger brothers love each other they will be harmonious. When all the people in the world love one another, then the strong will not overpower the weak, the many will not oppress the few, the wealthy will not mock the poor, the honoured will not disdain the humble, and the cunning will not deceive the simple. And it is all due to mutual love that calamities, strifes, complaints, and hatred are prevented from arising. Therefore the benevolent exalt it.

But the gentlemen of the world would say: 'So far so good. It is of course very excellent when love becomes universal. But it is only a difficult and distant ideal.'

Motse said: This is simply because the gentlemen of the world do not recognize what is to the benefit of the world, or understand what is its calamity. Now, to besiege a city, to fight in the fields, or to achieve a name at the cost of death – these are what men find difficult. Yet when the superior encourages them, the multitude can do them. Besides, universal love and mutual aid is quite different from these. Whoever loves others is loved by others; whoever benefits others is benefited by others; whoever hates others is hated by others; whoever injures others is injured by others. Then, what difficulty is there with it (universal love)? Only, the ruler fails to embody it in his government and the ordinary man in his conduct.[1]

Universal Love, II, Chapter 15.

Suppose a man enters the orchard of another and steals the other's peaches and plums. Hearing of it the public will condemn it; laying hold of him the authorities will punish him. Why? Because he injures others to profit himself. As to seizing dogs, pigs, chickens, and young pigs from another, it is even more unrighteous than to steal peaches and plums from his orchard. Why? Because it causes others to suffer more,[2] and it is more inhumane and criminal. When it comes to entering an-other's stable and appropriating the other's horses and oxen, it is more

1. Part of the second essay in *Universal Love*, of which there are three, with repetitions. Motse further proves his point by illustrations from ancient history and answers criticisms of Universal Love as 'impracticable', etc. The idea of Universal Love is closely connected with 'the will of Heaven' and is further developed all through Motse's works.

2. A clause seems to have been lost here, when we compare this sentence with the following sentences expressing the same meaning. The correct text here seems also to be, 'Because others are caused to suffer more: when others are caused to suffer more, it is more inhumane and criminal'

inhumane than to seize the dogs, pigs, chickens, and young pigs of another. Why? Because others are caused to suffer more; when others are caused to suffer more, then the act is more inhumane and criminal. Finally, as to murdering the innocent, stripping him of his clothing, dispossessing him of his spear and sword, it is even more unrighteous than to enter another's stable and appropriate his horses and oxen. Why? Because it causes others to suffer more; when others are caused to suffer more, then the act is more inhumane and criminal.

All the gentlemen of the world know that they should condemn these things, calling them unrighteous. But when it comes to the great attack of states, they do not know that they should condemn it. On the contrary, they applaud it, calling it righteous. Can this be said to be knowing the difference between righteousness and unrighteousness?

The murder of one person is called unrighteous and incurs one death penalty. Following this argument, the murder of ten persons will be ten times as unrighteous and there should be ten death penalties; the murder of a hundred persons will be a hundred times as unrighteous and there should be a hundred death penalties. All the gentlemen of the world know that they should condemn these things, calling them unrighteous. But when it comes to the great unrighteousness of attacking states, they do not know that they should condemn it. On the contrary, they applaud it, calling it righteous. And they are really ignorant of its being unrighteous. Hence they have recorded their judgement to bequeath to their posterity. If they did know that it is unrighteous, then why would they record their false judgement to bequeath to posterity?

Now, if there were a man who, upon seeing a little blackness, should say it is black, but, upon seeing much, should say it is white; then we should think he could not tell the difference between black and white. If, upon tasting a little bitterness one should say it is bitter, but, upon tasting much, should say it is sweet; then we should think he could not tell the difference between bitter and sweet. Now, when a little wrong is committed people know that they should condemn it, but when such a great wrong as attacking a state is committed, people do not know that they should condemn it. On the contrary, it is applauded, called righteous. Can this be said to be knowing the difference between the righteous and unrighteous? Hence we know the gentlemen of the world are confused about the difference between righteousness and unrighteousness.

Condemnation of Offensive War, I, Chapter 17.

Now, about a country going to war. If it is winter it will be too cold; if it is summer it will be too hot. So it should be neither in winter nor in summer. If it is spring it will take people away from sowing and planting; if it is autumn it will take people away from reaping and harvesting. Should they be taken away in either of these seasons, innumerable people would die of hunger and cold. And, when the army sets out, the bamboo arrows, the feather flags, the house tents, the armour, the shields, the sword hilts – innumerable quantities of these will break and rot and never come back. The spears, the lances, the swords, the poniards, the chariots, the carts – innumerable quantities of these will break and rot and never come back. Then innumerable horses and oxen will start out fat and come back lean or will not return at all. And innumerable people will die because their food will be cut off and cannot be supplied on account of the great distances of the roads. And innumerable people will be sick and die of the constant danger and the irregularity of eating and drinking and the extremes of hunger and over-eating. Then, the army will be lost in large numbers or entirely; in either case the number will be innumerable. And this means the spirits will lose their worshippers, and the number of these will also be innumerable.

Why then does the government deprive the people of their opportunities and benefits to such a great extent? It has been answered: 'I covet the fame of the victor and the possessions obtainable through the conquest. So I do it.'

Motse said: But when we consider the victory as such, there is nothing useful about it. When we consider the possessions obtained through it, it does not even make up for the loss. Now about the siege of a city of three *li* or a *kuo*[1] of seven *li* – if these could be obtained without the use of weapons or the killing of lives, it would be all right. But (as a matter of fact) those killed must be counted by the ten thousand, those widowed or left solitary must be counted by the thousand, before a city of three *li* or a *kuo* of seven *li* could be captured. Moreover the states of ten thousand chariots now have empty towns to be counted by the thousand, which can be entered without conquest; and their extensive lands to be counted by the ten thousand (of *mu*),[2] which can be cultivated without conquest. So, land is abundant but people are few. Now to pursue the people to death and aggravate the danger feared by

1. Outer city.

2. A *mu* is one sixth of an acre

both superiors and subordinates in order to obtain an empty city – this is to give up what is needed and to treasure what is already in abundance. Such an undertaking is not in accordance with the interest of the country. . . .

Condemnation of Offensive War, II, Chapter 18.

. . . What do I mean when I say people do not understand things of importance but understand trifles? Supposing someone entered the orchard and garden of another and took the other's peaches and prunes, melon and ginger, he will be punished by the superior when caught and condemned by the public when heard of. Why? Because he did not share the toil but takes the fruit and appropriates what is not his. How much more is this true with him who jumps over another's fence and maltreats the children of the other; of him who digs into another's storehouse and carries away the other's gold, jade, silk, and cloth; of him who breaks into another's fold and steals the other's oxen and horses; and of him who kills an innocent person? In the government of the lords of today all – from the one who kills an innocent person to the one who jumps over another's fence and maltreats the other's children, who digs into another's warehouse and carries away his gold, jade, silk, and cloth, who breaks into another's fold and steals his oxen and horses, and who enters another's orchard and garden and takes his peaches and prunes, melon and ginger, all these are punished quite the same as they would be even in the government of Yao, Shun, Yu, T'ang, Wen and Wu. Now the lords and chiefs in the world all attack and absorb others. This is a thousand times worse than killing one innocent individual, a thousand times worse than jumping over another's fence and maltreating his children or digging into another's storehouse and carrying away his gold, jade, silk, and cloth, a thousand and ten thousand times worse than breaking into another's fold and stealing his oxen and horses, or entering another's orchard and garden and taking his peaches and prunes, melons and ginger. Yet, they claim it to be righteous. . . .

The Will of Heaven, III, Chapter 28.

. . . Wu Matse said to Motse: 'Though you love universally the world cannot be said to be benefited; though I do not love (universally) the world cannot be said to be injured. Since neither of us has accomplished anything, what makes you then praise yourself and blame men?' Motse answered: Suppose a conflagration is on. One person is fetching water to extinguish it, and another is holding some fuel to reinforce it. Neither of them has yet accomplished anything, but which one do you value? Wu Matse answered that he approved of the intention of the person who fetches water and disapproved of the intention of the person who holds fuel. Motse said: (In the same manner) do I approve of my intention and disapprove of yours. . . .

Keng Chu, Chapter 46.

GOTAMA BUDDHA

c. 563-483 B.C.

ALTHOUGH such a wealth of flowery legend has sprung up around Gotama Buddha that it has become impossible to ascertain anything of his life with historical accuracy, no religion has committed itself more firmly to the way of non-violence than that which sprang from his teachings. Although Buddhism did not become as firmly established in its native India as in other Eastern countries, its influence there is unquestionably pervasive and permanent.

At a time when the Vedic religion had become enmeshed in priestcraft, metaphysics, and ritualism, the Buddha taught an ethics which was neither ascetic nor self-indulgent. Its cardinal principle was: 'A brother ought not intentionally to destroy the life of any being.' Two centuries later, Asoka, the great third-century Indian ruler, a convert to Buddhism, was to give up conquest to spread the Buddha's teachings as far as Egypt. Like the Buddha, he sought the Middle Way, a way which stressed gentleness, purity, and a concern for the needs of his fellow man.

The selections which appear below are taken from the *Dhammapada*, translated in 1872 by F. Max Müller. 'The Sermon on Abuse' is taken from *The Gospel of Buddha*, by Paul Carus, published in 1915.

A Refusal to Accept Anger

THE TWIN-VERSES

All that we are is the result of what we have thought: it is founded on our thoughts, it is made up of our thoughts. If a man speaks or acts with an evil thought, pain follows him, as the wheel follows the foot of the ox that draws the carriage.

All that we are is the result of what we have thought: it is founded on our thoughts, it is made up of our thoughts. If a man speaks or acts with a pure thought, happiness follows him, like a shadow that never leaves him.

'He abused me, he beat me, he defeated me, he robbed me' – in those who harbour such thoughts hatred will never cease.

43

'He abused me, he beat me, he defeated me, he robbed me' – in those who do not harbour such thoughts hatred will cease.

For hatred does not cease by hatred at any time: hatred ceases by love – this is an old rule.

The world does not know that we must all come to an end here; but those who know it, their quarrels cease at once.

PUNISHMENT

All men tremble at punishment, all men fear death; remember that you are like unto them, and do not kill, nor cause slaughter.

All men tremble at punishment, all men love life; remember that thou art like unto them, and do not kill, nor cause slaughter.

He who, seeking his own happiness, punishes or kills beings who also long for happiness, will not find happiness after death.

He who, seeking his own happiness, does not punish or kill beings who also long for happiness, will find happiness after death.

Do not speak harshly to anyone; those who are spoken to will answer thee in the same way. Angry speech is painful: blows for blows will touch thee.

If, like a shattered metal plate (gong), thou utter nothing, then thou hast reached Nirvāna; anger is not known to thee.

ANGER

Let a man leave anger, let him forsake pride, let him overcome all bondage! No sufferings befall the man who is not attached to name and form, and who calls nothing his own.

He who holds back rising anger like a rolling chariot, him I call a real driver; other people are but holding the reins.

Let a man overcome anger by love, let him overcome evil by good; let him overcome the greedy by liberality, the liar by truth!

Speak the truth; do not yield to anger; give, if thou art asked for little; by these three steps thou wilt go near the gods.

The sages who injure nobody, and who always control their body, they will go to the unchangeable place (Nirvāna), where, if they have gone, they will suffer no more.

Those who are ever watchful, who study day and night, and who strive after Nirvāna, their passions will come to an end.

This is an old saying, O Atula, this is not as if of today: 'They blame him who sits silent, they blame him who speaks much, they also blame him who says little; there is no one on earth who is not blamed.'

There never was, there never will be, nor is there now, a man who is always blamed, or a man who is always praised.

But he whom those who discriminate praise continually day after day, as without blemish, wise, rich in knowledge and virtue, who would dare to blame him, like a coin made of gold from the Gambū river? Even the gods praise him, he is praised even by Brāhman.

Beware of bodily anger, and control thy body! Leave the sins of the body, and with thy body practise virtue!

Beware of the anger of the tongue, and control thy tongue! Leave the sins of the tongue, and practise virtue with thy tongue!

Beware of the anger of the mind, and control thy mind! Leave the sins of the mind, and practise virtue with thy mind!

The wise who control their body, who control their tongue, the wise who control their mind, are indeed well controlled.

IMPURITY

He who destroys life, who speaks untruth, who in the world takes what is not given him, who goes to another man's wife; and the man who gives himself to drinking intoxicating liquors, he, even in this world, digs up his own root.

THE JUST

A man is not just if he carries a matter by violence; no, he who distinguishes both right and wrong, who is learned and guides others, not by violence, but by the same law, being a guardian of the law and intelligent, he is called just. . . .

. . . A man is not an elect (Ariya) because he injures living creatures; because he has pity on all living creatures, therefore is a man called Ariya. . . .

THE BRĀHMANA

. . . No one should attack a Brāhmana, but no Brāhmana, if attacked, should let himself fly at his aggressor! Woe to him who strikes a Brāhmana, more woe to him who flies at his aggressor!

It advantages a Brāhmana not a little if he holds his mind back from the pleasures of life; the more all wish to injure has vanished, the more all pain will cease.

Him I call indeed a Brāhmana who does not offend by body, word, or thought, and is controlled on these three points. . . .

. . . Him I call indeed a Brāhmana who, though he has committed no offence, endures reproach, stripes, and bonds: who has endurance for his force, and strength for his army.

Him I call indeed a Brāhmana who is free from anger, dutiful, virtuous, without appetites, who is subdued, and has received his last body. . . .

. . . Him I call indeed a Brāhmana who without hurting any creatures, whether feeble or strong, does not kill nor cause slaughter.

Him I call indeed a Brāhmana who is tolerant with the intolerant, mild with the violent, and free from greed among the greedy.

Him I call indeed a Brāhmana from whom anger and hatred, pride and hypocrisy have dropped like a mustard seed from the point of a needle.

Him I call indeed a Brāhmana who utters true speech, instructive and free from harshness, so that he offend no one.

Him I call indeed a Brāhmana who takes nothing in the world that is not given him, be it long or short, small or large, good or bad. . . .

THE SERMON ON ABUSE

And the Blessed One observed the ways of society and noticed how much misery came from malignity and foolish offences done only to gratify vanity and self-seeking pride.

And the Buddha said: 'If a man foolishly does me wrong, I will return to him the protection of my ungrudging love; the more evil comes from him the more good shall go from me; the fragrance of goodness always comes to me, and the harmful air of evil goes to him.'

A foolish man learning that the Buddha observed the principle of great love which commends the return of good for evil, came and abused him. The Buddha was silent, pitying his folly.

When the man had finished his abuse, the Buddha asked him, saying: 'Son, if a man declined to accept a present made to him, to whom would it belong?' And he answered: 'In that case it would belong to the man who offered it.'

'My son,' said the Buddha, 'thou hast railed at me, but I decline to accept thy abuse, and request thee to keep it thyself. Will it not be a source of misery to thee? As the echo belongs to the sound, and the shadow to the substance, so misery will overtake the evil-doer without fail.'

The abuser made no reply, and Buddha continued:

'A wicked man who reproaches a virtuous one is like one who looks up and spits at heaven; the spittle soils not the heaven, but comes back and defiles his own person.

'The slanderer is like one who flings dust at another when the wind is contrary; the dust does but return on him who threw it. The virtuous man cannot be hurt and the misery that the other would inflict comes back on himself.'

The abuser went away ashamed, but he came again and took refuge in the Buddha, the Dharma, and the Sangha.[1]

1. *Dharma*, the Law of the Path of Buddhist teachings; *Sangha*, the Buddhist Church. These, with Buddha, constitute the 'three refuges'.

TERTULLIAN

c.155–c.222

A CONVERT to Christianity in his late thirties, Quintus Septimus Florens Tertullianus is, after Augustine, generally considered the greatest of the early church writers in the West. Towards the end of his life he broke with the Catholic Church, cleaving to the teachings of the rigorously ascetic Montanist sect. At the time of writing *The Soldier's Chaplet*, Tertullian was already leaning in this direction, for the Montanists, while not directly impugning any particular Catholic doctrine, were putting into question with their 'New Prophecy' the very basis of Christian revelation and the hierarchic structure of the Church.

Although Tertullian sets out in his essay to defend the martyrdom of a Christian soldier who defied custom and the authorities by refusing to wear a laurel crown at an official ceremony, he soon broadens his concern by bringing up the question of whether it is at all permissible for a Christian to be a soldier:

> Shall it be held lawful to make an occupation of the sword, when the Lord proclaims that he who uses the sword shall perish by the sword? And shall the son of peace take part in the battle when it does not become him even to sue at law? And shall he apply the chain, and the prison, and the torture, and the punishment, who is not the avenger even of his own wrongs?

Tertullian indicates in this essay another tendency, one which was to become increasingly important with the rise of the historic Peace Churches of German origin: the conviction that not only was a Christian not permitted to enter military service, but he was likewise prohibited from assuming any civil offices.

The selections from *The Soldier's Chaplet* are taken from *The Writings of Tertullian* in the Ante-Nicene Christian Library.

The Soldier's Chaplet

Very lately it happened thus: while the bounty of our most excellent emperors was dispensed in the camp, the soldiers, laurel-crowned, were approaching. One of them, more a soldier of God, more steadfast than the rest of his brethren, who had imagined that they could serve two masters, his head alone uncovered, the useless crown in his hand– already even by that peculiarity known to everyone as a Christian – was nobly conspicuous. Accordingly, all began to mark him out, jeering him at a distance, gnashing on him near at hand. The murmur is wafted to the tribune, when the person had just left the ranks. The tribune at once puts the question to him, Why are you so different in your attire? He declared that he had no liberty to wear the crown with the rest. Being urgently asked for his reasons, he answered, I am a Christian. O soldier! boasting thyself in God. Then the case was considered and voted on; the matter was remitted to a higher tribunal; the offender was conducted to the prefects. At once he put away the heavy cloak, his dis-burdening commenced; he loosed from his foot the military shoe, beginning to stand upon holy ground; he gave up the sword, which was not necessary either for the protection of our Lord; from his hand like-wise dropped the laurel crown; and now, purple-clad with the hope of his own blood, shod with the preparation of the gospel, girt with the sharper word of God, completely equipped in the apostles' armour, and crowned more worthily with the white crown of martyrdom, he awaits in prison the largesse of Christ. Thereafter adverse judgements began to be passed upon his conduct – whether on the part of Christians I do not know, for those of the heathen are not different – as if he were headstrong and rash, and too eager to die, because, in being taken to task about a mere matter of dress, he brought trouble on the bearers of the Name – he, forsooth, alone brave among so many soldier-brethren, he alone a Christian. It is plain that as they have rejected the prophecies of the Holy Spirit, they are also purposing the refusal of martyrdom. So they murmur that a peace so good and long is endangered for them. Nor do I doubt that some are already turning their back on the Scrip-tures, are making ready their luggage, are equipped for flight from city to city; for that is all of the gospel they care to remember. I know, too, their pastors are lions in peace, deer in the fight. As to the questions asked for extorting confessions from us, we shall teach elsewhere. Now, as they put forth also the objection – But where are we forbidden to be crowned? – I shall take this point up, as more suitable to be treated of here, being the essence, in fact, of the present contention. So that, on the one hand, the inquirers who are ignorant, but anxious, may be in-structed; and on the other, those may be refuted who try to vindicate the sin, especially the laurel-crowned Christians themselves, to whom it is merely a question of debate, as if it might be regarded as either no trespass at all, or at least a doubtful one, because it may be made the subject of investigation. That it is neither sinless nor doubtful, I shall now, however, show.

Chapter 1

To begin with the real ground of the military crown, I think we must first inquire whether warfare is proper at all for Christians. What sense is there in discussing the merely accidental, when that on which it rests is to be condemned? Do we believe it lawful for a human oath to be superadded to one divine, for a man to come under promise to another master after Christ, and to abjure father, mother, and all nearest kinsfolk, whom even the law has commanded us to honour and love next to God Himself, to whom the gospel, too, holding them only of less account than Christ, has in like manner rendered honour? Shall it be held lawful to make an occupation of the sword, when the Lord proclaims that he who uses the sword shall perish by the sword? And shall the son of peace take part in the battle when it does not become him even to sue at law? And shall he apply the chain, and the prison, and the torture, and the punishment, who is not the avenger even of his own wrongs? Shall he, forsooth, either keep watch-service for others more than for Christ, or shall he do it on the Lord's day, when he does not even do it for Christ Himself? And shall he keep guard before the temples which he has renounced? And shall he take a meal where the apostle has forbidden him? And shall he diligently protect by night those whom in the day-time he has put to flight by his exorcisms, leaning and resting on the spear the while with which Christ's side was pierced? Shall he carry a flag, too, hostile to Christ? And shall *he* ask a watchword from the emperor who has already received one from God? Shall *he* be disturbed in death by the trumpet of the trumpeter, who expects to be aroused by the angel's trump? And shall the Christian be burned according to camp rule, when he was not permitted to burn incense to an idol, when to him Christ remitted the punishment of fire? Then how many other offences there are involved in the performances of camp offices, which we must hold to involve a transgression of God's law, you may see by a slight survey. The very carrying of the name over from the camp of light to the camp of darkness is a violation of it. Of course, if faith comes later, and finds any preoccupied with military service, their case is different, as in the instance of those whom John used to receive for baptism, and of those most faithful centurions, I mean the centurion whom Christ approves, and the centurion whom Peter instructs; yet, at the same time, when a man has become a believer, and faith has been sealed, there must be either an immediate abandonment of it, which has been the course with many; or all sorts of quibbling will have to be resorted to in order to avoid offending God, and that is not allowed even outside of military service; or, last of all, for God the fate must be endured which a citizen-faith has been no less ready to accept. Neither does military service hold out escape from punishment of sins, or exemption from martyrdom. Nowhere does the Christian change his character. There is one gospel, and the same Jesus, who will one day deny every one who denies, and acknowledge every one who acknowledges God – who will save, too, the life which has been lost for His sake; but, on the other hand, destroy that which for gain has been saved to His dishonour. With Him the faithful citizen is a soldier, just as the faithful soldier is a citizen. A state of faith admits no plea of necessity; they are under no necessity to sin, whose one necessity is, that they do not sin. For if one is pressed to the offering of sacrifice and the sheer denial of Christ by the necessity of torture or of punishment, yet discipline does not connive even at that necessity; because there is a higher necessity to dread denying and to undergo martyrdom, than to escape from suffering, and to render the homage required. In fact, an excuse of this sort overturns the entire essence of our sacrament, removing even the obstacle to voluntary sins; for it will be possible also to maintain that inclination is a necessity, as involving in it, forsooth, a sort of compulsion. I have, in fact, disposed of this very allegation of necessity with reference to the pleas by which crowns connected with official position are vindicated, in support of which it is in common use, since for this very reason offices must be either refused, that we may not fall into acts of sin, or martyrdoms endured that we may get quit of offices.

Chapter 11

Keep for God His own property untainted; He will crown it if He choose. Nay, then, He does even choose. He calls us to it. To him who conquers He says, 'I will give a crown of life.' Be *you*, too, faithful unto death, and fight *you*, too, the good fight, whose crown the apostle feels so justly confident has been laid up for him. The angel also, as he goes forth on a white horse, conquering and to conquer, receives a crown of victory; and another is adorned with an encircling rainbow (as it were in its fair colours) – a celestial meadow. In like manner, the elders sit crowned around, crowned too with a crown of gold, and the Son of Man Himself flashes out above the clouds. If such are the appearances in the vision of the seer, of what sort will be the realities in the actual manifestation? Look at those crowns. Inhale those odours. Why condemn you to a little chaplet, or a twisted headband, the brow which has been destined for a diadem? For Christ Jesus has made us even kings to God and His Father. What have you in common with the flower which is to die? You have a flower in the Branch of Jesse, upon which the grace of the Divine Spirit in all its fulness rested – a flower undefiled, unfading, everlasting, by choosing which the good soldier, too, has got promotion in the heavenly ranks. Blush, ye fellow-soldiers of his, henceforth not to be condemned even by him, but by some soldier of Mithras, who, at his initiation in the gloomy cavern, in the camp, it may well be said, of darkness, when at the sword's point a crown is presented to him, as though in mimicry of martyrdom, and thereupon put upon his head, is admonished to resist and cast it off, and, if you like, transfer it to his shoulder, saying that Mithras is his crown. And thenceforth he is never crowned; and he has that for a mark to show who he is, if anywhere he be subjected to trial in respect of his religion; and he is at once believed to be a soldier of Mithras if he throws the crown away – if he say that in his god he has his crown. Let us take note of the devices of the devil, who is wont to ape some of God's things with no other design than, by the faithfulness of his servants, to put us to shame, and to condemn us.

Chapter 15

DESIDERIUS ERASMUS

c.1466–1536

THE background of Erasmus, unquestionably the greatest humanist of the Renaissance, was theological. After entering a monastery, he was ordained a priest in 1492. He was, however, soon in rebellion against the disciplines of the Church and, from 1496 on, took pupils to support himself. Invited to England (1499–1500), he began there, under the influence of John Colet, to pursue the theological studies which were to be his lifework.

In 1504 his book *Enchiridion Militis Christiani* was published in Antwerp and in it he made his theological attitudes clear. He called for a return to the purity and simplicity of early Christianity, without, however, overtly attacking the ceremonialism in which he felt the Church had become enmeshed. His celebrated travels through Europe began approximately in this period, taking him to France, the Low Countries, Germany, England again, until he settled in Basle in 1521. These travels recall Mencius, who in the third century B.C. went from court to court in China, seeking to convert rulers to the way of benevolence. Erasmus, like Mencius, taught that war was not a natural prerogative of rule.

With the triumph of the Reformation, Erasmus left for Freiburg in 1529, where he remained until returning to Basle in 1535. In 1534–5 he refused a papal request to declare against the Reformation and upon his death he was neither confessed nor attended by a priest; his will left no monies for masses.

The two works of Erasmus which place him in the pacifist tradition are *Complaint of Peace* and *Antipolemus*, but a little known letter he wrote to Anthony a Bergis in 1513 also expresses his views on the subject. It is taken from a 1795 English edition entitled *Complaint of Peace*, translated by Vicesimus Knox.

Letter to Anthony a Bergis

Erasmus Roterodamus to Anthony a Bergis,
Abbot of St Bertin, sendeth health.

Most accomplished Father,

From the conversation of the bishop of Durham, and from my friend Andrew Ammonius the king's secretary, I have learned that you profess a warmth of affection for me which I may call paternal. It is this circumstance which makes me rejoice the more at the idea of returning to my country. I wish I possessed there an independent income, just enough to support me in a humble state of literary leisure. Not that I dislike England, or have any reason to be dissatisfied with the patronage of the Maecenas's, whom I have found in it. I have a great many intimate friends, and experience uncommon instances of kindness from many of the bishops. The archbishop of Canterbury fosters me with such peculiar affection, and embraces me with such cordiality, that he could not shew a greater love towards me if he were my brother or my father. I enjoy a little pension issuing from a living which he gave me, and allowed me to resign with an annuity out of it. My other Maecenas adds an equal sum out of his own purse; and many of the nobility contribute no inconsiderable addition to my income. I might have a great deal more, if I chose servilely to solicit or pay my court to great men, which I can by no means prevail upon myself to do.

But the war which is preparing, has altered the very temper and genius of this island. The price of every necessary of life increases every day, and the generosity of the people of course decreases. Indeed how can it be otherwise? People that are so often fleeced, must retrench in the liberality of their bounty. I assure you, I lately contracted a severe fit of the gravel, by being under the necessity of drinking bad beverage through the scarcity of good. Add to this, that as the whole island may be said, from the circumstance of its being surrounded by the sea, to be a place of confinement; so we are likely to be shut up still more closely by the wars. I see great commotions arising: whither they will tend, or how they will terminate, it is impossible to say. I only wish, God in his mercy would vouchsafe to still the raging sea which is agitating all Christendom.

I am often struck with astonishment and at a loss to account for the cause which can impel, I do not say Christians, but human creatures to such an extremity of madness and folly, as that they should rush head-long, with such ardour, at so great an expence of treasure, and with such dangers of every kind, to mutual destruction. For what is the business and chief concern of our whole lives, but to wage war with one another?

In the irrational part of the creation it is observable, that only those among the beasts who are called wild ever engage in war; and those not with one another, but with brutes of a different species; and they fight only with their own arms, the instruments of offence and defence supplied by nature. They do not attack with engines of destruction, invented by diabolical contrivance, nor on trifling causes and occasions, but either in defence of their young or for food. Our wars, for the most part, proceed either from ambition, from anger and malice, from the mere wantonness of unbridled power, or from some other mental distemper. The beasts of the forest meet not in battle array, with thousands assembled together and disciplined for murder.

To us, glorying as we do in the name of Christ, who taught nothing by his precept, and exhibited nothing in his example, but mildness and gentleness; who are members of one body, all of us one flesh, who grow in grace by one and the same spirit; who are fed by the same sacrament; who adhere to the same head; who are called to the same immortality; who hope for a sublime communion with God, that as Christ and the Father are one, so also we may be one with him; can any thing in this world be of such value as to provoke us to war? A state so destructive, so hideous, and so base, that even when it is founded on a just cause, it can never be pleasing to a good man. Do consider a moment, by what sort of persons it is actually carried into execution; by a herd of cut-throats, debauchees, gamesters, profligate wretches from the stews, the meanest and most sordid of mankind, hireling mankillers, to whom a little paltry pay is dearer than life. These are your fine fellows in war, who commit the very same villanies, with reward and with glory in the field of battle, which in society they formerly perpetrated, at the peril of the gallows. This filthy rabble of wretches must be admitted into your fields and your towns, in order that you may be enabled to carry on war: to these you must yourselves be in a state of subjection, that you may have it in your power to take vengeance of others in war.

Besides all this, consider what crimes are committed under the pretence of war, while the voice of salutary law is compelled to be silent amidst the din of arms; what plunder, what sacrilege, what ravages, what other indecent transactions, which cannot for shame be enumerated. Such a taint of men's morals cannot but continue its influence long after a war is terminated. Compute also the expence, which is so enormous, that even if you come off conqueror, you sit down with more loss than gain: though indeed, by what standard can you appreciate the lives and the blood of so many thousand human creatures?

But the greatest share of the calamities inseparable from a state of war, falls to those persons who have no interest, no concern whatever, either in the cause, or the success of the war: whereas the advantages of peace reach all men of every rank and degree. In war, he who conquers weeps over his triumphs. War draws such a troop of evils in its train, that the poets find reason for the fiction which relates, that war was brought from hell to earth by a deputation of devils.

I will not now dwell upon the picking of the people's pockets, the intrigues and collusion of the leading men, the vicissitudes of public affairs, which never can undergo violent revolutions without consequences of a most calamitous nature.

But if it is a desire of glory which drags us to war, be assured that the glory which is eagerly sought after, is no glory; that it is impossible to derive real honour from doing mischief; and that, if we must point out something glorious, it is infinitely more glorious to build and establish, than to ruin and lay waste a flourishing community. Now what will you say, when you reflect, that it is the people, yes, the lowest of the people, who build and establish by industry and wisdom, that which kings claim a privilege to subvert and destroy by their folly. If gain rather than glory is the object in view, be it remembered, that no war whatever did, at any time, succeed so fortunately as not to produce more loss than gain, more evil than good: and that no man ever injured his enemy in war, but previously he did many and great injuries to his own people. In short, when I see all human affairs rapidly ebbing and flowing, like the tide of the Euripus, what avails it to establish or extend empire with such vast exertions, when it must very soon, and on very slight occasions, devolve to some other possessor? With how much blood was the Roman empire raised to its exalted pitch of grandeur, and how soon did it decline and fall?

But you will say, the rights of kings must of necessity be prosecuted at all events. It is not for me to speak rashly of the rights of kings; but one thing I know, the strictest right is often the greatest wrong, and that some kings first determine upon a measure, because it accords with their inclination, and then go in quest of some colourable pretence, under which they may cloak their unjustifiable conduct; and amidst so many changes and chances in human affairs, amidst so many treaties made and unmade, what man alive can ever be long at a loss for a colourable pretence? But if it were a nice point in dispute, to whom the right of dominion belonged, what need, in settling a question which requires reason and argument only, what need can there be of spilling human blood? The welfare and happiness of the people have nothing at all to do in the dispute; it is merely a question whether they shall have the privilege of calling this man or that man their king, 'and paying taxes to Thomas instead of John, or to John instead of Thomas'.

There are pontiffs and bishops, there are wise and honest men, who could settle such a trifling and contemptible business as this, without going to war about it, and confounding all things divine as well as human. The pope, the bishops, the cardinals, the abbots, could not employ themselves in any way more consistently with their characters and stations, than in composing the differences of kings: here they ought to exert their authority, and to shew how much the sanctity of their characters and their religion can actually avail.

Pope Julius, a pontiff not of the very best repute in the world, was able to excite the storm of war; and shall Leo, a man of real learning, integrity, and piety, be unable to appease it? The pretext for undertaking the war was, that Pope Julius was in imminent danger. The cause is confessedly removed, but the war does not yet cease.

We ought also to remember, that all men are free, especially all Christian men. Now, when they have been flourishing a long time under any prince, and by this time acknowledge him as their lawful sovereign, what justifiable occasion can there be for disturbing the world, in attempting a revolution? Long consent of the people constituted a lawful sovereign among the heathens, and much more among Christians, with whom the kingly office is a ministerial trust, a chief magistracy, an administration of delegated power, and not a property or absolute dominion; so that if some part of the territory subject to a Christian king were taken away, he is relieved from an onus, a burthensome task, rather than robbed or injured.

But suppose one of the litigant parties will not agree to abide by the arbitration of good men chosen as referees? In this case how would you wish me to act? In the first place, if you are verily and truly a Christian,

I would have you bear the injury patiently, sit down with your heart at ease, and give up your right, be it what it will – Such would be the conduct of a Christian hero.

In the next place, if, waving your pretensions of Christianity, you are only a prudent, sensible man of the world; weigh well how much the prosecution of your right will cost you. If it will cost you too dearly, and it certainly will cost you too dearly, if you prosecute it by the sword; then never consent to assert a claim, which perhaps after all is a groundless one, by bringing so much certain mischief to the human race, by so many murders, by making so many childless parents and fatherless children, and by causing the sighs and tears of your own people, who have no concern in your right.

What do you suppose the Turks think, when they hear of Christian kings raging against each other, with all the madness of so many evils let loose? And raging for what? merely on account of a claim set up for power, for empire, and dominion.

Italy is now rescued from the French. And what is the great matter gained by so much blood spilt? what but that, where a Frenchman lately administered the powers of government, there some other man now administers the same powers? And to say the truth, the country flourished more before, than it flourishes now. But I will not enter farther into this part of the subject.

Now, if there are any systems which admit of war, I must maintain that they are founded on a gross principle, and favour of a Christianity degenerating, and likely to be overlaid by worldly influence. I do not know whether these systems, such as they are, justify war in the eyes of some men; but I observe, that whenever, through a zeal for defending the faith, the Christian peace is to be defended against the attack of barbarians, war is not at all opposed by men of acknowledged piety. But why, on these occasions, do a few maxims handed down from one to another by mere men, suggest themselves to our minds, rather than many positive precepts uttered by Christ himself, by the Apostles, by orthodox and approved fathers, concerning peace, and patience under all evil?

As to the usual arguments and means of justifying war, what is there that may not admit of defence in some mode or other; especially when they who have the management of the thing to be defended, are those, whose very villanies are always bepraised by the adulation of great numbers, and whose errors no man dares openly to reprehend? But in the mean time, it is very clear what all good-hearted men pray for, wish for, sigh for.

If you look narrowly into the case, you will find that they are, chiefly, the private, sinister, and selfish motives of princes, which operate as the real causes of all war.

But pray do you think it a conduct worthy of a rational creature, and not fitter for brutes or devils, to put the world in confusion, whenever one prince takes it into his head to be angry with another prince, or to pretend to be angry?

You and I may wish every thing that would be best, and most conducive to the happiness of the human race, but we can do no more than wish it. For my own part, all the little property I have in the world, I have among the English; and I will resign the whole of it with the greatest pleasure, on condition, that among Christian princes there may be established a Christian peace. Your influence may have considerable weight in accomplishing this end, since you have great interest with one potentate, Charles; a great deal with Maximilian; and stand very well with all the nobility and aristocracy of England. I do not doubt but by this time you have experienced what losses one's own friends may procure one in war; and must be sensible, that it will be doing your own business, and serving your own interest, if you endeavour to prevail with the great ones to put an end to the present war. I mention this, to hint to you that your labour will not be without its reward. I shall make all the haste I can to shake hands with you, as soon as I shall have it in my power to take my flight from this country. In the mean time, most respectable Father, farewel. My best wishes attend Ghilbert the physician, and Anthony Lutzenburg.

London.
Pridie Id. Mart. 1513.

HANS JAKOB CHRISTOFFEL VON GRIMMELSHAUSEN

*c.*1625–76

THE adventures of the hero in the great seventeenth-century classic, *The Adventurous Simplicissimus*, are largely drawn from the author's own experiences. He was kidnapped when only ten by Hessian soldiers and forthwith 'enlisted' into the Thirty Years War, the background for his novel. The grim humour and realistic portrayal of the horrors in that 'religious' war, his asides on the folly of man on the battlefield and at court, gave the work immediate renown, and this has continued to the present day.

The fourth chapter is reprinted here as an example of the large literary tradition which has influenced the polemic against war. That tradition is as varied as literature itself, sometimes humorous, sometimes evangelistic, sometimes satirical, and sometimes factual, as in such 'documentary' accounts as John Hersey's *Hiroshima*. Bayard Quincy Morgan is the translator of this excerpt from the first unexpurgated English translation of the novel, published in 1963.

Men of War

Although it was not my intention to lead the peace-loving reader along with these cavalrymen into my dad's house and home, since things will go foully enough there, yet the sequence of my history demands that I should bequeath to kind posterity the record of the kinds of atrocities that were practised now and again in this German war of ours, and in particular to attest by my own example that all such evils were often of necessity decreed for our benefit by the goodness of the Most High. For, dear reader, who would have told me that there is a God in Heaven, if no soldiers had destroyed my dad's house and by such seizure forced me out among people from whom I got sufficient information on the subject? Shortly before that time I could neither know nor imagine anything other than that my dad, my mom, I, and the others in our house were alone on the earth, because no other human beings and no other human dwellings were known to me besides the one which I entered and left from every day.

But soon thereafter I learned about the entry of humans into this world, and the fact that they must leave it again; I was a human being only in shape, and a Christian child only in name, but for the rest merely a *bestia*! But the Almighty beheld my ignorance with compassionate eyes and wanted to bring me to both, to the knowledge of him and of me. And although he had a thousand different ways of doing this, undoubtedly he wanted to make use only of the one whereby my dad and mom, as an example to others, would be punished on account of my negligent upbringing.

The first thing these horsemen did was to stable their horses; after which every man had his particular labour to perform, each of which resulted in some sort of ruin or destruction. For although some began to butcher, to boil, and to roast – so that it looked as if a jolly banquet were to be enjoyed – there were others who stormed through the house from top to bottom; and even the bed chamber was not safe, just as if the golden fleece of Colchis had been concealed there. Others made up great bundles of cloth, wearing apparel, and all sorts of household goods, as if they were going to set up a shop with second-hand goods somewhere; but whatever they had no mind to take along was smashed or slashed to bits; some of them thrust their swords through hay and straw, as if they hadn't enough sheep and swine to stab; some shook the feathers out of the bedding and in place thereof stuffed into the ticking salt pork, dried meat, or else tools and things, as if that made the ticking better to sleep on. Still others smashed the stove and the window panes, as if it were theirs to proclaim eternal summer; utensils of copper and pewter were hammered flat, and then they packed up the dented and damaged articles; sheets, tables, chairs, and benches they burned up, though all the while there were many cords of dry wood lying in the yard. Pots and dishes, finally, had to be smashed up too, either because they preferred eating what was roasted, or because they only had the intention of eating a single meal there.

Our maid was so dealt with in the stable that she was no longer able to come out, which is indeed a shame to relate. The farmhand they tied up and laid on the ground, stuck a gag between his jaws, and poured a milk pail full of liquid manure into him; this they called a Swedish drink, whereby they forced him to lead one party to another place where they took away people and cattle and brought them into our yard, among them my dad, my mom, and our Ursel as well.

Then they first began by taking the flints out of their pistols and in their stead screwing in the thumbs of the peasants, thus torturing the poor wretches as if it were intended to burn witches; indeed they were already shoving one of the captured peasants into the bake oven and putting fire in after him, despite the fact that he had not yet confessed anything. Another one they took and put a rope around his head, and then twisted it with a cudgel so tight that the blood burst out of his mouth, nose, and ears. In short, each one had his own scheme for tormenting the peasants, and so too each peasant had his own special torture. Only my dad, according to the notion I had at that time, was the most fortunate one, because he confessed with laughing lips what others had to say with agonies and pitiable lamentation, and this honour was without doubt done him because he was the householder; for they put him next to a fire, tied him so that he could move neither hand nor foot, and rubbed the soles of his feet with moistened salt, which our old nanny goat had to lick off again and thus tickle him so that he could have burst with laughing. This seemed so funny that to keep him company, or because I knew no better, I had to laugh too with all my might. Amid such laughter he confessed as he was supposed to do and opened up his hidden treasure, which was much richer in gold, pearls, and jewels than one would have expected among peasants.

Of the captured women, maid servants, and daughters I know nothing in particular to tell, because the soldiers did not let me see what they did with them. But this I know, that now and then one heard pitiful shrieking in the back corners; and I judge that my mom and our Ursel didn't fare any better than the others. In the midst of this misery I turned roasts and helped water the horses in the afternoon, by which means I came to our maid out in the stable looking most extraordinarily dishevelled.

I didn't recognize her, but she spoke to me with a feeble voice and said, 'Oh, boy, run off, or the riders will take you along with them! Be sure that you get away from here, for you see how bad. . . !' More than this she was unable to say.

EARLY
INTERNATIONALISM

MODERN efforts towards international organization received their impetus from non-governmental groups in England, America, France, and Switzerland, most of them the early peace societies of the nineteenth century. The dream of an international order either securing or guaranteeing the peace is much older, dating back at least to 1392 and Dante's *De Monarchia*. But Dante, like the originators of other early peace plans – Marsilius of Padua, Abbé Honoré Bonnor, King George Podiebad of Bohemia, Erasmus, Cardinal Wolsey, and Giulio Ferrero – did not imagine an *international* order of sovereign nations so much as a plan whereby one nation or one ruler would lead and control the others. There would, of course, be peace, but peace would be the 'by-product' of a prejudiced resolution to international rivalries. Dante found support for his view in the example of history; in *De Monarchia* he wrote, 'We shall not find at any time except under the divine monarch Augustus, when a perfect monarchy existed, that the world was everywhere quiet'. Wolsey saw his sovereign, Henry VIII, as head of an enlarged monarchy, and Podiebad's plan was aimed at the subjugation of the Turks. Even such advanced plans as the *Grand Design* of Henri IV of France and his minister Sully, had the reduction of Habsburg power in mind when it came to the question of peace.

But in 1623 *The New Cyneas* was published by Emeric Crucé, a plan which, in spite of some rather naïve details, seemed to have peace primarily in mind. It was one of the earliest direct attacks on chauvinism and in many ways in the tradition of Erasmus who, in his *Complaint of Peace* and other works, had questioned the 'divine' right of kings to make war.

The horrors Grimmelshausen related in *Simplicissimus* (1669) of the Thirty Years War and which Grotius must have experienced marked the increasing antipathy of thinking men to violence. Grotius' *De jure belli ac pacis* (1625) established the fundamental principle of international law, a term which was not coined, however, for another century and a half when Bentham published his monumental *Introduction to Principles and Morals*. Grotius stressed that all nations had common interests and that in this community lay mankind's great hope. The highest duty of a

Christian sovereign was not to win wars but to abolish them. Like Erasmus and Thomas More before him, he spoke out passionately against an international system which permitted persistent violence. Yet his major contribution lay in diminishing the injustices and inequalities of warfare. If wars could not be eliminated, they might perhaps be regulated. To speak of Grotius' contributions in this field seems slightly fanciful, however, in the twentieth century.

The end of the seventeenth century and the whole of the eighteenth saw a great burst of creative energy in the field of peace proposals of the internationalist sort. William Penn, John Bellers, the Abbé Saint-Pierre, Jeremy Bentham, and Immanuel Kant all concerned themselves with plans for international organization.

The increasing complexity and thoughtfulness of these plans could be seen clearly in Saint-Pierre's *Projet pour rendre la Paix perpetuelle*, published in 1713. Much influenced by the *Grand Design* written more than a century earlier, the Abbé's *projet* was easily the most comprehensive plan yet put forth to secure a lasting peace. Among literally thousands of details most minutely worked out lay the cardinal point: all states were to support a sovereign council. This council would be a tribunal with full executive power to decide all issues presented to it; the members were to desist from warfare in the event of dispute and to submit the issue to the council. Although the Abbé's proposals received more attention in Europe than any plan previously presented,[1] the complexity of Saint-Pierre's proposals kept the work generally inaccessible to the public, although it was well known in scholarly circles. Rousseau undertook its 'editing' between 1753 and 1758, producing a version which has since become more famous than the original; Rousseau unsurprisingly made the work of the Abbé the vehicle for his own ideas; in simplifying the material, he also amended it.

The last two great peace plans of the period were proposed by Jeremy Bentham in 1789 with his *Plan for a Universal and Perpetual Peace,* and by Immanuel Kant in 1795 with his *Perpetual Peace*. Bentham's plan envisaged a reduction of armaments, international institutions, but put all its faith in public opinion as a guarantor of international law.[2]

In earlier works Kant had already pointed out the necessity for some

1. See the extract from Leibnitz's letter to Saint-Pierre quoted in the Introduction (page 18). Leibnitz wrote also to a friend poking fun at the Abbe's *naïveté*.
2. As did the peace plan of the American, William Ladd, in 1840.

sort of a general league, an organization of all nations which would guarantee perpetual peace. The logic of history would provide the impetus for such an organization. In *Perpetual Peace* Kant declared war to be the natural state of mankind, peace the institution men must establish. He laid great stress on the constitution of this organization: it was to be republican in structure; international law was to be based on a federation of free states; the organization was to bring about a condition of international citizenship as the inevitable result of mankind's adopting the principle of universal hospitality.

The second half of the nineteenth century saw a proliferation in the number of peace conferences at the international level; the first one had met in London in 1843. It was principally at such meetings that specific internationalist proposals were presented along with methods for realizing them. These meetings, as has been mentioned, remained non-governmental until the end of the nineteenth century. Efforts were made to have leading figures, such as Victor Hugo, attend the conferences. The speeches generally had a high-flown, rhetorical air and were much applauded. Tolstoy's comment on them may be found in the Introduction. Selections from Hugo's speech to the Congrès de la Paix held in Paris in 1851 give a fairly good idea of the rhetoric adopted. However, these congresses did form the background for such later developments as the establishment of the World Court and both the League of Nations and the United Nations.

Emeric Crucé's 'A Holy Resolve', from *The New Cyneas*, and the extract from Victor Hugo's speech, from *Four Discourses,* were translated for this volume by the editor; the selection from Kant's *Perpetual Peace* was translated by M. Campbell Smith.

EMERIC CRUCÉ

c.1590–1648

A Holy Resolve

GREAT Princes, it is you who must accomplish this holy resolve. Mankind in general and your subjects in particular will be grateful to you. No conquest could win you so much acclaim; no victory deserves so many bonfires. What greater honour can you look for than to see peace proclaimed by your authority throughout the world? Your names will be noted in gilt in the chronicles: your reigns will be praised for having ushered in the return of the Golden Age. Alexander's conquests, Caesar's triumphs, the strategy of Hannibal and Sertorius, will be spoken of no more; their vanity will be recognized, for their glory was founded on murder and plunder, in which they should have found instead perpetual regrets and shame. Posterity will recognize in their place those brave heroes who have overcome the monsters of cruelty and barbarism, who have placed the universe under the justice of law – those men, in brief, who have shown themselves to be true images of God. Now this glorious honour is not to be acquired by pillage, slaughter, and hostile actions, but by consistent government, by lawful and regulated power, in contradistinction to the kingdom of tyranny, uneasiness, and short duration. . . .

How pleasant it would be to see men travel freely across frontiers and communicate with one another without any scruples whatsoever as to nation, ceremonies, or other such formalities, as if the earth were, as it is in truth, a common city for all. . . .

Someone will surely say, how will it be possible to make people so different in their ways and inclinations as the Turk and the Persian, the Frenchman and the Spaniard, the Chinaman and the Tartar, the Christian and the Jew or the Muslim, agree? I believe that such differences are but political, that they cannot ignore the affinities that exist and must exist between men. Geography . . . does not weaken the ties of blood. It can no longer set aside the unity of nature, the true foundation of friendship and human society.

Why should I, a Frenchman, bear ill will against an Englishman or an

Indian? I cannot, when I contemplate that they are men even as I, that I am like them subject to error and sin and that all nations are associated by a natural and, in consequence, indissoluble tie. . . .

It depends only on the rulers to bestow by anticipation this felicity on their people. For what do we need these arms? Will we always live like brutes? If we only behaved moderately in these affairs! . . . Men (unless impelled by hunger or other need) quarrel for mere trifles; sometimes out of sheer wantonness they begin a campaign, not the battle of one man with another, but ten thousand against ten thousand, so that they may enjoy the spectacle of seeing the dead piled on high, streams of blood flowing on the fields. Look at two armies about to assault each other: the fierce looks, the soldiers' faces made hideous, the threats and savage shouts on every side, the roar of the cannons; now the attack and the gruesome conflict, the butchering of men, some torn limb from limb, others half dead begging aid of their companions, begging them for the death stroke to cut their wretched and fast-fading lives short. Later the slaughter extends to the weak: old men are slaughtered, children killed or captured, women raped, houses of worship profaned – only injustice is sure. This is followed by two new evils: famine and pestilence, for husbandry ends in time of war. The population has nothing to eat and must therefore eat indiscriminately good and bad meat which, instead of being nourishment, produces . . . diseases.

How right, alas, was Heraclitus in deploring the blindness of man in bringing upon himself so many miseries, miseries which render his condition worse than that of beasts! Therefore it is not at all amazing that Gryllus, after being transformed into a pig, preferred to remain so, rather than to resume his natural shape. And wise Plotinus, who was ashamed of being a man and wished never to speak of his parents or birth. And why is it that today we see Timons aplenty, and men who withdraw from life? If we accuse them of hypochondria, they might reasonably reply that we have brought it down on them. The wickedness, sordidness, and cruelty they see around them every day are able to make them hate the world, and one would have to be insensible not to be touched. Now if the only considerations were life's brevity and the certainty of death, we ought to be ashamed of so much self-torture for an imaginary honour, and we would better imitate the ancient Egyptians who brought a skeleton or some other death-symbol into the midst of festivities in order to incite the company to drink deeply, to be merry as long as they had the chance. But we ought to aim at higher things, and take into consideration that God exists who punishes men's sins, and especially arrogance and cruelty. If these two vices were to be abandoned, wars would cease. The sword will be sheathed when we have seen the vanity of those opinions which lead us to take up arms.

IMMANUEL KANT

1724–1804

Perpetual Peace[1]

WE need not try to decide whether this satirical inscription (once found on a Dutch innkeeper's signboard above the picture of a church-yard) is aimed at mankind in general, or at the rulers of states in particular, unwearying in their love of war, or perhaps only at the philosophers who cherish the sweet dream of perpetual peace. The author of the present sketch would make one stipulation, however. The practical politician stands upon a definite footing with the theorist: with great self-complacency he looks down upon him as a mere pedant whose empty ideas can threaten no danger to the state (starting as it does from principles derived from experience), and who may always be permitted to knock down his eleven skittles at once without a worldly-wise statesman needing to disturb himself. Hence, in the event of a quarrel arising between the two, the practical statesman must always act consistently, and not scent danger to the state behind opinions ventured by the theoretical politician at random and publicly expressed. With which saving clause (*clausula salvatoria*) the author will herewith consider himself duly and expressly protected against all malicious mis-interpretation.

FIRST SECTION

—

CONTAINING THE PRELIMINARY ARTICLES OF
PERPETUAL PEACE BETWEEN STATES

1. – 'No treaty of peace shall be regarded as valid, if made with the secret reservation of material for a future war.'

For then it would be a mere truce, a mere suspension of hostilities, not peace. A peace signifies the end of all hostilities and to attach to it the

---

1. I have seen something of M. de St-Pierre's plan for maintaining perpetual peace in Europe. It reminds me of an inscription outside of a churchyard, which ran '*Pax Perpetua*. For the dead, it is true, fight no more. But the living are of another mind, and the mightiest among them have little respect for tribunals.'

epithet 'eternal' is not only a verbal pleonasm, but matter of suspicion. The causes of a future war existing, although perhaps not yet known to the high contracting parties themselves, are entirely annihilated by the conclusion of peace, however acutely they may be ferreted out of documents in the public archives. There may be a mental reservation of old claims to be thought out at a future time, which are, none of them, mentioned at this stage, because both parties are too much exhausted to continue the war, while the evil intention remains of using the first favourable opportunity for further hostilities. Diplomacy of this kind only Jesuitical casuistry can justify: it is beneath the dignity of a ruler, just as acquiescence in such processes of reasoning is beneath the dignity of his minister, if one judges the facts as they really are.

If, however, according to present enlightened ideas of political wisdom, the true glory of a state lies in the uninterrupted development of its power by every possible means, this judgement must certainly strike one as scholastic and pedantic.

2. – 'No state having an independent existence – whether it be great or small – shall be acquired by another through inheritance, exchange, purchase or donation.'

For a state is not a property (*patrimonium*), as may be the ground on which its people are settled. It is a society of human beings over whom no one but itself has the right to rule and to dispose. Like the trunk of a tree, it has its own roots, and to graft it on to another state is to do away with its existence as a moral person, and to make of it a thing. Hence it is in contradiction to the idea of the original contract without which no right over a people is thinkable.[1] Everyone knows to what danger the bias in favour of these modes of acquisition has brought Europe (in other parts of the world it has never been known). The custom of marriage between states, as if they were individuals, has survived even up to the most recent times, and is regarded as partly a new kind of industry by which ascendancy may be acquired through family alliances, without any expenditure of strength; partly as a device for territorial expansion. Moreover, the hiring out of the troops of one state to another to fight against an enemy not at war with their native

1. An hereditary kingdom is not a state which can be inherited by another state, but one whose sovereign power can be inherited by another physical person. The state then acquires a ruler, not the ruler as such (that is, as one already possessing another realm) the state.

country is to be reckoned in this connexion; for the subjects are in this way used and abused at will as personal property.

3. – 'Standing armies (*miles perpetuus*) shall be abolished in course of time.'

For they are always threatening other states with war by appearing to be in constant readiness to fight. They incite the various states to out-rival one another in the number of their soldiers, and to this number no limit can be set. Now, since owing to the sums devoted to this purpose, peace at last becomes even more oppressive than a short war, these standing armies are themselves the cause of wars of aggression, under-taken in order to get rid of this burden. To which we must add that the practice of hiring men to kill or to be killed seems to imply a use of them as mere machines and instruments in the hand of another (namely, the state) which cannot easily be reconciled with the right of humanity in our own person.[1] The matter stands quite differently in the case of voluntary periodical military exercise on the part of citizens of the state, who thereby seek to secure themselves and their country against attack from without.

The accumulation of treasure in a state would in the same way be regarded by other states as a menace of war, and might compel them to anticipate this by striking the first blow. For of the three forces, the power of arms, the power of alliance and the power of money, the last might well become the most reliable instrument of war, did not the difficulty of ascertaining the amount stand in the way. . . .

5. – 'No state shall violently interfere with the constitution and administration of another.'

For what can justify it in so doing? The scandal which is here pre-sented to the subjects of another state? The erring state can much more serve as a warning by exemplifying the great evils which a nation draws down on itself through its own lawlessness. Moreover, the bad example which one free person gives another (as *scandalum acceptum*) does no injury to the latter. In this connexion, it is true, we cannot count the case of a state which has become split up through internal corruption

1. A Bulgarian Prince thus answered the Greek Emperor who magnanimously offered to settle a quarrel with him, not by shedding the blood of his subjects, but by a duel: – 'A smith who has tongs will not take the red-hot iron from the fire with his hands.'

into two parts, each of them representing by itself an individual state which lays claim to the whole. Here the yielding of assistance to one faction could not be reckoned as interference on the part of a foreign state with the constitution of another, for here anarchy prevails. So long, however, as the inner strife has not yet reached this stage the interference of other powers would be a violation of the rights of an independent nation which is only struggling with internal disease. It would therefore itself cause a scandal, and make the autonomy of all states insecure.

6. – 'No state at war with another shall countenance such modes of hostility as would make mutual confidence impossible in a subsequent state of peace: such are the employment of assassins (*percussores*) or of poisoners (*venefici*), breaches of capitulation, the instigating and making use of treachery (*perduellio*) in the hostile state. . . .'

SECOND SECTION
—
CONTAINING THE DEFINITIVE ARTICLES OF A
PERPETUAL PEACE BETWEEN STATES

A state of peace among men who live side by side is not the natural state (*status naturalis*), which is rather to be described as a state of war: that is to say, although there is not perhaps always actual open hostility, yet there is a constant threatening that an outbreak may occur. Thus the state of peace must be *established*. For the mere cessation of hostilities is no guarantee of continued peaceful relations, and unless this guarantee is given by every individual to his neighbour – which can only be done in a state of society regulated by law – one man is at liberty to challenge another and treat him as an enemy.[1]

1. It is usually accepted that a man may not take hostile steps against anyone, unless the latter has already injured him by act. This is quite accurate, if both are citizens of a law-governed state. For, in becoming a member of this community, each gives the other the security he demands against injury, by means of the supreme authority exercising control over them both. The individual, however (or nation), who remains in a mere state of nature deprives me of this security and does me injury, by mere proximity. There is perhaps no active (*facto*) molestation, but there is a state of lawlessness (*status injustus*) which, by its very existence, offers a continual menace to me. I can therefore compel him, either to enter into relations with me under which we are both subject to law, or to withdraw from my neighbourhood. So that the postulate upon which the following articles are based

FIRST DEFINITIVE ARTICLE OF PERPETUAL PEACE

I. – 'The civil constitution of each state shall be republican.'

The only constitution which has its origin in the idea of the original contract, upon which the lawful legislation of every nation must be based, is the republican.[2] It is a constitution, in the first place, founded in

---

is: – 'All men who have the power to exert a mutual influence upon one another must be under a civil government of some kind.'

A legal constitution is, according to the nature of the individuals who compose the state:

(1) A constitution formed in accordance with the right of citizenship of the individuals who constitute a nation (*jus civitatis*).

(2) A constitution whose principle is international law which determines the relations of states (*jus gentium*).

(3) A constitution formed in accordance with cosmopolitan law, in as far as individuals and states, standing in an external relation of mutual reaction, may be regarded as citizens of one world-state (*jus cosmopoliticum*).

This classification is not an arbitrary one, but is necessary with reference to the idea of perpetual peace. For, if even one of these units of society were in a position physically to influence another, while yet remaining a member of a primitive order of society, then a state of war would be joined with these primitive conditions; and from this it is our present purpose to free ourselves.

2. Lawful, that is to say, external freedom cannot be defined, as it so often is, as the right [*Befugniss*] 'to do whatever one likes, so long as this does not wrong anyone else'. For what is this right? It is the possibility of actions which do not lead to the injury of others. So the explanation of a 'right' would be something like this: – 'Freedom is the possibility of actions which do not injure anyone. A man does not wrong another – whatever his action – if he does not wrong another': which is empty tautology. My external (lawful) freedom is rather to be explained in this way: it is the right through which I require not to obey any external laws except those to which I could have given my consent. In exactly the same way, external (legal) equality in a state is that relation of the subjects in consequence of which no individual can legally bind or oblige another to anything, without at the same time submitting himself to the law which ensures that he can, in his turn, be bound and obliged in like manner by this other.

The principle of lawful independence requires no explanation, as it is involved in the general concept of a constitution. The validity of this hereditary and inalienable right, which belongs of necessity to mankind, is affirmed and ennobled by the principle of a lawful relation between man himself and higher beings, if indeed he believes in such beings. This is so, because he thinks of himself, in accordance with these very principles, as a citizen of a transcendental world as well as of the world of sense. For, as far as my freedom goes, I am bound by no obligation even

accordance with the principle of the freedom of the members of society as human beings: secondly, in accordance with the principle of the dependence of all, as subjects, on a common legislation: and, thirdly, in accordance with the law of the equality of the members as citizens. It is then, looking at the question of right, the only constitution whose fundamental principles lie at the basis of every form of civil constitution. And the only question for us now is, whether it is also the one constitution which can lead to perpetual peace.

Now the republican constitution apart from the soundness of its origin, since it arose from the pure source of the concept of right, has also the prospect of attaining the desired result, namely, perpetual peace. And the reason is this. If, as must be so under this constitution, the consent of the subjects is required to determine whether there shall be war or not, nothing is more natural than that they should weigh the matter well, before undertaking such a bad business. For in decreeing war, they would of necessity be resolving to bring down the miseries of war upon their country. This implies: they must fight themselves; they

---

with regard to Divine Laws – which are apprehended by me only through my reason – except in so far as I could have given my assent to them; for it is through the law of freedom of my own reason that I first form for myself a concept of a Divine Will. As for the principle of equality, in so far as it applies to the most sublime being in the universe next to God – a being I might perhaps figure to myself as a mighty emanation of the Divine spirit – there is no reason why, if I perform my duty in the sphere in which I am placed, as that aeon does in his, the duty of obedience alone should fall to my share, the right to command to him. That this principle of equality (unlike the principle of freedom), does not apply to our relation to God is due to the fact that, to this Being alone, the idea of duty does not belong.

As for the right to equality which belongs to all citizens as subjects, the solution of the problem of the admissibility of an hereditary nobility hinges on the following question: – 'Does social rank – acknowledged by the state to be higher in the case of one subject than another – stand above desert, or does merit take precedence of social standing?' Now it is obvious that, if high position is combined with good family, it is quite uncertain whether merit, that is to say, skill and fidelity in office, will follow as well. This amounts to granting the favoured individual a commanding position without any question of desert; and to that the universal will of the people – expressed in an original contract which is the fundamental principle of all right – would never consent. For it does not follow that a nobleman is a man of noble character. In the case of the official nobility, as one might term the rank of higher magistracy – which one must acquire by merit – the social position is not attached like property to the person but to his office, and equality is not thereby disturbed; for, if a man gives up office, he lays down with it his official rank and falls back into the rank of his fellows.

must hand over the costs of the war out of their own property; they must do their poor best to make good the devastation which it leaves behind; and finally, as a crowning ill, they have to accept a burden of debt which will embitter even peace itself, and which they can never pay off on account of the new wars which are always impending. On the other hand, in a government where the subject is not a citizen holding a vote, (i.e. in a constitution which is not republican), the plunging into war is the least serious thing in the world. For the ruler is not a citizen, but the owner of the state, and does not lose a whit by the war, while he goes on enjoying the delights of his table or sport, or of his pleasure palaces and gala days. He can therefore decide on war for the most trifling reasons, as if it were a kind of pleasure party. Any justification of it that is necessary for the sake of decency he can leave without concern to the diplomatic corps who are always only too ready with their services. . . .

. . . Republicanism is the political principle of severing the executive power of the government from the legislature. Despotism is that principle in pursuance of which the state arbitrarily puts into effect laws which it has itself made: consequently it is the administration of the public will, but this is identical with the private will of the ruler. Of these three forms of a state, democracy, in the proper sense of the word, is of necessity despotism, because it establishes an executive power, since all decree regarding – and, if need be, against – any individual who dissents from them. Therefore the 'whole people', so-called, who carry their measure are really not all, but only a majority: so that here the universal will is in contradiction with itself and with the principle of freedom. . . .

SECOND DEFINITIVE ARTICLE OF PERPETUAL PEACE

II. – 'The law of nations shall be founded on a federation of free states.'

Nations, as states, may be judged like individuals who, living in the natural state of society – that is to say, uncontrolled by external law – injure one another through their very proximity. Every state, for the sake of its own security, may – and ought to – demand that its neigh-bour should submit itself to conditions similar to those of the civil society where the right of every individual is guaranteed. This would give rise to a federation of nations which, however, would not have to be a State of nations. That would involve a contradiction. For the term 'state' implies the relation of one who rules to those who obey – that is to say, of lawgiver to the subject people : and many nations in one state would constitute only one nation, which contradicts our hypothesis, since here we have to consider the right of one nation against another, in so far as they are so many separate states and are not to be fused into one. . . .

THIRD DEFINITIVE ARTICLE OF PERPETUAL PEACE

III. – 'The rights of men, as citizens of the world, shall be limited to the conditions of universal hospitality.'

We are speaking here, as in the previous articles, not of philanthropy, but of right; and in this sphere hospitality signifies the claim of a stranger entering foreign territory to be treated by its owner without hostility. The latter may send him away again, if this can be done without causing his death ; but, so long as he conducts himself peaceably, he must not be treated as an enemy. It is not a right to be treated as a guest to which the stranger can lay claim – a special friendly compact on his behalf would be required to make him for a given time an actual inmate – but he has a right of visitation. This right to present themselves to society belongs to all mankind in virtue of our common right of possession on the surface of the earth on which, as it is a globe, we cannot be infinitely scattered, and must in the end reconcile ourselves to existence side by side : at the same time, originally no one individual had more right than another to live in any one particular spot. Uninhabitable portions of the surface, ocean and desert, split up the human community, but in such a way that ships and camels – 'the ship of the desert' – make it possible for men to come into touch with one another across these unappropriated regions and to take advantage of our common claim to the face of the earth with a view to a possible inter-communication. The inhospitality of the inhabitants of certain sea coasts – as, for example, the coast of Barbary – in plundering ships in neighbouring seas or making slaves of shipwrecked mariners, or the behaviour of the Arab Bedouins in the deserts, who think that proximity to nomadic tribes constitutes a right to rob, is thus contrary to the law of nature. This right to hospitality, however – that is to say, the privilege of strangers arriving on foreign soil – does not amount to more than what is implied in a permission to make an attempt at intercourse with the original inhabitants. In this way far distant territories may enter into peaceful relations with one another. These relations may at last come under the public control of law, and thus the human race may be brought nearer the realization of a cosmopolitan constitution.

Let us look now, for the sake of comparison, at the inhospitable behaviour of the civilized nations, especially the commercial states of our continent. The injustice which they exhibit on visiting foreign lands and races – this being equivalent in their eyes to conquest – is such as to fill us with horror. America, the negro countries, the Spice Islands, the Cape, etc., were, on being discovered, looked upon as countries which belonged to nobody; for the native inhabitants were reckoned as nothing. In Hindustan, under the pretext of intending to establish merely commercial depots, the Europeans introduced foreign troops; and, as a result, the different states of Hindustan were stirred up to far-spreading wars. Oppression of the natives followed, famine, insurrection, perfidy and all the rest of the litany of evils which can afflict mankind. . . .

. . . A good political constitution, however, is not to be expected as a result of progress in morality; but rather, conversely, the good moral condition of a nation is to be looked for, as one of the first fruits of such a constitution. Hence the mechanism of nature, working through the self-seeking propensities of man (which of course counteract one another in their external effects), may be used by reason as a means of making way for the realization of her own purpose, the empire of right, and, as far as is in the power of the state, to promote and secure in this way internal as well as external peace. We may say, then, that it is the irresistible will of nature that right shall at last get the supremacy. What one here fails to do will be accomplished in the long run, although perhaps with much inconvenience to us. As Bouterwek says, 'If you bend the reed too much it breaks: he who would do too much does nothing.'

2. The idea of international law presupposes the separate existence of a number of neighbouring and independent states; and, although such a condition of things is in itself already a state of war, (if a federative union of these nations does not prevent the outbreak of hostilities) yet, according to the Idea of reason, this is better than that all the states should be merged into one under a power which has gained the ascendancy over its neighbours and gradually become a universal

monarchy. For the wider the sphere of their jurisdiction, the more laws lose in force; and soulless despotism, when it has choked the seeds of good, at last sinks into anarchy. Nevertheless it is the desire of every state, or of its ruler, to attain to a permanent condition of peace in this very way; that is to say, by subjecting the whole world as far as possible to its sway. But nature wills it otherwise. She employs two means to separate nations, and prevent them from intermixing: namely, the differences of language and of religion.[1] These differences bring with them a tendency to mutual hatred, and furnish pretexts for waging war. But, none the less, with the growth of culture and the gradual advance of men to great unanimity of principle, they lead to concord in a state of peace which, unlike the despotism we have spoken of (the churchyard of freedom) does not arise from the weakening of all forces, but is brought into being and secured through the equilibrium of these forces in their most active rivalry.

3. As nature wisely separates nations which the will of each state, sanctioned even by the principles of international law, would gladly unite under its own sway by stratagem or force; in the same way, on the other hand, she unites nations whom the principle of a cosmopolitan right would not have secured against violence and war. And this union she brings about through an appeal to their mutual interests. The commercial spirit cannot co-exist with war, and sooner or later it takes possession of every nation. For, of all the forces which lie at the command of a state, the power of money is probably the most reliable. Hence states find themselves compelled – not, it is true, exactly from motives of morality – to further the noble end of peace and to avert war, by means of mediation, wherever it threatens to break out, just as if they had made a permanent league for this purpose. For great alliances with a view to war can, from the nature of things, only very rarely occur, and still more seldom succeed.

In this way nature guarantees the coming of perpetual peace,

1. Difference of religion! A strange expression, as if one were to speak of different kinds of morality. There may indeed be different historical forms of belief – that is to say, the various means which have been used in the course of time to promote religion – but they are mere subjects of learned investigation, and do not really lie within the sphere of religion. In the same way there are many religious works – the *Zendavesta, Veda, Koran*, etc. – but there is only one religion, binding for all men and for all times. These books are each no more than the accidental mouthpiece of religion, and may be different according to differences in time and place.

through the natural course of human propensities: not indeed with sufficient certainty to enable us to prophesy the future of this ideal theoretically, but yet clearly enough for practical purposes. And thus this guarantee of nature makes it a duty that we should labour for this end, an end which is no mere chimera.

SECOND SUPPLEMENT

—

A SECRET ARTICLE FOR PERPETUAL PEACE

A secret article in negotiations concerning public right is, when looked at objectively or with regard to the meaning of the term, a contradiction. When we view it, however, from the subjective standpoint, with regard to the character and condition of the person who dictates it, we see that it might quite well involve some private consideration, so that he would regard it as hazardous to his dignity to acknowledge such an article as originating from him.

The only article of this kind is contained in the following proposition: – 'The opinions of philosophers, with regard to the conditions of the possibility of a public peace, shall be taken into consideration by states armed for war.'

It seems, however, to be derogatory to the dignity of the legislative authority of a state – to which we must of course attribute all wisdom – to ask advice from subjects (among whom stand philosophers) about the rules of its behaviour to other states. At the same time, it is very advisable that this should be done. Hence the state will silently invite suggestion for this purpose, while at the same time keeping the fact secret. This amounts to saying that the state will allow philosophers to discuss freely and publicly the universal principles governing the conduct of war and establishment of peace; for they will do this of their own accord, if no prohibition is laid upon them. The arrangement between states, on this point, does not require that a special agreement should be made, merely for this purpose; for it is already involved in the obligation imposed by the universal reason of man which gives the moral law. We would not be understood to say that the state must give a preference to the principles of the philosopher, rather than to the opinions of the jurist, the representative of state authority; but only that he should be heard. The latter, who has chosen for a symbol the scales of right and the sword of justice, generally uses that sword not merely to keep off all outside influences from the scales; for, when one pan of the balance will not go down, he throws his sword into it; and then *Vae victis!* The jurist, not being a moral philosopher, is under the greatest temptation to do this, because it is his business only to apply existing laws and not to investigate whether these are not themselves in need of improvement; and this actually lower function of his profession he looks upon as the nobler, because it is linked to power (as is the case also in both the other faculties, theology and medicine). Philosophy occupies a very low position compared with this combined power. So that it is said, for example, that she is the handmaid of theology; and the same has been said of her position with regard to law and medicine. It is not quite clear, however, 'whether she bears the torch before these gracious ladies, or carries the train'.

That kings should philosophize, or philosophers become kings, is not to be expected. But neither is it to be desired; for the possession of power is inevitably fatal to the free exercise of reason. But it is absolutely indispensable, for their enlightenment as to the full significance of their vocations, that both kings and sovereign nations, which rule themselves in accordance with laws of equality, should not allow the class of philosophers to disappear, nor forbid the expression of their opinions, but should allow them to speak openly. And since this class of men, by their very nature, are incapable of instigating rebellion or forming unions for purposes of political agitation, they should not be suspected of propagandism.

. . . Politics in the real sense cannot take a step forward without first paying homage to the principles of morals. And, although politics, *per se*, is a difficult art, in its union with morals no art is required; for in the case of a conflict arising between the two sciences, the moralist can cut asunder the knot which politics is unable to untie. Right must be held sacred by man, however great the cost and sacrifice to the ruling power. Here is no half-and-half course. We cannot devise a happy medium between right and expediency, a right pragmatically conditioned. But all politics must bend the knee to the principle of right, and may in that way, hope to reach, although slowly perhaps, a level whence it may shine upon men for all time. . . .

. . . If it is our duty to realize a state of public right, if at the same time there are good grounds for hope that this ideal may be realized, although only by an approximation advancing *ad infinitum*, then perpetual peace, following hitherto falsely so-called conclusions of peace, which have been in reality mere cessations of hostilities, is no mere empty idea. But rather we have here a problem which gradually works out its own solution and, as the periods in which a given advance takes place toward the realization of the ideal of perpetual peace will, we hope, become with the passing of time shorter and shorter, we must approach ever nearer to this goal.

VICTOR HUGO

1802–85

Address to the Congrès de la Paix
held in Paris, 1851

GENTLEMEN, is this religious idea, universal peace – the linking of the nations together by a common bond, the Gospel to become the supreme law, mediation to be substituted for war – is this religious idea a practical idea? Is this holy thought one that can be realized? Many practical minds … many politicians grown old … in the administration of affairs, answer 'No'. I answer with you; I answer unhesitatingly; I answer 'Yes', and I will make an attempt to prove my case later on.

But I will go farther and not only say that it is a realizable end, but that it is an unavoidable end. Its coming can be delayed or hastened; that is all.

The law of the world is not nor can it be different from the law of God. Now, the law of God is not war; it is peace. …

When one asserts these high truths, it is quite natural that the assertion should be met with incredulity; it is quite natural that in this hour of our trouble and anguish, the idea of a universal peace should be surprising and shocking, very much like the apparition of the impossible and the ideal. It is quite natural that one should shout 'Utopia'; as for me, modest and obscure worker in this great work of the nineteenth century, I accept this resistance of other minds without being either astonished or disheartened by it. Is it possible that men's minds should not be turned and their eyes blink in a kind of dizziness, when, in the midst of the darkness which still weighs upon us, the radiant door to the future is suddenly thrust open?

Gentlemen, if someone four centuries ago, at a time when war raged from parish to parish, from town to town, from province to province – if someone had said to Lorraine, to Picardy, to Normandy, to Brittany, to Auvergne, to Provence, to Dauphine, to Burgundy, 'A day will come when you will no longer wage war, when you will no longer raise men of arms against each other, when it will no longer be said that

Normans have attacked the men of Picardy, and the men of Lorraine have driven back those of Burgundy; that you will still have differences to settle, interests to discuss, certainly disputes to solve, but do you know what you will have in place of men on foot and horseback, in place of guns, falconets, spears, pikes, and swords? You will have a small box made of wood, which you will call a ballot box. And do you know what this box will bring forth? An assembly, an assembly in which you will all feel you live, an assembly which will be like your own soul, a supreme and popular council which will decide, judge, and solve everything in law, which will cause the sword to fall from every hand and justice to rise in every heart. And this event will say to you, 'There ends your right, here begins your duty. Lay down your arms! Live in peace!' On that day you will be conscious of a common thought, common interests, and a common destiny. You will clasp each other's hands and you will acknowledge that you are sons of the same blood and the same race. On that day you will no longer be hostile tribes, but a nation. You will no longer be Burgundy, Normandy, Brittany, Provence, you will be France. On that day your name will no longer be war, but civilization.

Well, you say today – and I am one of those who say it with you – all of us here, we say to France, to England, to Prussia, to Austria, to Spain, to Italy, to Russia, we say to them, 'A day will come when your weapons will fall from your hands, a day when war will seem absurd and be as impossible between Paris and London, St Petersburg and Berlin, Vienna and Turin, as today it would seem impossible between Rouen and Amiens, Boston and Philadelphia. A day will come when you France, you Russia, you Italy, you England, you Germany, all you continental nations, without losing your characteristics, your glorious individuality, will intimately dissolve into a superior unity and you will constitute the European brotherhood just as Normandy, Brittany, Burgundy, Lorraine, Alsace, and all our provinces, have dissolved into France. A day will come when there will be no battlefields, but markets opening to commerce and minds opening to ideas. A day will come when the bullets and bombs are replaced by votes, by universal suffrage, by the venerable arbitration of a great supreme senate which will be to Europe what Parliament is to England, the Diet to Germany, and the Legislative Assembly to France. A day will come when a cannon will be a museum-piece, as instruments of torture are today. And we will be amazed to think that these things once existed! A day will come when we shall see those two immense groups, the United States of America and the United States of Europe, stretching out their hands across the sea, exchanging their products, their arts, their works of genius, clearing up the globe, making deserts fruitful, ameliorating creation under the eyes of the Creator, and joining together to reap the well-being of all. . . .

Henceforth the goal of great politics, of true politics, is this: the recognition of all the nationalities, the restoration of the historical unity of nations and the uniting of the latter to civilization by peace, the relentless enlargement of the civilized group, the setting of an example to the still-savage nations; in short, and this recapitulates all I have said, the assurance that justice will have the last word, spoken in the past by might.

DEVELOPING THEORY
AND PRACTICE

THE QUAKERS

THE Quaker testimony against war is based on a conviction rather than a text, on a conviction that there is an abiding contradiction between war and the spirit of Christ. This conviction has never been based on a distinction between offensive and defensive wars, nor has there ever been a formal doctrine declared by the Society of Friends, nor a creed imposed on its members. The Quakers, unlike the Historic Peace Churches of German origin, have not extended their opposition to war to civil authorities and have supported them whenever such support did not conflict with their conception of the inward light – the divine spirit in all men.

The Society of Friends was founded c. 1650 by George Fox, from whose *Journal* selections printed below have been taken. Men like William Penn, John Bellers, and Robert Barclay were attracted early to the Society and wrote extensively in support of it.

The Quakers in America were well known for their excellent relations with the Indians, and from the first the Society of Friends maintained this to be the result of a 'friendship' established early between both groups; a short excerpt from William Penn's 1682 address to the Indians is included, as is a selection from John Woolman's *Journal* (1774) a minor American classic. Woolman was largely responsible for the fact that many Quakers voluntarily freed their slaves before the American Revolution, and his efforts should be seen in the light of the activities of men like Garrison who, when the Civil War broke out, subordinated their faith in non-violent resistance to the anti-slavery cause.

GEORGE FOX

1624–91

To Oliver Cromwell[1]

1654

I (WHO am of the world called George ffox) doe deny the carrying or drawing of any carnall sword against any, or against thee Oliver Crumwell or any men in presence of the lord God I declare it (God is my wittnesse, by whom I am moved to give this forth for truthes sake, from him whom the world calls George ffox, who is the son of God) who is sent to stand A wittnesse against all violence and against all the workes of darkenesse, and to turn people from the darknesse to the light, and to bring them from the occasion of the warre, and from the occasion of the Magistrates sword, which is A terrorism to the evill doers which actes contrary to the light of the lord Jesus Christ, which is A praise to them that doe well, which is A protection to them that doe well, and not the evill and such soldiers that are putt in that place no false accusers must bee, no violence must doe, but bee content with their wages, and that Magistrate beares not the sword in vaine, from under the occasion of that sword I doe seeke to bring people, my weapons are not carnall but spirituall, And my Kingdome is not of this world, therefore with the carnall weapon I doe not fight, but am from those things dead, from him who is not of the world, called of the world by the name George ffox, and this I am ready to seale with my blood, and this I am moved to give forth for the truthes sake, who A wittnesse stand against all unrighteousnesse and all ungodlynesse, who A suffrer is for the righteous seed sake, waiteing for the redemption of it, who A crowne that is mortal seeks not for, that fadeth away, but in the light dwells, which comprehends that Crowne, which light is the

---

1. After being arrested by soldiers of the Protector at a time when it was rumoured that people were plotting to take Cromwell's life, Fox was set at liberty after affirming in this letter that his intentions were not violent to Cromwell or any man. The incidents relating to this letter took place in 1654 and are in the sixth chapter of his *Journal*. The text of the letter is from the Cambridge edition of the *Journal*.

condemnation of all such; in which Light I wittnesse the Crowne that is Immortall that fades not away, from him who to all your soulls is A friend, for establishing of righteousnesse and cleansing the Land of evil doers, and A wittnesse against all wicked inventions of men and murderous plotts, which Answered shall be with the light in all your Consciences, which makes no Covenant with death, to which light in you all I speake, and am clear.

ff. G.

Who is of the world called George ffox who A new name hath which the world knowes not.

Wee are wittnesses of this Testimony whose names in the flesh is called

THO. ALDAM.   ROBERT CREVEN.

The Time of My Commitment

Now the time of my commitment to the house of correction being nearly ended, and there being many new soldiers raised, the commissioners would have made me captain over them, and the soldiers said they would have none but me. So the keeper of the house of correction was commanded to bring me before the commissioners and soldiers in the market-place; and there they offered me that preferment, as they called it, asking me, if I would not take up arms for the Commonwealth against Charles Stuart? I told them, I knew from whence all wars arose, even from lust, according to James's doctrine; and that I lived in the virtue of that life and power that took away the occasion of all wars. But they courted me to accept their offer, and thought I did but compliment them. But I told them, I was come into the covenant of peace, which was before wars and strife were. They said, they offered it in love and kindness to me, because of my virtue; and such like flattering words they used. But I told them, if that was their love and kindness, I trampled it under my feet. Then their rage got up, and they said, 'Take him away, jailer, and put him into the dungeon amongst the rogues and felons.' So I was had away and put into a lousy, stinking place, without any bed, amongst thirty felons, where I was kept almost half a year, unless it were at times; for they would sometimes let me walk in the garden, having a belief that I would not go away. Now when they had got me into Derby dungeon it was the belief and saying of the people that I should never come out; but I had faith in God, and believed I should be delivered in his time; for the Lord had said to me before, that I was not to be removed from the place yet, being set there for a service which he had for me to do. . . .

. . . All that pretend to fight for Christ, are deceived; for his kingdom is not of this world, therefore his servants do not fight. Fighters are not of Christ's kingdom, but are without Christ's kingdom; his kingdom starts in peace and righteousness, but fighters are in the lust; and all that would destroy men's lives, are not of Christ's mind, who came to save men's lives. Christ's kingdom is not of this world; it is peaceable: and all that are in strife, are not of his kingdom. All that pretend to fight for the Gospel, are deceived; for the Gospel is the power of God, which was before the devil, or fall of man was; and the gospel of peace was before fighting was. Therefore they that pretend fighting, are ignorant of the Gospel; and all that talk of fighting for Sion, are in darkness; for Sion needs no such helpers. All such as profess themselves to be ministers of Christ, or Christians, and go about to beat down the whore with outward, carnal weapons, the flesh and the whore are got up in themselves, and they are in a blind zeal; for the whore is got up by the inward ravening from the Spirit of God; and the beating down thereof, must be by the inward stroke of the sword of the Spirit within. All such as pretend Christ Jesus, and confess him, and yet run into the use of carnal weapons, wrestling with flesh and blood, throw away the spiritual weapons. They that would be wrestlers with flesh and blood, throw away Christ's doctrine; the flesh is got up in them, and they are weary of their sufferings. Such as would revenge themselves, are out of Christ's doctrine. Such as being stricken on one cheek, would not turn the other, are out of Christ's doctrine: and such as do not love one another, nor love enemies, are out of Christ's doctrine. . . .

WILLIAM PENN

1644–1718

Address to the American Indians

THE Great Spirit who made me and you, who rules the heavens and the earth, and who knows the innermost thoughts of men, knows that I and my friends have a hearty desire to live in peace and friendship with you, and to serve you to the utmost of our power. It is not our custom to use hostile weapons against our fellow creatures, for which reason we have come unarmed. Our object is not to do injury, and thus provoke the Great Spirit, but to do good.

We are met on the broad pathway of good faith and goodwill, so that no advantage is to be taken on either side, but all to be openness, brotherhood, and love. . . .

. . . I will not do as the Marylanders did, that is, call you children or brothers only; for parents are apt to whip their children too severely, and brothers sometimes will differ; neither will I compare the friendship between us to a chain, for the rain may rust it, or a tree may fall and break it, but I will consider you as the same flesh and blood with the Christians, and the same as if one man's body were to be divided into two parts.

November 1682

JOHN WOOLMAN

1720–72

A War Tax

A FEW years past, money being made current in our province for carrying on wars, and to be called in again by taxes laid on the inhabitants, my mind was often affected with the thoughts of paying such taxes; and I believe it right for me to preserve a memorandum concerning it. I was told, that Friends in England frequently paid taxes, when the money was applied to such purposes. I had conversation with several noted Friends on the subject, who all favoured the payment of such taxes; some of whom I preferred before myself, and this made me easier for a time; yet there was in the deeps of my mind, a scruple which I never could get over; and at certain times, I was greatly distressed on that account.

I all along believed that there were some upright-hearted men, who paid such taxes; but could not see that their example was a sufficient reason for me to do so, while I believed that the Spirit of Truth required of me, as an individual, to suffer patiently the distress of goods, rather than pay actively.

I have been informed that Thomas à Kempis lived and died in the profession of the Roman Catholic religion and in reading his writings, I have believed him to be a man of a true Christian spirit; as fully so, as many who died martyrs because they could not join with some superstitions in that church.

All true Christians are of the same spirit, but their gifts are diverse; Jesus Christ appointing to each one their peculiar office, agreeably to his infinite wisdom.

John Huss contended against the errors crept into the church, in opposition to the council of Constance; which the historian reports to have consisted of some thousand persons. He modestly vindicated the cause which he believed was right; and though his language and conduct toward his judges appear to have been respectful, yet he never could be moved from the principles settled in his mind. To use his own words: 'This I most humbly require and desire of you all, even for his sake who is the God of us all, that I be not compelled to the thing which my conscience doth repugn or strive against.' And again, in his answer to the emperor: 'I refuse nothing, most noble emperor, whatsoever the council shall decree or determine upon me, only this one thing I except, that I do not offend God and my conscience.' Fox's *Acts and Monuments*, page 233. At length, rather than act contrary to that which he believed the Lord required of him, he chose to suffer death by fire. Thomas à Kempis, without disputing against the articles then generally agreed to, appears to have laboured, by a pious example as well as by preaching and writing, to promote virtue and the inward spiritual religion: and I believe they were both sincere-hearted followers of Christ.

True charity is an excellent virtue: and to labour sincerely for their good, whose beliefs, in all points, do not agree with ours, is a happy state. To refuse the active payment of a tax which our Society generally paid, was exceedingly disagreeable; but to do a thing contrary to my conscience, appeared yet more dreadful. When this exercise came upon me, I knew of none under the like difficulty; and in my distress, I besought the Lord to enable me to give up all, that so I might follow him wheresoever he was pleased to lead me. Under this exercise I went to our Yearly meeting at Philadelphia, in the year 1755; at which a committee was appointed of some from each quarter, to correspond with the Meeting for Sufferings in London; and another to visit our Monthly and Quarterly Meetings; and after their appointment, before the last adjournment of the meeting, it was agreed that these two committees should meet together in Friends' school-house in the city, at a time then concluded on, to consider some things in which the cause of Truth was concerned. These committees meeting together, had a weighty conference in the fear of the Lord; at which time, I perceived there were many Friends under a scruple like that before-mentioned.

As scrupling to pay a tax on account of the application, hath seldom been heard of heretofore, even amongst men of integrity, who have steadily borne their testimony against war, in their time; I may here note some things which have occurred to my mind, as I have been inwardly exercised on that account. From the steady opposition which faithful Friends, in early times, made to wrong things then approved of, they were hated and persecuted by men living in the spirit of this world; and suffering with firmness, they were made a blessing to the church, and the work prospered. It equally concerns men in every age, to take heed to their own spirit; and in comparing their situation with ours, it looks to me that there was less danger of their being infected with the spirit of this world, in paying such taxes, than there is of us now. They had little or no share in civil government; and many of them declared, they were, through the power of God, separated from the spirit in which wars were; and being afflicted by the rulers on account of their testimony, there was less likelihood of uniting in spirit with them in things inconsistent with the purity of Truth. We, from the first settlement of this land, have known little or no troubles of that sort. Their profession for a time, was accounted reproachful; but at length, the uprightness of our predecessors being understood by the rulers, and their innocent sufferings moving them, our way of worship was tolerated; and many of our members in these colonies became active in civil government. Being thus tried with favour and prosperity, this world hath appeared inviting; our minds have been turned to the improvement of our country, to merchandize and sciences, amongst which are many things useful, being followed in pure wisdom; but in our present condition, that a carnal mind is gaining upon us, I believe will not be denied. Some of our members, who are officers in civil government, are, in one case or other, called upon in their respective stations to assist in things relative to the wars. Such being in doubt whether to act, or crave to be excused from their office, seeing their brethren united in the payment of a tax to carry on the said wars, might think their case not much different, and so quench the tender movings of the Holy Spirit in their minds; and thus, by small degrees, there might be an approach toward fighting, until we came so near it, as that the distinction would be little else but the name of a peaceable people.

It requires great self-denial and resignation of ourselves to God, to attain that state wherein we can freely cease from fighting when wrongfully invaded, if by our fighting there was a probability of overcoming the invaders. Whoever rightly attains to it, does, in some degree, feel that spirit in which our Redeemer gave his life for us; and through Divine goodness, many of our predecessors, and many now living, have learned this blessed lesson. But many others, having their religion chiefly by education, and not being enough acquainted with that cross which crucifies to the world, manifest a temper distinguishable from that of an entire trust in God. In calmly considering these things, it hath not appeared strange to me, that an exercise hath now fallen upon some, which, as to the outward means of it, is different from what was known to many of those who went before us.

Some time after the Yearly Meeting, a day being appointed and letters written to distant members, the said committees met at Philadelphia; and by adjournments, continued several days. The calamities of war were now increasing; the frontier inhabitants of Pennsylvania were frequently surprised, some slain, and many taken captive by the Indians; and while these committees sat the corpse of one so slain was brought in a wagon, and taken through the streets of the city, in his bloody garments, to alarm the people, and rouse them up to war.

Friends thus met were not all of one mind in relation to the tax; which, to such who scrupled it, made the way more difficult. To refuse an active payment at such a time, might be construed into an act of disloyalty, and appeared likely to displease the rulers, not only here but in England. Still there was a scruple so fastened upon the minds of many Friends, that nothing moved it: it was a conference the most weighty that ever I was at, and the hearts of many were bowed in reverence before the Most High. Some Friends of the said committees who appeared easy to pay the tax, after several adjournments, withdrew, others of them continued till the last. At length, an epistle of tender love and caution to Friends in Pennsylvania, was drawn by some Friends concerned, on that subject; and being read several times and corrected, was then signed by such of them as were free to sign it, and afterwards sent to the Monthly and Quarterly Meetings.

On the 9th day of the eighth month, in the year 1757, at night, orders came to the military officers in our county (Burlington), directing them to draft the militia and prepare a number of men to go as soldiers, to the relief of the English at fort William Henry, in New York government. A few days after, there was a general review of the militia at Mount Holly, and a number of men chosen and sent off under some officers. Shortly after, there came orders to draft three times as many, to hold themselves in readiness to march when fresh orders came; and on the 17th day of the eighth month, there was a meeting of the military officers at Mount Holly, who agreed on a draft, and orders were sent to the men so chosen, to meet their respective captains at set times and places; those in our township to meet at Mount Holly; amongst whom were a considerable number of our Society. My mind being affected herewith, I had fresh opportunity to see and consider the advantage of living in the real substance of religion where practice doth harmonize with principle. Amongst the officers are men of understanding, who have some regard to sincerity where they see it; and in the execution of their office, when they have men to deal with whom they

believe to be upright-hearted, to put them to trouble on account of
scruples of conscience, is a painful task, and likely to be avoided as much
as easily may be. But where men profess to be so meek and heavenly-
minded, and to have their trust so firmly settled in God, that they cannot
join in wars; and yet, by their spirit and conduct in common life,
manifest a contrary disposition, their difficulties are great at such a time.

Officers, who, in great anxiety, are endeavouring to get troops to
answer the demands of their superiors, seeing men who are insincere,
pretend a scruple of conscience, in hopes of being excused from a
dangerous employment, are likely to handle them roughly. In this time
of commotion some of our young men left the parts, and tarried abroad
till it was over; some came and proposed to go as soldiers; others
appeared to have a real tender scruple in their minds against joining in
wars, and were much humbled under the apprehension of a trial so near.
I had conversation with several of these to my satisfaction. At the set
time when the captain came to town, some of those last-mentioned
went and told him in substance as follows: – That they could not bear
arms for conscience' sake; nor could they hire any to go in their places,
being resigned as to the event of it: at length the captain acquainted
them all, that they might return home for the present, and required
them to provide themselves as soldiers, and to be in readiness to march
when called upon. This was such a time as I had not seen before; and
yet I may say, with thankfulness to the Lord, that I believed this trial
was intended for our good; and I was favored with resignation to him.
The French army taking the fort they were besieging, destroyed it and
went away: the company of men first drafted, after some days' march,
had orders to return home; and those on the second draft were no
more called upon on that occasion.

On the 4th day of the fourth month, in the year 1758, orders came to
some officers in Mount Holly, to prepare quarters a short time, for
about one hundred soldiers: an officer and two other men, all inhabitants of our town, came to my house; and the officer told me that he
came to speak with me, to provide lodging and entertainment for two
soldiers, there being six shillings a week per man allowed as pay for it.
The case being new and unexpected, I made no answer suddenly; but
sat a time silent, my mind being turned inward. I was fully convinced,
that the proceedings in wars are inconsistent with the purity of the
Christian religion: and to be hired to entertain men, who were then
under pay as soldiers, was a difficulty with me. I expected they had legal

authority for what they did; and after a short time, I said to the officer,
if the men are sent here for entertainment, I believe I shall not refuse to
admit them into my house; but the nature of the case is such, that I
expect I cannot keep them on hire: one of the men intimated, that he
thought I might do it consistently with my religious principles; to
which I made no reply, believing silence, at that time, best for me.
Though they spoke of two, there came only one, who tarried at my
house about two weeks, and behaved himself civilly; and when the
officer came to pay me, I told him I could not take pay for it, having
admitted him into my house in passive obedience to authority. I was on
horseback when he spoke to me; and as I turned from him, he said, he
was obliged to me: to which I said nothing; but thinking on the expression, I grew uneasy; and afterwards being near where he lived, I
went and told him on what grounds I refused taking pay for keeping the
soldier. . . .

WILLIAM GODWIN

1756–1836

GODWIN's great work of political science, *The Inquiry concerning Political Justice, and its Influence on General Virtue and Happiness* (1793), a statement of almost pure anarchism, places him in the main stream of English political radicalism. In it he attacked monarchy, capital punishment and the penal code in general, the institutions of property and marriage, founded as they were on law – for it was all law he was in protest against. Law was restrictive, and he believed in man's essential goodness, in his perfectibility; evil he laid at society's doorstep. He was opposed, therefore, to all control of man: law, violence which supported law, and war which extended violence.

He was a strong influence on Shelley, who eloped with his daughter, an action which drew Godwin's bitter hostility despite all he had written. In fact, the latter part of Godwin's life was a sad commentary on the individualism he espoused: in addition to opposing the elopement of his disciple, Shelley, with his daughter, he had himself married a second time in 1801; he accepted a more or less meaningless position as a gift from the hated government in 1833 – living quarters attached; and after his reconciliation with Shelley following the latter's marriage in 1816 he continued to demand, until Shelley's death, regular payments for his support.

But his earlier work stands as one of the great protests against violence and the tyranny of the State, one of the great affirmations of individualism. The selections below are taken from the second edition, London, 1796.

Set no value on anything, but . . .

It is perhaps impossible to shew that a single war ever did or could have taken place in the history of mankind, that did not in some way originate with those two great political monopolies, monarchy and aristocracy. . . .

What could be the source of misunderstanding between states, where no man or body of men found encouragement to the accumulation of privileges to himself at the expense of the rest. . . ?

One of the most essential principles of political justice is diametrically the reverse of that which impostors as well as patriots have too frequently agreed to recommend. Their perpetual exhortation has been, 'Love your country. Sink the personal existence of individuals in the existence of the community. Make little account of the particular men of whom the society consists, but aim at the general wealth, prosperity and glory. Purify your mind from the gross ideas of sense, and elevate it to the single contemplation of that abstract individual of which particular men are so many detached members, valuable only for the place they fill.'

The lessons of reason on this head are precisely opposite. 'Society is an ideal existence, and not on its own account entitled to the smallest regard. The wealth, prosperity and glory of the whole are unintelligible chimeras. Set no value on any thing, but in proportion as you are convinced of its tendency to make individual men happy and virtuous. Benefit by every practicable mode man wherever he exists; but be not deceived by the specious idea of affording services to a body of men, for which no individual man is the better. Society was instituted, not for the sake of glory, not to furnish splendid materials for the page of history, but for the benefit of its members. The love of our country, if we would speak accurately, is another of those specious illusions, which have been invented by impostors in order to render the multitude the blind instruments of their crooked designs. . . .'

Because individuals were liable to error, and suffered their apprehensions of justice to be perverted by a bias in favour of themselves, government was instituted. Because nations were susceptible of a similar weakness, and could find no sufficient umpire to whom to appeal, war was introduced. Men were induced deliberately to seek each other's lives, and to adjudge the controversies between them not according to the dictates of reason and justice, but as either should prove most successful in devastation and murder. This was no doubt in the first instance the extremity of exasperation and rage. But it has since been converted into a trade. One part of the nation pays another part to murder and be murdered in their stead; and the most trivial causes, a supposed insult or a sally of youthful ambition, has sufficed to deluge provinces with blood.

We can have no adequate idea of this evil, unless we visit, at least in imagination, a field of battle. Here men deliberately destroy each other by thousands without any resentment against or even knowledge of each other. The plain is strewed with death in all its various forms. Anguish and wounds display the diversified modes in which they can torment the human frame. Towns are burned, ships are blown up in the air while the mangled limbs descend on every side, the fields are laid desolate, the wives of the inhabitants exposed to brutal insult, and their children driven forth to hunger and nakedness. It would be despicable to mention, along with these scenes of horror, and the total subversion of all ideas of moral justice they must occasion in the auditors and spectators, the immense treasures which are coming in the form of taxes from those inhabitants whose residence is at a distance from the scene. . . .

The criminal justice, as it has been termed, of nations within themselves, has only three objects that it can be imagined to have in view – the reformation of the criminal, the restraining him from future excesses, and example. But none of these objects, whatever may be thought of them while confined to their original province, can possibly apply to the case of war between independent states. War, as we have already seen, perhaps never originates on the offending side in the sentiments of a nation, but of a comparatively small number of individuals: and, were it otherwise, there is something so monstrous in the idea of changing the principles of a whole country by the mode of military execution, that every man, not lost to sobriety and common sense, must inevitably shrink from it with horror.

Restraint appears to be sometimes necessary with respect to the offenders that exist in the midst of a community, because it is customary for such offenders to assault us with unexpected violence; but nations cannot move with such secrecy as to make an unforeseen attack an object of considerable apprehension. The only effectual means of restraint in this last case is by disabling, impoverishing and depopulating the country of our adversaries; and, if we recollected that they were men as well as ourselves, and the great mass of them innocent of the quarrel against us, we should be little likely to consider these expedients with complacency. The idea of making an example of an offending nation, is reserved for that God whom the Church by law established instructs us to adore. . . .

Treaties of alliance are in all cases wrong, in the first place, because all absolute promises are wrong, and neither individuals nor bodies of men ought to preclude themselves from the benefit of future improvement and deliberation. Secondly, they are wrong, because they are in all cases nugatory. Governments, and public men, will not, and ought not to hold themselves bound to the injury of the concerns they conduct, because a parchment, to which they or their predecessors were a party, requires it at their hands. If the concert demanded in time of need, approve itself to their judgement or correspond with their inclination, it will be yielded, though they were under no previous engagement for that purpose. Treaties of alliance serve to no other end, than to exhibit by their violation an appearance of profligacy and vice, which unfortunately becomes too often a powerful encouragement to the inconsistency of individuals. Add to this, that if alliances were engines as powerful, as they are really impotent, they could seldom be of use to a nation uniformly adhering to the principles of justice. They would be useless, because they are in reality ill calculated for any other purposes than those of ambition. They might be pernicious, because it would be beneficial for nations as it is for individuals, to look for resources at home, instead of depending upon the precarious compassion of their neighbours. . . .

This whole [diplomatic] system proceeds upon the idea of national grandeur and glory, as if in reality these words had any specific meaning. These contemptible objects, these airy names, have from the earliest page of history been made the ostensible colour for the most pernicious undertakings. Let us take a specimen of their value from the most innocent and laudable of pursuits. If I aspire to be a great poet or a great historian, so far as I am influenced by the dictates of reason, it is that I may be useful to mankind, and not that I may do honour to my country. Is Newton the better because he was an Englishman, or Galileo the worse because he was an Italian? Who can endure to put this high-sounding nonsense in the balance against the best interests of mankind, which will always suffer a mortal wound, when dexterity, artifice and concealment are made topics of admiration and applause? . . .

DAVID L. DODGE

1774–1852

DODGE was founder of the world's first peace society and the man who, with the publication of his first peace tract, *The Mediator's Kingdom Not of This World*, ushered in an era of intense peace pamphleteering. He was a well-to-do New York merchant, a Presbyterian, who, in contrast to the peace movement his efforts in large part established, made no distinction between offensive and defensive wars. In his major work, *War Inconsistent with the Religion of Jesus Christ* (1813), he drew attention to 'the fact ... that no man can, on gospel principles, draw a line of distinction between offensive and defensive war so as to make the former a crime and the latter a duty....'

His little-known *Autobiography* was written late in life at the request of his family; it was privately printed in 1857 together with a collection of his writings under the title *Memorial to Mr David L. Dodge*. It is from the *Autobiography* that the following selection is taken.

Dodge remained a merchant to the end of his life; far from reducing his effectiveness as a pacifist, it gave him some insight into the relationship between religion, society, and war. Not unnaturally perhaps, he overlooked the economic aspects of the problem, but he also wrote in *War Inconsistent with the Religion of Jesus Christ* that 'Newspapers must be ushered forth with flaming pieces to rouse, as it is called, the spirit of the countries, so as to impress upon the populace the idea that the approaching war is just and necessary, for all wars must be just and necessary on both sides'. Dymond attacked the press in this same period for the same reasons, but Dodge, whose own cause benefited so much from the increasing ease of communication, seems almost to prophesy the coming century and a half – the age of mass communication, mass war propaganda, and mass war.

By Gospel Authority

My parents again struggled, with severe labor and rigid economy, to free themselves from debt. After a few years' experiment on the new farm, which, by the way, was rough, but of strong soil and in rather an out-of-the-way place, our nearest neighbors being half a mile distant, my father was inclined to settle down for life. His spirit of enterprise seemed to be crushed, by hard service and misfortune. I, however, being an ambitious lad of about sixteen, was desirous that my parents should sell and move to Western New York, and grow up with some rising village. But they declined, and this led finally to my wandering from home after a season, by their reluctant consent.

I will now call to mind some of the events of my own life, though of no special interest to any one except to my children and near descendants, for whose sake I write. My earliest recollection extends to the time when I was but little over two years of age, and the place where my parents resided about that time, in the year 1776. When I was a young man I visited the place to see if my memory was correct, and found it perfectly so.

Several incidents I distinctly recollect, which occurred in the course of the two following years, as of my half-brother, William Earl, being brought home sick from the army, also the wagon manufactory, the names and visages of some of the workmen. I recollect our removal to our hired farm in 1779, and the cannonading when New London was burnt. At that time my father had employed a soldier at home on furlough for a few days, to cut bushes in a pasture, and I was with him to heap up the brush. As we listened, he said, there is fighting somewhere today. He then went and sat down under a large walnut tree, and I followed him. He occasionally uttered in substance such expressions as, 'There is hot work somewhere today'; 'Blood is flowing today'; 'Souls are passing into eternity', &c. Such exclamations, together with the expression of his countenance, fastened the day upon my memory. News came the next morning that the forts were stormed, the garrisons put to the sword, New London burnt, and the British were marching upon Norwich, and would proceed up into the country. My mother wrung her hands, and asked my father if we had not better pack up some things to secrete them. He replied, there would be ample time for this work after hearing again, before they could reach us. I particularly recollect the terrible snow-storm in the winter 1780, the intercourse of neighbors being kept up, mainly, on snow-shoes, and many females using them; the snow averaged five to eight feet deep.

I will here notice an event, as it illustrates the spirit of the times. There was a respectable farmer who resided in Brooklyn, by the name of John Baker, who was called an odd and singular man, because he openly denounced all kinds of carnal warfare as contrary to the Gospel; and, of course, refused to take any part in the revolutionary war. By some he was called a *Tory*, by others a *coward*, while he constantly declared it a matter of conscience. Yet he was drafted for the army, and his neighbors determined he should serve by compulsion. He declared he would die before he would serve as a warrior, and consequently fled to the woods in the fall of 1779. The clergy and the laity urged his compulsion, and the populace turned out and pursued him, as hounds would a fox, and finally they caught and bound him, like Sampson, 'with strong cords', placed him in a wagon, and sent two trusty patriots to convey him to Providence, to the troops stationed there. In the course of the night, however, he got hold of a knife, cut himself loose, and escaped to the woods. Subsequently he returned and secreted himself in a large, dense cedar swamp, about half a mile from our house. He made himself as comfortable a shelter as the thick boughs of the double spruce and cedar would permit. There he remained, without fire, during the severe winter of 1780, without the knowledge of any one, except his brother and my parents, to whom he made himself known to save himself from perishing. His brother furnished him, in the night, with some articles of food and clothing from his own house; and my father, by an understanding with him, was absent at certain times, while my mother would supply him with food, blankets, and other conveniences. There was a wall from the woods connected with the swamp, to our garden, forming the back fence. One day, as I was on a snow-bank in the rear of the garden, I looked over the fence and saw a man creeping along the side of the wall; as soon as he saw me he started and ran for the woods. I, with equal speed, made for the house, supposing he was a 'wild Indian', of which class of men I had heard many frightful stories, and screamed to my mother that the Indians had come, and fled into the back room and crept under the bed. The term 'wild' was applied to Indians on the frontiers at war with Americans, in distinction from a pretty numerous remnant of several tribes who lived quietly in the State. So frightened was I at a glimpse of poor Baker, that for several nights afterwards I dreamed frightful dreams about 'wild Indians'.

The facts relative to Mr Baker, I received from my parents, but do not recollect how he was released. Probably the compassion of the community was aroused, as there was reason to suppose that he might have perished by the severity of the winter. In after years, when a young man,

I have visited Mr Baker. He had one of the best cultivated farms in the vicinity, and I never heard a lisp against his character, except his opposition to war. . . .

We had in Hampton two officers who were captured by the Indians and were prisoners to them for a length of time during the revolutionary war. They started the project of another military gathering in Hampton. Volunteers were solicited from neighboring towns for soldiers and others to personate Indians. The day was appointed, the novelty of the scene excited attention and created high expectation.

They collected, as far as I recollect, nearly two hundred, to personate Indians. The night previous they encamped in a dense grove of woods, by a council fire, about three-quarters of a mile from the parade, where they were disguised in Indian dress, painted, and held a war dance, under the excitement of strong water. My father wisely prohibited me from witnessing the war dance, to my great grief. The military met about nine o'clock next morning. A scouting party of horse was sent out, and the troopers soon returned at full speed and reported an invading band of Indians. A display for battle was soon made and the troops marched, at quick time, toward the woods, and in the mean time the Indians had entered a bush pasture which joined the woods, and had crept near to the road. When all of a sudden, the Indians fired from the bushes, accompanied by the most unearthly whoop I ever heard. The infantry was ordered to display, scale the wall and charge the Indians in the pasture with bayonet, which was promptly executed, driving them before through the brush like a flock of sheep, both parties keeping up a scattering fire until they reached the woods, where the Indians made a stand behind trees, where the main battle was fought. The horse attempted to charge the Indians in the woods and were driven back, and the infantry also retreated, the Indians following, whooping and firing until they reached the open field. The horse made another charge and the Indians selected a trooper with a bald head and unhorsed him, and with their scalping-knife took his false scalp, and held it up as a trophy of victory. This excited a universal shout of laughter from the spectators. I need add no more particulars. I suppose the parts were pretty well sustained. There was a great collection to view the scene, and I suppose most of the ministers of the Gospel in the vicinity were present, as they were generally spectators of military parades, and often took parts in them. I have often, myself, seen the military form a hollow square, the drums all piled in the centre, and a minister led up by the officers under the flag, and offer up a prayer over the drums, after which they marched under the flag, at quick time, with the officers to their quarters to dine, while the soldiers followed, cross firing over their heads, as tokens of honor. No wonder the spirit of war pervaded the community. I simply glance at these things, that you may judge under what influence the youth of the country, at that day, were educated.

The county of Windham was famous for its patriotism. Very few able-bodied men were there who had not served more or less in the war; and, with few exceptions, those who survived and returned were generally addicted to low gambling, profanity, intemperance, and widely diffused a most unwholesome moral influence, which we might naturally expect as the fruits of war. I never heard of but one objection to the Indian farce, and that was so singular, I will mention it, though out of place. The person gravely remarked, that he thought it was impious to take the Lord's host and convert them into heathen idolaters. He had probably so often heard venerable ministers in their prayers and sermons call the militia of the country the Lord's host, his American Israel, &c., that he considered them set apart for sacred purposes.

About this time Shays' rebellion occurred, and many of the young men and some of the revolutionary soldiers went from our vicinity to join him; among the number, the young man who lived with us. They went off in the night. He was absent a number of days, when he entered a back door, and skulked in a corner of the kitchen. My father went out to him, and said, 'Abijah, I understand you have joined Shays in his rebellion.' He replied, 'I hav'n't joined him.' My father inquired if he had not run away for that purpose, which he admitted. He was then asked why he did not join him. He replied, 'I obtained a gun and powder, but couldn't get any bullets; and so I returned.' My father gave him an exhortation, and told him he had rather part with him than to have him remain unsteady, and he was at liberty to go if he chose. He staid a while, but was so much jeered at by his associates for his martial enterprise, that he left, to his own injury. Military glory was so much the theme of commendation by clergy and laity, that the amusements of youth were mainly of a military kind. There was a grenadier company formed in Hampton, of youth from twelve to fifteen years of age, in uniform, with wooden guns and paper caps, who were highly compli-mented by officers and old soldiers for their exact movements. There were also two artillery companies, having two small iron field pieces. I was, by permission, a member of the Down Town Company, and chosen first lieutenant. My father, who was an excellent wheelwright, took the wheels and axle of a hand-cart, and built a carriage for our cannon, and mounted it strongly for us. On muster day we went early to salute the colonel of the regiment and the militia officers. In return, they gave us a full supply of cherry rum. We were treated and complimented by the officers and soldiers, and joined in a sham fight, our pieces being in opposition. Gravel stones were added to the cartridges on both sides, without the observation of the officers, until some were slightly wounded. This led to interference, which finally caused the disbanding of our companies; but did not destroy the deadly hate of the rival companies, which often broke out in actual war, notwithstanding parental restraint. . . .

Early in 1792, a new subject interrupted my thoughts. A grenadier company of volunteers, not enrolled in the militia, was forming in Hampton. As I was not eighteen until the June following, I solicited my parents to permit me to enlist, to which they reluctantly consented on account of the expense. Most of our society of young men joined the company, the whole number of volunteers was about eighty. The commissioned officers were some of the most influential men in the town. Our thoughts and leisure were much occupied in attending to drills. I have seldom since seen a company exercise with more exactness. At our regimental review we were highly complimented for the beauty of our uniform and our soldier-like movements and deportment.

I will here mention an anecdote to illustrate the war-spirit we had imbibed. Soon after our regimental review, there was an ordination in a neighboring town. Most of our society, by agreement, went together and seated ourselves in the row of square pews next to the walls in the gallery. The house was soon filled to overflowing and the exercises progressed; all at once, a tremendous crash and jar occurred in the house, a general shriek and rush followed; one of our young corporals placed himself at the door of the pew and exclaimed to our young ladies not to be alarmed or leave their seats, for they were guarded by grenadiers, who know no fear nor ever shrink from danger, and all our girls quietly retained their seats, while many ladies were in a sad plight by attempting to escape through the windows and doors. The house was afterwards partially filled and the exercises closed without further alarm.

I will now glance at some of the moral effects of my wanderings. My association with the grenadier company drew off my thoughts from serious considerations, and fostered vanity and lightmindedness. Yet I occasionally had serious thoughts and reproofs of conscience. While teaching in Mansfield, for several weeks I boarded and lodged in the same room with a licentiate then preaching there on trial, but as far as I recollect, he never introduced a word on the subject of religion to me. He was affable and obliging, rendering me some assistance in my studies. We boarded in a religious family, had prayers morning and evening, with chaste conversation. The great theme of excitement, however, by clergy and laity at that day, was found in the events of the French revolution and the politics of the United States. These things rather stumbled me, thoughtful as I was; for I believed that, if the Bible were true, religion was paramount to all other considerations. . . .

Being at this time subject to military duty, and invited to join the Governor's Guards, the most popular uniform company in the State, I enlisted without much consideration. Indeed I was in the full belief of the duty and necessity of sustaining the military arm of power; but it proved a snare to me; it woke up anew my military spirit, which had in some measure died away, and drew away my thoughts to military glory, and quenched a thirst for spiritual things. This state of mind was for a while counteracted by an incident I will relate. While I was not slothful in business, yet I was not fervent in spirit serving the Lord. At a busy moment I heard our church bell, and inquired of my young men if they knew the occasion. They replied it was for the preparatory lecture. Though announced the previous sabbath I had forgotten the approaching communion. Mortified that my clerks would witness such neglect of duty, my languid conscience awoke, and urged to self-examination. I went to the lecture, which drew skilfully the lines of demarcation between saints and sinners; my place appeared among the latter. I immediately had solemn convictions of sin, which increased to the sabbath morning, when I went to meeting with desponding feelings. The communion was to be celebrated at the close of the morning service. I was more and more distressed as the services proceeded, and had fully decided not to remain at the communion, as I thought myself wholly unqualified. But just before the close of the morning services, a sudden view of Christ and his salvation for the chief of sinners, almost overwhelmed me; the darkness and terror fled away, and light and peace succeeded. During the celebration I could hardly command my feelings, I then continued more or less tranquil for a length of time, though I communicated my exercises to no one, lest I should appear vain-glorious. . . .

In this, or the following year, there were several daring highway robberies committed in the vicinity of Boston, and as I was in the habit of travelling to Boston in my chaise after goods, and often with large amounts of money, it became a question whether I ought not to arm myself for defence. As I had some doubts as to the propriety of arming myself with deathly weapons, I asked the opinion of some Christian friends, among whom was Mr Joseph Stewart, whose opinion I greatly respected. All concurred that it was my duty. I decided if it was duty, to arm effectually was also duty. I obtained large double barrel pistols, with a long spring dagger. I exercised myself with my pistols until I became expert in suddenly discharging them. As I commenced travelling armed, I was constantly looking out for robbers, and I presume often had suspicions of honest persons. On one occasion, as I was drawing out my deposits in the Hartford Bank, the cashier inquired if I was going to Boston. I told him I expected to start the next morning; he said he would thank me to take a bundle for him and leave it at the Massachusetts Bank. I did not like to deny him, and yet I did not like the responsibility of my own funds and his large package, which doubtless formed a large amount. I had business which called me by the way of Providence, R. I. I stopped at a tavern where I was acquainted; asked the landlord for a room by myself; he took me into a room with two beds. I observed he might wish to make use of the other bed. He answered, No; he had plenty of spare beds; I should not be disturbed. I put my trunk under the bed, my pistols under my pillow, locked the door, near the head of my bed, and put the key in my pocket. After supper, I retired to my room, examined every thing to see if all was safe from intrusion; examined my pistols, which were in the best of order; and soon after retired to bed with the door locked, and quickly fell asleep. In the night, a packet arrived from New York, with many passengers, who called up the landlord for lodgings. He, it seems, had wholly forgot his conducting me to bed, and came hastily to the door to open it, and gave it a sudden jar, and burst off the lock. The noise aroused me. While yet half asleep, I seized my pistols, and by a kind providence I so far awoke as to recognize him by the light of his candle;

by which means I just escaped taking his life. We were both frightened at the occurrence; and I do not know that I slept any more that night. . . .

Passing on to Boston alone in my chaise the next day, I pondered on the event, and tried to realize what would have been my situation and feelings had I taken his life; but especially in what light God would have viewed the transaction? I then resolved, by the help of God, to examine the question by the light of revelation, as to the duty of Christians arming themselves with deadly weapons for self-defence. I think this event occurred in 1805; and for two or three years following my mind dwelt more or less on the question; and I was surprised to find so little disquisition on the subject. When I turned to the spirit, and the examples of Christ, and the precepts of the Gospel, they appeared against it; but when I turned to theologians and moral philosophers, they generally appeared to favor it, except some of the early Christians, and those in the days of the Reformation, as Martin Luther, Erasmus, and a few others, until the times of the Moravians, Quakers, and some other denominations. I struggled hard to satisfy myself that defensive war, in extreme cases, might be tolerated by the Gospel; otherwise, the American revolution could not be justified. I here again met difficulty, as the precepts of the Gospel were especially against defensive warfare. I endeavored, during this period, to draw out arguments in favor of defence with deathly weapons, by conversing with many esteemed, pious, and well educated persons, taking myself opposite grounds. Some would decline controverting the question, as they had never examined it. Others would justify the recourse to deathly weapons, from the necessity of the case, appealing to hypothetical cases, which the supposed inherent laws of nature justified; while they wholly over-looked any divine warrant for the act, as well as God's promises of protection to his saints, in all cases, except witnesses for the truth, who receive the honor and reward of martyrs. Others, again, would justify defensive war, by the example of those whom they esteemed pious, especially the heroes of the American revolution, whose example seemed to be paramount to all other considerations. While I always endeavored to test the question by Gospel authority, yet my opponent generally avoided that standard, and would urge supposed conse-quences; such, for example, 'shall we stand still and let assassins into our houses, and let them murder ourselves and families?' As though assassins rolled out of the circle of God's providence, and that his promises of protection to the obedient were unmeaning. In this inquiring state of mind, no one circumstance led me so much to doubt the soundness of the sentiments of my opponents as their general want of faith in the promises and providential protection of God; and when I laid aside my pistols, exchanging them for the protection of the Lord God of Hosts, I was no more tormented with the fear of robbers. Indeed I was never fully settled in my mind on the subject, until it pleased my heavenly Father, in 1808 (while so low with the spotted fever, that two respectable physicians told me I should not probably live through the day), to shake me over the grave; when time appeared to be receding, and eternity opening with all its infinite importance, my mind being serene as the rising morning, this subject passed before it, when I had no more doubt, from the spirit and example of Christ and the precepts of the Gospel, that all kinds of carnal warfare were unlawful for the followers of Christ, than I had of my own existence. At this solemn moment the Word of God appeared a reality; a sure foundation on which to rest my eternal hopes. From this period, my war spirit appeared to be crucified and slain; and I felt regret that I had not borne some more public testimony against it.

I will drop a word of advice here to my descendants, that whatever indulgence you may grant your grand-children, I entreat you not to give them military toys, nor take them to visit military reviews; for not anything takes so strong hold of young and tender minds as martial music, and the gaudy trappings of military service. When they have accidentally caught the sounds of the music, and seen the brilliant parade of troops, then explain to them the nature and fruits of war, and that the parades were designed to foster the spirit and teach the art of war. This evil of witnessing reviews I know from long and sad experience, until my eyes were finally opened, by the providence of God, to examine and see their antichristian spirit and practice. . . .

RALPH WALDO EMERSON

1803–82

EMERSON delivered his lecture 'War' in Boston in 1838, a time in his life when he showed growing interest in experiments in contemporary reform. A year earlier he had delivered his much-quoted Phi Beta Kappa oration, 'The American Scholar', an eloquent appeal for independence, sincerity, realism, and experiment in American intellectual life. In 1838 the graduating class of the Harvard Divinity School heard him passionately protest 'the defects of historical Christianity' while affirming the need for a more intimate relationship 'with Deity'. Having earlier discovered that 'the writer shall not dig', one experiment he did not participate in was the one in communal living at Brook Farm, but in 1840 he and other Transcendentalists founded *The Dial*, which for four years was the organ of such writers as Thoreau and Margaret Fuller. It is in the light of Transcendentalist concern with Nature and social problems and Emerson's own characteristic optimism that 'War' should be seen today.

Familiar with the sacred books of the East in translation, he attempted when he became editor of *The Dial*, to make them better known; but despite their tradition, and despite 'War' for that matter, Emerson (who had by slow turns become an ardent abolitionist) actively supported the Union cause in the Civil War.

'War' was collected in 1849 in *Aesthetic Papers* by Elizabeth Peabody, another contributor to *The Dial*.

War

It has been a favorite study of modern philosophy to indicate the steps of human progress, to watch the rising of a thought in one man's mind, the communication of it to a few, to a small minority, its expansion and general reception, until it publishes itself to the world by destroying the existing laws and institutions, and the generation of new. Looked at in this general and historical way, many things wear a very different face from that they show near by, and one at a time – and, particularly, war. War, which to sane men at the present day begins to look like an epidemic insanity, breaking out here and there like the cholera or influenza, infecting men's brains instead of their bowels – when seen in the remote past, in the infancy of society, appears a part of the connexion of events, and, in its place, necessary.

As far as history has preserved to us the slow unfoldings of any savage tribe, it is not easy to see how war could be avoided by such wild, passionate, needy, ungoverned, strong-bodied creatures. For in the infancy of society, when a thin population and improvidence make the supply of food and of shelter insufficient and very precarious, and when hunger, thirst, ague and frozen limbs universally take precedence of the wants of the mind and the heart, the necessities of the strong will certainly be satisfied at the cost of the weak, at whatever peril of future revenge. It is plain, too, that in the first dawnings of the religious sentiment, *that* blends itself with their passions and is oil to the fire. Not only every tribe has war-gods, religious festivals in victory, but *religious wars*.

The student of history acquiesces the more readily in this copious bloodshed of the early annals, bloodshed in God's name too, when he learns that it is a temporary and preparatory state, and does actively forward the culture of man. War educates the senses, calls into action the will, perfects the physical constitution, brings men into such swift and close collision in critical moments that man measures man. On its own scale, on the virtues it loves, it endures no counterfeit, but shakes the whole society until every atom falls into the place its specific gravity assigns it. It presently finds the value of good sense and of foresight, and Ulysses takes rank next to Achilles. The leaders, picked men of a courage and vigor tried and augmented in fifty battles, are emulous to distinguish themselves above each other by new merits, as clemency, hospitality, splendor of living. The people imitate the chiefs. The strong tribe, in which war has become an art, attack and conquer their neighbors, and teach them their arts and virtues. New territory, augmented numbers and extended interests call out new virtues and abilities, and the tribe makes long strides. And, finally, when much progress has been made, all its secrets of wisdom and art are disseminated by its invasions. Plutarch, in his essay 'On the Fortune of Alexander', considers the invasion and conquest of the East by Alexander as one of the most bright and pleasing pages in history; and it must be owned he gives sound reason for his opinion. It had the effect of uniting into one great interest the divided commonwealths of Greece, and infusing a new and more enlarged public spirit into the councils of their statesmen. It carried the arts and language and philosophy of the Greeks into the sluggish and barbarous nations of Persia, Assyria and India. It introduced the arts of husbandry among tribes of hunters and shepherds. It weaned the Scythians and Persians from some cruel and licentious practices to a more civil way of life. It introduced the sacredness of marriage among them. It built seventy cities, and sowed the Greek customs and humane laws over Asia, and united hostile nations under one code. It brought different families of the human race together – to blows at first, but afterwards to truce, to trade and to intermarriage. It would be very easy to show analogous benefits that have resulted from military movements of later ages.

Considerations of this kind lead us to a true view of the nature and office of war. We see it is the subject of all history; that it has been the principal employment of the most conspicuous men; that it is at this moment the delight of half the world, of almost all young and ignorant persons; that it is exhibited to us continually in the dumb show of brute nature, where war between tribes, and between individuals of the same tribe, perpetually rages. The miscroscope reveals miniature butchery in atomies and infinitely small biters that swim and fight in an illuminated drop of water; and the little globe is but a too faithful miniature of the large.

What does all this war, beginning from the lowest races and reaching up to man, signify? Is it not manifest that it covers a great and beneficent principle, which nature had deeply at heart? What is that principle? – It is self-help. Nature implants with life the instinct of self-help, perpetual struggle to be, to resist opposition, to attain to freedom, to attain to a mastery and the security of a permanent, self-defended being; and to each creature these objects are made so dear that it risks its life continually in the struggle for these ends.

But whilst this principle, necessarily, is inwrought into the fabric of every creature, yet it is but *one* instinct; and though a primary one, or we may say the very first, yet the appearance of the other instincts immediately modifies and controls this; turns its energies into harmless, useful and high courses, showing thereby what was its ultimate design; and finally, takes out its fangs. The instinct of self-help is very early unfolded in the coarse and merely brute form of war, only in the childhood and imbecility of the other instincts, and remains in that form only until their development. It is the ignorant and childish part of mankind that is the fighting part. Idle and vacant minds want excitement, as all boys kill cats. Bull-baiting, cockpits and the boxer's ring are the enjoyment of the part of society whose animal nature alone has been developed. . . . .

. . . Nothing is plainer than that the sympathy with war is a juvenile and temporary state. Not only the moral sentiment, but trade, learning and whatever makes intercourse, conspire to put it down. Trade, as all men know, is the antagonist of war. Wherever there is no property, the people will put on the knapsack for bread; but trade is instantly endangered and destroyed. And, moreover, trade brings men to look each other in the face, and gives the parties the knowledge that these enemies over sea or over the mountain are such men as we; who laugh and grieve, who love and fear, as we do. And learning and art, and especially religion, weave ties that make war look like fratricide, as it is. And as all history is the picture of war, as we have said, so it is no less true that it is the record of the mitigation and decline of war. Early in the eleventh and twelfth centuries, the Italian cities had grown so populous and strong, that they forced the rural nobility to dismantle their castles, which were dens of cruelty, and come and reside in the towns. The Popes, to their eternal honor, declared religious jubilees, during which all hostilities were suspended throughout Christendom, and man had a breathing space. The increase of civility has abolished the use of poison and of torture, once supposed as necessary as navies now. And, finally, the art of war, what with gunpowder and tactics, has made, as all men know, battles less frequent and less murderous. . . .

. . . The scandal which we feel in such facts certainly shows that we have got on a little. All history is the decline of war, though the slow decline. All that society has yet gained is mitigation: the doctrine of the right of war still remains.

For ages (for ideas work in ages, and animate vast societies of men) the human race has gone on under the tyranny – shall I so call it? – of this first brutish form of their effort to be men; that is, for ages they have shared so much of the nature of the lower animals, the tiger and the shark, and the savages of the water-drop. They have nearly exhausted all the good and all the evil of this form: they have held as fast to this degradation as their worst enemy could desire; but all things have an end, and so has this. The eternal germination of the better has unfolded new powers, new instincts, which were really concealed under this rough and base rind. The sublime question has startled one and another happy soul in different quarters of the globe – Cannot love be, as well as hate? Would not love answer the same end, or even a better? Cannot peace be, as well as war?

This thought is no man's invention, neither St Pierre's nor Rousseau's, but the rising of the general tide in the human soul – and rising highest, and first made visible, in the most simple and pure souls, who have therefore announced it to us beforehand; but presently we all see it. It has now become so distinct as to be a social thought: societies can be formed on it. It is expounded, illustrated, defined, with different degrees of clearness; and its actualization, or the measures it should inspire, predicted according to the light of each seer.

The idea itself is the epoch; the fact that it has become so distinct to any small number of persons as to become a subject of prayer and hope, of concert and discussion – *that* is the commanding fact. This having come, much more will follow. Revolutions go not backward. The star once risen, though only one man in the hemisphere has yet seen its upper limb in the horizon, will mount and mount, until it becomes visible to other men, to multitudes, and climbs the zenith of all eyes. And so it is not a great matter how long men refuse to believe the advent of peace: war is on its last legs; and a universal peace is as sure as is the prevalence of civilization over barbarism, of liberal governments over feudal forms. The question for us is only *How soon?* . . .

. . . Thus always we are daunted by the appearances; not seeing that their whole value lies at bottom in the state of mind. It is really a thought that built this portentous war-establishment, and a thought shall also melt it away. Every nation and every man instantly surround themselves with a material apparatus which exactly corresponds to their moral state, or their state of thought. Observe how every truth and every error, each a *thought* of some man's mind, clothes itself with societies, houses, cities, language, ceremonies, newspapers. Observe the ideas of the present day – orthodoxy, scepticism, missions, popular education, temperance, anti-masonry, anti-slavery; see how each of these abstractions has embodied itself in an imposing apparatus in the community; and how timber, brick, lime and stone have flown into convenient shape, obedient to the master-idea reigning in the minds of many persons. . . .

. . . It follows of course that the least change in the man will change his circumstances; the least enlargement of his ideas, the least mitigation of his feelings in respect to other men; if, for example, he could be inspired with a tender kindness to the souls of men, and should come to feel that every man was another self with whom he might come to join, as left hand works with right. Every degree of the ascendancy of this feeling would cause the most striking changes of external things: the tents would be struck; the men-of-war would rot ashore; the arms rust; the cannon would become street-posts; the pikes, a fisher's harpoon; the marching regiment would be a caravan of emigrants, *peaceful* pioneers at the fountains of the Wabash and the Missouri. . . .

. . . War and peace thus resolve themselves into a mercury of the state of cultivation. At a certain stage of his progress, the man fights, if he be of a sound body and mind. At a certain higher stage, he makes no offensive demonstration, but is alert to repel injury, and of an unconquerable heart. At a still higher stage, he comes into the region of holiness; passion has passed away from him; his war-like nature is all converted into an active medicinal principle; he sacrifices himself, and accepts with alacrity wearisome tasks of denial and charity; but, being attacked, he bears it and turns the other cheek, as one engaged, throughout his being, no longer to the service of an individual but to the common soul of all men.

Since the peace question has been before the public mind, those who affirm its right and expediency have naturally been met with objections more or less weighty. There are cases frequently put by the curious – moral problems, like those problems in arithmetic which in long winter evenings the rustics try the hardness of their heads in ciphering out. And chiefly it is said – Either accept this principle for better, for worse, carry it out to the end, and meet its absurd consequences; or else, if you pretend to set an arbitrary limit, a 'Thus far, no farther', then give up the principle, and take that limit which the common sense of all mankind has set, and which distinguishes offensive war as criminal, defensive war as just. Otherwise, if you go for no war, then be consistent, and give up self-defence in the highway, in your own house. Will you push it thus far? Will you stick to your principle of non-resistance when your strong-box is broken open, when your wife and babes are insulted and slaughtered in your sight? If you say yes, you only invite the robber and assassin; and a few bloody-minded desperadoes would soon butcher the good.

In reply to this charge of absurdity on the extreme peace doctrine, as shown in the supposed consequences, I wish to say that such deductions consider only one half of the fact. They look only at the passive side of the friend of peace, only at his passivity; they quite omit to consider his activity. But no man, it may be presumed, ever embraced the cause of peace and philanthropy for the sole end and satisfaction of being plundered and slain. A man does not come the length of the spirit of martyrdom without some active purpose, some equal motive, some flaming love. If you have a nation of men who have risen to that height of moral cultivation that they will not declare war or carry arms, for they have not so much madness left in their brains, you have a nation of lovers, of benefactors, of true, great and able men. Let me know more of that nation; I shall not find them defenceless, with idle hands springing at their sides. I shall find them men of love, honor and truth; men of an immense industry; men whose influence is felt to the end of the earth; men whose very look and voice carry the sentence of honor and shame; and all forces yield to their energy and persuasion. Whenever we see the doctrine of peace embraced by a nation, we may be assured it will not be one that invites injury; but one, on the contrary, which has a friend in the bottom of the heart of every man, even of the violent and the base; one against which no weapon can prosper; one which is looked upon as the asylum of the human race and has the tears and the blessings of mankind.

In the second place, as far as it respects individual action in difficult and extreme cases, I will say, such cases seldom or never occur to the good and just man; nor are we careful to say, or even to know, what in such crises is to be done. A wise man will never impawn his future being and action, and decide beforehand what he shall do in a given extreme event. Nature and God will instruct him in that hour.

The question naturally arises, How is this new aspiration of the human mind to be made visible and real? How is it to pass out of thoughts into things?

Not, certainly, in the first place, *in the way of routine and mere forms* – the universal specific of modern politics; not by organizing a society, and going through a course of resolutions and public manifestoes, and being thus formally accredited to the public and to the civility of the newspapers. We have played this game to tediousness. In some of our cities they choose noted duellists as presidents and officers of anti-duelling societies. Men who love that bloated vanity called public opinion think all is well if they have once got their bantling through a sufficient course of speeches and cheerings, of one, two, or three public meetings; as if *they* could do anything: they vote and vote, cry hurrah on both sides, no man responsible, no man caring a pin. The next season an Indian war, or an aggression on our commerce by Malays; or the party this man votes with have an appropriation to carry through Congress: instantly he wags his head the other way, and cries, Havoc and war!

This is not to be carried by public opinion, but by private opinion, by private conviction, by private, dear and earnest love. For the only hope of this cause is in the increased insight, and it is to be accomplished by the spontaneous teaching, of the cultivated soul, in its secret experience and meditation – that it is now time that it should pass out of the state of beast into the state of man; it is to hear the voice of God, which bids the devils that have rended and torn him come out of him and let him now be clothed and walk forth in his right mind.

Nor, in the next place, is the peace principle to be carried into effect by fear. It can never be defended, it can never be executed, by cowards. Everything great must be done in the spirit of greatness. The manhood that has been in war must be transferred to the cause of peace, before war can lose its charm, and peace be venerable to men.

The attractiveness of war shows one thing through all the throats of artillery, the thunders of so many sieges, the sack of towns, the jousts of chivalry, the shock of hosts – this namely, the conviction of man universally, that a man should be himself responsible, with goods, health and life, for his behavior; that he should not ask of the State protection; should ask nothing of the State; should be himself a kingdom and a state; fearing no man; quite willing to use the opportunities and advantages that good government throw in his way, but nothing daunted, and not really the poorer if government, law and order went by the board; because in himself reside infinite resources; because he is sure of himself, and never needs to ask another what in any crisis it behooves him to do. . . .

. . . This self-subsistency is the charm of war; for this self-subsistency is essential to our idea of man. But another age comes, a truer religion and ethics open, and a man puts himself under the dominion of principles. I see him to be the servant of truth, of love and of freedom, and immoveable in the waves of the crowds. The man of principle, that is, the man who, without any flourish of trumpets, titles of lordship or train of guards, without any notice of his action abroad, expecting none, takes in solitude the right step uniformly, on his private choice and disdaining consequences – does not yield, in my imagination, to any man, He is willing to be hanged at his own gate, rather than consent to any compromise of his freedom or the suppression of his conviction. I regard no longer those names that so tingled in my ear. This is a baron of a better nobility and a stouter stomach.

The cause of peace is not the cause of cowardice. If peace is sought to be defended or preserved for the safety of the luxurious and the timid, it is a sham, and the peace will be base. War is better, and the peace will be broken. If peace is to be maintained, it must be by brave men, who have come up to the same height as the hero, namely, the will to carry their life in their hand, and stake it at any instant for their principle, but who have gone one step beyond the hero, and will not seek another man's life; – men who have, by their intellectual insight or else by their moral elevation, attained such a perception of their own intrinsic worth, that they do not think property or their own body a sufficient good to be saved by such dereliction of principle as treating a man like a sheep. . . .

WILLIAM LLOYD GARRISON

1805–79

WILLIAM LLOYD GARRISON's lifelong work within the pacifist tradition has been widely neglected by biographers who have emphasized his career as an abolitionist. Until the Civil War, certainly, slavery was the major issue of the day. But Garrison's leadership of numerous national and international anti-slavery societies and his editorship of the *Liberator* and the *Non-Resistant* were both intimately connected with his crusade to abolish slavery without resort to violence.

In 1838, together with Adin Ballou, Edmund Quincy, and Maria W. Chapman, he founded in Boston the New England Non-Resistance Society. A convention had been called to consider non-resistance as the true basis of peace, and on 20 September, the Declaration of Principles (sometimes called the Declaration of Sentiments) which he had drawn up, was adopted by the large majority of the 150 delegates present. The text is reprinted in its entirety below. At the time Garrison declared his conviction that 'Mankind shall hail the 20th of September with more exultation and gratitude than Americans now do the 4th of July'.

He took great pains, as did Adin Ballou, to specify what non-resistance was and what it was not. With Garrison it was anything but passive: '. . . it is a state of activity, ever fighting the good fight, ever foremost to assail unjust power, ever struggling for "liberty, equality, fraternity", in no national sense, but in a world-wide spirit. It is passive only in this sense – that it will not return evil for evil. . . .' However, when war came over the slavery question, Garrison, while still maintaining that non-resistance remained his faith and conviction, could declare the Government 'entirely right'. He counselled abolitionists: 'Now that civil war has begun and a whirlwind of violence and excitement is to sweep the country, it is for abolitionists to "stand still and see the salvation of God", rather than to attempt to add anything to the general commotion'.

Non-resistance Society:
Declaration of Principles, 1838

Assembled in Convention from various sections of the American Union for the promotion of peace on earth, and good will among men, we, the undersigned, regard it as due to ourselves, to the cause which we love, to the country in which we live, and to the world, to publish a DECLARATION, expressive of the principles we cherish, the purpose we aim to accomplish, and the measures we shall adopt to carry forward the work of peaceful, universal reformation.

We cannot acknowledge allegiance to any human government; neither can we oppose any such government by a resort to physical force. We recognize but one KING and LAWGIVER, one JUDGE and RULER of mankind. We are bound by the laws of a kingdom which is not of this world; the subjects of which are forbidden to fight; in which MERCY and TRUTH are met together, and RIGHTEOUSNESS and PEACE have kissed each other; which has no state lines, no national partitions, no geographical boundaries; in which there is no distinction of rank, or division of caste, or inequality of sex; the officers of which are PEACE, its exactors RIGHTEOUSNESS, its walls SALVATION, and its gates PRAISE; and which is destined to break in pieces and consume all other kingdoms.

Our country is the world, our countrymen are all mankind. We love the land of our nativity only as we love all other lands. The interests, rights, liberties of American citizens are no more dear to us, than are those of the whole human race. Hence, we can allow no appeal to patriotism, to revenge any national insult or injury. The PRINCE OF PEACE, under whose stainless banner we rally, came not to destroy, but to save, even the worst of enemies. He has left us an example, that we should follow his steps. GOD COMMANDETH HIS LOVE TOWARD US, IN THAT, WHILE WE WERE YET SINNERS, CHRIST DIED FOR US.

We conceive, that if a nation has no right to defend itself against foreign enemies, or to punish its invaders, no individual possesses that right in his own case. The unit cannot be of greater importance than the aggregate. If one man may take life, to obtain or defend his rights, the same license must necessarily be granted to communities, states, and nations. If *he* may use a dagger or a pistol, *they* may employ cannon, bomb-shells, land and naval forces. The means of self-preservation must be in proportion to the magnitude of interests at stake, and the number of lives exposed to destruction. But if a rapacious and blood-thirsty soldiery, thronging these shores from abroad, with intent to commit rapine and destroy life, may not be resisted by the people or magistracy, then ought no resistance to be offered to domestic troublers of the public peace, or of private security. No obligations can rest upon Americans to regard foreigners as more sacred in their persons than themselves, or to give them a monopoly of wrong-doing with impunity.

The dogma, that all the governments of the world are approvingly ordained of God, and that THE POWERS THAT BE in the United States, in Russia, in Turkey, are in accordance with his will, is not less absurd than impious. It makes the impartial Author of human freedom and equality, unequal and tyrannical. It cannot be affirmed, that THE POWERS THAT BE, in any nation, are actuated by the spirit, or guided by the example of Christ, in the treatment of enemies; therefore, they cannot be agreeable to the will of God; and, therefore, their overthrow, by a spiritual regeneration of their subjects, is inevitable.

We register our testimony, not only against all wars, whether offensive or defensive, but all preparations of war; against every naval ship, every arsenal, every fortification; against the militia system and a standing army; against all military chieftains and soldiers; against all monuments commemorative of victory over a foreign foe, all trophies won in battle, all celebrations in honor of military or naval exploits; against all appropriations for the defence of a nation by force and arms, on the part of any legislative body; against every edict of government requiring of its subjects military service. Hence, we deem it unlawful to bear arms, or to hold a military office.

As every human government is upheld by physical strength, and its laws are enforced virtually at the point of the bayonet, we cannot hold any office which imposes upon its incumbent the obligation to compel men to do right, on pain of imprisonment or death. We therefore voluntarily exclude ourselves from every legislative and judicial body, and repudiate all human politics, worldly honors, and stations of authority. If we cannot occupy a seat in the legislature, or on the bench, neither can we elect others to act as our substitutes in any such capacity.

It follows, that we cannot sue any man at law to compel him by force to restore anything which he may have wrongfully taken from us or others; but, if he had seized our coat, we shall surrender up our cloak rather than subject him to punishment.

We believe that the penal code of the old covenant, AN EYE FOR AN EYE AND A TOOTH FOR A TOOTH, has been abrogated by JESUS CHRIST; and that under the new covenant, the forgiveness instead of the punishment of enemies has been enjoined upon all his disciples, in all cases whatsoever. To extort money from enemies, or set them upon a pillory, or cast them into prison, or hang them upon a gallows, is obviously not to forgive, but to take retribution. VENGEANCE IS MINE— I WILL REPAY, SAITH THE LORD.

The history of mankind is crowded with evidence, proving that physical coercion is not adapted to moral regeneration; that the sinful dispositions of man can be subdued only by love; that evil can be exterminated from the earth only by goodness; that it is not safe to rely upon an arm of flesh, upon man whose breath is in his nostrils, to preserve us from harm; that there is great security in being gentle, harmless, long-suffering, and abundant in mercy; that it is only the meek who shall inherit the earth, for the violent who resort to the sword are destined to perish with the sword. Hence, as a measure of sound policy – of safety to property, life and liberty – of public quietude and private enjoyment – as well as on the ground of allegiance to HIM who is KING OF KINGS and LORD OF LORDS – we cordially adopt the non-resistance principle; being confident that it provides for all possible consequences, will insure all things needful to us, is armed with omnipotent power, and must ultimately triumph over every assailing force.

We advocate no Jacobinical doctrines. The spirit of Jacobinism is the spirit of retaliation, violence, and murder. It neither fears God, nor regards man. *We* would be filled with the spirit of CHRIST. If we abide by our principles, it is impossible for us to be disorderly, or plot treason, or participate in any evil work; we shall submit to every ordinance of man, FOR THE LORD'S SAKE; obey all the requirements of government, except such as we deem contrary to the commands of the Gospel; and in no case resist the operation of law, except by meekly submitting to the penalty of disobedience.

But, while we shall adhere to the doctrine of non-resistance and passive submission to enemies, we purpose, in a moral and spiritual sense, to speak and act boldly in the cause of GOD; to assail iniquity in high places, and in low places; to apply our principles to all existing civil, political, legal and ecclesiastical institutions; and to hasten the time, when the kingdoms of this world will have become the kingdoms of our LORD and of his CHRIST, and he shall reign forever.

It appears to us a self-evident truth, that whatever the Gospel is designed to destroy at any period of the world, being contrary to it, ought now to be abandoned. If, then, the time is predicted, when swords shall be beaten into ploughshares, and spears into pruning hooks, and men shall not learn the art of war any more, it follows that all who manufacture, sell, or wield those deadly weapons, do thus array themselves against the peaceful dominion of the SON OF GOD on earth.

Having thus briefly, but frankly, stated our principles and purpose, we proceed to specify the measures we propose to adopt, in carrying our object into effect.

We expect to prevail, through THE FOOLISHNESS OF PREACHING — striving to commend ourselves unto every man's conscience, in the sight of GOD. From the press, we shall promulgate our sentiments as widely as practicable. We shall endeavor to secure the cooperation of all persons, of whatever name or sect. The triumphant progress of the cause of TEMPERANCE and of ABOLITION in our land, through the instrumentality of benevolent and voluntary associations, encourages us to combine our own means and efforts for the promotion of a still greater cause. Hence, we shall employ lecturers, circulate tracts and publications, form societies, and petition our state and national governments, in relation to the subject of UNIVERSAL PEACE. It will be our leading object to devise ways and means for effecting a radical change in the views, feelings and practices of society, respecting the sinfulness of war and the treatment of enemies.

In entering upon the great work before us, we are not unmindful that, in its prosecution, we may be called to test our sincerity, even as in a fiery ordeal. It may subject us to insult, outrage, suffering, yea, even death itself. We anticipate no small amount of misconception, misrepresentation, calumny. Tumults may arise against us. The ungodly and violent, the proud and pharisaical, the ambitious and tyrannical, principalities and powers, and spiritual wickedness in high places, may combine to crush us. So they treated the MESSIAH, whose example we are humbly striving to imitate. If we suffer with him, we know that we shall reign with him. We shall not be afraid of their terror, neither be troubled. Our confidence is in the LORD ALMIGHTY, not in man.

Having withdrawn from human protection, what can sustain us but that faith which overcomes the world? We shall not think it strange concerning the fiery trial which is to try us, as though some strange thing had happened unto us; but rejoice, inasmuch as we are partakers of CHRIST'S sufferings. Wherefore, we commit the keeping of our souls to GOD, in well-doing, as unto a faithful Creator. FOR EVERY ONE THAT FORSAKES HOUSES, OR BRETHREN, FATHER, OR MOTHER, OR WIFE, OR CHILDREN, OR LANDS, FOR CHRIST'S SAKE, SHALL RECEIVE A HUNDREDFOLD, AND SHALL INHERIT EVERLASTING LIFE.

Firmly relying upon the certain and universal triumph of the sentiments contained in this DECLARATION, however formidable may be the opposition arrayed against them – in solemn testimony of our faith in their divine origin – we hereby affix our signatures to it; commending it to the reason and conscience of mankind, giving ourselves no anxiety as to what may befall us, and resolving, in the strength of the LORD GOD, calmly and meekly to abide the issue.

ADIN BALLOU

1803–90

IT is not Adin, but his kinsman Hosea Ballou (1771–1852), a Universalist clergyman, who is chiefly remembered today, an injustice Tolstoy perhaps anticipated in 1893 in *The Kingdom of God is Within You*. Remarking on an obituary which appeared in the *Religio-Philosophic Journal* of 23 August 1890, Tolstoy wrote that the article in question noted only that Ballou was 'a spiritual guide to the community, that he delivered between eight and nine thousand sermons, married one thousand couples, and wrote about five hundred articles, but not a word is said about the aim to which he devoted all his life – the word "non-resistance" is not even used'.

The work for which he should be remembered, and from which selections have been taken, is *Christian Non-resistance*, published in Philadelphia in 1846. It is the first systematic attempt at defining the term and studying the subject; in his preface he was astute and honest enough to write: 'Here is a little book in illustration and defense of a very unpopular doctrine', and later, prophetically, 'It is a book for the Future, rather than the Present'. His writings were so overlooked in the last years of his life that the original text of Ballou's *The Catechism of Non-resistance*, which Tolstoy was able to quote at length, has never been found. And a reference work like Stanley Kunitz's *American Authors, 1600–1900* (1938) recalls him, correctly enough, as the founder of the Hopedale Community (founded on 'brotherly love and the Gospel of Jesus Christ'), lists his works, but omits mention of *Christian Non-resistance*. The work was reprinted, however, in 1910 in Philadelphia.

Ballou was closely associated with Garrison; they were both founding spirits of the New England Non-resistance Society in 1838, of which Ballou was chosen president in 1843.

Christian Non-resistance

The term non-resistance itself . . . demands attention. It requires very considerable qualifications. I use it as applicable *only* to the conduct of human beings towards human begins – not towards the inferior animals, inanimate things, or satanic influences. If an opponent, willing to make me appear ridiculous, should say – 'You are a non-resistant, and therefore must be *passive* to all assailing beings, things and influences, to satan, man, beast, bird, serpent, insect, rocks, timbers, fires, floods, heat, cold and storm' – I should answer, *not so*; my non-resistance relates solely to conduct between human beings. This is an important limitation of the term. But I go further, and disclaim using the term to express *absolute passivity*, even towards *human* beings. I claim the right to offer the utmost *moral* resistance, not sinful, of which God has made me capable, to every manifestation of evil among mankind. Nay, I hold it my *duty* to offer such moral resistance. In this sense my very non-resistance becomes the highest kind of *resistance* to evil. This is another important qualification of the term. But I do not stop here. There is an uninjurious, benevolent *physical* force. There are cases in which it would not only be allowable, but in the highest degree commendable, to *restrain* human beings by this kind of force. Thus, maniacs, the insane, the delirious sick, ill natured children, the intellectually or *morally* non-compos mentis, the intoxicated and the violently passionate, are frequently disposed to perpetrate outrages and inflict injuries, either on themselves or others, which ought to be kindly and uninjuriously prevented by the muscular energy of their friends. And in cases where deadly violence is inflicted with deliberation and malice aforethought, one may nobly throw his body as a temporary barrier between the destroyer and his helpless victim, choosing to die in that position, rather than be a passive spectator. Thus another most important qualification is given to the term non-resistance. It is not non-resistance to animals and inanimate things, nor to satan, but only to human beings. Nor is it *moral* non-resistance to human beings, but chiefly physical. Nor is it physical non-resistance to all human beings, under all circumstances, but only so far as to abstain totally from the infliction of personal injury, as a means of resistance. It is simply non-resistance of injury with injury – evil with evil.

Will the opposer exclaim – 'This is no non-resistance at all; the term is mischosen!' I answer. So said the old opposers of the Temperance Reformation, respecting the term 'total abstinence'. They began by insisting that the term *must* be taken unqualifiedly, and pronounced total abstinence an *absurdity*. It was replied – 'we limit its application to the use of ardent spirits and intoxicating liquors'. 'Then you exclude these substances from the arts and from external applications, do you?' rejoined the opposers. 'No,' replied the advocates of the cause, 'we mean *total abstinence* from the *internal* use – the *drinking* of those liquors.' 'But are they not sometimes necessary for medical purposes?' said the opposers, 'and *then* may they not be taken internally?' 'Certainly, with proper precautions,' was the reply; 'we mean by *total abstinence*, precisely *this* and no more, 🖝 the entire disuse of all ardent spirits and intoxicating liquors, *as a beverage*'. 'That,' exclaimed the objectors (despairing of a reductio ad absurdum), 'is *no total* abstinence *at all; the* term is mischosen!' Nevertheless, it was a most significant term. It had in it an almost talismanic power. It expressed better than any other just what was meant, and wrought a prodigious change in public opinion and practice. The term *non-resistance* is equally significant and talismanic. It signifies total abstinence from all resistance of injury with injury. It is thus far *non-resistance* – no farther.

The almost universal opinion and practice of mankind has been on the side of resistance of injury *with* injury. It has been held justifiable and *necessary*, for individuals the nations to inflict any amount of *injury* which would effectually resist a supposed greater injury. The consequence has been universal suspicion, defiance, armament, violence, torture and bloodshed. The earth has been rendered a vast slaughter-field – a theatre of reciprocal cruelty and vengeance – strewn with human skulls, reeking with human blood, resounding with human groans, and steeped with human tears. Men have become drunk with mutual revenge; and they who could inflict the greatest amount of injury, in pretended defence of life, honor, rights, property, institutions and laws, have been idolized as the heroes and rightful sovereigns of the world. Non-resistance explodes this horrible delusion; announces the impossibility of overcoming evil with evil; and, making its appeal directly to all the *injured* of the human race, enjoins on them, in the name of God, never more to *resist injury with injury*; assuring them that by adhering to the law of love under all provocations, and scrupulously suffering wrong, rather than inflicting it, they shall gloriously 'overcome evil with good', and exterminate all their enemies by turning them into faithful friends. . . .

THE TERM INJURY

. . . I use this term in a somewhat peculiar sense, to signify any moral influence or physical force exerted by one human being upon another, the legitimate *effect* of which is to destroy or impair *life*, to destroy or impair the *physical faculties*, to destroy or impair the *intellectual powers*, to destroy, impair or pervert the *moral and religious sentiment*, or to destroy or impair the *absolute welfare*, all things considered, of the person on whom such influence or force is exerted; whether that person be innocent or guilty, harmless or offensive, injurious or uninjurious, sane or insane, compos mentis or non-compos, adult or infant. Some of the lexicographers define an '*injury*' to be 'hurt, harm or mischief, *unjustly* done to a person'; thereby implying that any hurt, harm or mischief done to one who *deserves* nothing better, or can be considered as justly liable to it, *is no injury at all*. I reject entirely every such qualification of the term. I hold an *injury* to be an *injury*, whether *deserved* or *undeserved*, whether intended or unintended, whether well meant or ill meant, determining the fact in accordance with the foregoing definition. But, says the inquirer – 'what if it can be proved justifiable, by the law of God, to inflict personal injury in certain cases on the offensive and guilty?' Then, of course, it will be proved that non-resistance is a false doctrine. 'What if it can be proved that the infliction of small injuries may prevent much greater evils?' Then it will be proved that we may do evil that good may come, which will forever keep the world just where it is. 'What if it can be shown that the person who inflicts an injury honestly intended it for a benefit?' That will only prove him *honestly mistaken*, and so undeserving of blame. 'What if a man inflicts death or any other injury, according to established human laws, but does it without malice, or revenge, or any malevolent intent?' Then he does an *anti-christian* act, without conscience as to its real nature. The act must be condemned; he must be credited for his motives; due allowance must be made for his misapprehension of duty; and light poured into his mind to superinduce a better conscience, that he may be brought to act the Christian part. But in no case must we lose sight of the inquiry, whether an *injury* has been done. And in determining this, we must not ask whether the recipient were guilty or innocent, whether the thing done were well or ill intended, whether it were done in a right or a wrong spirit. If it be in fact an *injury*, it is contrary to the doctrine of Christian non-resistance; and no person knowing it to be such can repeat it under any pretext whatsoever, without violating the law of God. This is the sense and signification of the terms *injury*, *injurer*, *injurious*, &c., as used in these pages. The objector may here interpose critical queries, with a view to test the soundness of my definition. He may suppose that a man's leg, hand, or eye, is so diseased as to require amputation, in order to save his life. But such member is one of his physical faculties, which must not be destroyed or impaired, because that would be an *injury*. I answer. The diseased member is already lost. The question is not whether the friendly surgeon shall destroy or impair it; but only whether he shall amputate it, in order to preserve the life and remaining faculties. No *injury*, but an absolute *benefit* is proposed. This case is clear. But suppose the minister of the *law* is ordered to amputate a sound leg, hand or eye, as a punishment, or for an example to deter others from the commission of crime. This is absolute *injury*, done under good pretexts indeed, but on that account none the less an *injury*. Again; a child dangerously sick requires some medical application, very disagreeable, yet indispensable to his recovery, which can only be applied by physical force. Or an insane adult is in the same circumstances. Or a person infected with hydrophobia and subject to terrible paroxysms of the disease, needs to be confined; and yet for want of judgement, even in his intervals, refuses to be. Or a man subject to violent impulses of propensity or passion, rendering him dangerous to all around him when excited, needs to be excluded from general society, or otherwise watched and restrained by keepers, in order to prevent serious mischief to others; and yet he resents and resists all entreaties to submit to such restriction. Or a wicked man is exceedingly alarmed, disturbed and offended by a truthful exposure of his iniquitous proceedings, or by the faithful remonstrances and rebukes of some good man. Now in all such cases the *will* must be crossed, the personal freedom abridged, and the feelings pained. Must it not be an *injury* to coerce, restrain, expose and reprove such persons, however necessary to their and the public good, and however kindly executed? Is it not generally more intolerable to be *crossed* in one's *will*, and wounded in one's *feelings*, than to be beaten, maimed and otherwise maltreated? Answer. It is not man's imaginations, thoughts and feelings, that determine what *is*, or *is not injurious* to him. Love itself may 'heap coals of fire on a man's head'. Truth may torment his mind. The most benevolent restraint may be painful to his feelings. He may be made, for a while, quite unhappy by crossing his evil will. He may prefer to be smitten and mutilated, rather than be exposed in his secret iniquities, or endure the faithful reproof of the upright. Such persons often prefer an *injury* to a benefit. They are not, for the time being, in a state of mind to understand and choose what is best for them. Therefore their wills, feelings and opinions are not the indices of their own *good* – much less that of others. Is it *good* for a capricious obstinate child to be indulged in opposing a necessary medical application? Is it *good* for an insane or delirious sick adult to have his own *will*, even to the commission of murder and self-destruction? Is it *good* for a man to have unlimited freedom, when he will almost certainly make it a curse to himself and others, by gross involuntary outrage, or uncontrollable passion? Is it *good* for a wicked man, under specious hypocritical disguises, to perpetrate the most atrocious mischief, unexposed and unreproved? These things are not good for mankind. On the contrary, it is good for them to be crossed, restrained, coerced and reproved, by all uninjurious moral and physical forces, which benevolence prompts and wisdom dictates. To cross their wills, and pain their feelings, by such means, under such circumstances, is not an *injury*, but a substantial *good*, to them and all who are connected with them. It may be said – 'these things cannot be done *uninjuriously*. It would be impracticable'. Cannot unreasonable children be nursed, delirious adults controlled, dangerously distempered people prevented from doing themselves and others harm, outrageous non-compos persons restrained, hypocrites exposed, and sinners reproved without *inflicting injury* on them! Then can nothing good be done without doing evil. Imperfection is indeed incidental to all human judgement and conduct; and therefore it is probable that some mistakes and some accidental injuries might happen. But the reason and common sense of mankind, once fairly pledged to the true principle of action, would seldom fail to discharge all these duties to general satisfaction. Still it may be asked: 'What is to be done if uninjurious force should prove inadequate? May life be sacrificed, limbs broken, the flesh mangled, or any other injuries allowed in extreme cases?' Never. The principle of *non-injury* must be held inviolable. It is worth worlds, and must be preserved at all hazards. What cannot be done uninjuriously must be left undone. But these extreme cases are mostly imaginary. The truth is, that what cannot be done uninjuriously can scarcely ever be done at all. Or if done, had better have been let alone. Experience in the case of the insane has already proved that incomparably more can be done by *uninjurious* forces, scrupulously and judiciously employed, than by any admixtures of the injurious element. Presuming that my definition and use of the terms *injure, injury, injurer, injurious*, &c., cannot be misunderstood, I pass on.

THE TERM CHRISTIAN NON-RESISTANCE

Whence originated the term *Christian non-resistance*? Non-resistance comes from the injunction, 'resist not evil', Matt. 5: 39. The words '*resist not*', being changed from the form of a *verb* to that of a substantive, give us *non-resistance*. This term is considered more strikingly significant than any other, of the *principle* involved, and the *duty* enjoined in our Saviour's precept. Hence its adoption and established use. It is denominated *Christian* non-resistance, to distinguish it, as the genuine primitive doctrine, from mere *philosophical, sentimental* and *necessitous* non-resistance. Literally, then, *Christian non-resistance* is the original non-resistance taught and exemplified by Jesus Christ; the bearings, limitations and applications of which are to be learned from the Scriptures of the New Testament. And what are those bearings, limitations and applications? I have already given an imperfect view of them in the previous definitions. But I will be more explicit. What I aim at is to carry the obligations of non-resistance just as far and no farther than Jesus Christ has. It is easy to go beyond, or to fall short of his limits. Ultra radicals go beyond him. Ultra conservatives fall short of him. Even those of both these classes, who profess to abide implicitly by his teachings, construe and interpret his language so as to favor their respective errors. The ultra radicals seize on strong figurative, hyperbolic, or *intensive* forms of expression, and make him *seem* to mean *much more* than he *could have intended*. The ultra conservatives ingeniously fritter away and nullify the very essence of his precepts, in such a manner as to make him *seem* to mean *much less* than he *must have intended*. There is, however, a general rule for such cases, which can scarcely fail to expose the errors of both classes, in respect to any given text. It is this: 'Consider the context; consider parallel texts; consider examples; consider the known spirit of Christianity.' Any construction or interpretation of the recorded language of Christ, or of his apostles, in which all *these concur*, is sound. Any other is probably erroneous.

THE KEY TEXT OF NON-RESISTANCE

Now let us examine Matt. 5 : 39. 'I say unto you, resist not evil,' &c. This single text, from which, as has been stated, the term non-resistance took its rise, if justly construed, furnishes a complete key to the true bearings, limitations and applications of the doctrine under discussion. This is precisely one of those precepts which may be easily made to mean *much more*, or *much less*, than its author intended. It is in the *intensive*, condensed form of expression, and can be understood only by a due regard to its context. What did the divine teacher mean by the word '*evil*', and what by the word '*resist*'? There are several kinds of *evil*. 1. Pain, loss, damage, suffered from causes involving no moral agency, or *natural evil*. 2. Sin in general, or *moral evil*. 3. Temptations to sin, or *spiritual evil;* and 4. Personal wrong, insult, outrage, injury – or *personal evil*. Which of these kinds of evil does the context show to have been in our Saviour's mind when he said, '*resist not evil*'? Was he speaking of fires, floods, famine, disease, serpents, wild beasts, or any other mere *natural evil agents*? No. Then of course he does not prohibit our resisting *such evil*. Was he speaking of sin in general? No. Then of course he does not prohibit our resisting *such evil* by suitable means. Was he speaking of temptations addressed to our propensities and passions, enticing us to commit sin? No. Then of course he does not prohibit our resisting the *devil*, withstanding the *evil* suggestions of our own carnal mind, and suppressing our *evil* lusts. Was he speaking of *personal evil*, injury personally inflicted by man on man? Yes. 'Ye have heard that it hath been said, an eye for an eye, and a tooth for a tooth; but I say unto you that ye resist not evil,' i.e. personal outrage, insult, affront – *injury*. The word '*evil*' necessarily means, in this con-nexion, *personal injury*, or evil inflicted by human beings on human beings.

But what did Jesus mean by the words '*resist not*'? There are various kinds of *resistance*, which may be offered to personal injury, when threatened or actually inflicted. There is *passive* resistance – a dead silence, a sullen inertia, a complete muscular helplessness – an utter refusal to speak or move. Does the context show that Jesus contem-plated, pro or con, any such resistance in his prohibition? No. There is an active righteous moral resistance – a meek firm remonstrance, rebuke, reproof, protestation. Does the connexion show that Jesus prohibits this kind of resistance? No. There is an active, firm, compound, moral and physical resistance, *uninjurious* to the evil doer, and only calculated to restrain him from deadly violence or extreme outrage. Was Jesus contemplating such modes of resisting personal injury? Does the context show that he intended to prohibit all resistance of evil by such means? No. There is a determined resistance of *personal injury* by means of *injury inflicted*; as when a man deliberately takes life to save life, destroys an assailant's eye to save an eye, inflicts a violent blow to prevent a blow; or, as when, in retaliation, he takes life for life, eye for eye, tooth for tooth, hand for hand, &c.; or, as when, by means of governmental agencies, he causes an injurious person to be punished by the infliction of some injury equivalent to the one he had inflicted or attempted. It was of such resistance as this, that our Saviour was speaking. It is such resistance as this, that he prohibits. His obvious doctrine is: ☛ *Resist not personal injury with personal injury.* . . .

WHAT A CHRISTIAN NON-RESISTANT CANNOT
CONSISTENTLY DO

1. He cannot kill, maim or otherwise *absolutely injure* any human being, in personal self-defence, or for the sake of his family, or any thing he holds dear.

2. He cannot participate in any lawless conspiracy, mob, riotous assembly, or disorderly combination of individuals, to cause or countenance the commission of any such absolute personal injury.

3. He cannot be a member of any voluntary association, however orderly, respectable or allowable by law and general consent, *which declaratively* holds as *fundamental truth*, or claims as an essential right, or distinctly inculcates as sound doctrine, or approves as commendable in practice, *war, capital* punishment, or any other absolute personal injury.

4. He cannot be an *officer* or *private*, chaplain or retainer, in the army, navy or militia of any nation, state, or chieftain.

5. He cannot be an officer, elector, agent, legal prosecutor, passive constituent, or approver of any government, as a sworn or otherwise pledged supporter thereof, whose civil constitution and fundamental laws, require, authorize or tolerate war, slavery, capital punishment, or the infliction of any absolute personal injury.

6. He cannot be a member of any chartered corporation, or body politic, whose articles of compact oblige or authorize its official func-

tionaries to resort for compulsory aid, in the conducting of its affairs, to a government of constitutional violence.

7. Finally, he cannot do any act, either in person or by proxy; nor abet or encourage any act in others; nor demand, petition for, request, advise or approve the doing of any act, by an individual, association or government, *which* act would inflict, *threaten* to inflict, or *necessarily* cause to *be* inflicted *any absolute personal injury*, as herein before defined.

Such are the necessary bearings, limitations and applications of the doctrine of Christian non-resistance. Let the reader be careful not to misunderstand the positions laid down. The platform of principle and action has been carefully founded, and its essential peculiarities plainly delineated. Let it not be said that the doctrine goes against all religion, government, social organization, constitution, laws, order, rules and regulations. It goes against none of these things, *per se*. It goes for them, in the highest and best sense. It goes only against *such* religion, government, social organization, constitution, laws, order, rules, regulations and restraints, as are unequivocally contrary to the law of Christ; as sanction taking 'life for life, eye for eye, tooth for tooth'; as are based on the assumption, that it is *right* to resist *injury with injury, evil with evil.*

THE CONCLUSION

But the Son of the Highest, the great self-sacrificing Non-Resistant, is our prophet, priest and king. Though the maddened inhabitants of the earth have so long turned a deaf ear to his voice, he shall yet be heard. He declares that *good* is the only antagonist of *evil*, which can conquer the deadly foe. Therefore he enjoins on his disciples the duty of resisting *evil only* with *good*. This is the sub-principle of Christian non-resistance. 'Evil can be overcome only with *good*.' Faith, then, in the inherent superiority of *good* over *evil*, truth over error, right over wrong, love over hatred, is the immediate moral basis of our doctrine. Accordingly we transfer all the faith we have been taught to cherish in *injury*, to *beneficence, kindness,* and *uninjurious treatment*, as the only all-sufficient enginery of war against *evil doers*. No longer seeking or expecting to put down evil with evil, we lift up the cross for an ensign, and surmounting it with the glorious banner of love, exult in the divine motto displayed on its immaculate folds, 'RESIST NOT INJURY WITH INJURY'. Let this in all future time be the specific rule of our conduct, the magnetic needle of our pathway across the troubled waters of human reform, till all men, all governments and all social institutions shall have been moulded into moral harmony with the grand comprehensive commandment of the living God 'THOU SHALT LOVE THY NEIGHBOUR AS THYSELF'. Then shall *Love* (God by his sublimest name) 'be all in all'.

> The earth, so long a slaughter-field,
> Shall yet an Eden bloom;
> The *tiger* to the *lamb* shall yield,
> And *War* descend the tomb:
> For all shall feel the Saviour's love,
> Reflected from the cross –
> That love, that non-resistant love,
> Which triumphed on the cross.

HENRY DAVID THOREAU

1817–62

ALTHOUGH Thoreau wrote, 'I do not wish to kill or be killed, but I foresee circumstances in which both of these things would by me be unavoidable', the example he set in his life and writings places him in the very heart of the non-violent tradition. His work was well known to Tolstoy and Gandhi, both of whom expressed their indebtedness to the American.

With its emphasis on the individual conscience, on protest, justice, and non-violent resistance to the civil power, more than any other short work of modern times, Thoreau's essay 'Civil Disobedience' has informed the pacifist tradition. It was originally given as a lecture in 1848 (Elizabeth Peabody gives 1847 as the date) and titled 'Resistance to Civil Government'. With some changes it first appeared in print in Elizabeth Peabody's anthology, *Aesthetic Papers*, published in 1849.

In all likelihood, the well-known story of Emerson's visit to Thoreau in jail for having refused to pay his poll-tax, is apocryphal. The story runs that when Emerson questioned Thoreau on the reasons for his imprisonment Thoreau replied by questioning his friend as to why he was not there with him. But Emerson must have known the reasons for Thoreau's imprisonment, since Bronson Alcott had established a precedent a few years earlier; nor is there any record of such a visit. But the story being a pleasant and revealing one, it does not die easily.

Civil Disobedience

I heartily accept the motto – 'That government is best which governs least'; and I should like to see it acted up to more readily and systematically. Carried out, it finally amounts to this, which also I believe – 'That government is best which governs not at all'; and when men are prepared for it, that will be the kind of government which they will have. Government is at best but an expedient; but most governments are usually, and all governments are sometimes, inexpedient. The objections which have been brought against a standing army, and they are many and weighty, and deserve to prevail, may also at last be brought against a standing government. The standing army is only an arm of the standing government. The government itself, which is only the mode which the people have chosen to execute their will, is equally liable to be abused and perverted before the people can act through it. Witness the present Mexican war, the work of comparatively a few individuals using the standing government as their tool; for, in the outset, the people would not have consented to this measure.

This American government – what is it but a tradition, though a recent one, endeavoring to transmit itself unimpaired to posterity, but each instant losing some of its integrity? It has not the vitality and force of a single living man; for a single man can bend it to his will. It is a sort of wooden gun to the people themselves; and, if ever they should use it in earnest as a real one against each other, it will surely split. But it is not the less necessary for this; for the people must have some complicated machinery or other, and hear its din, to satisfy that idea of government which they have. Governments show thus how successfully men can be imposed on, even impose on themselves, for their own advantage. It is excellent, we must all allow; yet this government never of itself furthered any enterprise, but by the alacrity with which it got out of its way. *It* does not keep the country free. *It* does not settle the West. *It* does not educate. The character inherent in the American people has done all that has been accomplished; and it would have done somewhat more, if the government had not sometimes got in its way. For government is an expedient by which men would fain succeed in letting one another alone; and, as has been said, when it is most expedient, the governed are most let alone by it. Trade and commerce, if they were not made of India rubber, would never manage to bounce over the obstacles which legislators are continually putting in their way; and, if one were to judge these men wholly by the effects of their actions, and not partly by their intentions, they would deserve to be classed and punished with those mischievous persons who put obstructions on the railroads.

But, to speak practically and as a citizen, unlike those who call themselves no-government men, I ask for, not at once no government, but *at once* a better government. Let every man make known what kind of government would command his respect, and that will be one step toward obtaining it.

After all, the practical reason why, when the power is once in the hands of the people, a majority are permitted, and for a long period continue, to rule, is not because they are most likely to be in the right, nor because this seems fairest to the minority, but because they are physically the strongest. But a government in which the majority rule in all cases cannot be based on justice, even as far as men understand it. Can there not be a government in which majorities do not virtually decide right and wrong, but conscience? – in which majorities decide only those questions to which the rule of expediency is applicable? Must the citizen ever for a moment, or in the least degree, resign his conscience to the legislator? Why has every man a conscience, then? I think that we should be men first, and subjects afterward. It is not desirable to cultivate a respect for the law, so much as for the right. The only obligation which I have a right to assume, is to do at any time what I think right. It is truly enough said, that a corporation has no conscience; but a corporation of conscientious men is a corporation *with* a conscience. Law never made men a whit more just; and, by means of their respect for it, even the well-disposed are daily made the agents of injustice. A common and natural result of an undue respect for law is, that you may see a file of soldiers, colonel, captain, corporal, privates, powder-monkeys and all, marching in admirable order over hill and dale to the wars, against their wills, aye, against their common sense and consciences, which makes it very steep marching indeed, and produces a palpitation of the heart. They have no doubt that it is a damnable business in which they are concerned; they are all peaceably inclined. Now, what are they? Men at all? or small moveable forts and magazines, at the service of some unscrupulous man in power? Visit the Navy Yard, and behold a marine, such a man as an American government can make, or such as it can make a man with its black arts, a mere shadow and reminiscence of humanity, a man laid out alive and standing, and already, as one may say, buried under arms with funeral accompaniments, though it may be

'Not a drum was heard, nor a funeral note,
   As his corse to the ramparts we hurried;
Not a soldier discharged his farewell shot
   O'er the grave where our hero we buried.'

The mass of men serve the State thus, not as men mainly, but as machines, with their bodies. They are the standing army, and the militia, jailers, constables, *posse comitatus*, &c. In most cases there is no free exercise whatever of the judgement or of the moral sense; but they put themselves on a level with wood and earth and stones; and wooden men can perhaps be manufactured that will serve the purpose as well. Such command no more respect than men of straw, or a lump of dirt. They have the same sort of worth only as horses and dogs. Yet such as these even are commonly esteemed good citizens. Others, as most legislators, politicians, lawyers, ministers, and officeholders, serve the State chiefly with their heads; and, as they rarely make any moral distinctions, they are as likely to serve the devil, without intending it, as God. A very few, as heroes, patriots, martyrs, reformers in the great sense, and *men*, serve the State with their consciences also, and so necessarily resist it for the most part; and they are commonly treated by it as enemies. A wise man will only be useful as a man, and will not submit to be 'clay', and 'stop a hole to keep the wind away', but leave that office to his dust at least:

> 'I am too high-born to be propertied,
> To be a secondary at control,
> Or useful serving-man and instrument
> To any sovereign state throughout the world.'

He who gives himself entirely to his fellow men appears to them useless and selfish; but he who gives himself partially to them is pronounced a benefactor and philanthropist.

How does it become a man to behave toward this American government today? I answer that he cannot without disgrace be associated with it. I cannot for an instant recognize that political organization as *my* government which is the *slave's* government also.

All men recognize the right of revolution; that is, the right to refuse allegiance to and to resist the government, when its tyranny or its inefficiency are great and unendurable. But almost all say that such is not the case now. But such was the case, they think, in the Revolution of '75. If one were to tell me that this was a bad government because it taxed certain foreign commodities brought to its ports, it is most probable that I should not make an ado about it, for I can do without them: all machines have their friction; and possibly this does enough good to counterbalance the evil. At any rate, it is a great evil to make a stir about it. But when the friction comes to have its machine, and oppression and robbery are organized, I say, let us not have such a machine any longer. In other words, when a sixth of the population of a nation which has undertaken to be the refuge of liberty are slaves, and a whole country is unjustly overrun and conquered by a foreign army, and subjected to military law, I think that it is not too soon for honest men to rebel and revolutionize. What makes this duty the more urgent is the fact, that the country so overrun is not our own, but ours is the invading army.

Paley, a common authority with many on moral questions, in his chapter on the 'Duty of Submission to Civil Government', resolves all civil obligation into expediency; and he proceeds to say, 'that so long as the interest of the whole society requires it, that is, so long as the established government cannot be resisted or changed without public inconveniency, it is the will of God that the established government be obeyed, and no longer.' – 'This principle being admitted, the justice of every particular case of resistance is reduced to a computation of the quantity of the danger and grievance on the one side, and of the probability and expense of redressing it on the other.' Of this, he says, every man shall judge for himself. But Paley appears never to have contemplated those cases to which the rule of expediency does not apply, in which a people, as well as an individual, must do justice, cost what it may. If I have unjustly wrested a plank from a drowning man, I must restore it to him though I drown myself. This, according to Paley, would be inconvenient. But he that would save his life, in such a case, shall lose it. This people must cease to hold slaves, and to make war on Mexico, though it cost them their existence as a people.

In their practice, nations agree with Paley; but does any one think that Massachusetts does exactly what is right at the present crisis?

> 'A drab of state, a cloth-o'-silver slut,
>   To have her train borne up, and her soul trail in the dirt.'

Practically speaking, the opponents to a reform in Massachusetts are not a hundred thousand politicians at the South, but a hundred thousand merchants and farmers here, who are more interested in commerce and agriculture than they are in humanity, and are not prepared to do justice to the slave and to Mexico, *cost what it may*. I quarrel not with far-off foes, but with those who, near at home, cooperate with, and do the bidding of those far away, and without whom the latter would be harmless. We are accustomed to say, that the mass of men are unprepared; but improvement is slow, because the few are not materially wiser or better than the many. It is not so important that many should be as good as you, as that there be some absolute goodness somewhere; for that will leaven the whole lump. There are thousands who are *in opinion* opposed to slavery and to the war, who yet in effect do nothing to put an end to them; who, esteeming themselves children of Washington and Franklin, sit down with their hands in their pockets, and say that they know not what to do, and do nothing; who even postpone the question of freedom to the question of free-trade, and quietly read the prices-current along with the latest advices from Mexico, after dinner, and, it may be, fall asleep over them both. What is the price-current of an honest man and patriot today? They hesitate, and they regret, and sometimes they petition; but they do nothing in earnest and with effect. They will wait, well disposed, for others to remedy the evil, that they may no longer have it to regret. At most, they give only a cheap vote, and a feeble countenance and Godspeed, to the right, as it goes by them. There are nine hundred and ninety-nine patrons of virtue to one virtuous man; but it is easier to deal with the real possessor of a thing than with the temporary guardian of it.

All voting is a sort of gaming, like chequers or backgammon, with a slight moral tinge to it, a playing with right and wrong, with moral questions; and betting naturally accompanies it. The character of the voters is not staked. I cast my vote, perchance, as I think right; but I am not vitally concerned that that right should prevail. I am willing to leave it to the majority. Its obligation, therefore, never exceeds that of expediency. Even voting *for the right* is *doing* nothing for it. It is only expressing to men feebly your desire that it should prevail. A wise man will not leave the right to the mercy of chance, nor wish it to prevail through the power of the majority. There is but little virtue in the action of masses of men. When the majority shall at length vote for the abolition of slavery, it will be because they are indifferent to slavery, or because there is but little slavery left to be abolished by their vote. *They* will then be the only slaves. Only *his* vote can hasten the abolition of slavery who asserts his own freedom by his vote.

I hear of a convention to be held at Baltimore, or elsewhere, for the selection of a candidate for the Presidency, made up chiefly of editors, and men who are politicians by profession; but I think, what is it to any independent, intelligent, and respectable man what decision they may come to, shall we not have the advantage of his wisdom and honesty, nevertheless? Can we not count upon some independent votes? Are there not many individuals in the country who do not attend conventions? But no: I find that the respectable man, so called, has immediately drifted from his position, and despairs of his country, when his country has more reason to despair of him. He forthwith adopts one of the candidates thus selected as the only *available* one, thus proving that he is himself *available* for any purposes of the demagogue. His vote is of no more worth than that of any unprincipled foreigner or hireling native, who may have been bought. Oh for a man who is a *man*, and, as my neighbor says, has a bone in his back which you cannot pass your hand through! Our statistics are at fault: the population has been returned too large. How many *men* are there to a square thousand miles in this country? Hardly one. Does not America offer any inducement for men to settle here? The American has dwindled into an Odd Fellow – one who may be known by the development of his organ of gregariousness, and a manifest lack of intellect and cheerful self-reliance; whose first and chief concern, on coming into the world, is to see that the almshouses are in good repair; and, before yet he has lawfully donned the virile garb, to collect a fund for the support of the widows and orphans that may be; who, in short, ventures to live only by the aid of the mutual insurance company, which has promised to bury him decently.

It is not a man's duty, as a matter of course, to devote himself to the eradication of any, even the most enormous wrong; he may still properly have other concerns to engage him; but it is his duty, at least, to wash his hands of it, and, if he gives it no thought longer, not to give it practically his support. If I devote myself to other pursuits and contemplations, I must first see, at least, that I do not pursue them sitting upon another man's shoulders. I must get off him first, that he may pursue his contemplations too. See what gross inconsistency is tolerated. I have heard some of my townsmen say, 'I should like to have them order me out to help put down an insurrection of the slaves, or to march to Mexico – see if I would go'; and yet these very men have each, directly by their allegiance, and so indirectly, at least, by their money, furnished a substitute. The soldier is applauded who refuses to serve in an unjust war by those who do not refuse to sustain the unjust government which makes the war; is applauded by those whose own act and authority he disregards and sets at nought; as if the State were penitent to that degree that it hired one to scourge it while it sinned, but not to that degree that it left off sinning for a moment. Thus, under the name of order and civil government, we are all made at last to pay homage to and support our own meanness. After the first blush of sin, comes its indifference; and from immoral it becomes, as it were, *un-*moral, and not quite unnecessary to that life which we have made.

The broadest and most prevalent error requires the most disinterested virtue to sustain it. The slight reproach to which the virtue of patriotism is commonly liable, the noble are most likely to incur. Those who, while they disapprove of the character and measures of a government, yield to it their allegiance and support, are undoubtedly its most conscientious supporters, and so frequently the most serious obstacles to reform. Some are petitioning the State to dissolve the Union, to disregard the requisitions of the President. Why do they not dissolve it themselves – the union between themselves and the State – and refuse to pay their quota into its treasury? Do not they stand in the same relation to the State, that the State does to the Union? And have not the same reasons prevented the State from resisting the Union, which have prevented them from resisting the State?

How can a man be satisfied to entertain an opinion merely, and enjoy *it*? Is there any enjoyment in it, if his opinion is that he is aggrieved? If you are cheated out of a single dollar by your neighbor, you do not rest satisfied with knowing that you are cheated, or with saying that you are cheated, or even with petitioning him to pay you your due; but you take effectual steps at once to obtain the full amount, and see that you are never cheated again. Action from principle – the perception and the performance of right – changes things and relations; it is essentially revolutionary, and does not consist wholly with any thing which was. It not only divides states and churches, it divides families; aye, it divides the *individual*, separating the diabolical in him from the divine.

Unjust laws exist: shall we be content to obey them, or shall we endeavor to amend them, and obey them until we have succeeded, or shall we transgress them at once? Men generally, under such a government as this, think that they ought to wait until they have persuaded the majority to alter them. They think that, if they should resist, the remedy would be worse than the evil. But it is the fault of the government itself that the remedy *is* worse than the evil. *It* makes it worse. Why is it not more apt to anticipate and provide for reform? Why does it not cherish its wise minority? Why does it cry and resist before it is hurt? Why does it not encourage its citizens to be on the alert to point out its faults, and *do* better than it would have them? Why does it always crucify Christ, and excommunicate Copernicus and Luther, and pronounce Washington and Franklin rebels?

One would think, that a deliberate and practical denial of its authority, was the only offence never contemplated by government; else, why has it not assigned its definite, its suitable and proportionate penalty? If a man who has no property refuses but once to earn nine shillings for the State, he is put in prison for a period unlimited by any law that I know, and determined only by the discretion of those who placed him there; but if he should steal ninety times nine shillings from the State, he is soon permitted to go at large again.

If the injustice is part of the necessary friction to the machine of government, let it go, let it go: perchance it will wear smooth – certainly the machine will wear out. If the injustice has a spring, or a pulley, or a rope, or a crank, exclusively for itself, then perhaps you may consider whether the remedy will not be worse than the evil; but if it is of such a nature that it requires you to be the agent of injustice to another, then, I say, break the law. Let your life be a counter friction to stop the machine. What I have to do is to see, at any rate, that I do not lend myself to the wrong which I condemn.

As for adopting the ways which the State has provided for remedying the evil, I know not of such ways. They take too much time, and a man's life will be gone. I have other affairs to attend to. I came into this world, not chiefly to make this a good place to live in, but to live in it, be it good or bad. A man has not every thing to do, but something; and because he cannot do *every thing*, it is not necessary that he should do *something* wrong. It is not my business to be petitioning the governor or the legislature any more than it is theirs to petition me; and, if they should not hear my petition, what should I do then? But in this case the State has provided no way: its very Constitution is the evil. This may seem to be harsh and stubborn and unconciliatory; but it is to treat with the utmost kindness and consideration the only spirit that can appreciate or deserves it. So is all change for the better, like birth and death which convulse the body.

I do not hesitate to say, that those who call themselves abolitionists should at once effectually withdraw their support, both in person and property, from the government of Massachusetts, and not wait till they constitute a majority of one, before they suffer the right to prevail through them. I think that it is enough if they have God on their side, without waiting for that other one. Moreover, any man more right than his neighbors, constitutes a majority of one already.

I meet this American government, or its representative the State government, directly, and face to face, once a year, no more, in the person of its tax-gatherer; this is the only mode in which a man situated as I am necessarily meets it; and it then says distinctly, Recognize me; and the simplest, the most effectual, and, in the present posture of affairs, the indispensablest mode of treating with it on this head, of expressing your little satisfaction with and love for it, is to deny it then. My civil neighbor, the tax-gatherer, is the very man I have to deal with – for it is, after all, with men and not with parchment that I quarrel – and he has voluntarily chosen to be an agent of the government. How shall he ever know well what he is and does as an officer of the government, or as a man, until he is obliged to consider whether he shall treat me, his neighbor, for whom he has respect, as a neighbor and well-disposed man, or as a maniac and disturber of the peace, and see if he can get over this obstruction to his neighborliness without a ruder and more impetuous thought or speech corresponding with his action? I know this well, that if one thousand, if one hundred, if ten men whom I could name – if ten *honest* men only – aye, if *one* HONEST man, in this State of Massachusetts, *ceasing to hold slaves*, were actually to withdraw from this copartnership, and be locked up in the county jail therefor, it would be the abolition of slavery in America. For it matters not how small the beginning may seem to be: what is once well done is done for ever. But we love better to talk about it: that we say is our mission. Reform keeps many scores of newspapers in its service, but not one man. If my esteemed neighbor, the State's ambassador, who will devote his days to the settlement of the question of human rights in the Council Chamber, instead of being threatened with the prisons of Carolina, were to sit down the prisoner of Massachusetts, that State which is so anxious to foist the sin of slavery upon her sister – though at present she can discover only an act of inhospitality to be the ground of a quarrel with her – the Legislature would not wholly waive the subject the following winter.

Under a government which imprisons any unjustly, the true place for a just man is also in prison. The proper place today, the only place which Massachusetts has provided for her freer and less desponding spirits, is in her prisons, to be put out and locked out of the State by her own act, as they have already put themselves out by their principles. It is there that the fugitive slave, and the Mexican prisoner on parole, and the Indian come to plead the wrongs of his race, should find them; on that separate, but more free and honorable ground, where the State places those who are not *with* her but *against* her – the only house in a slave-state in which a free man can abide with honor. If any think that their influence would be lost there, and their voices no longer afflict the ear of the State, that they would not be as an enemy within its walls, they do not know by how much truth is stronger than error, nor how much more eloquently and effectively he can combat injustice who has experienced a little in his own person. Cast your whole vote, not a strip of paper merely, but your whole influence. A minority is powerless while it conforms to the majority; it is not even a minority then; but it is irresistible when it clogs by its whole weight. If the alternative is to keep all just men in prison, or give up war and slavery, the State will not hesitate which to choose. If a thousand men were not to pay their tax-bills this year, that would not be a violent and bloody measure, as it would be to pay them, and enable the State to commit violence and shed innocent blood. This is, in fact the definition of a peaceable revolution if any such is possible. If the tax-gatherer, or any other public officer, asks me, as one has done, 'But what shall I do?' my answer is, 'If you really wish to do any thing, resign your office.' When the subject has refused allegiance, and the officer has resigned his office, then the revolution is accomplished. But even suppose blood should flow. Is there not a sort of blood shed when the conscience is wounded? Through this wound a man's real manhood and immortality flow out, and he bleeds to an everlasting death. I see this blood flowing now.

I have contemplated the imprisonment of the offender, rather than the seizure of his goods – though both will serve the same purpose – because they who assert the purest right, and consequently are most dangerous to a corrupt State, commonly have not spent much time in accumulating property. To such the State renders comparatively small service, and a slight tax is wont to appear exorbitant, particularly if they are obliged to earn it by special labor with their hands. If there were one who lived wholly without the use of money, the State itself would hesitate to demand it of him. But the rich man – not to make any invidious comparison – is always sold to the institution which makes him rich. Absolutely speaking, the more money, the less virtue; for money comes between a man and his objects, and obtains them for him; and it was certainly no great virtue to obtain it. It puts to rest many questions which he would otherwise be taxed to answer; while the only new question which it puts is the hard but superfluous one, how to spend it. Thus his moral ground is taken from under his feet. The opportunities of living are diminished in proportion as what are called the 'means' are increased. The best thing a man can do for his culture when he is rich is to endeavour to carry out those schemes which he entertained when he was poor. Christ answered the Herodians according to their condition. 'Show me the tribute-money,' said he; – and one took a penny out of his pocket; – If you use money which has the image of Cæsar on it, and which he has made current and valuable, that is, *if you are men of the State*, and gladly enjoy the advantages of Cæsar's government, then pay him back some of his own when he demands it; 'Render therefore to Cæsar that which is Cæsar's, and to God those things which are God's' – leaving them no wiser than before as to which was which; for they did not wish to know.

When I converse with the freest of my neighbors, I perceive that, whatever they may say about the magnitude and seriousness of the question, and their regard for the public tranquillity, the long and the short of the matter is, that they cannot spare the protection of the existing government, and they dread the consequences of disobedience to it to their property and families. For my own part, I should not like to think that I ever rely on the protection of the State. But, if I deny the authority of the State when it presents its tax-bill, it will soon take and waste all my property, and so harass me and my children without end. This is hard. This makes it impossible for a man to live honestly and at the same time comfortably in outward respects. It will not be worth the while to accumulate property; that would be sure to go again. You must hire or squat somewhere, and raise but a small crop, and eat that soon. You must live within yourself, and depend upon yourself, always tucked up and ready for a start, and not have many affairs. A man may grow rich in Turkey even, if he will be in all respects a good subject of the Turkish government. Confucius said – 'If a State is governed by the principles of reason, poverty and misery are subjects of shame; if a State is not governed by the principles of reason, riches and honors are the subjects of shame.' No: until I want the protection of Massachusetts to be extended to me in some distant southern port, where my liberty is endangered, or until I am bent solely on building up an estate at home by peaceful enterprise, I can afford to refuse allegiance to Massachusetts, and her right to my property and life. It costs me less in every sense to incur the penalty of disobedience to the State, than it would to obey. I should feel as if I were worth less in that case.

Some years ago, the State met me in behalf of the church, and commanded me to pay a certain sum toward the support of a clergyman whose preaching my father attended, but never I myself. 'Pay it,' it said, 'or be locked up in the jail.' I declined to pay. But, unfortunately, another man saw fit to pay it. I did not see why the schoolmaster should be taxed to support the priest, and not the priest the schoolmaster; for I was not the State's schoolmaster, but I supported myself by voluntary subscription. I did not see why the lyceum should not present its tax-bill, and have the State to back its demand, as well as the church. However, at the request of the selectmen, I condescended to make some such statement as this in writing: – 'Know all men by these presents, that I, Henry Thoreau, do not wish to be regarded as a member of any incorporated society which I have not joined.' This I gave to the town-clerk; and he has it. The State, having thus learned that I did not wish to be regarded as a member of that church, has never made a like demand on me since; though it said that it must adhere to its original presumption that time. If I had known how to name them, I should then have signed off in detail from all the societies which I never signed on to; but I did not know where to find a complete list.

I have paid no poll-tax for six years. I was put into a jail once on this account, for one night; and, as I stood considering the walls of solid stone, two or three feet thick, the door of wood and iron, a foot thick, and the iron grating which strained the light, I could not help being struck with the foolishness of that institution which treated me as if I were mere flesh and blood and bones, to be locked up. I wondered that it should have concluded at length that this was the best use it could put me to, and had never thought to avail itself of my services in some way. I saw that, if there was a wall of stone between me and my townsmen, there was a still more difficult one to climb or break through, before they could get to be as free as I was. I did not for a moment feel confined, and the walls seemed a great waste of stone and mortar. I felt as if I alone of all my townsmen had paid my tax. They plainly did not know how to treat me, but behaved like persons who are underbred. In every threat and in every compliment there was a blunder; for they thought that my chief desire was to stand the other side of that stone wall. I could not but smile to see how industriously they locked the door on my meditations, which followed them out again without let or hindrance, and *they* were really all that was dangerous. As they could not reach me, they had resolved to punish my body; just as boys, if they cannot come at some person against whom they have a spite, will abuse his dog. I saw that the State was half-witted, that it was timid as a lone woman with her silver spoons, and that it did not know its friends from its foes, and I lost all my remaining respect for it, and pitied it.

Thus the State never intentionally confronts a man's sense, intellectual or moral, but only his body, his senses. It is not armed with superior wit or honesty, but with superior physical strength. I was not born to be forced. I will breathe after my own fashion. Let us see who is the strongest. What force has a multitude? They only can force me who obey a higher law than I. They force me to become like themselves. I do not hear of *men* being *forced* to live this way or that by masses of men. What sort of life were that to live? When I meet a government which says to me, 'Your money or your life', why should I be in haste to give it my money? It may be in a great strait, and not know what to do: I cannot help that. It must help itself; do as I do. It is not worth the while to snivel about it. I am not responsible for the successful working of the machinery of society. I am not the son of the engineer. I perceive that, when an acorn and a chestnut fall side by side, the one does not remain inert to make way for the other, but both obey their own laws, and spring and grow and flourish as best they can, till one, perchance, overshadows and destroys the other. If a plant cannot live according to its nature, it dies; and so a man.

The night in prison was novel and interesting enough. The prisoners in their shirt-sleeves were enjoying a chat and the evening air in the doorway, when I entered. But the jailer said, 'Come, boys, it is time to lock up'; and so they dispersed, and I heard the sound of their steps returning into the hollow apartments. My room-mate was introduced to me by the jailer, as 'a first-rate fellow and a clever man'. When the door was locked, he showed me where to hang my hat, and how he managed matters there. The rooms were whitewashed once a month; and this one, at least, was the whitest, most simply furnished, and probably the neatest apartment in the town. He naturally wanted to know where I came from, and what brought me there; and, when I had told him, I asked him in my turn how he came there, presuming him to be an honest man, of course; and, as the world goes, I believe he was. 'Why,' said he, 'they accuse me of burning a barn; but I never did it.' As near as I could discover, he had probably gone to bed in a barn when drunk, and smoked his pipe there; and so a barn was burnt. He had the reputation of being a clever man, had been there some three months waiting for his trial to come on, and would have to wait as much longer; but he was quite domesticated and contented, since he got his board for nothing, and thought that he was well treated.

He occupied one window, and I the other; and I saw, that, if one stayed there long, his principal business would be to look out the window. I had soon read all the tracts that were left there, and examined where former prisoners had broken out, and where a grate had been sawed off, and heard the history of the various occupants of that room; for I found that even here there was a history and a gossip which never circulated beyond the walls of the jail. Probably this is the only house in the town where verses are composed, which are afterward printed in a circular form, but not published. I was shown quite a long list of verses which were composed by some young men who had been detected in an attempt to escape, who avenged themselves by singing them.

I pumped my fellow prisoner as dry as I could, for fear I should never see him again; but at length he showed me which was my bed, and left me to blow out the lamp.

It was like travelling into a far country, such as I had never expected to behold, to lie there for one night. It seemed to me that I never had heard the town-clock strike before, nor the evening sounds of the village; for we slept with the windows open, which were inside the grating. It was to see my native village in the light of the middle ages, and our Concord was turned into a Rhine stream, and visions of knights and castles passed before me. They were the voices of old Burghers that I heard in the streets. I was an involuntary spectator and auditor of whatever was done and said in the kitchen of the adjacent village-inn – a wholly new and rare experience to me. It was a closer view of my native town. I was fairly inside of it. I never had seen its institutions before. This is one of its peculiar institutions; for it is a shire town. I began to comprehend what its inhabitants were about.

In the morning, our breakfasts were put through the hole in the door, in small oblong-square tin pans, made to fit, and holding a pint of chocolate, with brown bread, and an iron spoon. When they called for the vessels again, I was green enough to return what bread I had left; but my comrade seized it, and said that I should lay that up for lunch or dinner. Soon after, he was let out to work at haying in a neighboring field, whither he went every day, and would not be back till noon; so he bade me good-day, saying that he doubted if he should see me again.

When I came out of prison – for some one interfered, and paid the tax – I did not perceive that great changes had taken place on the common, such as he observed who went in a youth, and emerged a tottering and gray-headed man; and yet a change had to my eyes come over the scene – the town, and State, and country – greater than any that mere time could effect. I saw yet more distinctly the State in which I lived. I saw to what extent the people among whom I lived could be trusted as good neighbors and friends; that their friendship was for summer weather only; that they did not greatly purpose to do right; that they were a distinct race from me by their prejudices and super-stitions, as the Chinamen and Malays are; that, in their sacrifices to humanity, they ran no risks, not even to their property; that, after all, they were not so noble but they treated the thief as he had treated them, and hoped, by a certain outward observance and a few prayers, and by walking in a particular straight though useless path from time to time, to save their souls. This may be to judge my neighbors harshly; for I believe that most of them are not aware that they have such an institution as the jail in their village.

It was formerly the custom in our village, when a poor debtor came out of jail, for his acquaintances to salute him, looking through their fingers, which were crossed to represent the grating of a jail window, 'How do ye do?' My neighbors did not thus salute me, but first looked at me, and then at one another, as if I had returned from a long journey. I was put into jail as I was going to the shoemaker's to get a shoe which was mended. When I was let out the next morning, I proceeded to finish my errand, and, having put on my mended shoe, joined a huckleberry party, who were impatient to put themselves under my conduct; and in half an hour – for the horse was soon tackled – was in the midst of a huckleberry field, on one of our highest hills, two miles off; and then the State was nowhere to be seen.

This is the whole history of 'My Prisons'.

I have never declined paying the highway tax, because I am as desirous of being a good neighbor as I am of being a bad subject; and, as for supporting schools, I am doing my part to educate my fellow countrymen now. It is for no particular item in the tax-bill that I refuse to pay it. I simply wish to refuse allegiance to the State, to withdraw and stand aloof from it effectually. I do not care to trace the course of my dollar, if I could, till it buys a man, or a musket to shoot one with –

the dollar is innocent – but I am concerned to trace the effects of my allegiance. In fact, I quietly declare war with the State, after my fashion, though I will still make what use and get what advantage of her I can, as is usual in such cases.

If others pay the tax which is demanded of me, from a sympathy with the State, they do but what they have already done in their own case, or rather they abet injustice to a greater extent than the State requires. If they pay the tax from a mistaken interest in the individual taxed, to save his property or prevent his going to jail, it is because they have not considered wisely how far they let their private feelings interfere with the public good.

This, then, is my position at present. But one cannot be too much on his guard in such a case, lest his action be biased by obstinacy, or an undue regard for the opinions of men. Let him see that he does only what belongs to himself and to the hour.

I think sometimes, Why, this people mean well; they are only ignorant; they would do better if they knew how: why give your neighbors this pain to treat you as they are not inclined to? But I think, again, this is no reason why I should do as they do, or permit others to suffer much greater pain of a different kind. Again, I sometimes say to myself, When many millions of men, without heat, without ill-will, without personal feeling of any kind, demand of you a few shillings only, without the possibility, such is their constitution, of retracting or altering their present demand, and without the possibility, on your side, of appeal to any other millions, why expose yourself to this overwhelming brute force? You do not resist cold and hunger, the winds and the waves, thus obstinately; you quietly submit to a thousand similar necessities. You do not put your head into the fire. But just in proportion as I regard this as not wholly a brute force, but partly a human force, and consider that I have relations to those millions as to so many millions of men, and not of mere brute or inanimate things, I see that appeal is possible, first and instantaneously, from them to the Maker of them, and, secondly, from them to themselves. But, if I put my head deliberately into the fire, there is no appeal to fire or to the Maker of fire, and I have only myself to blame. If I could convince myself that I have any right to be satisfied with men as they are, and to treat them accordingly, and not according, in some respects, to my requisitions and expectations of what they and I ought to be, then, like a good Mussulman and fatalist, I should endeavor to be satisfied with things as they are, and say it is the will of God. And, above all, there is this difference between resisting this and a purely brute or natural force, that I can resist this with some effect; but I cannot expect, like Orpheus, to change the nature of the rocks and trees and beasts.

I do not wish to quarrel with any man or nation. I do not wish to split hairs, to make fine distinctions, or set myself up as better than my neighbors. I seek rather, I may say, even an excuse for conforming to the laws of the land. I am but too ready to conform to them. Indeed I have reason to suspect myself on this head; and each year, as the tax-gatherer comes round, I find myself disposed to review the acts and position of the general and state governments, and the spirit of the people, to discover a pretext for conformity. I believe that the State will soon be able to take all my work of this sort out of my hands, and then I shall be no better a patriot than my fellow-countrymen. Seen from a lower point of view, the Constitution, with all its faults, is very good; the law and the courts are very respectable; even this State and this American government are, in many respects, very admirable and rare things, to be thankful for, such as a great many have described them; but seen from a point of view a little higher, they are what I have described them; seen from a higher still, and the highest, who shall say what they are, or that they are worth looking at or thinking of at all?

However, the government does not concern me much, and I shall bestow the fewest possible thoughts on it. It is not many moments that I live under a government, even in this world. If a man is thought-free, fancy-free, imagination-free, that which *is not* never for a long time appearing *to be* to him, unwise rulers or reformers cannot fatally interrupt him.

I know that most men think differently from myself; but those whose lives are by profession devoted to the study of these or kindred subjects, content me as little as any. Statesmen and legislators, standing so completely within the institution, never distinctly and nakedly behold it. They speak of moving society, but have no resting-place without it. They may be men of a certain experience and discrimination, and have no doubt invented ingenious and even useful systems, for which we sincerely thank them; but all their wit and usefulness lie within certain not very wide limits. They are wont to forget that the world is not governed by policy and expediency. Webster never goes behind government, and so cannot speak with authority about it. His words are wisdom to those legislators who contemplate no essential reform in the existing government; but for thinkers, and those who legislate for all time, he never once glances at the subject. I know of those whose serene and wise speculations on this theme would soon reveal the limits of his mind's range and hospitality. Yet, compared with the cheap professions of most reformers, and the still cheaper wisdom and eloquence of politicians in general, his are almost the only sensible and valuable words, and we thank Heaven for him. Comparatively, he is always strong, original, and, above all, practical. Still his quality is not wisdom, but prudence. The lawyer's truth is not Truth, but consistency, or a consistent expediency. Truth is always in harmony with herself, and is not concerned chiefly to reveal the justice that may consist with wrong-doing. He well deserves to be called, as he has been called, the Defender of the Constitution. There are really no blows to be given by him but defensive ones. He is not a leader, but a follower. His leaders are the men of '87. 'I have never made an effort,' he says, 'and never propose to make an effort; I have never countenanced an effort, and never mean to countenance an effort, to disturb the arrangement as originally made, by which the various States came into the Union.' Still thinking of the sanction which the Constitution gives to slavery, he says, 'Because it was a part of the original compact – let it stand.' Notwithstanding his special acuteness and ability, he is unable to take a fact out of its merely political relations, and behold it as it lies absolutely to be disposed of by the intellect – what, for instance, it behoves a man to do here in America today with regard to slavery, but ventures, or is driven, to make some such desperate answer as the following, while professing to speak absolutely, and as a private man – from which what new and singular code of social duties might be inferred? – 'The manner,' says he, 'in which the government of those States where slavery exists are to regulate it, is for their own considerations, under their responsibility to their constituents, to the general laws of propriety, humanity, and justice, and to God. Associations formed elsewhere, springing from a feeling of humanity, or any other cause, have nothing whatever to do with it. They have never received any encouragement from me, and they never will.'[1]

They who know of no purer sources of truth, who have traced up its stream no higher, stand, and wisely stand, by the Bible and the Constitution, and drink at it there with reverence and humility; but they who behold where it comes trickling into this lake or that pool, gird up their

1. These extracts have been inserted since the Lecture was read. [*Thoreau's note.*]

loins once more, and continue their pilgrimage toward its fountain-head.

No man with a genius for legislation has appeared in America. They are rare in the history of the world. There are orators, politicians, and eloquent men, by the thousand; but the speaker has not yet opened his mouth to speak, who is capable of settling the much-vexed questions of the day. We love eloquence for its own sake, and not for any truth which it may utter, or any heroism it may inspire. Our legislators have not yet learned the comparative value of free-trade and of freedom, of union, and of rectitude, to a nation. They have no genius or talent for comparatively humble questions of taxation and finance, commerce and manufactures and agriculture. If we were left solely to the wordy wit of legislators in Congress for our guidance, uncorrected by the seasonable experience and the effectual complaints of the people, America would not long retain her rank among the nations. For eighteen hundred years, though perchance I have no right to say it, the New Testament has been written; yet where is the legislator who has wisdom and practical talent enough to avail himself of the light which it sheds on the science of legislation?

The authority of government, even such as I am willing to submit to – for I will cheerfully obey those who know and can do better than I, and in many things even those who neither know or can do so well – is still an impure one: to be strictly just, it must have the sanction and consent of the governed. It can have no pure right over my person and property but what I concede to it. The progress from an absolute to a limited monarchy, from a limited monarchy to a democracy, is a progress toward a true respect for the individual. Is a democracy, such as we know it, the last improvement possible in government? Is it not possible to take a step further towards recognizing and organizing the rights of man? There will never be a really free and enlightened State, until the State comes to recognize the individual as a higher and independent power, from which all its own power and authority are derived, and treats him accordingly. I please myself with imagining a State at last which can afford to be just to all men, and to treat the individual with respect as a neighbor; which even would not think it inconsistent with its own repose, if a few were to live aloof from it, not meddling with it, nor embraced by it, who fulfilled all the duties of neighbors and fellow-men. A State which bore this kind of fruit, and suffered it to drop off as fast as it ripened, would prepare the way for a still more perfect and glorious State, which also I have imagined, but not yet anywhere seen.

LEO TOLSTOY

1828–1910

At the age of fifty-seven, with the writing of *War and Peace* and *Anna Karenina* behind him, Tolstoy underwent a spiritual crisis which was to change him irrevocably. At that time he turned against organized Christianity and insisted on a simpler Gospel based on 'The Law of Love'. Tolstoy's rejection of violence was absolute, his attack on society devastating; what Godwin had attacked on secular grounds, Tolstoy opposed for religious reasons. In his great work, *The Kingdom of God Is Within You* (1893), he left few stones unturned as he attacked the respectable violence of an industrial system which exploited men ruthlessly and a Church which had left the way of Christ. Tolstoy spoke of a faith informed by reason and a God present in all men: 'I believe that He is in me and I in Him.' He was excommunicated in 1901, but this only made formal what he had himself earlier proclaimed.

At the time of his death he was easily the most famous man in the world, and Gandhi in his writings often affirmed his debt to the Russian. Gandhi was, in fact, one of the early Indian translators of 'Letter to a Hindu' which Tolstoy wrote two years before his death. In it he attacked the violent resistance of Tarakuatta Das to aggression, which echoed Gandhi's sentiments; Gandhi had by then begun campaigns of passive resistance in the Transvaal. He wrote to Tolstoy in 1909 and a correspondence sprang up between the two men whose views were at once so similar and so different, for Gandhi always believed in working with governments.

The little-known 'Letter to a Non-commissioned Officer' appears, without a date, in Volume 20 of *The Novels and Other Works of Lyof N. Tolstoi* (New York: Scribner's, 1902). The letter displays much of that passionate attack on established institutions which made Tolstoy the great exponent in our time of the Christian anarchist position.

Letter to a Non-commissioned Officer

You are surprised that soldiers are taught that it is right to kill people in certain cases and in war, while in the books admitted to be holy by those who so teach, there is nothing like such a permission, but, on the contrary, not only is all murder forbidden but all insulting of others is forbidden also, and we are told not to do to others what we do not wish done to us. And you ask, is not this a fraud? And if it is a fraud, then for whose sake is it done?

Yes, it is a fraud, committed for the sake of those accustomed to live on the sweat and blood of other men, and who have therefore perverted, and still pervert, Christ's teaching, which was given to man for his good, but which has now, in its perverted form, become the chief source of human misery.

The thing has come about in this way:

The government, and all those people of the upper classes that are near the government, and that live by the work of others, need some means of dominating the workers, and this means they find in their control of the army. Defence against foreign enemies is only an excuse. The German government frightens its subjects about the Russians and the French, the French government frightens its people about the Germans, the Russian government frightens its people about the French and the Germans, and that is the way with all governments. But neither the Germans, nor the Russians, nor the French, desire to fight their neighbours and other people; but, living in peace, they dread war more than anything else in the world. The government and the upper governing classes, to excuse their domination of the labourers, behave like a gipsy who whips his horse before he turns a corner and then pretends he cannot hold it in. They provoke their own people and some foreign government, and then pretend that for the well-being or for the defence of their people they must declare war, which again brings profit only to generals, officers, functionaries, merchants, and, in general, to the rich. In reality war is an inevitable result of the existence of armies; and armies are only needed by governments in order to dominate their own working-classes.

The thing is a crime, but the worst of it is that the government, in order to have a plausible basis for its domination of the people, has to pretend that it holds the highest religious teaching known to man (i.e. the Christian), and that it brings up its subjects in this teaching. That teaching, however, is in its nature opposed not only to murder, but to all violence, and, therefore, the governments, in order to dominate the people and to be considered Christian, had to pervert Christianity and to hide its true meaning from the people, and thus deprive men of the well-being Christ brought them.

This perversion was accomplished long ago, in the time of that scoundrel the Emperor Constantine, who for doing it was enrolled among the saints. All subsequent governments, especially our Russian government, do their utmost to preserve this perverted understanding, and not to allow the people to see the real meaning of Christianity; because, having seen the real meaning of Christianity, the people would perceive that the governments, with their taxes, soldiers, prisons, gallows, and false priests, are not only not the pillars of Christianity they profess to be, but are its greatest enemies.

In consequence of this perversion those frauds which have surprised you are possible, and all those terrible misfortunes occur from which people suffer.

The people are oppressed, robbed, poor, ignorant, dying of hunger. Why? Because the land is in the hands of the rich; the people are enslaved in mills and in factories, obliged to earn money because taxes are demanded from them, and the price of their labour is diminished while the price of things they need is increased.

How are they to escape? By taking the land from the rich? But if this is done, soldiers will come and will kill the rebels or put them in prison. Take the mills and factories? The same will happen. Organize and support a strike? But it is sure to fail. The rich will hold out longer than the workers, and the armies are always on the side of the capitalists. The people will never extricate themselves from the want in which they are kept, as long as the army is in the hands of the governing classes.

But who compose these armies that keep the people in this state of slavery? Who are these soldiers that will fire at the peasants who take the land, or at the strikers who will not disperse, and at the smugglers who bring in goods without paying taxes, that put in prison and there guard those who refuse to pay taxes? The soldiers are these same peasants who are deprived of land, these same strikers who want better wages, these same taxpayers who want to be rid of these taxes.

And why do these people shoot at their brothers? Because it has been instilled into them that the oath they were obliged to take on entering the service is binding, and that, though it is generally wrong to murder people, it is right to do so at the command of their superiors. That is to say that that fraud is played off upon them which has occurred to you. But here we meet the question: How is it that sensible people – often people who can read, and even educated people – believe in such an evident lie? However little education a man may have, he cannot but know that Christ did not sanction murder, but taught kindness, meekness, forgiveness of injuries, love of one's enemies – and therefore he cannot help seeing that on the basis of Christian teaching he cannot pledge himself in advance to kill all whom he may be ordered to kill.

The question is: How can sensible people believe, as all now serving in the army have believed and still believe, such an evident fraud? The answer is that it is not this one fraud by itself that takes people in, but they have from childhood been deprived of the proper use of their reason by a whole series of frauds, a whole system of frauds, called the Orthodox Faith, which is nothing but the grossest idolatry. In this faith people are taught that God is triple, that besides this triple God there is a Queen of Heaven, and besides this queen there are various saints whose corpses have not decayed, and besides these saints there are ikons of the Gods and of the Queen of Heaven, to which one should offer candles and pray with one's hands; and that the most important and holy thing on earth is the pap, which the parson makes of wine and white bread on Sundays behind a railing; and that after the parson has whispered over it, the wine is no longer wine, and the white bread is not bread, but they are the blood and flesh of one of the triple Gods, etc.

All this is so stupid and senseless that it is quite impossible to understand what it all means. And the very people who teach this faith do not tell you to understand it, but only tell you to believe it; and people trained to do it from childhood can believe any kind of nonsense that is told them. And when men have been so befooled that they believe that God hangs in the corner, or sits in a morsel of pap which the parson gives out in a spoon; that to kiss a board or some relics, and to put candles in front of them, is useful for life here and hereafter – they are called on to enter the military service, where they are humbugged to any extent, being made to swear on the Gospels (in which swearing is prohibited) that they will do just what is forbidden in those Gospels, and then taught that to kill people at the word of those in command is not a sin, but that to refuse to submit to those in command is a sin. So that the fraud played off on soldiers, when it is instilled into them that they may without sin kill people at the wish of those in command, is not an isolated fraud, but is bound up with a whole system of fraud, without which this one fraud would not deceive them.

Only a man who is quite befooled by the false faith called Orthodoxy, palmed off upon him for the true Christian faith, can believe that there is no sin in a Christian entering the army, promising blindly to obey any man who ranks above him in the service, and, at the will of others, learning to kill, and committing that most terrible crime, forbidden by all laws.

A man free from the pseudo-Christian faith called Orthodox will not believe that.

And that is why the so-called Sectarians – i.e. Christians who have repudiated the Orthodox teaching and acknowledge Christ's teaching as explained in the Gospels, and especially in the Sermon on the Mount – are not tricked by this deception, but have frequently refused, and still do refuse, to be soldiers, considering such occupation incompatible with Christianity and preferring to bear all kinds of persecution, as hundreds and thousands of people are doing; in Russia among the Dukhobors and Molokans, in Austria the Nazarenes, and in Sweden, Switzerland, and Germany among members of the Evangelical sects. The government knows this, and is therefore exceedingly anxious that the general Church fraud, without which its power could not be maintained, should be commenced with every child from early infancy, and should be continually maintained in such a way that none may avoid it. The government tolerates anything else, drunkenness and vice (and not only tolerates, but even organizes drunkenness and vice – they help to stupefy people), but by all the means in its power it hinders those who have escaped from its trap from assisting others to escape.

The Russian government perpetrates this fraud with special craft and cruelty. It orders all its subjects to baptize their children during infancy into the false faith called Orthodoxy, and it threatens to punish them if they disobey. And when the children are baptized, i.e. are reckoned as Orthodox, then under threats of criminal penalties they are forbidden to discuss the faith into which, without their wish, they were baptized; and for such discussion of that faith, as well as for renouncing it and passing to another, they are actually punished. So that about all Russians it cannot be said that they believe the Orthodox faith – they do not know whether they believe it or not, but were converted to it during infancy and kept in it by violence, i.e. by the fear of punishment. All Russians were entrapped into Orthodoxy by a cunning fraud, and are kept in it by cruel force. Using the power it wields, the government perpetrates and maintains this fraud, and the fraud upholds its power.

And, therefore, the only means to free people from their many miseries lies in freeing them from the false faith instilled in them by government, and in their imbibing the true Christian teaching which is hidden by this false teaching. The true Christian teaching is very simple, clear, and obvious to all, as Christ said. But it is simple and accessible only when man is freed from that falsehood in which we were all educated, and which is passed off upon us as God's truth.

Nothing needful can be poured into a vessel full of what is useless. We must first empty out what is useless. So it is with the acquirement of true Christian teaching. We have first to understand that all the stories telling how God six thousand years ago made the world; how Adam sinned and the human race fell; and how the Son of God, a God born of a virgin, came on earth and redeemed man; and all the fables in the Old Testament and in the Gospels, and all the lives of the saints with their stories of miracles and relics – are nothing but a gross hash of Jewish superstitions and priestly frauds. Only to a man quite free from this deception can the clear and simple teaching of Christ, which needs no explanation, be accessible and comprehensible. That teaching tells us nothing of the beginning, or of the end, of the world, or about God and His purpose, or in general about things which we cannot, and need not, know; but it speaks only of what man must do to save himself, i.e. how best to live the life he has come into, in this world, from birth to death. For this purpose it is only necessary to act to others as we wish them to act to us. In that is all the law and the prophets, as Christ said. And to act in that way we need neither ikons, nor relics, nor church services, nor priests, nor catechisms, nor governments, but on the contrary, we need perfect freedom from all that; for to do to others as we wish them to do to us is only possible when a man is free from the fables which the priests give out as the only truth, and is not bound by promises to act as other people may order. Only such a man will be capable of fulfilling – not his own will nor that of other men – but the will of God.

And the will of God is not that we should fight and oppress the weak, but that we should acknowledge all men to be our brothers and should serve one another.

These are the thoughts your letter has aroused in me. I shall be very glad if they help to clear up the questions you are thinking about.

Letter to a Hindu

I

I received your letter and the two issues of the magazine. Both were intensely interesting to me; indeed, the oppression of a majority by the minority of a people and the corruption which flows from it, is a phenomenon which has always occupied my mind and, at present, is entirely occupying my attention. I will endeavour to convey to you what I think both in a particular and general way, about the causes from which these dreadful calamities have arisen, and do arise, of which you write in your letter, and which are also mentioned in the two numbers of the Hindu magazine you sent me.

The causes, owing to which this astonishing spectacle arises, of the majority of the labouring classes submitting to a mere handful of idlers, whom it permits to dispose not only of its labours but also of its very life, are always, and everywhere, the same; whether the oppressors and the oppressed belong to the same nation, or, whether, as in the case in India and in other countries, the dominant class belongs to an entirely different nation from those oppressed.

It appears especially strange of India, for here we have a people of 200 millions of individuals, highly endowed with spiritual and physical powers, in absolute subjection to a small clique, composed of persons utterly alien to it in thought and aspiration, and altogether inferior to those whom they enslave.

These causes, as one can easily see from your letter, from the articles in 'Free Hindustan', from the highly interesting writings of the Hindu Swami Vive Kananda and others, are in accord with that which causes the distress of all the peoples of our times; in the absence of a rational religious teaching which, while elucidating the meaning of life to all people alike, would also make clear the higher law which should be a guide to conduct, and in the substitution for them of the more than dubious propositions of a false religion and a pseudo-science, and in the immoral conclusion called civilization, derived from both.

One has already seen, not only from your letter and from the articles in 'Free Hindustan', but also from the entire Hindu political literature of our times, that the majority of the leaders of public opinion among the native races of India, while no longer ascribing any significance to those religious teachings which were, and are, professed by the Hindu peoples, now find the sole possibility of deliverance of this people from the oppression it endures, in embracing those anti-religious and subtly immoral forms of social order in which the English and other pseudo-Christian nations live today. Nothing shows more clearly the total absence of religious consciousness in the minds of the present-day leaders of Hindu peoples than does this tendency to instil into the hearts of the natives acceptance of the forms of life in operation amongst European nations. Meanwhile, in the absence of true religious consciousness and the guidance of conduct flowing from it, which is common in our times to all the nations of the East and the West, from Japan to England and America, lies the chief, if not the sole, cause of the enslavement of all the Indian peoples by the English.

II

In order to make my thoughts clear I must go back a considerable time.

We do not know, and cannot know (I boldly say – we need not) how mankind lived millions or even tens of thousands of years ago; but in all those times of which we have any reliable knowledge we find that humanity has lived in separate tribes, classes and nations, in which the majority, submitting to the apparently inevitable, has permitted the coercive rule of one or several persons of the minority. We know this beyond a doubt. Notwithstanding the external diversity of events and persons, such an organization of human life has manifested itself in a similar way in all the countries of whose previous history we know any-thing. And such an order of life, the further back you go, was always looked upon as the necessary basis for harmonious intercourse, both by the rulers and the ruled.

Thus it was everywhere. And in spite of such an external order of life having existed for centuries and continuing even until now, a long time ago – thousands of years before our time, in the midst of different nations and often from out of the very centre of this order of life resting on coercion, one and the same thought has been expressed – that in every individual one spiritual source manifests itself which gives life to everything existing, that this spiritual source endeavours to unite with everything that is in harmony with it, and attains this unification by love. This thought in its various forms has been voiced with more or less completeness and lucidity at different times and in various places. It has been expressed in Brahmanism, Judaism, Mazdaism (the teaching of Zoroastra), in Buddhism, Taoism, Confucianism, and the writings of the Greek and Roman sages, and in Christianity and Mohammedanism. The fact that one and the same thought has been expressed in the midst of the most diverse nations and at different times and places, indicates that this thought was inherent in human nature and contained the truth in itself. But this truth as declared to those who considered that the only possible way of uniting people into societies was by the exercise of violence on the part of one set to others, appeared to be in opposition to the existing order. Indeed, at the time of its first appearance, it was expressed in such a vague and fragmentary manner, that, although the people embraced it as a theory, they were unable to accept it as an authoritative guidance for conduct. Besides, in regard to all the renderings of this truth as it was gradually proclaimed amongst people whose order of life was founded on violence, one and the same thing always occurred, viz.: those who enjoyed the benefits derived from power, realizing that the recognition by the people of this truth undermined their position, consciously or unconsciously distorted the truth by every means in their power, robing it with attributes and meanings totally foreign to it, and also opposed its dissemination by downright violence. Thus this truth which is natural to humanity *that human life should be guided by the spiritual source which forms the foundations of human life and manifests itself in love* in order to permeate man's consciousness, had to struggle with the incompleteness of its expression and the intentional and unintentional distortions of it, as well as with deliberate violence which compels, by means of punishments and persecutions, the acceptance of that explanation of the religious law established by the authorities, and which is opposed to this revealed truth. Such a misrepresentation and obscuration of the new, but, as yet, imperfectly explained truth, took place everywhere, in Confucianism, Taoism, Buddhism, Christianity, in Mohammedanism and also in your Brahmanism.

III

This has occurred everywhere. The fact that love is the highest moral feeling was accepted universally, but the truth itself was interwoven with many and varied falsehoods, which so distorted it, that out of this recognition of love as the highest moral feeling, nothing but mere words remain. The theory was advanced that this highest moral feeling is applicable to the individual life only, (i.e, for home life), whereas, in social life, all forms of violence – prisons, executions, wars, – involving acts diametrically opposed to even the feeblest perception of love, were regarded as indispensable for the protection of the majority against evil doers. Although common sense clearly indicates, that if one set of people can arrogate to themselves the right to decide as to which people are to be subjected to all kinds of coercion for the supposed welfare of the many, it naturally follows that those few individuals to whom violence is so applied could also come to the same conclusion with regard to those who subjected them to violence; and although the great religious teachers – Brahman, Buddhist and, especially, Christian – anticipating this perversion of the law of love, directed attention to the one inevitable condition of love: the enduring of affronts, injuries, and all kinds of violence, without resisting the evil by evil – mankind continued to accept what was incompatible: the beneficence of love, and, with it, the resistance of evil by violence which is absolutely opposed to love. And teachings voicing this, in spite of the palpable contradiction embodied in them, have taken such a deep hold upon the people that, while believing in the benignity of love, they fail to question the lawfulness of an order of life founded on coercion, and including the imposition not only of tortures but also of death, by some persons upon others.

For a long time people lived quite unconsciously in this obvious contradiction. But the day came when this contradiction began to stagger the more thoughtful people of different nations, and the ancient simple truth that it was natural for people to help and to love, instead of torturing and killing each other, began to dawn upon the minds of men and grew clearer every day, while the belief in those false interpretations by which the deviations from it were justified, grew weaker and weaker.

In ancient times the fraudulent belief that so-called monarchs, Tsars, sultans, rajahs, shahs, and other heads of states, enjoyed peculiar divine rights, was the chief means by which the use of violence was justified. But, as time went on, the belief that the special rights of monarchs were sanctioned by God became weaker and weaker. This faith declined in equal degree, and almost simultaneously, in the Christian, in the Brahman, in the Buddhist and in the Confucian spheres, and it has recently become so feeble that it can no longer serve, as it once did, as a justification of acts openly opposed to common sense and to genuine religious feeling. People saw more and more distinctly, and today the majority see quite clearly, the absurdity and the immorality of the submission of their will to that of others like themselves, who require of them acts not only contrary to their material welfare, but which are also a violation of their moral feeling.

It is, therefore, perfectly natural that people who have lost faith in the divine authority of all manner of potentates should endeavour to free themselves from it. Unfortunately, however, not only have these monarchs, considered to be divinely appointed beings, availed themselves of the advantages accruing from ruling over nations, but, during their domination, and owing to the existence of these pseudo-supernatural beings, an ever increasing number of persons have sprung up who established themselves near the courts and, under the guise of governing the people, lived upon their labours. And this governing class has taken steps that, as the old religious fraud that the divine rule of monarchs was instituted by God Himself decays in influence, another and similar deception should take its place, and having superseded the old one, should continue, in the same way as the old one, to keep nations in slavery to a limited number of rulers.

IV

New superstitions have replaced the obsolete outlived religious superstitions. These are as groundless as those they superseded, but they are still new; hence their inconsistency cannot at once be detected by the majority. And besides, people who make use of power propagate them and support them in such a skilful manner that these justifications appear incontrovertible to many, even those who suffer from what they justify. These new superstitions are termed scientific.

By the word 'scientific' is meant the same as the word 'religion' implied, namely: All that was called *religion* was always supposed to be undoubtedly true for the simple reason that it was named *religion*; exactly in the same way all that is now named '*science*' is always expected to be undoubtedly true for the simple reason that it is named *science*. Thus, in this case the obsolete religious justification of violence, which consisted in the assumption of the uniqueness and divinity of personages being in power, and put in power by God, ('There is no power but from God'), was replaced by the justification that, as the coercion of some by others always has been, it is proved that such violence must continue indefinitely. This notion, that mankind should not live according to reason and conscience, but in obedience to that which has for a long time been taking place amongst them, is embodied in what 'science' terms the 'historical' law. The second 'scientific' justification is, that because, amongst plants and animals a struggle for existence goes on which always culminates in the survival of the fittest, the same struggle should go on amongst men, being endowed with the attributes of reason and love, faculties which are absent from beings submitting to the law of struggle and selection. In this consists the second 'scientific' justification of violence.

The third 'scientific' justification of violence, the most prominent, and, unfortunately, the most widespread, is, in reality, the oldest religious justification very slightly changed in aspect. It runs as follows: In social life the use of violence against some for the welfare of many is inevitable; therefore, however desirable love amongst people may be, coercion is indispensable. The difference between the justification of violence by pseudo-science and that of pseudo-religion lies in the different answers that they give to the question 'Why such and such people, and not others, have the right to decide whom violence may, and must, be used against' – science does not say that these decisions are just because they are pronounced by personages who possess a divine power – but that these decisions represent the will of the people, which under a constitutional form of government, is supposed to express itself in all the decisions and actions of those who, at any given time, are in power.

Such are the scientific justifications of coercion, which are not only groundless but simply absurd; but they are so necessary to people occupying privileged positions that they as implicitly believe in them and as confidently propagate them, as they formerly did the doctrine of the immaculate conception.

The unhappy majority, weighed down by toil, is so dazzled by the display which accompanies the dissemination of these 'scientific truths', that, under this new influence, it accepts all these scientific follies as a sacred truth as readily as it formerly accepted the pseudo-religious justifications, and continues to submit slavishly to new potentates who are just as cruel, but who have somewhat increased in number.

V

Thus it has been going on, and still is, in the Christian world. There seemed hope that in the vast Brahman-Buddhist, Confucian worlds this new scientific superstition would not find place, and that the Chinese, the Japanese and the Hindus, having seen the falsity of religious impositions which justify violence, would proceed direct to the conception of the law of love inherent in humanity, which has been so clearly enunciated by the great teachers of the East. But it appears that the scientific superstition which replaced the religious one is getting a firmer and firmer grip upon the Oriental nations. It has now a specially strong hold on the land of the extreme East, Japan, and not only on its leaders, but on the majority of the people, and is the precursor of the greatest calamities. It has taken hold of China with her 400 million inhabitants, and also of your India with her 200 millions, or, at least, the bulk of the people who look upon themselves, as you do, as the leaders of these peoples.

In your magazine you include, as the basic principle which should direct the activity of your people, the following thought as an epigram: '*Resistance to aggression is not simply justifiable but imperative; non-resistance hurts both altruism and egoism.*'

Love is the only means of saving people from all those disasters which they undergo.

In this case, the only means of liberating your people from slavery lies in love. Love as the religious foundation of human life was proclaimed among your people with striking force and lucidity in remote antiquity. Love, so long as resistance to evil by violence is permitted, is a contradiction in itself and loses its inner sense and all its meaning. And what follows? In the twentieth century you, a member of one of the most religious of peoples, lightheartedly, and with confidence in your scientific enlightenment, and, hence, in your undoubted righteousness – you deny this law, repeating – pardon me – that colossal stupidity which your European teachers, at first the servants of theology, then of science, defenders of violence, enemies of the truth, have instilled into you.

You say that the English have enslaved and keep the Hindus in subjection because the latter have not resisted sufficiently and do not resist violence by force.

But it is just the contrary. If the English have enslaved the Hindus, it is simply because the Hindus recognized, and do recognize, coercion as the main and fundamental principle of their social order. In the name of this principle they submitted to their little Tsars, the Princes, in the name of it they struggled with each other, fought with Europeans, with the English, and, at present, are preparing to struggle with them again.

A commercial company enslaved a nation comprising 200 millions. Tell this to a man free from superstition and he will fail to grasp what these words mean. What does it mean that 30 thousand people, not athletes, but rather weak and ill-looking, have enslaved 200 millions of vigorous, clever, strong, freedom-loving people? Do not the figures alone make it clear that not the English, but the Hindus themselves are the cause of their slavery?

For the Hindus to complain that the English have enslaved them is like people who are addicted to drink complaining that vendors of wine who have settled in their midst have enslaved them. You tell them that they can abstain from drinking, but they answer that they are so accustomed to it that they cannot abstain, that they find it necessary to keep up their energy by wine. Is not that the case with all the people, the millions of people, who submit to thousands or even hundreds of individuals of their own nation, or those of foreign nations?

If the Hindus have been enslaved by violence, it is because they themselves have lived, and continue to live by violence, and fail to recognize the eternal law of love inherent in humanity.

'Pitiful and ignorant is the man who seeks what he has already got, but is unaware that he has it. Yes, pitiful and ignorant is the man who does not know the bliss of that love which surrounds him, which I gave him.' – (Krishna).

If man only lives in accord with the law of love, which includes non-resistance, which has already been revealed to him and is natural to his heart, and, hence, does not participate in any form of violence, not only will hundreds not enslave millions, but even millions will be unable to enslave one individual. Do not resist evil, but also do not participate in evil yourselves; in the violent deeds of the administration, of the law courts, of the collection of taxes, and, what is more important, of the soldiers. Then no one in the world can enslave you.

VI

The same thing happens to the humanity of our times, Eastern or Western, as to every individual when he is passing from one age to another (childhood to youth, youth to manhood). During these transition periods he loses what has been, hitherto, his guide in life; and not having yet acquired a new one suited to his age, he lives without any guidance, becoming a prey to restlessness and irritability, and, ultimately, turns to amusements and intoxicants, to distract his attention from the misery and selfishness of his life. Such a condition may last a long time.

But, even in the transition of an individual from one age to another, the time must inevitably come when life can no longer continue in the same old rut, in senseless anxiety and restlessness. The man must understand that because he has outgrown the previous guidance, it does not follow that he must necessarily live without any rational guidance whatever. He must formulate for himself a view of life corresponding to his age, and, having elucidated it, he should be guided by it.

Similar crises must of necessity occur in the ever-changing life of humanity. And I am of opinion that the time has arrived for such a transition of humanity from one age to another, and not in the sense that it has arrived now, viz.: 1908, but in the sense that the inherent contradiction of human life, i.e. the contradiction between the consciousness of the beneficence of the law of love, and the system of life built upon the law of violence, opposed to love, which has produced in humanity the senseless, irritating, anxious life of martyrdom which has lasted for centuries, has in our time reached an unbearable intensity. The only solution of this contradiction is a recognition of the truth that the law of human life is the law of love, cherished by all humanity from the most remote antiquity, coupled with the final rejection of the outlived law of violence.

The recognition of this truth in its full significance is only possible for men when they free themselves completely from all religious as well as scientific superstitions, and the mass of spurious distortions and misinterpretations flowing therefrom by means of which truth has been hidden for centuries from mankind.

In order to save a sinking ship it is necessary to throw overboard the ballast which, though it might have been indispensable at one time, would cause destruction. It is exactly the same with religious and scientific superstitions which hide this salutary truth from men. If people are to embrace the truth, not with the vagueness of childhood, nor with the one-sided uncertainty of interpretation given to them by religious and scientific teachers, but in such a manner that it should become the highest law of human life, they must effect the complete liberation of this truth from *all* those superstitions, pseudo-religious as well as pseudo-scientific, which now obscure it. Not a partial, timid liberation, which considers tradition sanctified by antiquity and the habits of the people, such as was effected by Guru-nanaka, the founder of the religion of the Sakas, and in Christianity by Luther, or similar reformers in other religions in the religious sphere, but a complete deliverance of the religious truth from all the ancient religions, as well as the modern scientific superstitions.

If people only freed themselves from beliefs in all kinds of Ormuzds, Brahmas, Sabbaoths, their incarnation in Krishnas and Christs, from beliefs in paradise and hell, in angels and demons, in reincarnation, resurrections and the idea of the *interference of God in the life of the Universe*; freed themselves, chiefly, from the belief in the infallibility of the various Vedas, Bibles, Gospels, Tripitakas, Korans, etc. If people only freed themselves also from blindly believing all sorts of scientific doctrines about infinitesimally small atoms, molecules, about all kinds of infinitely great, and infinitely remote, worlds, about their movements and their origin, about forces; from the implicit faith in all manner of theoretical scientific laws to which man is supposed to be subjected; the historic and economic laws, the laws of struggle and survival, etc. – if people only freed themselves from this terrible accumulation of the idle exercise of our lower capacities of mind and memory which is called the sciences, from all the innumerable divisions of all sorts of histories, anthropologies, homiletics, bacteriologies, jurisprudences, cosmographics, strategies, whose name is legion: if only people would unburden themselves from this ruinous intoxicating ballast – that simple, explicit law of love, accessible to all, which is so natural to mankind, and which solves all questions and perplexities, would, of its own accord, become clear and obligatory.

VII

To escape from the self-inflicted calamities which have reached the highest degree of intensity men do not require new explanations and justifications of old religious superstitions, such as Vive-Kanandas, Babe Bharatis and others have formulated in your country, and an infinite number of similar new interpreters and expounders of whom no one stands in need in our Christian world; nor do they require the innumerable sciences about matters which not only are not essential but mostly harmful (in the spiritual realm there is nothing indifferent; what is not useful is always harmful). The Hindu, as well as the Englishman, the Frenchman, the German, the Russian, do not require constitutions, revolutions, conferences, congresses, or any new ingenious devices for submarine navigation, aerial navigation, powerful explosives, or all kinds of conveniences for the enjoyment of the rich ruling classes; nor new schools and universities with instruction in innumerable sciences, nor the augmentation of papers and books, the gramophones and cinematographs, nor those childish and, mostly, corrupt stupidities which are called arts : one thing only is needful : the knowledge of that simple lucid truth which can be contained in the soul of every man who has not been perverted by religious and scientific superstitions – that the law of human life is the law of love which gives the highest happiness to every individual as well as to all mankind.

If people would only free their consciousness from those mountains of nonsense which hide from them the indubitable eternal truth inherent in mankind, one and the same in all the great religions of the world. The truth would then reveal itself at once in spite of the mass of pseudo-religious nonsense which now conceals it. And as soon as this truth is revealed to the consciousness of people, all that stupidity which now conceals it, will disappear of its own accord and, with it, also that evil from which humanity now suffers.

'Children, look upwards with your beclouded eyes, and a world full of joy and love will disclose itself to you, a rational world made by my wisdom, the only real world. Then you will know what Love has done with you, what Love has bestowed upon you, and what Love demands from you' – (Krishna).

14 December 1908.
Yasnaya Poliana.

THEORY AND PRACTICE
IN THE TWENTIETH
CENTURY

WILLIAM JAMES

1842–1910

'THE Moral Equivalent of War' was given wide publicity by pacifists upon its appearance in the February 1910 publication of the Association for International Conciliation. Here was a proposal by an eminent psychologist–philosopher, a plan which called for mankind's surplus energies to be directed, not into destructive pursuits, but into adventurous and idealistic enterprise. Although funds were never forthcoming to put James's proposal to a 'pragmatic' test, various organizations have followed the lines he marked out, among them the Friends Service Committee, Service Civil International, the Unitarian Service Committee, and perhaps one day the Peace Corps.

The Moral Equivalent of War

The war against war is going to be no holiday excursion or camping party. The military feelings are too deeply grounded to abdicate their place among our ideals until better substitutes are offered than the glory and shame that come to nations as well as to individuals from the ups and downs of politics and the vicissitudes of trade. There is something highly paradoxical in the modern man's relation to war. Ask all our millions, north and south, whether they would vote now (were such a thing possible) to have our war for the Union expunged from history and the record of a peaceful transition to the present time substituted for that of its marches and battles, and probably hardly a handful of eccentrics would say yes. Those ancestors, those efforts, those memories and legends, are the most ideal part of what we now own together, a sacred spiritual possession worth more than all the blood poured out. Yet ask those same people whether they would be willing in cold blood to start another civil war now to gain another similar possession, and not one man or woman would vote for the proposition. In modern eyes, precious though wars may be, they must not be waged solely for the sake of the ideal harvest. Only when forced upon one, only when an enemy's injustice leaves us no alternative, is a war now thought permissible.

It was not thus in ancient times. The earlier men were hunting men, and to hunt a neighboring tribe, kill the males, loot the village and possess the females, was the most profitable, as well as the most exciting, way of living. Thus were the more martial tribes selected, and in chiefs and peoples a pure pugnacity and love of glory came to mingle with the more fundamental appetite for plunder.

Modern war is so expensive that we feel trade to be a better avenue to plunder; but modern man inherits all the innate pugnacity and all the love of glory of his ancestors. Showing war's irrationality and horror is of no effect upon him. The horrors make the fascination. War is the *strong* life; it is life *in extremis*; war-taxes are the only ones men never hesitate to pay, as the budgets of all nations show us.

History is a bath of blood. The Iliad is one long recital of how Diomedes and Ajax, Sarpedon and Hector *killed*. No detail of the wounds they made is spared us, and the Greek mind fed upon the story. Greek history is a panorama of jingoism and imperialism – war for war's sake, all the citizens being warriors. It is horrible reading, because of the irrationality of it all – save for the purpose of making 'history' – and the history is that of the utter ruin of civilization in intellectual respects perhaps the highest the earth has ever seen.

Those wars were purely piratical. Pride, gold, women, slaves, excitement, were their only motives. In the Peloponnesian war, for example, the Athenians ask the inhabitants of Melos (the island were the 'Venus of Milo' was found), hitherto neutral, to own their lordship. The envoys meet, and hold a debate which Thucydides gives in full, and which, for sweet reasonableness of form, would have satisfied Matthew Arnold. 'The powerful exact what they can,' said the Athenians, 'and the weak grant what they must.' When the Meleans say that sooner than be slaves they will appeal to the gods, the Athenians reply: 'Of the gods we believe and of men we know that, by a law of their nature, wherever they can rule they will. This law was not made by us, and we are not the first to have acted upon it; we did but inherit it, and we know that you and all mankind, if you were as strong as we are, would do as we do. So much for the gods; we have told you why we expect to stand as high in their good opinion as you.' Well, the Meleans still refused, and their town was taken. 'The Athenians,' Thucydides quietly says, 'thereupon put to death all who were of military age and made slaves of the women and children. They then colonized the island, sending thither five hundred settlers of their own.'

Alexander's career was piracy pure and simple, nothing but an orgy of power and plunder, made romantic by the character of the hero. There was no rational principle in it, and the moment he died his generals and governors attacked one another. The cruelty of those times is incredible. When Rome finally conquered Greece, Paulus Æmilius was told by the Roman Senate to reward his soldiers for their toil by 'giving' them the old kingdom of Epirus. They sacked seventy cities and carried off a hundred and fifty thousand inhabitants as slaves. How many they killed I know not; but in Etolia they killed all the senators, five hundred and fifty in number. Brutus was 'the noblest Roman of them all', but to reanimate his soldiers on the eve of Philippi he similarly promises to give them the cities of Sparta and Thessalonica to ravage, if they win the fight.

Such was the gory nurse that trained societies to cohesiveness. We inherit the warlike type; and for most of the capacities of heroism that the human race is full of we have to thank this cruel history. Dead men tell no tales, and if there were any tribes of other type than this they have left no survivors. Our ancestors have bred pugnacity into our bone and marrow, and thousands of years of peace won't breed it out of us. The popular imagination fairly fattens on the thought of wars. Let public opinion once reach a certain fighting pitch, and no ruler can withstand it. In the Boer War both governments began with bluff but couldn't stay there; the military tension was too much for them. In 1898 our people had read the word 'war' in letters three inches high for three months in every newspaper. The pliant politician McKinley was swept away by their eagerness, and our squalid war with Spain became a necessity.

At the present day, civilized opinion is a curious mental mixture. The military instincts and ideals are as strong as ever, but are confronted by reflective criticisms which sorely curb their ancient freedom. Innumerable writers are showing up the bestial side of military service. Pure loot and mastery seem no longer morally avowable motives, and pretexts must be found for attributing them solely to the enemy. England and we, our army and navy authorities repeat without ceasing, arm solely for 'peace', Germany and Japan it is who are bent on loot and glory. 'Peace' in military mouths today is a synonym for 'war expected'. The word has become a pure provocative, and no government wishing peace sincerely should allow it ever to be printed in a newspaper. Every up-to-date dictionary should say that 'peace' and 'war' mean the same thing, now *in posse*, now *in actu*. It may even reasonably be said that the intensely sharp competitive *preparation* for war by the nations *is the real war*, permanent, unceasing; and that the battles are only a sort of public verification of the mastery gained during the 'peace'-interval.

It is plain that on this subject civilized man has developed a sort of double personality. If we take European nations, no legitimate interest of any one of them would seem to justify the tremendous destructions which a war to compass it would necessarily entail. It would seem as though common sense and reason ought to find a way to reach agreement in every conflict of honest interests. I myself think it our bounden duty to believe in such international rationality as possible. But, as things stand, I see how desperately hard it is to bring the peace-party and the war-party together, and I believe that the difficulty is due to certain deficiencies in the program of pacificism which set the militarist imagination strongly, and to a certain extent justifiably, against it. In the whole discussion both sides are on imaginative and sentimental ground. It is but one utopia against another, and everything one says must be abstract and hypothetical. Subject to this criticism and caution, I will try to characterize in abstract strokes the opposite imaginative forces, and point out what to my own very fallible mind seems the best utopian hypothesis, the most promising line of conciliation.

In my remarks, pacifist though I am, I will refuse to speak of the bestial side of the war-*regime* (already done justice to by many writers) and consider only the higher aspects of militaristic sentiment. Patriotism no one thinks discreditable; nor does anyone deny that war is the romance of history. But inordinate ambitions are the soul of every patriotism, and the possibility of violent death the soul of all romance. The militarily patriotic and romantic-minded everywhere, and especially the professional military class, refuse to admit for a moment that war may be a transitory phenomenon in social evolution. The notion of a sheep's paradise like that revolts, they say, our higher imagination. Where then would be the steeps of life? If war had ever stopped, we should have to re-invent it, on this view, to redeem life from flat degeneration.

Reflective apologists for war at the present day all take it religiously. It is a sort of sacrament. Its profits are to the vanquished as well as to the victor; and quite apart from any question of profit, it is an absolute good, we are told, for it is human nature at its highest dynamic. Its 'horrors' are a cheap price to pay for rescue from the only alternative supposed, of a world of clerks and teachers, of co-education and zo-ophily, of 'consumers' leagues' and 'associated charities', of in-dustrialism unlimited, and feminism unabashed. No scorn, no hardness, no valor any more! Fie upon such a cattleyard of a planet!

So far as the central essence of this feeling goes, no healthy-minded person, it seems to me, can help to some degree partaking of it. Militar-ism is the great preserver of our ideals of hardihood, and human life with no use for hardihood would be contemptible. Without risks or prizes for the darer, history would be insipid indeed; and there is a type of military character which everyone feels that the race should never cease to breed, for everyone is sensitive to its superiority. The duty is incumbent on mankind, of keeping military characters in stock – of keeping them, if not for use, then as ends in themselves and as pure pieces of perfection – so that Roosevelt's weaklings and mollycoddles may not end by making everything else disappear from the face of nature.

This natural sort of feeling forms, I think, the innermost soul of army-writings. Without any exception known to me, militarist authors take a highly mystical view of their subject, and regard war as a biological or sociological necessity, uncontrolled by ordinary psycho-logical checks and motives. When the time of development is ripe the war must come, reason or no reason, for the justifications pleaded are in-variably fictitious. War is, in short, a permanent human *obligation*. General Homer Lea, in his recent book *The Valor of Ignorance*, plants himself squarely on this ground. Readiness for war is for him the essence of nationality, and ability in it the supreme measure of the health of nations.

Nations, General Lea says, are never stationary – they must necessarily expand or shrink, according to their vitality or decrepitude. Japan now is culminating; and by the fatal law in question it is impossible that her statesmen should not long since have entered, with extraordinary foresight, upon a vast policy of conquest – the game in which the first moves were her wars with China and Russia and her treaty with Eng-land, and of which the final objective is the capture of the Philippines, the Hawaiian Islands, Alaska, and the whole of our coast west of the Sierra Passes. This will give Japan what her ineluctable vocation as a state absolutely forces her to claim, the possession of the entire Pacific Ocean; and to oppose these deep designs we Americans have, according to our author, nothing but our conceit, our ignorance, our commercialism, our corruption, and our feminism. General Lea makes a minute technical comparison of the military strength which we at present could oppose to the strength of Japan, and concludes that the islands, Alaska, Oregon, and Southern California, would fall almost without resistance, that San Francisco must surrender in a fortnight to a Japanese investment, that in three or four months the war would be over, and our republic, unable to regain what it had heedlessly neglected to protect sufficiently, would then 'disintegrate', until perhaps some Cæsar should arise to weld us again into a nation.

A dismal forecast indeed! Yet not unplausible, if the mentality of Japan's statesmen be of the Cæsarian type of which history shows so many examples, and which is all that General Lea seems able to imagine. But there is no reason to think that women can no longer be the mothers of Napoleonic or Alexandrian characters; and if these come in Japan and find their opportunity, just such surprises as *The Valor of Ignorance* paints may lurk in ambush for us. Ignorant as we still are of the innermost recesses of Japanese mentality, we may be foolhardy to disregard such possibilities.

Other militarists are more complex and more moral in their considerations. The *Philosophie des Krieges*, by S. R. Steinmetz, is a good example. War, according to this author, is an ordeal instituted by God, who weighs the nations in its balance. It is the essential form of the State, and the only function in which peoples can employ all their powers at once and convergently. No victory is possible save as the resultant of a totality of virtues, no defeat for which some vice or weakness is not responsible. Fidelity, cohesiveness, tenacity, heroism, conscience, education, inventiveness, economy, wealth, physical health and vigor – there isn't a moral or intellectual point of superiority that doesn't tell, when God holds his assizes and hurls the peoples upon one another. *Die Weltgeschichte ist das Weltgericht;*[1] and Dr Steinmetz does not believe that in the long run chance and luck play any part in apportioning the issues.

The virtues that prevail, it must be noted, are virtues anyhow, superiorities that count in peaceful as well as in military competition; but the strain on them, being infinitely intenser in the latter case, makes war infinitely more searching as a trial. No ordeal is comparable to its winnowings. Its dread hammer is the welder of men into cohesive

1. *Universal history is the tribunal of humanity.*

states, and nowhere but in such states can human nature adequately develop its capacity. The only alternative is 'degeneration'.

Dr Steinmetz is a conscientious thinker, and his book, short as it is, takes much into account. Its upshot can, it seems to me, be summed up in Simon Patten's word, that mankind was nursed in pain and fear, and that the transition to a 'pleasure-economy' may be fatal to a being wielding no powers of defence against its disintegrative influences. If we speak of the *fear of emancipation from the fear-régime*, we put the whole situation into a single phrase; fear regarding ourselves now taking the place of the ancient fear of the enemy.

Turn the fear over as I will in my mind, it all seems to lead back to two unwillingnesses of the imagination, one æsthetic, and the other moral; unwillingness, first to envisage a future in which army-life, with its many elements of charm, shall be forever impossible, and in which the destinies of peoples shall nevermore be decided quickly, thrillingly, and tragically, by force, but only gradually and insipidly by 'evolution'; and, secondly, unwillingness to see the supreme theater of human strenuousness closed, and the splendid military aptitudes of men doomed to keep always in a state of latency and never show themselves in action. These insistent unwillingnesses, no less than other æsthetic and ethical insistencies, have, it seems to me, to be listened to and respected. One cannot meet them effectively by mere counter-insistency on war's expensiveness and horror. The horror makes the thrill; and when the question is of getting the extremest and supremest out of human nature, talk of expense sounds ignominious. The weakness of so much merely negative criticism is evident – pacificism makes no converts from the military party. The military party denies neither the bestiality nor the horror, nor the expense; it only says that these things tell but half the story. It only says that war is *worth* them; that, taking human nature as a whole, its wars are its best protection against its weaker and more cowardly self, and that mankind cannot *afford* to adopt a peace-economy.

Pacificists ought to enter more deeply into the æsthetical and ethical point of view of their opponents. Do that first in any controversy, says J. J. Chapman, *then move the point*, and your opponent will follow. So long as antimilitarists propose no substitute for war's disciplinary function, no *moral equivalent* of war, analogous, as one might say, to the mechanical equivalent of heat, so long they fail to realize the full inwardness of the situation. And as a rule they do fail. The duties, penalties, and sanctions pictured in the utopias they paint are all too weak and tame to touch the military-minded. Tolstoy's pacificism is the only exception to this rule, for it is profoundly pessimistic as regards all this world's values, and makes the fear of the Lord furnish the moral spur provided elsewhere by the fear of the enemy. But our socialistic peace-advocates all believe absolutely in this world's values; and instead of the fear of the Lord and the fear of the enemy, the only fear they reckon with is the fear of poverty if one be lazy. This weakness pervades all the socialistic literature with which I am acquainted. Even in Lowes Dickinson's exquisite dialogue, high wages and short hours are the only forces invoked for overcoming man's distaste for repulsive kinds of labor. Meanwhile men at large still live as they always have lived, under a pain-and-fear economy – for those of us who live in an ease-economy are but an island in the stormy ocean – and the whole atmosphere of present-day utopian literature tastes mawkish and dish-watery to people who still keep a sense for life's more bitter flavors. It suggests, in truth, ubiquitous inferiority.

Inferiority is always with us, and merciless scorn of it is the keynote of the military temper. 'Dogs, would you live forever?' shouted Frederick the Great. 'Yes,' say our utopians, 'let us live forever, and raise our level gradually.' The best thing about our 'inferiors' today is that they are as tough as nails, and physically and morally almost as insensitive. Utopianism would see them soft and squeamish, while militarism would keep their callousness, but transfigure it into a meritorious characteristic, needed by 'the service', and redeemed by that from the suspicion of inferiority. All the qualities of a man acquire dignity when he knows that the service of the collectivity that owns him needs them. If proud of the collectivity, his own pride rises in proportion. No collectivity is like an army for nourishing such pride; but it has to be confessed that the only sentiment which the image of pacific cosmopolitan industrialism is capable of arousing in countless worthy breasts is shame at the idea of belonging to *such* a collectivity. It is obvious that the United States of America as they exist today impress a mind like General Lea's as so much human blubber. Where is the sharpness and precipitousness, the contempt for life, whether one's own, or another's? Where is the savage 'yes' and 'no', the unconditional duty? Where is the conscription? Where is the blood-tax? Where is anything that one feels honored by belonging to?

Having said thus much in preparation, I will now confess my own utopia. I devoutly believe in the reign of peace and in the gradual advent of some sort of a socialistic equilibrium. The fatalistic view of the war-function is to me nonsense, for I know that war-making is due to definite motives and subject to prudential checks and reasonable criticisms, just like any other form of enterprise. And when whole nations are the armies, and the science of destruction vies in intellectual refinement with the sciences of production, I see that war becomes absurd and impossible from its own monstrosity. Extravagant ambitions will have to be replaced by reasonable claims, and nations must make common cause against them. I see no reason why all this should not apply to yellow as well as to white countries, and I look forward to a future when acts of war shall be formally outlawed as between civilized peoples.

All these beliefs of mine put me squarely into the antimilitarist party. But I do not believe that peace either ought to be or will be permanent on this globe, unless the states pacifically organized preserve some of the old elements of army-discipline. A permanently successful peace-economy cannot be a simple pleasure-economy. In the more or less socialistic future toward which mankind seems drifting we must still subject ourselves collectively to those severities which answer to our real position upon this only partly hospitable globe. We must make new energies and hardihood continue the manliness to which the military mind so faithfully clings. Martial virtues must be the enduring cement; intrepidity, contempt of softness, surrender of private interest, obedience to command, must still remain the rock upon which states are built – unless, indeed, we wish for dangerous reactions against commonwealths fit only for contempt, and liable to invite attack whenever a center of crystallization for military-minded enterprise gets formed anywhere in their neighborhood.

The war-party is assuredly right in affirming and reaffirming that the martial virtues, although originally gained by the race through war, are absolute and permanent human goods. Patriotic pride and ambition in their military form are, after all, only specifications of a more general competitive passion. They are its first form, but that is no reason for supposing them to be its last form. Men now are proud of belonging to a conquering nation, and without a murmur they lay down their persons and their wealth, if by so doing they may fend off subjection. But who can be sure that *other aspects of one's country* may not, with time and education and suggestion enough, come to be regarded with similarly effective feelings of pride and shame? Why should men not some day feel that it is worth a blood-tax to belong to a collectivity superior in *any* ideal respect? Why should they not blush with indignant shame if the community that owns them is vile in any way whatsoever? Individuals, daily more numerous, now feel this civic passion. It is only a question of blowing on the spark till the whole population gets incandescent, and on the ruins of the old morals of military honor, a stable system of morals of civic honor builds itself up. What the whole community comes to believe in grasps the individual as in a vise. The war-function has grasped us so far; but constructive interests may some day seem no less imperative, and impose on the individual a hardly lighter burden.

Let me illustrate my idea more concretely. There is nothing to make one indignant in the mere fact that life is hard, that men should toil and suffer pain. The planetary conditions once for all are such, and we can stand it. But that so many men, by mere accidents of birth and opportunity, should have a life of *nothing else* but toil and pain and hardness and inferiority imposed upon them, should have *no* vacation, while others natively no more deserving never get any taste of this campaigning life at all – *this* is capable of arousing indignation in reflective minds. It may end by seeming shameful to all of us that some of us have nothing but campaigning, and others nothing but unmanly ease. If now – and this is my idea – there were, instead of military conscription a conscription of the whole youthful population to form for a certain number of years a part of the army enlisted against *Nature*, the injustice would tend to be evened out, and numerous other goods to the commonwealth would follow. The military ideals of hardihood and discipline would be wrought into the growing fiber of the people; no one would remain blind as the luxurious classes now are blind, to man's relations to the globe he lives on, and to the permanently sour and hard foundations of his higher life. To coal and iron mines, to freight-trains, to fishing fleets in December, to dish-washing, clothes-washing, and window-washing, to road-building and tunnel-making, to foundries and stoke-holes, and to the frames of skyscrapers, would our gilded youths be drafted off, according to their choice, to get the childishness knocked out of them, and to come back into society with healthier sympathies and soberer ideas. They would have paid their blood-tax, done their own part in the immemorial human warfare against nature; they would tread the earth more proudly, the women would value them more highly, they would be better fathers and teachers of the following generation.

Such a conscription, with the state of public opinion that would have required it, and the many moral fruits it would bear, would preserve in the midst of a pacific civilization the manly virtues which the military party is so afraid of seeing disappear in peace. We should get toughness without callousness, authority with as little criminal cruelty as possible, and painful work done cheerily because the duty is temporary, and threatens not, as now, to degrade the whole remainder of one's life. I spoke of the 'moral equivalent' of war. So far, war has been the only force that can discipline a whole community, and until an equivalent discipline is organized, I believe that war must have its way. But I have no serious doubt that the ordinary prides and shames of social man, once developed to a certain intensity, are capable of organizing such a moral equivalent as I have sketched, or some other just as effective for preserving manliness of type. It is but a question of time, of skillful propagandism, and of opinion-making men seizing historic opportunities.

The martial type of character can be bred without war. Strenuous honor and disinterestedness abound elsewhere. Priests and medical men are in a fashion educated to it, and we should all feel some degree of it imperative if we were conscious of our work as an obligatory service to the state. We should be *owned*, as soldiers are by the army, and our pride would rise accordingly. We could be poor, then, without humiliation, as army officers now are. The only thing needed henceforward is to inflame the civic temper as past history has inflamed the military temper. H. G. Wells, as usual, sees the center of the situation. 'In many ways,' he says, 'military organization is the most peaceful of activities. When the contemporary man steps from the street of clamorous, insincere advertisement, push, adulteration, underselling, and intermittent employment into the barrackyard, he steps on to a higher social plane, into an atmosphere of service and cooperation and of infinitely more honorable emulations. Here at least men are not flung out of employment to degenerate because there is no immediate work for them to do. They are fed and drilled and trained for better services. Here at least a man is supposed to win promotion by self-forgetfulness and not by self-seeking. And beside the feeble and irregular endowment of research by commercialism, its little short-sighted snatches at profit by innovation and scientific economy, see how remarkable is the steady and rapid development of method and appliances in naval and military affairs! Nothing is more striking than to compare the progress of civil conveniences which has been left almost entirely to the trader, to the progress in military apparatus during the last few decades. The house-appliances of today, for example, are little better than they were fifty years ago. A house of today is still almost as ill-ventilated, badly heated by wasteful fires, clumsily arranged and furnished as the house of 1858. Houses a couple of hundred years old are still satisfactory places of residence, so little have our standards risen. But the rifle or battleship of fifty years ago was beyond all comparison inferior to those we possess; in power, in speed, in convenience alike. No one has a use now for such superannuated things.'

Wells adds that he thinks that the conception of order and discipline, the tradition of service and devotion, of physical fitness, unstinted exertion and universal responsibility, which universal military duty is now teaching European nations, will remain a permanent acquisition, when the last ammunition has been used in the fireworks that celebrate the final peace. I believe as he does. It would be simply preposterous if the only force that could work ideals of honor and standards of efficiency into English or American natures should be the fear of being killed by the Germans or the Japanese. Great indeed is Fear; but it is not, as our military enthusiasts believe and try to make us believe, the only stimulus known for awakening the higher ranges of men's spiritual energy. The amount of alteration in public opinion which my utopia postulates is vastly less than the difference between the mentality of those black warriors who pursued Stanley's party on the Congo with their cannibal warcry of 'Meat! Meat!' and that of the 'general-staff' of any civilized nation. History has seen the latter interval bridged over: the former one can be bridged over much more easily.

RANDOLPH BOURNE

1886–1918

DEFORMED at birth, born poor into an old American family, from the time of his student days at Columbia Randolph Bourne became, for many young Americans of his day, the spokesman of their generation. He placed himself in the stream of political radicalism, and his 'non-literary' writings mercilessly attacked American big business and the nascent military-industrial complex. After his death at the age of 32, his writings on pacifism were collected in *Untimely Papers* (1919), among them his long, incomplete essay, 'The State'.

Bourne's writing of 'The War and the Intellectuals' came as a direct result of his pacifist experience; as the war fever in all countries grew more virulent, he sadly watched the departure from the pacifist ranks of many of the men with whom he had worked and under whose influence he had come as a student and young journalist. In particular, the support John Dewey, his most significant intellectual influence, gave to intervention, and the articles Dewey wrote chiding pacifists for their non-conformity, infuriated him and called forth from his pen article after article of despair, disillusionment, and fury. This selection is taken from *The History of a Literary Radical*.

The War and the Intellectuals

To those of us who still retain an irreconcilable animus against war, it has been a bitter experience to see the unanimity with which the American intellectuals have thrown their support to the use of war-technique in the crisis in which America found herself. Socialists, college professors, publicists, new-republicans, practitioners of literature, have vied with each other in confirming with their intellectual faith the collapse of neutrality and the riveting of the war-mind on a hundred million more of the world's people. And the intellectuals are not content with confirming our belligerent gesture. They are now complacently asserting that it was they who effectively willed it against the hesitation and dim perceptions of the American democratic masses. A war made deliberately by the intellectuals! A calm moral verdict, arrived at after a penetrating study of inexorable facts! Sluggish masses, too remote from the world-conflict to be stirred, too lacking in intellect to perceive their danger! An alert intellectual class, saving the people in spite of themselves biding their time with Fabian strategy until the nation could be moved into war without serious resistance! An intellectual class, gently guiding a nation through sheer force of ideas into what the other nations entered only through predatory craft or popular hysteria or militarist madness! A war free from any taint of self-seeking, a war that will secure the triumph of democracy and internationalize the world! This is the picture which the more self-conscious intellectuals have formed of themselves, and which they are slowly impressing upon a population which is being led no man knows whither by an indubitable intellectualized President. And they are right, in that the war certainly did not spring from either the ideals or the prejudices, from the national ambitions or hysterias, of the American people, however acquiescent the masses prove to be, and however clearly the intellectuals prove their putative intuition.

Those intellectuals who have felt themselves totally out of sympathy with this drag toward war will seek some explanation for this joyful leadership. They will want to understand this willingness of the American intellect to open the sluices and flood us with the sewage of the war spirit. We cannot forget the virtuous horror and stupefaction which filled our college professors when they read the famous manifesto of their ninety-three German colleagues in defense of their war. To the American academic mind of 1914 defense of war was inconceivable. From Bernhardi it recoiled as from a blasphemy, little dreaming that two years later would find it creating its own cleanly reasons for imposing military service on the country and for talking of the rough rude currents of health and regeneration that war would send through the American body politic. They would have thought any one mad who talked of shipping American men by the hundreds of thousands – conscripts – to die on the fields of France. Such a spiritual change seems catastrophic when we shoot our minds back to those days when neutrality was a proud thing. But the intellectual progress has been so gradual that the country retains little sense of the irony. The war sentiment, begun so gradually but so perseveringly by the preparedness advocates who came from the ranks of big business, caught hold of one after another of the intellectual groups. With the aid of Roosevelt, the murmurs became a monotonous chant, and finally a chorus so mighty that to be out of it was at first to be disreputable and finally almost obscene. And slowly a strident rant was worked up against Germany which compared very creditably with the German fulminations against the greedy power of England. The nerve of the war-feeling centered, of course, in the richer and older classes of the Atlantic seaboard, and was keenest where there were French and English business and particularly social connections. The sentiment then spread over the country as a class-phenomenon, touching everywhere those upperclass elements in each section who identified themselves with this Eastern ruling group. It must never be forgotten that in every community it was the least liberal and least democratic elements among whom the preparedness and later the war sentiment was found. The farmers were apathetic, the small business men and workingmen are still apathetic toward the war. The election was a vote of confidence of these latter classes in a President who would keep the faith of neutrality. The intellectuals, in other words, have identified themselves with the least democratic forces in American life. They have assumed the leadership for war of those very classes whom the American democracy has been immemorially fighting. Only in a world where irony was dead could an intellectual class enter war at the head of such illiberal cohorts in the avowed cause of world-liberalism and world-democracy. No one is left to point out the undemocratic nature of this war-liberalism. In a time of faith, skepticism is the most intolerable of all insults.

Our intellectual class might have been occupied, during the last two years of war, in studying and clarifying the ideals and aspirations of the American democracy, in discovering a true Americanism which would not have been merely nebulous but might have federated the different ethnic groups and traditions. They might have spent the time in endeavoring to clear the public mind of the cant of war, to get rid of old mystical notions that clog our thinking. We might have used the time for a great wave of education, for setting our house in spiritual order. We could at least have set the problem before ourselves. If our intellectuals were going to lead the administration, they might conceivably have tried to find some way of securing peace by making neutrality effective. They might have turned their intellectual energy not to the problem of jockeying the nation into war, but to the problem of using our vast neutral power to attain democratic ends for the rest of the world and ourselves without the use of the malevolent technique of war. They might have failed. The point is that they scarcely tried. The time was spent not in clarification and education, but in a mulling over of nebulous ideals of democracy and liberalism and civilization which had never meant anything fruitful to those ruling classes who now so glibly used them, and in giving free rein to the elementary instinct of self-defense. The whole era has been spiritually wasted. The outstanding feature has been not its Americanism but its intense colonialism. The offense of our intellectuals was not so much that they were colonial – for what could we expect of a nation composed of so many national elements? – but that it was so one-sidedly and partisanly colonial. The official, reputable expression of the intellectual class has been that of the English colonial. Certain portions of it have been even more loyalist than the King, more British even than Australia. Other colonial attitudes have been vulgar. The colonialism of the other American stocks was denied a hearing from the start. America might have been made a meeting-ground for the different national attitudes. An intellectual class, cultural colonists of the different European nations, might have threshed out the issues here as they could not be threshed out in Europe. Instead of this, the English colonials in university and press took command at the start, and we became an intellectual Hungary where thought was subject to an effective process of Magyarization. The reputable opinion of the American intellectuals became more and more either what could be read pleasantly in London, or what was written in an earnest effort to put Englishmen straight on their war-aims and war-technique. This Magyarization of thought produced as a counter-reaction a peculiarly offensive and inept German apologetic, and the two partisans divided the field between them. The great masses, the other ethnic groups, were inarticulate. American public opinion was almost as little prepared for war in 1917 as it was in 1914.

The sterile results of such an intellectual policy are inevitable. During the war the American intellectual class has produced almost nothing in the way of original and illuminating interpretation. Veblen's *Imperial Germany*; Patten's *Culture and War*, and addresses; Dewey's *German Philosophy and Politics*; a chapter or two in Weyl's *American Foreign Policies*; – is there much else of creative value in the intellectual repercussion of the war? It is true that the shock of war put the American intellectual to an unusual strain. He had to sit idle and think as spectator not as actor. There was no government to which he could docilely and loyally tender his mind as did the Oxford professors to justify England in her own eyes. The American's training was such as to make the fact of war almost incredible. Both in his reading of history and in his lack of economic perspective he was badly prepared for it. He had to explain to himself something which was too colossal for the modern mind, which outran any language or terms which we had to interpret it in. He had to expand his sympathies to the breaking-point, while pulling the past and present into some sort of interpretative order. The intellectuals in the fighting countries had only to rationalize and justify what their country was already doing. Their task was easy. A neutral, however, had really to search out the truth. Perhaps perspective was too much to ask of any mind. Certainly the older colonials among our college professors let their prejudices at once dictate their thought. They have been comfortable ever since. The war has taught them nothing and will teach them nothing. And they have had the satisfaction, under the rigor of events, of seeing prejudice submerge the intellects of their younger colleagues. And they have lived to see almost their entire class, pacifists and democrats too, join them as apologists for the 'gigantic irrelevance' of war.

We have had to watch, therefore, in this country the same process which so shocked us abroad – the coalescence of the intellectual classes in support of the military programme. In this country, indeed, the socialist intellectuals did not even have the grace of their German brothers and wait for the declaration of war before they broke for cover. And when they declared for war they showed how thin was the intellectual veneer of their socialism. For they called us in terms that might have emanated from any bourgeois journal to defend democracy and civilization, just as if it was not exactly against those very bourgeois democracies and capitalist civilizations that socialists had been fighting for decades. But so subtle is the spiritual chemistry of the 'inside' that all this intellectual cohesion – herd-instinct become herd-intellect – which seemed abroad so hysterical and so servile, comes to us here in highly rational terms. We go to war to save the world from subjugation! But the German intellectuals went to war to save their culture from barbarization! And the French went to war to save their beautiful France! And the English to save international honor! And Russia, most altruistic and self-sacrificing of all, to save a small State from destruction! Whence is our miraculous intuition of our moral spotlessness? Whence our confidence that history will not unravel huge economic and imperialist forces upon which our rationalizations float like bubbles? The Jew often marvels that his race alone should have been chosen as the true people of the cosmic God. Are not our intellectuals equally fatuous when they tell us that our war of all wars is stainless and thrillingly achieving for good?

An intellectual class that was wholly rational would have called insistently for peace and not for war. For months the crying need has been for a negotiated peace, in order to avoid the ruin of a deadlock. Would not the same amount of resolute statesmanship thrown into intervention have secured a peace that would have been a subjugation for neither side? Was the terrific bargaining power of a great neutral ever really used? Our war followed, as all wars follow, a monstrous failure of diplomacy. Shamefacedness should now be our intellectuals' attitude, because the American play for peace was made so little more than a polite play. The intellectuals have still to explain why, willing as they now are to use force to continue the war to absolute exhaustion, they were not willing to use force to coerce the world to a speedy peace.

Their forward vision is no more convincing than their past rationality. We go to war now to internationalize the world! But surely their League to Enforce Peace is only a palpable apocalyptic myth, like the syndicalists' myth of the 'general strike'. It is not a rational programme so much as a glowing symbol for the purpose of focusing belief, of setting enthusiasm on fire for international order. As far as it does this it has pragmatic value, but as far as it provides a certain radiant mirage of idealism for this war and for a world-order founded on mutual fear, it is dangerous and obnoxious. Idealism should be kept for what is ideal. It is depressing to think that the prospect of a world so strong that none dare challenge it should be the immediate ideal of the American intellectual. If the League is only a makeshift, a coalition into which we enter to restore order, then it is only a description of existing fact, and the idea should be treated as such. But if it is an actually prospective outcome of the settlement, the keystone of American policy, it is neither realizable nor desirable. For the programme of such a League contains no provision for dynamic national growth or for international economic justice. In a world which requires recognition of economic internationalism far more than of political internationalism, an idea is reactionary which proposes to petrify and federate the nations as political and economic units. Such a scheme for international order is a dubious justification for American policy. And if American policy had been sincere in its belief that our participation would achieve international beatitude, would we not have made our entrance into the war conditional upon a solemn general agreement to respect in the final settlement those principles of international order? Could we have afforded, if our war was to end war by the establishment of a league of honor, to risk the defeat of our vision and our betrayal in the settlement? Yet we are in the war, and no such solemn agreement was made, nor has it ever been suggested.

The case of the intellectuals seems, therefore, only very speciously rational. They could have used their energy to force a just peace or at least to devise other means than war for carrying through American policy. They could have used their intellectual energy to ensure that our participation in the war meant the international order which they wish. Intellect was not so used. It was used to lead an apathetic nation into an irresponsible war, without guarantees from those belligerents whose cause we were saving. The American intellectual, therefore, has been rational neither in his hindsight nor his foresight. To explain him we must look beneath the intellectual reasons to the emotional disposition. It is not so much what they thought as how they felt that explains our intellectual class. Allowing for colonial sympathy, there was still the personal shock in a world-war which outraged all our preconceived notions of the way the world was tending. It reduced to rubbish most of the humanitarian internationalism and democratic nationalism which had been the emotional thread of our intellectuals' life. We had suddenly to make a new orientation. There were mental conflicts. Our latent colonialism strove with our longing for American unity. Our desire for peace strove with our desire for national responsibility in the world. That first lofty and remote and not altogether unsound feeling of our spiritual isolation from the conflict could not last. There was the itch to be in the great experience which the rest of the world was having. Numbers of intelligent people who had never been stirred by the horrors of capitalistic peace at home were shaken out of their slumber by the horrors of war in Belgium. Never having felt responsibility for labor wars and oppressed masses and excluded races at home, they had a large fund of idle emotional capital to invest in the oppressed nationalities and ravaged villages of Europe. Hearts that had felt only ugly contempt for democratic strivings at home beat in tune with the struggle for freedom abroad. All this was natural, but it tended to over-emphasize our responsibility. And it threw our thinking out of gear.

The task of making our own country detailedly fit for peace was abandoned in favor of a feverish concern for the management of the war, advice to the fighting governments on all matters, military, social and political, and a gradual working up of the conviction that we were ordained as a nation to lead all erring brothers toward the light of liberty and democracy. The failure of the American intellectual class to erect a creative attitude toward the war can be explained by these sterile mental conflicts which the shock to our ideals sent raging through us.

Mental conflicts end either in a new and higher synthesis or adjustment, or else in a reversion to more primitive ideas which have been outgrown but to which we drop when jolted out of our attained position. The war caused in America a recrudescence of nebulous ideals which a younger generation was fast outgrowing because it had passed the wistful stage and was discovering concrete ways of getting them incarnated in actual institutions. The shock of the war threw us back from this pragmatic work into an emotional bath of these old ideals. There was even a somewhat rarefied revival of our primitive Yankee boastfulness, the reversion of senility to that republican childhood when we expected the whole world to copy our republican institutions. We amusingly ignored the fact that it was just that Imperial German régime, to whom we are to teach the art of self-government, which our own Federal structure, with its executive irresponsible in foreign policy and with its absence of parliamentary control, most resembles. And we are missing the exquisite irony of the unaffected homage paid by the American democratic intellectuals to the last and most detested in Britain's tory premiers as the representative of a 'liberal' ally, as well as the irony of the selection of the best hated of America's bourbon 'old guard' as the missionary of American democracy to Russia.

The intellectual state that could produce such things is one where reversion has taken place to more primitive ways of thinking. Simple syllogisms are substituted for analysis, things are known by their labels, our heart's desire dictates what we shall see. The American intellectual class, having failed to make the higher syntheses, regresses to ideas that can issue in quick, simplified action. Thought becomes an easy rationalization of what is actually going on or what is to happen inevitably tomorrow. It is true that certain groups did rationalize their colonialism and attach the doctrine of the inviolability of British sea-power to the doctrine of a League of Peace. But this agile resolution of the mental conflict did not become a higher synthesis, to be creatively developed. It gradually merged into a justification for our going to war. It petrified into a dogma to be propagated. Criticism flagged and emotional propaganda began. Most of the socialists, the college professors and the practitioners of literature, however, have not even reached this high-water mark of synthesis. Their mental conflicts have been resolved much more simply. War in the interests of democracy! This was almost the sum of their philosophy. The primitive idea to which they regressed became almost insensibly translated into a craving for action. War was seen as the crowning relief of their indecision. At last action, irresponsibility, the end of anxious and torturing attempts to reconcile peace-ideals with the drag of the world towards Hell. An end to the pain of trying to adjust the facts to what they ought to be! Let us consecrate the facts as ideal! Let us join the greased slide towards war! The momentum increased. Hesitations, ironies, consciences, considerations – all were drowned in the elemental blare of doing something aggressive, colossal. The new-found Sabbath 'peacefulness of being at war'! The thankfulness with which so many intellectuals lay down and floated with the current betrays the hesitation and suspense through which they had been. The American university is a brisk and happy place these days. Simple, unquestioning action has superseded the knots of thought. The thinker dances with reality.

With how many of the acceptors of war has it been mostly a dread of intellectual suspense? It is a mistake to suppose that intellectuality necessarily makes for suspended judgements. The intellect craves certitude. It takes effort to keep it supple and pliable. In a time of danger and disaster we jump desperately for some dogma to cling to. The time comes, if we try to hold out, when our nerves are sick with fatigue, and we seize in a great healing wave of release some doctrine that can be immediately translated into action. Neutrality meant suspense, and so it became the object of loathing to frayed nerves. The vital myth of the League of Peace provides a dogma to jump to. With war the world becomes motor again and speculation is brushed aside like cobwebs. The blessed emotion of self-defense intervenes too, which focused millions in Europe. A few keep up a critical pose after war is begun, but since they usually advise action which is in one-to-one correspondence with what the mass is already doing, their criticism is little more than a rationalization of the common emotional drive.

The results of war on the intellectual class are already apparent. Their thought becomes little more than a description and justification of what is going on. They turn upon any rash one who continues idly to speculate. Once the war is on, the conviction spreads that individual thought is helpless, that the only way one can count is as a cog in the great wheel. There is no good holding back. We are told to dry our unnoticed and ineffective tears and plunge into the great work. Not only is every one forced into line, but the new certitude becomes idealized. It is a noble realism which opposes itself to futile obstruction and the cowardly refusal to face facts. This realistic boast is so loud and sonorous that one wonders whether realism is always a stern and intelligent grappling with realities. May it not be sometimes a mere surrender to the actual, an abdication of the ideal through a sheer fatigue from intellectual suspense? The pacifist is roundly scolded for refusing to face the facts, and for retiring into his own world of sentimental desire. But is the realist, who refuses to challenge or criticize facts, entitled to any more credit than that which comes from following the line of least resistance? The realist thinks he at least can control events by linking himself to the forces that are moving. Perhaps he can. But if it is a question of controlling war, it is difficult to see how the child on the back of a mad elephant is to be any more effective in stopping the beast than is the child who tries to stop him from the ground. The ex-humanitarian, turned realist, sneers at the snobbish neutrality, colossal conceit, crooked thinking, dazed sensibilities, of those who are still unable to find any balm of consolation for this war. We manufacture consolations here in America while there are probably not a dozen men fighting in Europe who did not long ago give up every reason for their being there except that nobody knew how to get them away.

But the intellectuals whom the crisis has crystallized into an acceptance of war have put themselves into a terrifyingly strategic position. It is only on the craft, in the stream, they say, that one has any chance of controlling the current forces for liberal purposes. If we obstruct, we surrender all power for influence. If we responsibly approve we then retain our power for guiding. We will be listened to as responsible thinkers, while those who obstructed the coming of war have committed intellectual suicide and shall be cast into outer darkness. Criticism by the ruling powers will only be accepted from those intellectuals who are in sympathy with the general tendency of the war. Well, it is true that they may guide, but if their stream leads to disaster and the frustration of national life, is their guiding any more than a preference whether they shall go over the right-hand or the left-hand side of the precipice? Meanwhile, however, there is comfort on board. Be with us, they call, or be negligible, irrelevant. Dissenters are already excommunicated. Irreconcilable radicals, wringing their hands among the débris, become the most despicable and impotent of men. There seems no choice for the intellectual but to join the mass of acceptance. But again the terrible dilemma arises – either support what is going on, in which case you count for nothing because you are swallowed in the mass and great incalculable forces bear you on; or remain aloof, passively resistant, in which case you count for nothing because you are outside the machinery of reality.

Is there no place left, then, for the intellectual who cannot yet crystallize, who does not dread suspense, and is not yet drugged with fatigue? The American intellectuals, in their preoccupation with reality, seem to have forgotten that the real enemy is War rather than imperial Germany. There is work to be done to prevent this war of ours from passing into popular mythology as a holy crusade. What shall we do with leaders who tell us that we go to war in moral spotlessness, or who make 'democracy' synonymous with a republican form of government? There is work to be done in still shouting that all the revolutionary by-products will not justify the war, or make war anything else than the most noxious complex of all the evils that afflict men. There must be some to find no consolation whatever, and some to sneer at those who buy the cheap emotion of sacrifice. There must be some irreconcilables left who will not even accept the war with walrus tears. There must be some to call unceasingly for peace, and some to insist that the terms of settlement shall be not only liberal but democratic. There must be some intellectuals who are not willing to use the old discredited counters again and to support a peace which would leave all the old inflammable materials of armament lying about the world. There must still be opposition to any contemplated 'liberal' world-order founded on military coalitions. The 'irreconcilable' need not be disloyal. He need not even be 'impossibilist'. His apathy towards war should take the form of a heightened energy and enthusiasm for the education, the art, the interpretation that make for life in the midst of the world of death. The intellectual who retains his animus against war will push out more boldly than ever to make his case solid against it. The old ideals crumble; new ideals must be forged. His mind will continue to roam widely and ceaselessly. The thing he will fear most is premature crystallization. If the American intellectual class rivets itself to a 'liberal' philosophy that perpetuates the old errors, there will then be need for 'democrats' whose task will be to divide, confuse, disturb, keep the intellectual waters constantly in motion to prevent any such ice from ever forming.

MOHANDAS K. GANDHI

1869–1948

In the twentieth century no one has contributed more to the theory and practice of non-violence than Mahatma Gandhi. He was born in India, educated in England as a lawyer, and it was in South Africa that he first took part in political life. It was there that he organized the first campaigns of non-violent resistance aimed at the discriminatory legislation in effect against the large Indian population.

In 1900 he completely relinquished his lucrative law practice, and in 1905 he gave up all Western ways, living abstinently, and rigidly following the precepts of Hinduism. Gandhi supported Great Britain in World War I in the belief that this might hasten the day of Indian independence; when neither this nor other necessary reforms were forthcoming, he organized the *satyagraha* (literally, truth-force) campaigns on behalf of Indian independence which captured the imagination of the Indian masses and the rest of the world.

His statement to the court reprinted below is taken from his newspaper *Young India* of 15 March 1922. The reasons for the arrest are taken up in the account.

The influences on Gandhi range from the *Bhagavad-Gita* to the *Sermon on the Mount*, from Thoreau to Ruskin and Tolstoy. Gandhi's influence is evident in the fight for Negro rights in America, the non-violent resistance of the Norwegians under the Nazi occupation, the work of Danilo Dolci in Sicily, and the fight led by Albert Luthuli for African freedom. While the ascetic dedication Gandhi demanded of *satyagrahis* makes it unlikely that any campaigns quite like his will ever be waged in the West, the significance of non-violence as a way of life and as a political tool was apparent immediately to pacifists everywhere. The work and writings of Clarence Marsh Case and Richard Gregg did much to publicize events in India.

The history of civil disobedience is at least as ancient as Antigone's defiance of Creon in Greek tragedy, but until the time of Gandhi it had been generally practised at the level of the individual conscience; Thoreau's refusal to pay a tax which would support an imperialist war is a prime example. The success of Gandhi in South Africa and India focused attention on such resistance, and raised civil disobedience to the level of group relations.

India won its independence in August 1947, largely through the efforts of Gandhi and the men around him. To his great disappointment, the subcontinent was partitioned into what is now India and Pakistan. He was shot and killed on 30 January 1948 at a prayer meeting in New Delhi by a young Hindu who held Gandhi responsible for the partition. The meeting had been called to protest against the violence which had broken out between the two main religious communities immediately upon independence.

'The Doctrine of the Sword' is reprinted from *Young India* of 11 August 1920; it is a piece in which Gandhi makes an important qualification to his non-violent principles, and statements from it have often been used as apologies for violent resistance in special circumstances. Martin Buber's defence of such resistance by the Jews to the Nazi terror and of the fight for the Jewish homeland quotes a statement made by Gandhi in 1922 which repeats part of Gandhi's argument in this essay.

Arrest and Trial

The long expected has happened at last. The wished for, longed for consummation has been reached. Mr Gandhi pined for his arrest and imprisonment by the Government under which it became intolerable for him to live. His heart's desire has been fulfilled. He now feels himself free, though imprisoned.

Even from the 8th instant the rumour of his arrest began to thicken. He left for Ajmere that day on an urgent invitation from Mr Chhotani by an afternoon train, and it was even whispered that he might be arrested on the way. Nothing however happened then. In the meantime, the rumour was growing from hour to hour. A suspicious telegram from Ajmere made Mrs Gandhi and some others to run up to the Sabarmati Station to see him safely return. He reached the *Ashram* in the afternoon of the 10th as free as ever and as if bursting under the weight of his simple and child-like joy.

At the *Ashram* the rumour of the last two days was being received with calm and stolid indifference. For there have been so many final partings since he had decided to start Civil Disobedience in November last that the ideas of arrest, imprisonment or even worse became quite common and familiar. So the daily routine of work of the *Ashram* was not disturbed in the least by these rumours. Only when the day wore on, the evening came and the bell rang out the hour of prayer, there was a sudden hush all around as all the *Ashramites* proceeded with anxious and hasty steps to join their *Bapu* in his last prayer, perhaps for a long time to come. He was unusually light and happy and played with the children like one of their own spreading the contagion of his lightness and happiness all round.

After the prayer he returned to his work as usual and dictated replies to some correspondence. During this time friends continued to come to see him from the city bringing tit-bits of news all of which went to confirm the prevailing rumour.

Mr Gandhi arose at about quarter to ten[1] for his last ablutions before retiring and the small assembly that had all this time surrounded him began to disperse. Mr Banker who had come with Mr Shvaib and Anasuyabai to confirm the strength of the rumour also departed at that time. A few minutes after, Mr Shvaib returned with Anasuyabai and brought the news that Mr Banker was arrested and that the S. P. was waiting on the road for Mr Gandhi's arrest. The news spread in a minute throughout the *Ashram* quarters, and almost all the inmates, men, women and children, hastened to Mr Gandhi to bid him farewell and have his blessings. At his desire, his favourite Gujarati hymn which describes the qualities of a true *vaishnava* was sung in chorus. After this, he accosted each of the *Ashramites* in suitable terms, encouraged them all by his sprightliness and abundant joy and then prepared to surrender himself. While proceeding from his residence to the Police Officer on the road, he expressed himself several times that he felt very happy and gratified over the arrest.

Maulana Hasrat Mohani who travelled with Mr Gandhi from Ajmere by the same train and stopped at Ahmedabad came to the *Ashram* just before the arrival of the Police Commissioner and when Mr Gandhi had retired for his ablutions. Mr Gandhi was supremely happy when he met the Maulana just before his arrest. They embraced each other with

1. Mr Gandhi was arrested at 10.30 p.m. by Mr Healey, the Superintendent of Police, Ahmedabad, on a complaint in respect of four articles in *Young India*, namely, 'Disaffection a Virtue', of 15 June 1921 and three others referred to elsewhere. Mr Shvaib took up the editorship till Mr C. Rajagopalachari, who was appointed editor, took charge.

feelings of mutual esteem and regard. The Maulana seemed to have been deeply moved by this and assured Mr Gandhi that he would give his whole-hearted support to the cause of non-violent Non-co-operation.

Both Mr Gandhi and Mr Banker were taken to the Sabarmati Jail. Mrs Gandhi with a small company of four or five was allowed to accompany them and see them lodged in their quarters, which consists of a row of eight rooms with an open verandah about 10 feet wide and a fairly large courtyard with a line of small trees in the middle. The two rooms given to them are furnished each with an iron cot, a mattress, two sheets, a pillow, a blanket and a carpet. Light is provided in the evening. The doors of the rooms are made of wooden frames, the planks about six inches wide with thick iron bars fixed in them, the distance between two bars being a little over an inch. The whole place was scrupulously clean.

The next day they were produced before the trying Magistrate, Mr Allan Brown, I.C.S., who held his court at the Commissioner's office, outside the city proper and under the shelter of the cantonment and easily accessible by rail from Sabarmati. The news was kept a secret. Yet a good many spectators who were permitted by the Magistrate attended the trial. Five witnesses consisting of the D.S.P., Mr Mealey, the Registrar of the Bombay High Court, Mr Dinshaw Gharda, Mr Chatfield, the District Magistrate of Ahmedabad, a Sub-Inspector and a C.I.D. subordinate of police were examined by the prosecutor on the Government side. There were two issues on which these evidences were taken and articles from 'Young India' were read before the Court, viz., (1) proving the editorship and (2) proving the intention of the articles. These were simple issues upon which several precious hours of the day were uselessly spent simply to keep up the forms of law. But it appeared to be unreasonable that so much time should be taken to prove a self-evident fact. There was also an air of artificiality or theatricality about the whole business. The dignity and aloofness maintained by the trying Magistrate even while taking down statements from his friends, colleagues and superiors had an element of acting which was admirably done; similarly the deference shown to the chair of justice, irrespective of the person who may occupy it for the time being. Perhaps these are matters of tradition which grow upon those whose daily duty is to practise them. But to a new observer they appear incongruous, out of place and unnatural, although dignified and invested with gravity and splendour.

THE GREAT TRIAL, 23 MARCH, 1922

At the Circuit House at Shahi Bag, the trial of Mr Gandhi and Mr Banker commenced on Saturday noon, the 18 March, before Mr C. N. Broomsfield, I.C.S., District and Sessions Judge of Ahmedabad.

Sir J. T. Strangman with Rao Bahadur Girdharlal conducted the prosecution, while the accused were undefended. The Judge took his seat at 12 noon, and said there was a slight mistake in the charges framed, which he corrected. The charges were then read out by the Registrar, the offence being in three articles[1] published in the *Young India* of 29 September, 15 December of 1921 and 23 February 1922. The offending articles were then read out: first of them was, 'Tampering with Loyalty'; the second, 'The Puzzle and Its Solution'; and the last was 'Shaking the Manes'.

The Judge said the law required that the charge should not only be read out, but explained. In this case, it would not be necessary for him to say much by way of explanation. The charge in each case was that of bringing or attempting to bring into hatred or contempt or exciting or attempting to excite disaffection towards His Majesty's Government, established by law in British India. Both the accused were charged with the three offences under section 124 A, contained in the articles read out, written by Mr Gandhi and printed by Mr Banker. The words 'hatred and contempt' were words the meaning of which was sufficiently obvious. The word 'disaffection' was defined under the section, where they were told that disaffection included disloyalty and feelings of enmity, and the word used in the section had also been interpreted by the High Court of Bombay in a reported case as meaning political alienation or discontent, a spirit of disloyalty to Government or existing authority. The charges having been read out, the Judge called upon the accused to plead to the charges. He asked Mr Gandhi, whether he pleaded guilty or claimed to be tried.

MR GANDHI: I plead guilty to all the charges. I observe that the King's name has been omitted from the charge, and it has been properly omitted.

THE JUDGE: Mr Banker, do you plead guilty, or do you claim to be tried?

MR BANKER: I plead guilty.

1. The complaint in respect of the earlier article, 'Disaffection a Virtue', seems to have been dropped subsequently after inquiry by the Magistrate.

Sir J. Strangman then wanted the Judge to proceed with the trial fully; but the Judge said he did not agree with what had been said by the Counsel. The Judge said that from the time he knew he was going to try the case, he had thought over the question of sentence, and he was prepared to hear anything that the Counsel might have to say, or Mr Gandhi wished to say, on the sentence. He honestly did not believe that the mere recording of evidence in the trial which Counsel had called for would make no [sic] difference to them, one way or the other. He, therefore, proposed to accept the pleas.

Mr Gandhi smiled at this decision.

The Judge said nothing further remained but to pass sentence and before doing so, he liked to hear Sir J. T. Strangman. He was entitled to base his general remarks on the charges against the accused and on their pleas.

SIR J. T. STRANGMAN: It will be difficult to do so. I ask the Court that the whole matter may be properly considered. If I stated what has happened before the Committing Magistrate, then I can show that there are many things which are material to the question of the sentence.

The first point, he said, he wanted to make out, was that the matter which formed the subject of the present charges formed a part of the campaign to spread disaffection openly and systematically to render Government impossible and to overthrow it. The earliest article that was put in from *Young India* was dated 25 May 1921, which said that it was the duty of a Non-cooperator to create disaffection towards the Government. The counsel then read out portions of articles written by Mr Gandhi in the *Young India*.

Court said, nevertheless, it seemed to it that the Court could accept plea, on the materials of which the sentence had to be based.

Sir J. Strangman said the question of sentence was entirely for the Court to decide. The Court was always entitled to deal in a more general manner in regard to the question of the sentence, than the particular matter resulting in the conviction. He asked leave to refer to articles before the Court, and what result might have been produced, if the trial had proceeded in order to ascertain what the facts were. He was not going into any matter which involved dispute.

The Judge said there was not the least objection.

Sir J. Strangman said he wanted to show that these articles were not isolated. They formed part of an organized campaign, but so far as *Young India* was concerned, they would show that from the year

1921. The Counsel then read out extracts from the paper, dated 8 June, on the duty of a non-cooperator, which was to preach disaffection towards the existing government and preparing the country for Civil Disobedience. Then in the same number, there was an article on disobedience. Then in the same number there was an article on 'Disaffection – a virtue' or something to that effect. Then there was an article on the 28 July 1921, in which it was stated that 'we have to destroy the system'. Again, on 30 September 1921, there was an article headed, 'Punjab Prosecutions', where it was stated that a non-cooperator worth his name should preach disaffection. That was all so far as *Young India* was concerned. They were earlier in date than the article 'Tampering with Loyalty', and it was referred to the Governor of Bombay. Continuing, he said the accused was a man of high educational qualifications and evidently from his writings a recognized leader. The harm that was likely to be caused was considerable. They were the writings of an educated man, and not the writings of an obscure man, and the Court must consider to what the results of a campaign of the nature disclosed in the writings must inevitably lead. They had examples before them in the last few months. He referred to the occurrences in Bombay last November and Chauri Chaura, leading to murder and destruction of property, involving many people in misery and misfortune. It was true that in the course of those articles they would find Non-violence was insisted upon as an item of the campaign and an item of the creed. But what was the use of preaching Non-violence when he preached disaffection towards Government or openly instigated others to overthrow it? The answer to that question appeared to him to come from Chauri Chaura, Madras and Bombay. These were circumstances which he asked the Court to take into account in sentencing the accused, and it would be for the Court to consider those circumstances which involve sentences of severity.

As regards the second accused, his offence was lesser. He did the publication and he did not write. His offence nevertheless was a serious one. His instructions were that he was a man of means and he asked the Court to impose a substantial fine in addition to such term of imprisonment as might be inflicted. He quoted Section 10 of the Press Act as bearing on the question of fine. When making a fresh declaration, he said a deposit of Rs. 1,000 to Rs. 10,000 was asked in many cases.

COURT: Mr Gandhi, do you wish to make a statement on the question of sentence?

MR GANDHI: I would like to make a statement.

COURT: Could you give me in writing to put it on record?

MR GANDHI: I shall give it as soon as I finish it reading.

Before reading his written statement, Mr Gandhi spoke a few words as introductory remarks to the whole statement. He said:

Before I read this statement, I would like to state that I entirely endorse the learned Advocate-General's remarks in connexion with my humble self. I think that he was entirely fair to me in all the statements that he has made, because it is very true and I have no desire whatsoever to conceal from this Court the fact that to preach disaffection towards the existing system of Government has become almost a passion with me, and the learned Advocate-General is also entirely in the right when he says that my preaching of disaffection did not commence with my connexion with *Young India*, but that it commenced much earlier; and in the statement that I am about to read, it will be my painful duty to admit before this Court that it commenced much earlier than the period stated by the Advocate-General. It is the most painful duty with me, but I have to discharge that duty knowing the responsibility that rests upon my shoulders, and I wish to endorse all the blame that the learned Advocate-General has thrown on my shoulders in connexion with the Bombay occurrences, Madras occurrences and the Chauri Chaura occurrences. Thinking over these deeply and sleeping over them night after night, it is impossible for me to dissociate myself from the diabolical crimes of Chauri Chaura or the mad outrages of Bombay. He is quite right when he says that as a man of responsibility, a man having received a fair share of education, having had a fair share of experience of this world, I should have known the consequences of every one of my acts. I knew that I was playing with fire. I ran the risk, and if I was set free, I would still do the same. I have felt it this morning that I would have failed in my duty, if I did not say what I said here just now.

I wanted to avoid violence, I want to avoid violence. Non-violence is the first article of my faith. It is also the last article of my creed. But I had to make my choice. I had either to submit to a system which I considered had done an irreparable harm to my country, or incur the risk of the mad fury of my people bursting forth when they understood the truth from my lips. I know that my people have sometimes gone mad. I am deeply sorry for it and I am therefore here to submit not to a light penalty but to the highest penalty. I do not ask for mercy. I do not plead any extenuating act. I am here, therefore, to invite and cheerfully submit to the highest penalty that can be inflicted upon me for what in law is a deliberate crime and what appears to me to be the highest duty of a citizen. The only course open to you, the Judge, is, as I am just going to say in my statement, either to resign your post, or inflict on me the severest penalty, if you believe that the system and law you are assisting to administer are good for the people. I do not expect that kind of conversion, but by the time I have finished with my statement, you will perhaps have a glimpse of what is raging within my breast to run this maddest risk which a sane man can run.

The Statement was then read out.

Statement

I owe it perhaps to the Indian public and to the public in England to placate which this prosecution is mainly taken up that I should explain why from a staunch loyalist and cooperator I have become an uncompromising disaffectionist and Non-cooperator. To the Court too I should say why I plead guilty to the charge of promoting disaffection towards the Government established by law in India.

My public life began in 1893 in South Africa in troubled weather. My first contact with British authority in that country was not of a happy character. I discovered that as a man and an Indian I had no rights. More correctly, I discovered that I had no rights as a man, because I was an Indian.

But I was not baffled. I thought that this treatment of Indians was an excrescence upon a system that was intrinsically and mainly good. I gave the Government my voluntary and hearty cooperation, criticizing it freely where I felt it was faulty but never wishing its destruction.

Consequently when the existence of the Empire was threatened in 1899 by the Boer challenge, I offered my services to it, raised a volunteer ambulance corps and served at several actions that took place for the relief of Ladysmith. Similarly in 1906, at the time of the Zulu revolt, I raised a stretcher-bearer party and served till the end of the 'rebellion'. On both these occasions I received medals and was even mentioned in dispatches. For my work in South Africa I was given by Lord Hardinge a Kaiser-i-Hind Gold Medal. When the war broke out in 1914 between England and Germany, I raised a volunteer ambulance corps in London consisting of the then resident Indians in London, chiefly students. Its work was acknowledged by the authorities to be valuable. Lastly, in

India, when a special appeal was made at the War Conference in Delhi in 1918 by Lord Chelmsford for recruits, I struggled at the cost of my health to raise a corps in Kheda and the response was being made when the hostilities ceased and orders were received that no more recruits were wanted. In all these efforts at service I was actuated by the belief that it was possible by such services to gain a status of full equality in the Empire for my countrymen.

The first shock came in the shape of the Rowlatt Act, a law designed to rob the people of all real freedom. I felt called upon to lead an intensive agitation against it. Then followed the Punjab horrors beginning with the massacre at Jallianwala Bagh and culminating in crawling orders, public floggings and other indescribable humiliations. I discovered too that the plighted word of the Prime Minister to the Mussalmans of India regarding the integrity of Turkey and the holy places of Islam was not likely to be fulfilled. But in spite of the fore-bodings and the grave warnings of friends, at the Amritsar Congress in 1919, I fought for cooperation and working the Montagu-Chelmsford reforms, hoping that the Prime Minister would redeem his promise to the Indian Mussalmans, that the Punjab wound would be healed and that the reforms, inadequate and unsatisfactory though they were, marked a new era of hope in the life of India.

But all that hope was shattered. The Khilafat promise was not to be redeemed. The Punjab crime was white-washed and most culprits went not only unpunished but remained in service and some continued to draw pensions from the Indian revenue, and in some cases were even rewarded. I saw too that not only did the reforms not mark a change of heart, but they were only a method of further draining India of her wealth and of prolonging her servitude.

I came reluctantly to the conclusion that the British connexion had made India more helpless than she ever was before, politically and economically. A disarmed India has no power of resistance against any aggressor if she wanted to engage in an armed conflict with him. So much is this the case that some of our best men consider that India must take generations before she can achieve the Dominion status. She has become so poor that she has little power of resisting famines. Before the British advent, India spun and wove in her millions of cottages just the supplement she needed for adding to her meagre agricultural resources. This cottage industry, so vital for India's existence, has been ruined by incredibly heartless and inhuman processes as described by

English witnesses. Little do town-dwellers know how the semi-starved masses of India are slowly sinking to lifelessness. Little do they know that their miserable comfort represents the brokerage they get for the work they do for the foreign exploiter, that the profits and the broker-age are sucked from the masses. Little do they realize that the Government established by law in British India is carried on for this exploitation of the masses. No sophistry, no jugglery in figures can explain away the evidence that the skeletons in many villages present to the naked eye. I have no doubt whatsoever that both England and the town dwellers of India will have to answer, if there is a God above, for this crime against humanity which is perhaps unequalled in history. The law itself in this country has been used to serve the foreign exploiter. My unbiased examination of the Punjab Martial Law cases has led me to believe that at least ninety-five per cent of convictions were wholly bad. My experience of political cases in India leads me to the conclusion that in nine out of every ten the condemned men were totally innocent. Their crime consisted in the love of their country. In ninety-nine cases out of a hundred justice has been denied to Indians against Europeans in courts in India. This is not an exaggerated picture. It is the experience of almost every Indian who has had anything to do with such cases. In my opinion, the administration of the law is thus prostituted consciously or unconsciously for the benefit of the exploiter.

The greatest misfortune is that Englishmen and their Indian associates in the country do not know that they are engaged in the crime I have attempted to describe. I am satisfied that many Englishmen and Indian officials honestly believe that they are administering one of the best systems devised in the world and that India is making steady though slow progress. They do not know that a subtle but effective system of terrorism and an organized display of force on the one hand, and the deprivation of all powers of retaliation or self-defence on the other, have emasculated the people and induced in them the habit of simulation. This awful habit has added to the ignorance and self-deception of the administrators. Section 124-A under which I am happily charged is perhaps the prince among the political sections of the Indian Penal Code designed to suppress the liberty of the citizen. Affection cannot be manufactured or regulated by law. If one has no affection for a person or system, one should be free to give the fullest expression to his dis-affection, so long as he does not contemplate, promote or incite to violence. But the section under which Mr Banker and I are charged is one under which mere promotion of disaffection is a crime. I have studied some of the cases tried under it, and I know that some of the most loved of Indian patriots have been convicted under it. I consider it a privilege, therefore, to be charged under that section. I have endeavoured to give in their briefest outline the reasons for my disaffection. I have no personal ill-will against a single administrator, much less can I have any disaffection towards the King's person. But I hold it to be a virtue to be disaffected towards a Government which in its totality has done more harm to India than any previous system. India is less manly under the British rule than she ever was before. Holding such a belief, I consider it to be a sin to have affection for the system. And it has been a precious privilege for me to be able to write what I have in the various articles, tendered in evidence against me.

In fact, I believe that I have rendered a service to India and England by showing in Non-cooperation the way out of the unnatural state in which both are living. In my humble opinion, Non-cooperation with evil is as much a duty as is cooperation with good. But in the past, Non-cooperation has been deliberately expressed in violence to the evil doer. I am endeavouring to show to my countrymen that violent Non-cooperation only multiplies evil and that as evil can only be sustained by violence, withdrawal of support of evil requires complete abstention from violence. Non-violence implies voluntary submission to the penalty for Non-cooperation with evil. I am here, therefore, to invite and submit cheerfully to the highest penalty that can be inflicted upon men for what in law is a deliberate crime and what appears to me to be the highest duty of a citizen. The only course open to you, the Judge, is either to resign your post and thus dissociate yourself from evil, if you feel that the law you are called upon to administer is an evil and that in reality I am innocent; or to inflict on me the severest penalty if you believe that the system and the law you are assisting to administer are good for the people of this country and that my activity is therefore injurious to the public weal.

MR BANKER: I only want to say that I had the privilege of printing these articles and I plead guilty to the charge. I have got nothing to say as regards the sentence.

The Judgment

The following is the full text of the judgment:
Mr Gandhi, you have made my task easy in one way by pleading

guilty to the charge. Nevertheless, what remains, namely, the determination of a just sentence, is perhaps as difficult a proposition as a judge in this country could have to face. The law is no respecter of persons. Nevertheless, it will be impossible to ignore the fact that you are in a different category from any person I have ever tried or am likely to have to try. It would be impossible to ignore the fact that in the eyes of millions of your countrymen, you are a great patriot and a great leader. Even those who differ from you in politics look upon you as a man of high ideals and of noble and of even saintly life. I have to deal with you in one character only. It is not my duty and I do not presume to judge or criticize you in any other character. It is my duty to judge you as a man subject to the law, who by his own admission has broken the law and committed what to an ordinary man must appear to be a grave offence against the State. I do not forget that you have consistently preached against violence and that you have on many occasions, as I am willing to believe, done much to prevent violence. But having regard to the nature of your political teaching and the nature of many of those to whom it was addressed, how you could have continued to believe that violence would not be the inevitable consequence, it passes my capacity to understand.

There are probably few people in India, who do not sincerely regret that you should have made it impossible for any government to leave you at liberty. But it is so. I am trying to balance what is due to you against what appears to me to be necessary in the interest of the public, and I propose in passing sentence to follow the precedent of a case in many respects similar to this case that was decided some twelve years ago, I mean the case against Bal Gangadhar Tilak under the same section. The sentence that was passed upon him as it finally stood was a sentence of simple imprisonment for six years. You will not consider it unreasonable, I think, that you should be classed with Mr Tilak, i.e., a sentence of two years simple imprisonment on each count of the charge; six years in all, which I feel it my duty to pass upon you, and I should like to say in doing so that, if the course of events in India should make it possible for the Government to reduce the period and release you, no one will be better pleased than I.

THE JUDGE to Mr Banker: I assume you have been to a large extent under the influence of your chief. The sentence that I propose to pass upon you is simple imprisonment for six months on each of the first two counts, that is to say, simple imprisonment for one year and a fine of a thousand rupees on the third count, with six months' simple imprisonment in default.

Mr Gandhi on the Judgment

Mr Gandhi said: I would say one word. Since you have done me the honour of recalling the trial of the late Lokamany a Bal Gangadhar Tilak, I just want to say that I consider it to be the proudest privilege and honour to be associated with his name. So far as the sentence itself is concerned, I certainly consider that it is as light as any judge would inflict on me, and so far as the whole proceedings are concerned, I must say that I could not have expected greater courtesy.

Then the friends of Mr Gandhi crowded round him, as the Judge left the court, and fell at his feet. There was much sobbing on the part of both men and women. But all the while, Mr Gandhi was smiling and cool and giving encouragement to everybody who came to him. Mr Banker also was smiling and taking this in a light-hearted way. After all his friends had taken leave of him, Mr Gandhi was taken out of the court to the Sabarmati Jail.

And thus the great trial finished.

The Doctrine of the Sword

In this age of the rule of brute force, it is almost impossible for any one to believe that any one else could possibly reject the law of the final supremacy of brute force. And so I receive anonymous letters advising me that I must not interfere with the progress of Non-cooperation, even though popular violence may break out. Others come to me and, assuming that secretly I must be plotting violence, inquire when the happy moment for declaring open violence is to arrive. They assure me that the English will never yield to anything but violence secret or open. Yet others, I am informed, believe that I am the most rascally person living in India, because I never give out my real intention and that they have not a shadow of a doubt that I believe in violence just as much as most people do.

Such being the hold that the doctrine of the sword has on the majority of mankind, and as success of Non-cooperation depends principally on absence of violence during its pendency and as my views in this matter affect the conduct of a large number of people, I am anxious to state them as clearly as possible.

I do believe that, where there is only a choice between cowardice and violence, I would advise violence. Thus when my eldest son asked me what he should have done, had he been present when I was almost fatally assaulted in 1908, whether he should have run away and seen me killed or whether he should have used his physical force which he could and wanted to use, and defended me, I told him that it was his duty to defend me even by using violence. Hence it was that I took part in the Boer War, the so called Zulu rebellion and the late War. Hence also do I advocate training in arms for those who believe in the method of violence. I would rather have India resort to arms in order to defend her honour than that she should in a cowardly manner become or remain a helpless witness to her own dishonour.

But I believe that non-violence is infinitely superior to violence, forgiveness is more manly than punishment. Forgiveness adorns a soldier. But abstinence is forgiveness only when there is the power to punish: it is meaningless when it pretends to proceed from a helpless creature. A mouse hardly forgives a cat when it allows itself to be torn to pieces by her. I therefore appreciate the sentiment of those who cry out for the condign punishment of General Dyer and his ilk. They would tear him to pieces if they could. But I do not believe India to be helpless. I do not believe myself to be a helpless creature. Only I want to use India's and my strength for a better purpose.

Let me not be misunderstood. Strength does not come from physical capacity. It comes from an indomitable will. An average Zulu is any way more than a match for an average Englishman in bodily capacity. But he flees from an English boy, because he fears the boy's revolver or those who will use it for him. He fears death and is nerveless in spite of his burly figure. We in India may in a moment realize that one hundred thousand Englishmen need not frighten three hundred million human beings. A definite forgiveness would therefore mean a definite recognition of our strength. With enlightened forgiveness must come a mighty wave of strength in us, which would make it impossible for a Dyer and a Frank Johnson to heap affront upon India's devoted head. It matters little to me that for the moment I do not drive my point home. We feel too down-trodden not to be angry and revengeful. But I must not refrain from saying that India can gain more by waiving the right of punishment. We have better work to do, a better mission to deliver to the world.

I am not a visionary. I claim to be a practical idealist. The religion of non-violence is not meant merely for the Rishis and saints. It is meant for the common people as well. Non-violence is the law of our species as violence is the law of the brute. The spirit lies dormant in the brute and he knows no law but that of physical might. The dignity of man requires obedience to a higher law – to the strength of the spirit.

I have therefore ventured to place before India the ancient law of self-sacrifice. For Satyagraha and its off-shoots, non-cooperation and civil resistance, are nothing but new names for the law of suffering. The Rishis, who discovered the law of non-violence in the midst of violence, were greater geniuses than Newton. They were themselves greater warriors than Wellington. Having themselves known the use of arms, they realized their uselessness and taught a weary world that its salvation lay not through violence but through non-violence.

Non-violence in its dynamic condition means conscious suffering. It does not mean meek submission to the will of the evil-doer, but it means the putting of one's whole soul against the will of the tyrant. Working under this law of our being, it is possible for a single individual to defy the whole might of an unjust empire to save his honour, his religion, his soul and lay the foundation for that empire's fall or its regeneration.

And so I am not pleading for India to practise non-violence, because it is weak. I want her to practise non-violence being conscious of her strength and power. No training in arms is required for realization of her strength. We seem to need it, because we seem to think that we are but a lump of flesh. I want India to recognize that she has a soul that cannot perish and that can rise triumphant above every physical weakness and defy the physical combination of a whole world. What is the meaning of Rama, a mere human being, with his host of monkeys, pitting himself against the insolent strength of ten-headed Ravan surrounded in supposed safety by the raging waters on all sides of Lanka? Does it not mean the conquest of physical might by spiritual strength? However, being a practical man, I do not wait till India recognizes the practicability of the spiritual life in the political world. India considers herself to be powerless and paralysed before the machine-guns, the tanks and the aeroplanes of the English. And she takes up Non-cooperation out of her weakness. It must still serve the same purpose, namely, bring her delivery from the crushing weight of British injustice, if a sufficient number of people practise it.

I isolate this Non-cooperation from Sinn Feinism, for, it is so conceived as to be incapable of being offered side by side with violence. But I invite even the school of violence to give this peaceful Non-cooperation a trial. It will not fail through its inherent weakness. It may fail because of poverty of response. Then will be the time for real danger. The high-souled men, who are unable to suffer national humiliation any longer, will want to vent their wrath. They will take to violence. So far as I know, they must perish without delivering themselves or their country from the wrong. If India takes up the doctrine of the sword, she may gain momentary victory. Then India will cease to be the pride of my heart. I am wedded to India, because I owe my all to her. I believe absolutely that she has a mission for the world. She is not to copy Europe blindly. India's acceptance of the doctrine of the sword will be the hour of my trial. I hope I shall not be found wanting. My religion has no geographical limits. If I have a living faith in it, it will transcend my love for India herself. My life is dedicated to service of India through the religion of non-violence which I believe to be the root of Hinduism.

Meanwhile, I urge those who distrust me, not to disturb the even working of the struggle that has just commenced, by inciting to violence in the belief that I want violence. I detest secrecy as a sin. Let them give Non-violent Non-cooperation a trial and they will find that I had no mental reservation whatsoever.

From *Young India*, 11 August 1920

ALAIN

1868–1951

ALAIN (the pen-name of Émile-Auguste Chartier) is considered, with Bergson and Bachelard, one of the three great French philosophers of modern times. He developed no new philosophic system in his long career, but his study of ancient and modern philosophy and his remarkable gifts as a teacher – among his students were Simone Weil, André Maurois, and André Prévost – brought his work to wide attention in the last part of his life; earlier he had attracted renown for his defence of Dreyfus in the short articles he wrote for *La Dépêche de Rouen*.

All his life he was a defender of the individual conscience against the tyranny of the State, an attitude which became more pronounced after the First World War, in which he served. His best-known book in England and America is *Mars, or the Truth About War* (1930), from which these selections are taken. They have been translated by Doris Mudie and Elizabeth Hill.

On Passions

I must explain more fully the main idea of this book, which is that passions and not interests govern the world, and I am particularly anxious to return to this question when I think of the very incomplete descriptions of human nature current nowadays, according to which all our actions are explained by a more or less hidden personal interest. If we are to accept this, then there is such a contrast between the man of my books and the man in the trenches, that one would like to imagine some superhuman miracle which would inevitably lead us back to the very engrained idea that war has been divinely decreed and is consequently inevitable. That is why I shall never be able to explain at too great a length the mechanism of passions and its terrible effects. You should know to begin with that Descartes has said the last word on the subject in his treatise on the passions, and the secret is well hidden there in spite of its apparent simplicity. But in case you have not yet grasped the meaning of this profound work I will explain here the same doctrine above all by examples, and without giving any details as to the structure of the human body.

The first thing I must say on the subject is that I have never yet met the man, so often described, who follows in all his actions the calculations of self-interest. Now every one has experienced more or less the strange madness of love; a man can die of love, want to die of love, want to kill and kill the person he loves, which results in a convulsion and a revolt that casts him into a still greater and more desperate misery. Observe in which sense this madness is belligerent, in the full sense of the word. Yes, the jealous man throws himself fearlessly against his own interest as though he were taking pleasure in tearing himself to pieces. I do not insist on the wild delights of revenge, about which I can scarcely speak except from hearsay, but it is sufficiently well known that this feeling can make a man accept great suffering in the hope of causing still greater suffering to another. It is also clear that in all these passions there is at bottom a presentiment of a fearful deed and a type of fatality that is horrifying. It is I, and yet it is stronger than I am, and this is what the word passion expresses so well.

Anger is the common form of passion in its paroxysm; of all passions, even of fear. And it is then that we can see how quickly a man can forget his prudent calculations in his own interest and even his own safety. Anger, even if it is the result of minor causes, ordinarily leads us to extravagant deeds like hitting, smashing, and even destroying things. And I venture to say that the greatest anger is when a man is angry for being angry and knows that he is giving way to it and feels it rising inside him like a physical storm. The word irritation, in its double sense, explains this if we were only to think of it logically. The child cries louder and louder mainly because crying sets up an irritation, just as some people aggravate a cough.

I also want to remind you of some of the follies of passion which are always contrary to one's interest and often to conversation; not least among which is the folly of fear, for fear always increases the danger as can be seen on board a ship. The disputants get irritated almost always to the point of hurling words at each other, which they later regret.

The gambler, the better, the drunkard soon fall headlong into their passion as into an abyss, with the idea, it seems to me, that they are destined to it, condemned to it, and that they might as well plunge into it at once. Properly speaking, it is a form of giddiness. Have you not known litigants who, although they are almost sure of losing their case, pursue it to the bitter end merely for the pleasure of ruining the other party? Of course, it could be said, and not without some measure of truth, that lawsuits are caused by greed. But there is also poetry in lawsuits, and, after meditating as we should on oysters and shells, we should still not be protected against this prosecuting obstinacy which, in ruining another, ruins itself. Is that not war in miniature?

The Causes

Where are all my words leading to? To make war known by its real causes which will turn people away from religious fatalism. This feeling is a very strong one and here are the factors which compose it. On the one hand the periodic catastrophe which every one deplores and to which every one gives his consent; which is effected by human wills and against human wills; which it would be sufficient to deny but which one cannot deny, which is foreseen and which inevitably happens; which succeeds by the precautions that are taken against it; which imposes itself because it is feared; which because it has been insanity will be like insanity. And this throws some into passive waiting and others into an impatience to follow their destiny. Both think like Tolstoy that history is controlled by some hidden and unchangeable law. Thus the superhuman appears above the smoke.

On the other hand, the memory of dead heroes, glory, marches, and parades awakens and stirs up uncontrollable emotions in the coldest hearts; human force is adored; I insist on that; and it is not only accepted as necessary but is very genuinely adored. This cult is the only cult at present; no other religion reduces the effects of this one; and it does not find any unbelievers because it cannot find any who are insensible to it; the only way to escape the celebration of victory was not to go to it. Fatalism is beautified by the emotions which memory revives so successfully. There arises a mysticism about war and a fanaticism. Its doctrine is more or less an enthusiastic pessimism.

Against which I say that we must understand war by its causes. And first of all, in order to guard against the emotions which are æsthetic, we must analyse the rhythm of contagion and understand the price of a man in the audience, but much more so for the man who is the actor; we must seize the curious relation, but one which is, however, explicable, according to which, when emotions are made the criterion, the cult takes the place of the God. Use your imagination and prepare other celebrations. It is terrifying to think that the mob does not know of any other active sacrament than the military one. For the Beautiful has supreme power over us all and thus our ugly industrialism is far more harmful than it is thought to be.

As for the war that is prophesied and always prepared for, and the evil prophets whom the event justifies, say to yourselves first of all that inasmuch as they persuade, the event will come about, since it is brought about by men. And, above all, understand why all those who love power love war deep down in themselves and thus, without always confessing it to themselves, they place all their hopes on the great traditional game, when actually the councils of war and the councils of peace have the same aim, and that by the negligence of the citizens it is always men of that type who direct human affairs, who explain them, and who prophesy them. And understand that the leaders of war go to war in hope, not only because the menace of war gives them power, but also because the war itself makes them kings without counter-balance against an acceptable risk and which is always less the older they are in years, and the higher they are in rank. By these views the remedies become apparent and within reach of every one; for it is sufficient to refuse to believe. Once again, say 'No!'

RICHARD GREGG

1885–

PUBLISHED first in India in 1934, *The Power of Nonviolence*, from which this selection is taken, was a pioneering work; although Gandhi's activities were known abroad, Gregg's book, by synthesizing the ideals of Christian brotherhood with the psychological techniques underlying *satyagraha*, offered a basis for nonviolent approaches to social and political problems in the West. In connexion with the reprinting in this anthology of the second chapter of his book, Mr Gregg has written on how he came to understand the working of nonviolent resistance:

After three years practising law and six years of industrial relations work I was employed in the early 1920s by a federation of railway employees who were on a nation-wide strike. At the height of the strike when feelings were most bitter I chanced upon a book about Mahatma Gandhi and his ideas, with some quotations from him. The contrast between his way of handling conflicts and what I was in the midst of was so great that I was deeply moved. We lost the strike and my job evaporated. I wrote to Gandhi in India and asked if I might come out and learn about it at first hand. The answer was favourable, so after a year of study and work on agriculture, I set sail on 1 January 1925. I stayed in India nearly four years, living in Indian fashion. Seven months of that time I lived in Gandhi's *ashram*.

I saw that non-violent resistance worked, but could not understand why. My Hindu friends explained it in terms of Hindu philosophy and religion, but somehow that did not carry conviction to me. Once in Delhi I picked up a book about Japanese jiu-jitsu. It explained that the jiu-jitsu wrestler overcomes his opponent not by pushing harder against the push of the opponent, but by yielding faster than the opponent pushes, thus depriving him of the support of the expected violent resistance and causing him to lose his balance. I realized then that non-violent resistance is a sort of jiu-jitsu purely in the moral and psychological realm. Then later, while spending the night at an inn in the Himalayas I picked up a military journal left behind by a British army officer. It contained an article on Von Clausewitz's principles of military strategy. I had never read about that subject before. I suddenly saw that non-violent resistance carries out all the eleven principles of military strategy, only on the moral and psychological level. These two analogies gave me the clue and explanation of the power of non-violence. The rest was just a matter of following up fully the psychological implications, thus putting the whole matter in terms of Western thinking.

When I went to India I had no thought of writing about what I might discover. But realizing the immense and deep involvement of violence in the very foundations of Western civilization, I felt when I came to understand the workings of non-violence that I must try to explain in Western terminology its validity, power, and importance.

Moral Jiu-Jitsu

Most people hitherto have been skeptical of nonviolent resistance simply because they did not understand how it could possibly work. They might be less skeptical once they could see how the method could operate and be effective. Let us then try to understand first how non-violent resistance works. Later we may estimate the probabilities of its success in general use. Modern psychology enables us to understand the emotional, mental and moral mechanisms involved. So let us analyse the matter and pay attention to one part of the problem at a time. We will consider first its operation by individuals and later its use by organized groups of people.

If one man attacks another with physical violence and the victim hits back, the violent response gives the attacker a certain reassurance and moral support. It shows that the position of violence on the victim's scale of moral values is the same as that of the attacker. A mere display of either fear or anger by the victim is sufficient to have this effect. It makes the attacker sure of his own *savoir-faire*, of his choice of methods, of his knowledge of human nature and hence of his opponent. He can rely on the victim to react in a definite way. The attacker's morale is sustained, his sense of values is vindicated.

But suppose the assailant, using physical violence, attacks a different sort of person. The attitude of this new opponent is fearless, calm, steady; because of a different belief, training or experience he has much self-control. He does not respond to the attacker's violence with counter-violence. Instead, he accepts the blows good-temperedly, stating his belief as to the truth of the matter in dispute, asking for an examination of both sides of the dispute, and stating his readiness to abide by the truth. He offers resistance, but only in moral terms. He states his readiness to prove his sincerity by his own suffering rather than by inflicting suffering on the assailant. He accepts blow after blow, showing no signs of fear or resentment, keeping steadily good-humored and kindly in look of eye, tone of voice, and posture of body and arms. To violence he opposes nonviolent resistance.

The assailant's first thought may be that his opponent is afraid of him, that he is a coward, ready to give way and acknowledge defeat. But the opponent's look and posture show not fear but courage. His steady resistance of will reveals no subservience. His unflinching endurance of pain is startling, particularly because, as F. C. Bartlett has pointed out, 'it is easier and requires less courage to attack than to withstand fire without retaliation'.[1]

At such an unusual and unexpected reaction the assailant will be surprised. If at first he was inclined to be scornful or contemptuous of the victim as a coward, those feelings rapidly become displaced by curiosity and wonder. As the psychologist Shand points out, 'Wonder tends to exclude repugnance, disgust and contempt in relation to its object.'[2]

Thus nonviolent resistance acts as a sort of moral jiu-jitsu. The nonviolence and goodwill of the victim act in the same way that the lack of physical opposition by the user of physical jiu-jitsu, does, causing the attacker to lose his moral balance. He suddenly and unexpectedly loses the moral support which the usual violent resistance of most victims would render him. He plunges forward, as it were, into a new world of values. He feels insecure because of the novelty of the situation and his ignorance of how to handle it. He loses his poise and self-confidence. The victim not only lets the attacker come, but, as it were, pulls him forward by kindness, generosity and voluntary suffering, so that the attacker loses his moral balance. The user of nonviolent resistance, knowing what he is doing and having a more creative purpose, keeps his moral balance. He uses the leverage of a superior wisdom to subdue the rough direct force of his opponent.[3]

Another way to state it is that between two persons in physically violent combat there may appear to be complete disagreement, but in reality they conduct their fight on the basis of a strong fundamental agreement that violence is a sound mode of procedure. Hence, if one of the parties eliminates that basic agreement, announcing by his actions

1. F. C. Bartlett, *Psychology and the Soldier*, p. 175 (Cambridge: Cambridge University Press 1927).

2. See A. F. Shand, *The Foundations of Character*, p. 448 (New York: Macmillan 1914).

3. See W. B. Cannon, *Bodily Changes in Pain, Hunger, Fear and Rage* (New York: Appleton 1927).

that he has abandoned the method used by his ancestors almost as early as the beginning of animal life, it is no wonder that the other is startled and uncertain. His instincts no longer tell him instantly what to do. He feels that he has plunged into a new world.

Just as in jiu-jitsu, violence itself helps to overthrow its user. There are several reasons for this, besides the element of surprise.

First, prolonged anger is very exhausting. Undoubtedly anger at first gives an access of muscular and sometimes mental energy. But it also consumes energy very rapidly, and if long sustained it may completely exhaust the person feeling it.[1]

Second, part of the energy of the assailant is reverted and used up against himself. The steadfast appeals of an individual nonviolent resister work in the personality of the violent attacker, arousing the latter's more decent and kindly motives and putting them in conflict with his fighting, aggressive instincts. Thus the attacker's personality is divided. The appeals, like commercial advertising, may require considerable repetition before they become effective, but the result is pretty sure. They act on the principle of 'summation of stimuli'.[2]

The violent assailant realizes that he has made a mistake in thinking at first that his opponent was a coward. He is bothered by the thought that he may have made or might in future make another mistake about this unusual opponent, and that another mistake might be more embarrassing. He therefore becomes more cautious.

If there are onlookers, the assailant soon loses still more poise. Instinctively he dramatizes himself before them and becomes more aware of his position. With the audience as a sort of mirror, he realizes the contrast between his own conduct and that of the victim. In relation to the onlookers, the attacker with his violence perhaps begins to feel a little excessive and undignified – even a little ineffective – and by contrast with the victim, less generous and in fact brutal. He realizes that the onlookers see that he has misjudged the nature of his adversary, and realizes that he has lost prestige. He somewhat loses his inner self-respect, gets a sense of inferiority. Of course he does not want to acknowledge it, but his feelings betray themselves in hesitance of

1. See G. W. Crile, *Origin and Nature of the Emotions*, esp. pp. 30, 52, 61 (Philadelphia: W. B. Saunders 1915). Also William Ernest Hocking, *Morale and Its Enemies*, p. 53f. (New Haven: Yale University Press 1918).

2. See T. Burrow, *The Social Basis of Consciousness* (New York: Harcourt Brace 1927).

manner, speech or glance. The onlookers perceive it, and he himself senses a further loss of public support.

If anyone feels inclined to doubt such a reaction of the outsiders against the assailant's violence, let him recall what happens during a labor strike if any striker loses his temper and destroys property or attacks any person. Immediately the employers blazon the news in the press and try to make it appear that all the strikers are men of violence and that public safety is threatened. They play on the fears of the public and then persuade the authorities to call out extra police or soldiers. Public opinion, swayed by the press, reacts strongly against the strikers and their cause is lost. Violence which is not opposed by violence, but by courageous nonviolence, if it is in the open, is sure sooner or later to react against the attacker.

The disadvantage of the attacker increases by reason of a further loss of inner assurance. He becomes increasingly aware that the victim's scale of values is different from his own. He dimly realizes that the courage of the nonviolent opponent is higher than mere physical bravery or recklessness – that it is somehow a clearer and stronger realization of human nature or perhaps of some ultimate powers or realities in the background of life. He is surprised into an uncertainty of his own valuations and methods.

A final disadvantage and continuing cause of relative weakness in the attacker is that he is in a suggestible and receptive state of mind and emotion, more so than the nonviolent resister. The reasons for this are several. The emotion of the struggle of course tends to make both parties suggestible.[1] But the surprising conduct and attitude of the victim suddenly present a new idea to the attacker.[2] 'The effect of surprise is to make us attend to the event that surprises us. Wonder tends to arrest and detail the attention on the thing which excites it.'[3] The struggle is a process of mutual interacting influence. As this process proceeds, there is a cumulative effect of the several disabilities of the violent assailant as above described, together with advantages of the nonviolent opponent which we are about to set forth. This cumulative effect acts upon the subconscious and imagination of the attacker to keep him more sug-

1. See Baudouin, *Suggestion and Auto-Suggestion*, p. 143 (New York: Dodd, Mead 1931).

2. See William Ernest Hocking, *Human Nature and Its Remaking*, 2nd ed., p. 374 (New Haven: Yale University Press 1928).

3. Shand, above cited, pp. 430, 448.

gestible than the nonviolent resister. Thus the assailant has less chance of influencing the resister than the latter has of influencing him.

In this moral jiu-jitsu, the nonviolent person has superior position, poise and power for many reasons. First, he has taken the moral initiative. His conduct is new, unexpected, and unpredictable to the person habituated to violence. Second, he is not surprised. He knows, by reasoning or by intuition and faith, what is really taking place in such a struggle, and how to control the process. Third, his self-control and lack of anger conserve his energy. Moreover, he is not in as suggestible a condition as his assailant.

He has still another element of superior power: he has demonstrated his sincerity and deep conviction. To be willing to suffer and die for a cause is an incontestable proof of sincere belief, and perhaps in most cases the only incontestable proof. Nonviolence coupled with voluntary suffering is just such an incontestable proof of sincerity. Voluntary suffering is probably also a sure sign that the whole being of the sufferer – body, mind, will and spirit – is integrated and at work with singleness of purpose. This means that immense and unpredictable resources of energy are in action and ready to endure. The sight and realization of this is profoundly impressive and moving.

Again, the victim's refusal to use violence indicates his respect for the personality and moral integrity of the assailant. From childhood we all tend to like people who show respect for our personality. This tendency operates even between the parties to a conflict. Such respect for the personality of the opponent was one of the important elements in the practice of medieval European chivalry, and added much to the charm and power of that code. Respect for personality is a prerequisite for real freedom and fine human association. It is proof of unselfishness and of moral poise and understanding. If, as at least two distinguished psychologists believe,[1] the self-regarding sentiment is the foundation of all the higher morality,[2] a demonstration of respect for personality exercises a much deeper and more far-reaching influence than is generally realized. This respect, shown by the nonviolent resister, gradually tends to put his attacker to shame and to enhance the respect of any onlookers toward the former.

Both opponents feel a desire and need for the approbation of others.

1. William McDougal and A. G. Tansley.
2. See Erich Fromm, *The Art of Loving* (New York: Harper 1957), for his conception of self-love.

Social approval and opprobrium are very strong forces. They act through and are a part of the herd or gregarious instinct that is so powerful in mankind.[1] The desire for outside approval is strikingly shown by the increasing emphasis on the uses of propaganda by major nations since World War I. Again, it is demonstrated in labor disputes in which both parties are at great pains to win public support and sympathy. All politicians recognize the force of public opinion.

For these reasons, in a struggle between a violent person and a non-violent resister, if there are any onlookers or a public that hears of the conflict, the nonviolent resister gains a strong advantage from their reaction. When the public sees the gentle person's courage and fortitude, notes his generosity and good will toward the attacker, and hears his repeated offers to settle the matter fairly, peaceably and openly, they are filled with surprise, curiosity and wonder. If they have been hostile to the victim before, they at least pause to think. His good humor, fairness and kindness arouse confidence. Sooner or later his conduct wins public sympathy, admiration and support, and also the respect of the violent opponent himself. Gandhi's chivalrous and generous conduct toward the South African government when it was threatened by a railway strike is an instance of this sort. Once the respect of the opponent has been secured, a long step has been taken toward a satisfactory solution of the controversy, no matter whether it be public or private.

But what is the psychology of the affair if the assailant is filled with the sort of cruelty or greed, pride, bigotry, or hardness that seems to grow on what it feeds on?

Cruelty is a complex of fear, anger and pride.[2] Greed is a distorted desire for security and completion. In a sense it is a fear of lack. Pride is another mistaken sense of divisiveness. Bigotry is an obstinate, narrow religious pride.

In all such instances, the tendency of nonviolent resistance is to remove fear, anger and any foreboding or dread of loss or sense of separateness ... and to replace these with feelings of security, unity, sympathy and good will. Since fear and anger are elements of cruelty, the removal of fear and anger will tend to reduce cruelty. Shand tells us that 'wonder tends to exclude repugnance, disgust and contempt in

---

1. See E. J. Kempf, *Autonomic Functions and the Personality*, pp. 93ff. (New York: Nervous and Mental Diseases Publishing Co. 1921). Also W. Trotter, *Instincts of the Herd in Peace and War* (New York: Macmillan 1916).

2. See Shand, *The Foundations of Character*, p. 268f, above cited.

relation to its object'.[1] Insofar as these may be elements involved in pride, the wonder evoked by the conduct of the nonviolent person also tends to reduce pride and hence to reduce cruelty. Insofar as cruelty is due to a desire for power or a feeling of superiority, the ability of nonviolence to win the support of the outside public presently makes the cruel person realize that the kind of power he has valued is disadvantageous and that perhaps he is not so superior as he had previously supposed.

Aside from its effect on the spectators, nonviolent resistance gradually creates even in the violent opponent himself a gradual realization of human unity and a different idea of what kind of power is desirable. Cruelty may be partly due to a defect in the cruel person's imagination or to dullness of observation, and in this event, dramatic scenes of prolonged nonviolent resistance act to stimulate his imagination and powers of observation, and thereby to reduce his cruelty. If avarice or desire for revenge are factors in a particular case of cruelty, these also are reduced by prolonged nonviolent resistance.

The attacker gradually loses divisive emotions in relation to the victim: fear, anger, hatred, indignation, pride, vanity, scorn, contempt, disdain, disgust, anxiety, worry, apprehension. These feelings are not merely thwarted or suppressed by the use of nonviolence; their very basis is uprooted.

The art of jiu-jitsu is based on a knowledge of balance and how to disturb it. In a struggle of moral jiu-jitsu, the retention of moral balance seems to depend upon the qualities of one's relationship to moral truth. Hence part of the superior power of the nonviolent resister seems to lie in the nature of his character.

He must have primarily that disposition best known as love – an interest in people so deep, and determined, and lasting as to be creative; a profound knowledge of or faith in the ultimate possibilities of human nature; a courage based upon a conscious or subconscious realization of the underlying unity of all life and eternal values or eternal life of the human spirit; a strong and deep desire for and love of truth; and a humility that is not cringing or self-deprecatory or timid but is rather a true sense of proportion in regard to people, things, qualities and ultimate values. These human traits of love, faith, courage, honesty and humility exist in greater or less strength in *every* person. By self-training and discipline they can be developed sufficiently to make a good non-

1. Same, p. 448.

violent 'soldier' out of any ordinary human being. Of course, leaders of a nonviolent movement require these qualities to an unusual degree, just as generals require military qualities more highly developed than those of the common soldier.

Love is the most important of all these qualities of the nonviolent person; it may even be considered the origin of all the others. If the word 'love' in such a context seems too sentimental, call it a sort of intelligence or knowledge. This love must be strong and clear-sighted, not mawkish or sentimental. It does not hint that it is going to 'do good to' the other person, nor does it make a parade of itself. It must be patient and full of insight, understanding and imagination. It must be enduring, kind and unselfish. It is wonderful but it is not superhuman or exceedingly rare. We have all seen such love in many mothers of all classes, nations and races, as well as in the best teachers. Its creativeness in these instances is well known.

If through love for your enemy you can create in him respect or admiration for you, this provides the best possible means by which your new idea or suggestion to him will become an auto-suggestion within him, and it will also help nourish that auto-suggestion.

Anger, as well as love, can be creative, for both are expressions or modes of energy. But love contains more energy and endurance than anger. Love involves the very principle and essence of continuity of life itself. If considered as an instrument, it can be more efficiently and effectively wielded, has better aim, has a better fulcrum or point of vantage, than anger. Love gains a stronger and more lasting approval from the rest of mankind. The probabilities in favor of its winning over anger in the long run are strong.

But if one party to a contest cannot develop toward the conflict or toward his opponent an attitude that is creative or akin to love, he should certainly be honest and true to himself. 'Unless I am, in fact, so much of a seer to be a lover of my enemy,' says Hocking, 'it is both futile and false to assume the behavior of love; we can generally rely on the enemy to give such conduct its true name.'[1] As long as men have uncontrollable anger or enmity in their feelings it is better to express it honestly and courageously than to be hypocritical and refuse to fight out of cowardice. In reference to such a situation Gandhi once said to me, 'If you have a sword in your bosom, take it out and use it like a man.' Christ, searching for a change in men more profound and

1. Hocking, *Human Nature and Its Remaking*, above cited, p. 376.

important than immediate external acts, told them to get rid of anger and greed, knowing, I believe, that if this took place, war would disappear.

Courageous violence, to try to prevent or stop a wrong, is better than cowardly acquiescence. Cowardice is more harmful morally than violence. The inner attitude is more important than the outer act, though it is vitally important always to be true to oneself, to make one's outer conduct a true reflection and expression of one's inner state. Fear develops out of an assumption of relative weakness. Since all men have the innate possibility of moral strength, to be afraid is really a denial of one's moral potential powers and is therefore very harmful. Violence and anger at least show faith in one's own moral powers and thus provide at least a basis for further growth. He who refrains from fighting because he is afraid, really hates his opponent in his heart and wishes that circumstances would change so that he could hurt or destroy his opponent. The energy of his hate is present but suppressed. If one lacks the discipline or conviction to resist wrong or violence without counter-violence, then I agree with Gandhi that it is better to be violent than to be cowardly.[1]

But he who has the courage to fight and yet refrains, is the true non-violent resister. Because the coward fears, he cannot love, and thus cannot be successful in nonviolent resistance. He cannot use this moral

1. In *Young India* for 5 Nov. 1925, Gandhi wrote in answer to a question why he had enlisted men for service in World War I:

'As a citizen not then and not even now, a reformer leading an agitation against institution of war, I had to advise and lead men who believed in war but who from cowardice, or from base motives or from anger against the British Government refrained from enlisting. I did not hesitate to advise them that so long as they believed in war and professed loyalty to the British constitution they were in duty bound to support it by enlistment. Though I do not believe in the use of arms, and though it is contrary to the religion of *Ahimsa* which I profess, I should not hesitate to join an agitation for a repeal of the debasing Arms Act which I have considered amongst the blackest crimes of the British Government against India. I do not believe in retaliation, but I did not hesitate to tell the villagers of Bettiah four years ago that they who knew nothing of *Ahimsa* were guilty of cowardice in failing to defend the honour of their women-folk and their property by force of arms. And I have not hesitated, as the correspondent should know, only recently to tell the Hindus that if they do not believe in out-and-out *Ahimsa* and cannot practise it, they will be guilty of a crime against their religion and humanity if they fail to defend by force of arms the honour of their women against any kidnapper who chooses to take away their women.' M. K. Gandhi, *Nonviolence in Peace and War*, vol. 1, p. 49f. (Ahmedabad, India: Navajivan 1948).

jiu-jitsu effectively. It is better to refrain from outward violent acts through fearless self-control of anger than to act violently, but getting rid of anger is the only sure way. True nonviolent resistance, where the outer act is an expression of inner attitude, gradually creates among all beholders an awareness of essential human unity. But if one's inner condition is of anger or hate, it causes a cowardly inconsistency with the superficial nonviolence of one's deed, which is soon detected by others and perhaps openly called hypocrisy. This inconsistency makes impossible any considerable increase in the awareness of essential unity.

As to the outcome of a struggle waged by nonviolence, we must understand one point thoroughly. The aim of the nonviolent resister is not to injure, or to crush and humiliate his opponent, or to 'break his will', as in a violent fight. The aim is to convert the opponent, to change his understanding and his sense of values so that he will join wholeheartedly with the resister in seeking a settlement truly amicable and truly satisfying to both sides. The nonviolent resister seeks a solution under which both parties can have complete self-respect and mutual respect, a settlement that will implement the new desires and full energies of both parties. The nonviolent resister seeks to help the violent attacker to re-establish his moral balance on a level higher and more secure than that from which he first launched his violent attack. The function of the nonviolent type of resistance is not to harm the opponent nor impose a solution against his will, but to help both parties into a more secure, creative, happy, and truthful relationship.

ALBERT EINSTEIN

1879–1955

and SIGMUND FREUD

1856–1939

ALBERT EINSTEIN, though best known for his scientific contributions, worked on behalf of peace for more than half a century. In that time he travelled all over the world and wrote constantly in support of peace activity. In a letter he wrote in 1929 to Paul Hutchinson, editor of *The Christian Century*, he disclosed the absolutist nature of his pacifist thought before the Second World War:

> My pacifism is an instinctive feeling, a feeling that possesses me because the murder of men is disgusting. My attitude is not derived from any intellectual theory but is based on my deepest antipathy to every kind of cruelty and hatred. I might go on to rationalize this reaction, but that would really be *a posteriori* thinking. I am an absolute pacifist. One of the main objects of my life is to oppose, at every turning, the ancient European tradition of warfare. That tradition still retains its power, but even so I am not discouraged. I believe in taking a holy oath never to participate in any act of violence.

In the late thirties, after his forced emigration from Germany, continuing to call himself a pacifist, he supported the Allied effort, maintaining that only through strong international organization could the peace be maintained.

Sigmund Freud was more or less a stranger to peace activities, but all his writings display a strong concern for the problems of violence and aggression in men's lives. His correspondence with Einstein over a period of years on this subject culminated in this little-known exchange of letters reprinted below. It was published first by the International Institute of Intellectual Cooperation in 1933 under the title, 'Why War?' (translated by Stuart Gilbert). In spite of the serious reservations Freud held with regard to the practical peaceful alternatives open to nations in an aggressive world, Freud pronounces himself a pacifist, and embraces attitudes quite similar to those which Einstein in later years was to adopt.

Why War?

Dear Mr Freud:

The proposal of the League of Nations and its International Institute of Intellectual Cooperation at Paris that I should invite a person, to be chosen by myself, to a frank exchange of views on any problem that I might select affords me a very welcome opportunity of conferring with you upon a question which, as things now are, seems the most insistent of all the problems civilization has to face. This is the problem: Is there any way of delivering mankind from the menace of war? It is common knowledge that, with the advance of modern science, this issue has come to mean a matter of life and death for civilization as we know it; nevertheless, for all the zeal displayed, every attempt at its solution has ended in a lamentable breakdown.

I believe, moreover, that those whose duty it is to tackle the problem professionally and practically are growing only too aware of their impotence to deal with it, and have now a very lively desire to learn the views of men who, absorbed in the pursuit of science, can see world problems in the perspective distance lends. As for me, the normal objective of my thought affords no insight into the dark places of human will and feeling. Thus, in the inquiry now proposed, I can do little more than to seek to clarify the question at issue and, clearing the ground of the more obvious solutions, enable you to bring the light of your far-reaching knowledge of man's instinctive life to bear upon the problem. There are certain psychological obstacles whose existence a layman in the mental sciences may dimly surmise, but whose interrelations and vagaries he is incompetent to fathom; you, I am convinced, will be able to suggest educative methods, lying more or less outside the scope of politics, which will eliminate these obstacles.

As one immune from nationalist bias, I personally see a simple way of dealing with the superficial (i.e., administrative) aspect of the problem; the setting up, by international consent, of a legislative and judicial body to settle every conflict arising between nations. Each nation would undertake to abide by the orders issued by this legislative body, to invoke its decision in every dispute, to accept its judgements unreservedly and to carry out every measure the tribunal deems necessary for the execution of its decrees. But here, at the outset, I come up against a difficulty; a tribunal is a human institution which, in proportion as the power at its disposal is inadequate to enforce its verdicts, is all the more prone to suffer these to be deflected by extrajudicial pressure. This is a fact with which we have to reckon; law and might inevitably go hand in hand, and juridical decisions approach more nearly the ideal justice demanded by the community (in whose name and interests these verdicts are pronounced) in so far as the community has effective power to compel respect of its juridical ideal. But at present we are far from possessing any supranational organization competent to render verdicts of incontestable authority and enforce absolute submission to the execution of its verdicts. Thus I am led to my first axiom : The quest of international security involves the unconditional surrender by every nation, in a certain measure, of its liberty of action – its sovereignty that is to say – and it is clear beyond all doubt that no other road can lead to such security.

The ill success, despite their obvious sincerity, of all the efforts made during the last decade to reach this goal leaves us no room to doubt that strong psychological factors are at work which paralyse these efforts. Some of these factors are not far to seek. The craving for power which characterizes the governing class in every nation is hostile to any limitation of the national sovereignty. This political power hunger is often supported by the activities of another group, whose aspirations are on purely mercenary, economic lines. I have especially in mind that small but determined group, active in every nation, composed of individuals who, indifferent to social considerations and restraints, regard warfare, the manufacture and sale of arms, simply as an occasion to advance their personal interests and enlarge their personal authority.

But recognition of this obvious fact is merely the first step toward an appreciation of the actual state of affairs. Another question follows hard upon it : How is it possible for this small clique to bend the will of the majority, who stand to lose and suffer by a state of war, to the service of their ambitions? (In speaking of the majority I do not exclude soldiers of every rank who have chosen war as their profession, in the belief that they are serving to defend the highest interests of their race, and that attack is often the best method of defence.) An obvious answer to this question would seem to be that the minority, the ruling class at present, has the schools and press, usually the Church as well, under its thumb. This enables it to organize and sway the emotions of the masses, and makes its tool of them.

Yet even this answer does not provide a complete solution. Another question arises from it : How is it that these devices succeed so well in rousing men to such wild enthusiasm, even to sacrifice their lives? Only one answer is possible. Because man has within him a lust for hatred and destruction. In normal times this passion exists in a latent state, it emerges only in unusual circumstances; but it is a comparatively easy task to call it into play and raise it to the power of a collective psychosis. Here lies, perhaps, the crux of all the complex factors we are considering, an enigma that only the expert in the lore of human instincts can resolve.

And so we come to our last question. Is it possible to control man's mental evolution so as to make him proof against the psychosis of hate and destructiveness? Here I am thinking by no means only of the so-called uncultured masses. Experience proves that it is rather the so-called 'intelligentsia' that is most apt to yield to these disastrous collective suggestions, since the intellectual has no direct contact with life in the raw but encounters it in its easiest, synthetic form – upon the printed page.

To conclude: I have so far been speaking only of wars between nations; what are known as international conflicts. But I am well aware that the aggressive instinct operates under other forms and in other circumstances. (I am thinking of civil wars, for instance, due in earlier days to religious zeal, but nowadays to social factors; or, again, the persecution of racial minorities.) But my insistence on what is the most typical, most cruel and extravagant form of conflict between man and man was deliberate, for here we have the best occasion of discovering ways and means to render all armed conflicts impossible.

I know that in your writings we may find answers, explicit or implied, to all the issues of this urgent and absorbing problem. But it would be of the greatest service to us all were you to present the problem of world peace in the light of your most recent discoveries, for such a presentation well might blaze the trail for new and fruitful modes of action.

Yours very sincerely,

A. Einstein

Dear Mr Einstein:

When I learned of your intention to invite me to a mutual exchange of views upon a subject which not only interested you personally but seemed deserving, too, of public interest, I cordially assented. I expected you to choose a problem lying on the borderland of the knowable, as it stands today, a theme which each of us, physicist and psychologist, might approach from his own angle, to meet at last on common ground, though setting out from different premisses. Thus the question which you put me – what is to be done to rid mankind of the war menace? – took me by surprise. And, next, I was dumbfounded by the thought of my (of *our*, I almost wrote) incompetence; for this struck me as being a matter of practical politics, the statesman's proper study. But then I realized that you did not raise the question in your capacity of scientist or physicist, but as a lover of his fellow men, who responded to the call of the League of Nations much as Fridtjof Nansen, the polar explorer, took on himself the task of succouring homeless and starving victims of the World War. And, next, I reminded myself that I was not being called on to formulate practical proposals but, rather, to explain how this question of preventing wars strikes a psychologist.

But here, too, you have stated the gist of the matter in your letter – and taken the wind out of my sails! Still, I will gladly follow in your wake and content myself with endorsing your conclusions, which, however, I propose to amplify to the best of my knowledge or surmise.

You begin with the relations between might and right, and this is assuredly the proper starting point for our inquiry. But, for the term *might*, I would substitute a tougher and more telling word: *violence*. In right and violence we have today an obvious antinomy. It is easy to prove that one has evolved from the other and, when we go back to origins and examine primitive conditions, the solution of the problem follows easily enough. I must crave your indulgence if in what follows I speak of well-known, admitted facts as though they were new data; the context necessitates this method.

Conflicts of interest between man and man are resolved, in principle, by the recourse to violence. It is the same in the animal kingdom, from which man cannot claim exclusion; nevertheless, men are also prone to conflicts of opinion, touching, on occasion, the loftiest peaks of abstract thought, which seem to call for settlement by quite another method. This refinement is, however, a late development. To start with, group force was the factor which, in small communities, decided points of ownership and the question which man's will was to prevail. Very soon physical force was implemented, then replaced, by the use of various adjuncts; he proved the victor whose weapon was the better, or handled the more skilfully. Now, for the first time, with the coming of weapons, superior brains began to oust brute force, but the object of the conflict remained the same: one party was to be constrained, by the injury done him or impairment of his strength, to retract a claim or a refusal. This end is most effectively gained when the opponent is definitely put out of action – in other words, is killed. This procedure has two advantages: the enemy cannot renew hostilities, and, secondly, his fate deters others from following his example. Moreover, the slaughter of a foe gratifies an instinctive craving – a point to which we shall revert hereafter. However, another consideration may be set off against this will to kill: the possibility of using an enemy for servile tasks if his spirit be broken and his life spared. Here violence finds an outlet not in slaughter but in subjugation. Hence springs the practice of giving quarter; but the victor, having from now on to reckon with the craving for revenge that rankles in his victim, forfeits to some extent his personal security.

Thus, under primitive conditions, it is superior force – brute violence, or violence backed by arms – that lords it everywhere. We know that in the course of evolution this state of things was modified, a path was traced that led away from violence to law. But what was this path? Surely it issued from a single verity: that the superiority of one strong man can be overborne by an alliance of many weaklings, that *l'union fait la force*. Brute force is overcome by union; the allied might of scattered units makes good its right against the isolated giant. Thus we may define 'right' (i.e., law) as the might of a community. Yet it, too, is nothing else than violence, quick to attack whatever individual stands in its path, and it employs the selfsame methods, follows like ends, with but one difference; it is the communal, not individual, violence that has its way. But, for the transition from crude violence to the reign of law, a certain psychological condition must first obtain. The union of the majority must be stable and enduring. If its sole *raison d'être* be the discomfiture of some overweening individual and, after his downfall, it be dissolved, it leads to nothing. Some other man, trusting to his superior power, will seek to reinstate the rule of violence, and the cycle will repeat itself unendingly. Thus the union of the people must be permanent and well organized; it must enact rules to meet the risk of possible revolts; must set up machinery insuring that its rules – the laws – are observed and that such acts of violence as the laws demand are duly carried out. This recognition of a community of interests engenders among the members of the group a sentiment of unity and fraternal solidarity which constitutes its real strength.

So far I have set out what seems to me the kernel of the matter: the suppression of brute force by the transfer of power to a larger combination, founded on the community of sentiments linking up its members. All the rest is mere tautology and glosses. Now the position is simple enough so long as the community consists of a number of equipollent individuals. The laws of such a group can determine to what extent the individual must forfeit his personal freedom, the right of using personal force as an instrument of violence, to insure the safety of the group. But such a combination is only theoretically possible; in practice the situation is always complicated by the fact that, from the outset, the group includes elements of unequal power, men and women, elders and children, and, very soon, as a result of war and conquest, victors and the vanquished – i.e. masters and slaves – as well. From this time on the common law takes notice of these inequalities of power, laws are made by and for the rulers, giving the servile classes fewer rights. Thenceforward there exist within the state two factors making for legal instability, but legislative evolution, too: first, the attempts by members of the ruling class to set themselves above the law's restrictions and, secondly, the constant struggle of the ruled to extend their rights and see each gain embodied in the code, replacing legal disabilities by equal laws for all. The second of these tendencies will be particularly marked when there takes place a positive mutation of the balance of power within the community, the frequent outcome of certain historical conditions. In such cases the laws may gradually be adjusted to the changed conditions or (as more usually ensues) the ruling class is loath to rush in with the new developments, the result being insurrections and civil wars, a period when law is in abeyance and force once more the arbiter, followed by a new régime of law. There is another factor of constitutional change, which operates in a wholly pacific manner, viz.: the cultural evolution of the mass of the community; this factor, however, is of a different order and can only be dealt with later.

Thus we see that, even within the group itself, the exercise of violence cannot be avoided when conflicting interests are at stake. But the common needs and habits of men who live in fellowship under the same sky favour a speedy issue of such conflicts and, this being so, the possibilities of peaceful solutions make steady progress. Yet the most casual glance at world history will show an unending series of conflicts between one community and another or a group of others, between large and smaller units, between cities, countries, races, tribes and kingdoms, almost all of which were settled by the ordeal of war. Such war ends either in pillage or in conquest and its fruits, the downfall of the loser. No single all-embracing judgement can be passed on these wars of aggrandizement. Some, like the war between the Mongols and the Turks, have led to unmitigated misery; others, however, have furthered the transition from violence to law, since they brought larger units into being, within whose limits a recourse to violence was banned and a new régime determined all disputes. Thus the Roman conquest brought that boon, the *pax Romana*, to the Mediterranean lands. The French kings' lust for aggrandizement created a new France, flourishing in peace and unity. Paradoxical as its sounds, we must admit that warfare well might serve to pave the way to that unbroken peace we so desire, for it is war that brings vast empires into being, within whose frontiers all warfare is proscribed by a strong central power. In practice, however, this end is not attained, for as a rule the fruits of victory are but short-lived, the new-created unit falls asunder once again, generally because there can be no true cohesion between the parts that violence has welded. Hitherto, moreover, such conquests have only led to aggregations which, for all their magnitude, had limits, and disputes between these units could be resolved only by recourse to arms. For humanity at large the sole result of all these military enterprises was that, instead of frequent, not to say incessant, little wars, they had now to face great wars which, for all they came less often, were so much the more destructive.

Regarding the world of today the same conclusion holds good, and you, too, have reached it, though by a shorter path. There is but one sure way of ending war and that is the establishment, by common consent, of a central control which shall have the last word in every conflict of interests. For this, two things are needed: first, the creation of such a supreme court of judicature; secondly, its investment with adequate executive force. Unless this second requirement be fulfilled, the first is unavailing. Obviously the League of Nations, acting as a Supreme Court, fulfils the first condition; it does not fulfil the second. It has no force at its disposal and can only get it if the members of the new body, its constituent nations, furnish it. And, as things are, this is a forlorn hope. Still we should be taking a very shortsighted view of the League of Nations were we to ignore the fact that here is an experiment the like of which has rarely – never before, perhaps, on such a scale – been attempted in the course of history. It is an attempt to acquire the authority (in other words, coercive influence), which hitherto reposed exclusively in the possession of power, by calling into play certain idealistic attitudes of mind. We have seen that there are two factors of cohesion in a community: violent compulsion and ties of sentiment ('identifications', in technical parlance) between the members of the group. If one of these factors becomes inoperative, the other may still suffice to hold the group together. Obviously such notions as these can only be significant when they are the expression of a deeply rooted sense of unity, shared by all. It is necessary, therefore, to gauge the efficacy of such sentiments. History tells us that, on occasion, they have been effective. For example, the Panhellenic conception, the Greeks' awareness of superiority over their barbarian neighbours, which found expression in the Amphictyonies, the Oracles and Games, was strong enough to humanize the methods of warfare as between Greeks, though inevitably it failed to prevent conflicts between different elements of the Hellenic race or even to deter a city or group of cities from joining forces with their racial foe, the Persians, for the discomfiture of a rival. The solidarity of Christendom in the Renaissance age was no more effective, despite its vast authority, in hindering Christian nations, large and small alike, from calling in the Sultan to their aid. And, in our times, we look in vain for some such unifying notion whose authority would be unquestioned. It is all too clear that the nationalistic ideas, paramount today in every country, operate in quite a contrary direction. Some there are who hold that the Bolshevist conceptions may make an end of war, but, as things are, that goal lies very far away and, perhaps, could only be attained after a spell of brutal internecine warfare. Thus it would seem that any effort to replace brute force by the might of an ideal is, under present conditions, doomed to fail. Our logic is at fault if we ignore the fact that right is founded on brute force and even today needs violence to maintain it.

I now can comment on another of your statements. You are amazed that it is so easy to infect men with the war fever, and you surmise that man has in him an active instinct for hatred and destruction, amenable to such stimulations. I entirely agree with you. I believe in the existence of this instinct and have been recently at pains to study its manifestations. In this connexion may I set out a fragment of that knowledge of the instincts, which we psychoanalysts, after so many tentative essays and gropings in the dark, have compassed? We assume that human instincts are of two kinds: those that conserve and unify, which we call 'erotic' (in the meaning Plato gives to Eros in his Symposium), or else 'sexual' (explicitly extending the popular connotation of 'sex'); and, secondly, the instincts to destroy and kill, which we assimilate as the aggressive or destructive instincts. These are, as you perceive, the well-known opposites, Love and Hate, transformed into theoretical entities; they are, perhaps, another aspect of those eternal polarities, attraction and repulsion, which fall within your province. But we must be chary of passing overhastily to the notions of good and evil. Each of these instincts is every whit as indispensable as its opposite, and all the phenomena of life derive from their activity, whether they work in concert or in opposition. It seems that an instinct of either category can operate but rarely in isolation; it is always blended ('alloyed', as we say) with a certain dosage of its opposite, which modifies its aim or even, in certain circumstances, is a prime condition of its attainment. Thus the instinct of self-preservation is certainly of an erotic nature, but to gain its end this very instinct necessitates aggressive action. In the same way the love instinct, when directed to a specific object, calls for an admixture of the acquisitive instinct if it is to enter into effective possession of that object. It is the difficulty of isolating the two kinds of instinct in their manifestations that has so long prevented us from recognizing them.

If you will travel with me a little further on this road, you will find that human affairs are complicated in yet another way. Only exceptionally does an action follow on the stimulus of a single instinct, which is *per se* a blend of Eros and destructiveness. As a rule several motives of similar composition concur to bring about the act. This fact was duly noted by a colleague of yours, Professor G. C. Lichtenberg, sometime Professor of Physics at Göttingen; he was perhaps even more eminent as a psychologist than as a physical scientist. He evolved the notion of a 'Compass-card of Motives' and wrote: 'The efficient motives impelling man to act can be classified like the thirty-two winds and described in the same manner; e.g., *Food-Food-Fame* or *Fame-Fame-Food*'. Thus, when a nation is summoned to engage in war, a whole gamut of human motives may respond to this appeal – high and low motives, some openly avowed, others slurred over. The lust for aggression and destruction is certainly included; the innumerable cruelties of history and man's daily life confirms its prevalence and strength. The stimulation of these destructive impulses by appeals to idealism and the erotic instinct naturally facilitate their release. Musing on the atrocities recorded on history's page, we feel that the ideal motive has often served as a camouflage for the lust of destruction; sometimes, as with the cruelties of the Inquisition, it seems that, while the ideal motives occupied the foreground of consciousness, they drew their strength from the destructive instincts submerged in the unconscious. Both interpretations are feasible.

You are interested, I know, in the prevention of war, not in our theories, and I keep this fact in mind. Yet I would like to dwell a little longer on this destructive instinct which is seldom given the attention that its importance warrants. With the least of speculative efforts we are led to conclude that this instinct functions in every living being, striving to work its ruin and reduce life to its primal state of inert matter. Indeed, it might well be called the 'death instinct'; whereas the erotic instincts vouch for the struggle to live on. The death instinct becomes an impulse to destruction when, with the aid of certain organs, it directs its action outward, against external objects. The living being, that is to say, defends its own existence by destroying foreign bodies. But, in one of its activities, the death instinct is operative *within* the living being and we have sought to trace back a number of normal and pathological phenomena to this *introversion* of the destructive instinct. We have even committed the heresy of explaining the origin of human conscience by some such 'turning inward' of the aggressive impulse. Obviously when this internal tendency operates on too large a scale, it is no trivial matter; rather, a positively morbid state of things; whereas the diversion of the destructive impulse toward the external world must have beneficial effects. Here is then the biological justification for all those vile, pernicious propensities which we are now combating. We can but own that they are really more akin to nature than this our stand against them, which, in fact, remains to be accounted for.

All this may give you the impression that our theories amount to a species of mythology and a gloomy one at that! But does not every natural science lead ultimately to this – a sort of mythology? Is it otherwise today with our physical sciences?

The upshot of these observations, as bearing on the subject in hand, is that there is no likelihood of our being able to suppress humanity's aggressive tendencies. In some happy corners of the earth, they say, where nature brings forth abundantly whatever man desires, there flourish races whose lives go gently by, unknowing of aggression or constraint. This I can hardly credit; I would like further details about these happy folk. The Bolshevists, too, aspire to do away with human aggressiveness by insuring the satisfaction of material needs and enforcing equality between man and man. To me this hope seems vain.

Meanwhile they busily perfect their armaments, and their hatred of outsiders is not the least of the factors of cohesion among themselves. In any case, as you too have observed, complete suppression of man's aggressive tendencies is not in issue; what we may try is to divert it into a channel other than that of warfare.

From our 'mythology' of the instincts we may easily deduce a formula for an indirect method of eliminating war. If the propensity for war be due to the destructive instinct, we have always its counter-agent, Eros, to our hand. All that produces ties of sentiment between man and man must serve us as war's antidote. These ties are of two kinds. First, such relations as those toward a beloved object, void though they be of sexual intent. The psychoanalyst need feel no compunction in mentioning 'love' in this connexion; religion uses the same language: Love thy neighbour as thyself. A pious injunction, easy to enounce, but hard to carry out! The other bond of sentiment is by way of identification. All that brings out the significant resemblances between men calls into play this feeling of community, identification, whereon is founded, in large measure, the whole edifice of human society.

In your strictures on the abuse of authority I find another suggestion for an indirect attack on the war impulse. That men are divided into the leaders and the led is but another manifestation of their inborn and irremediable inequality. The second class constitutes the vast majority; they need a high command to make decisions for them, to which decisions they usually bow without demur. In this context we would point out that men should be at greater pains than heretofore to form a superior class of independent thinkers, unamenable to intimidation and fervent in the quest of truth, whose function it would be to guide the masses dependent on their lead. There is no need to point out how little the rule of politicians and the Church's ban on liberty of thought encourage such a new creation. The ideal conditions would obviously be found in a community where every man subordinated his instinctive life to the dictates of reason. Nothing less than this could bring about so thorough and so durable a union between men, even if this involved the severance of mutual ties of sentiment. But surely such a hope is utterly utopian, as things are. The other indirect methods of preventing war are certainly more feasible, but entail no quick results. They conjure up an ugly picture of mills that grind so slowly that, before the flour is ready, men are dead of hunger.

As you see, little good comes of consulting a theoretician, aloof from worldly contact, on practical and urgent problems! Better it were to tackle each successive crisis with means that we have ready to our hands. However, I would like to deal with a question which, though it is not mooted in your letter, interests me greatly. Why do we, you and I and many another, protest so vehemently against war, instead of just accepting it as another of life's odious importunities? For it seems a natural thing enough, biologically sound and practically unavoidable. I trust you will not be shocked by my raising such a question. For the better conduct of an inquiry it may be well to don a mask of feigned aloofness. The answer to my query may run as follows: Because every man has a right over his own life and war destroys lives that were full of promise; it forces the individual into situations that shame his manhood, obliging him to murder fellow men, against his will; it ravages material amenities, the fruits of human toil, and much besides. Moreover, wars, as now conducted, afford no scope for acts of heroism according to the old ideals and, given the high perfection of modern arms, war today would mean the sheer extermination of one of the combatants, if not of both. This is so true, so obvious, that we can but wonder why the conduct of war is not banned by general consent. Doubtless either of the points I have just made is open to debate. It may be asked if the community, in its turn, cannot claim a right over the individual lives of its members. Moreover, all forms of war cannot be indiscriminately condemned; so long as there are nations and empires, each prepared callously to exterminate its rival, all alike must be equipped for war. But we will not dwell on any of these problems; they lie outside the debate to which you have invited me. I pass on to another point, the basis, as it strikes me, of our common hatred of war. It is this: We cannot do otherwise than hate it. Pacifists we are, since our organic nature wills us thus to be. Hence it comes easy to us to find arguments that justify our standpoint.

This point, however, calls for elucidation. Here is the way in which I see it. The cultural development of mankind (some, I know, prefer to call it civilization) has been in progress since immemorial antiquity. To this *processus* we owe all that is best in our composition, but also much that makes for human suffering. Its origins and causes are obscure, its issue is uncertain, but some of its characteristics are easy to perceive. It well may lead to the extinction of mankind, for it impairs the sexual function in more than one respect, and even today the uncivilized races and the backward classes of all nations are multiplying more rapidly than the cultured elements. This process may, perhaps, be likened to the effects of domestication on certain animals – it clearly involves physical changes of structure – but the view that cultural development is an organic process of this order has not yet become generally familiar. The psychic changes which accompany this process of cultural change are striking, and not to be gainsaid. They consist in the progressive rejection of instinctive ends and a scaling down of instinctive reactions. Sensations which delighted our forefathers have become neutral or unbearable to us; and, if our ethical and aesthetic ideals have undergone a change, the causes of this are ultimately organic. On the psychological side two of the most important phenomena of culture are, firstly, a strengthening of the intellect, which tends to master our instinctive life, and, secondly, an introversion of the aggressive impulse, with all its consequent benefits and perils. Now war runs most emphatically counter to the psychic disposition imposed on us by the growth of culture; we are therefore bound to resent war, to find it utterly intolerable. With pacifists like us it is not merely an intellectual and affective repulsion, but a constitutional intolerance, an idiosyncrasy in its most drastic form. And it would seem that the aesthetic ignominies of warfare play almost as large a part in this repugnance as war's atrocities.

How long have we to wait before the rest of men turn pacifist? Impossible to say, and yet perhaps our hope that these two factors – man's cultural disposition and a well-founded dread of the form that future wars will take – may serve to put an end to war in the near future, is not chimerical. But by what ways or byways this will come about, we cannot guess. Meanwhile we may rest on the assurance that whatever makes for cultural development is working also against war.

With kindest regards and, should this exposé prove a disappointment to you, my sincere regrets,

Yours,

Sigmund Freud

REINHOLD NIEBUHR

1892–

At first widely known as a Christian pacifist and a prominent member of the Fellowship of Reconciliation, with his publication in 1932 of *Moral Man and Immoral Society* Niebuhr took the first step towards a reconciliation with 'conservative' Christianity. In Luther's tract, *On the Civil Power* (1523), the reformer had drawn a sharp line between those Christians who strictly followed the gospel and those who were Christians in name only, those for whom the restraint of the civil power was intended, for whom it was necessary.

Niebuhr, who in an earlier piece ('A Critique of Pacifism', 1927) had taken up the problem of individual-versus-group relations, drew his lines slightly differently from Luther, but their sense was the same: Christians act differently as individuals and as members of groups; it was necessary to distinguish between a private and public ethic. While it was possible to follow Jesus's teachings in relations between men, it was very often impossible between groups of men, although the teachings were relevant in both cases – Love was the 'impossible possibility'. This Niebuhr made clear in the fourth chapter of *An Interpretation of Christian Ethics* ('The Relevance of an Impossible Ethical Idea'). D. R. Robertson, in his introduction to the shorter writings of Niebuhr, states that 'Niebuhr intends to underline ... the impossibility of love as a wholly adequate social ethic. Love is the final or highest possibility of man toward man; it is the peak of fulfillment of his nature as a social being.' In the affairs of men, however, something less rules.

It was not until 1933 that Niebuhr formally left the f.o.r. In *The Christian Century* of 3 January 1934, he published the reasons for his decision; the article is reprinted below. His exit from the f.o.r.'s ranks did not mean, however, that he and those who followed him were abandoning their opposition to war; that would come later with the rising threat of the dictatorships. It was not the issue of war, but the issue of the working-class struggle, that led Niebuhr to leave the f.o.r., for earlier he had made plain his view that in some circumstances force was justified. Since the f.o.r. believed that love was the only effective basis for the resolution of society's evils (which did not make the organization conservative by any means; the social gospel has always been a prominent part of its creed) Niebuhr's continued membership became impossible.

The present 'nuclear pacifist' position is an outgrowth in large part of Niebuhr's recent writings, in which he suggests that the policy of the mutual nuclear deterrent is bankrupt and questions its legitimacy in the light of Christian principles.

Why I Leave the F.O.R.

Historically the Fellowship of Reconciliation is an organization of pacifists, born during the war, and holding to the Quaker position on war beyond the confines of the Quaker fellowship. In a sense the Fellowship has been a kind of Quaker conventicle inside of the traditional church. Gradually the effort to present a Christian testimony against war forced an increasingly large number of F.O.R. members to oppose the capitalistic social system as a breeder of war and injustice. As long as they could believe that the injustice of capitalism could be abolished by moral suasion there seemed to be no particular conflict between their pacifism and their socialism. They held to the generally accepted position of Christian socialists who believed that the peculiar contribution of religion to the social struggle must be an insistence upon nonviolent or even noncoercive methods of social change. In the recent poll of the membership it was revealed that 21 per cent of the membership still believed that the Fellowship should endeavor through 'method of love' to bring about a new social order 'without identifying itself with either the underprivileged or the privileged class'.

This position probably mirrors quite accurately the conviction of a very considerable portion of the liberal Protestant Church, which has not yet recognized that it is practically impossible to be completely neutral in a social struggle and that the effort at neutrality is morally more dangerous in a class conflict than in an international war because it works to the advantage of entrenched interests against advancing forces.

NEUTRALITY IN THE CLASS STRUGGLE

Another 22 per cent of the Fellowship believe in 'identifying itself with the just aims of the workers' but 'without the use of any form of coercion'. Taking these two groups together we find that almost half of the Fellowship disavows any form of coercion. Since this type of ethical perfectionism is not related with any ascetic withdrawal from the world, which might give it consistency, it may be assumed that it is a good revelation of the failure of liberal protestantism to recognize the coercive character of political and economic life. To refuse the use of any coercive methods means that it is not recognized that everyone is using them all the time, that we all live in and benefit or suffer from a political and economic order that maintains its cohesion partially by the use of various forms of political and economic coercion.

THE DISMISSAL OF MR MATTHEWS

Another group in the Fellowship (47 per cent to be exact) believes in the use of some form of coercion short of violence. One part of the group believes in 'assisting the organization of the workers and in leading them in strikes for a living wage' and also in organizing them into a political party that will use 'nonviolent political and economic coercive measures' and a smaller number in this group go as far as willingness to support the workers in an armed conflict but without themselves participating in the attendant violence in any way.

If the two groups that abjure any form of coercion and those which will not participate in any type of violent coercion are taken together, they represent about 90 per cent of the Fellowship. This is quite natural and logical in an organization of pacifists. It is idle, therefore, to make it appear that the action of the council, which dismissed J. B. Matthews from his position as secretary, was in any sense irregular or unfair. It was the only logical step for the Fellowship to take. Furthermore, though I share, roughly speaking, the political position of Mr Matthews, I do not agree with the publicity that those who are supporting him have released since the dismissal.

I am not a good enough Marxian to declare that convictions are determined purely by class interests and that every pacifist is therefore a conscious or unconscious tool of capitalism. I think it is quite probable that there are wealthy Quakers who abhor all violence without recognizing to what degree they are the beneficiaries of an essentially violent system. In fact, I have known Philadelphia Quakers to give hearty approval to Mr Hoover's treatment of the bonus army. At the same time I am not willing to attribute to men like Nevin Sayre, John

Haynes Holmes, and Kirby Page, who represent the middle section of the Fellowship and who believe in the use of nonviolent coercion as a means of attaining social justice, the 'class interests' that have been ascribed to them by those who opposed them.

The pacifist position, whether in its pure form of nonresistance or in the more qualified form of nonviolent resistance, has always been held by a minority in the Christian church. It may be plausibly argued that such pacifism will benefit entrenched interests more than it will help the proponents of a higher social justice when the day of crisis comes. But to suggest that it is dictated by class interests not only does injustice to these courageous champions of justice, but it presses the economic interpretation of history to precisely that point where it becomes absurd. Anyone who recognizes the terrible tension between the Christian ideal of love and the hard realities of life is certainly bound to respect the effort of those who, recognizing the horrors of violence, make non-violence an absolute in their social ethic.

WE ARE NOT PACIFIST!

While respecting this position of the pure and the qualified pacifists, I am bound to admit that I cannot share their position. For this reason I am forced to associate myself with 20 per cent of the Fellowship who are pacifists only in the sense that they will refuse to participate in an international armed conflict. Perhaps it would clear the issue if we admitted that we were not pacifists at all. We probably all recognize the terrible possibilities of violence. We regard an international armed conflict as so suicidal that we are certain that we will not participate in it.

In the case of the social struggle that is being waged between the privileged and the disinherited classes in every Western nation, some of us, at least, know that there are possibilities that modern civilization will drift into barbarism with the disintegration of the capitalistic system. We believe that not only fascism but communism has the perils of barbarism in it. The peril of the latter arises not so much from its preaching of violence as from its preaching of hatred. Hatred is very blinding; and those who are blind cannot be good enough statesmen to become the instruments of a new unity amid the complexities of Western civilization. We would certainly have as much sense of responsibility toward the avoidance of barbaric civil strife as any other intelligent and responsible person.

The reason we cannot, in spite of our scruples, maintain our connection with the majority of the Fellowship is because we regard all problems of social morality in pragmatic rather than absolute terms. The only absolute law that we recognize is the law of love, and that is an ideal that transcends all law. The purely Marxian section of this 10 per cent minority would probably not recognize the validity of the ideal of love at all. They would think of the social struggle simply as a contest between two classes in which the one class is fated to play the role of creating a classless society. Those of us who are Christian Marxians would renounce some of the utopianism implied in this belief. We believe rather that the world of nature and history is a world in which egoism, collective and individual, will never be completely overcome and in which the law of love will remain both an ideal for which men must strive and a criterion that will convict every new social structure of imperfection.

A PRAGMATIC PROBLEM

We realize that the problem of social justice is a pragmatic and even a technical one. Modern capitalism breeds injustice because of the disproportions of economic power that it tolerates and upon which it is based. We expect no basic economic justice without a destruction of the present disproportion of power and we do not expect the latter without a social struggle. Once we have accepted the fact of the reality of the social struggle we do not feel that we can stop where the middle portion of the Fellowship has stopped. We are unable to stop there because we can find no stable absolute in the shifting situation of the social struggle where everything must be finally decided in pragmatic terms.

If we should agree with one portion of this middle section that we will use nonviolent coercion in behalf of the disinherited but will discourage any coercion that may issue in violence, we feel that we would give an undue moral advantage to that portion of the community which is always using nonviolent coercion against the disinherited. This is precisely what the liberal church is constantly tempted to do. It is furthermore usually oblivious to the fact that nonviolence may be covert violence. Children do starve and old people freeze to death in the poverty of our cities, a poverty for which everyone who has more than the bare necessities of life must feel some responsibility.

We cannot agree with another group of these qualified pacifists who would participate in an armed social conflict but who would not personally participate in its violence, contenting themselves with non-combatant services, because we have come to believe that such an attitude represents an abortive effort to maintain personal purity while holding an organic relation to a social movement that is bound to result in some degree of violence in the day of crisis.

IS THIS DIVISION ACADEMIC?

The outsider may think that those careful definitions of just what degree of violence or nonviolence one accepts in a social struggle represent academic hairsplitting. I quite admit that this discussion as to just what any of us would do in the day of crisis is very unrealistic in many ways. As a Marxian and as a Christian it reveals to me the futility of finding a moral absolute in the relativities of politics. If anyone should suggest that those of us who have thus renounced the pacifist position ought not any longer to regard ourselves as Christian, I would answer that it is only a Christianity that suffers from modern liberal illusions that has ever believed that the law of love could be made an absolute guide of conduct in social morality and politics. As a Marxian and as a Christian I recognize the tragic character of man's social life, and the inevitability of conflict in it arising from the inability of man ever to bring his egoism completely under the dominion of conscience.

As a Marxian I will try to guide that conflict to a goal that guarantees a basic economic justice and creates a society that makes modern technical civilization sufferable. As a Christian I will know that even the justice of a socialist commonwealth will reveal the imperfections of natural man and will not destroy the contest of wills and interests which will express itself in every society. As a Christian I will achieve at least enough contrition before the absolute demands that God makes upon me and that I never completely fulfil to be able to deal with those who oppose me with a measure of forgiveness. Christianity means more than any moral attitude that can express itself in social politics. But it must at least mean that the social struggle is fought without hatred. Nonhatred is a much more important sign and symbol of Christian faith than non-violence.

THE CHOICE OF THE RADICAL

To make the matter short, the Fellowship controversy has revealed that there are radical Christians who can no longer express themselves in pacifist terms. For some of them pacifism was the last remnant of Christianity in their radicalism. With pacifism dissipated they are inclined to disavow their Christian faith or to be quiescent about it. Others of us have merely discovered the profundity of the Christian faith when we ceased to interpret it in merely moralistic demands.

I think we ought to leave the Fellowship of Reconciliation with as good grace as possible. Perhaps we could even prove that there are some of the fruits of the spirit within us by leaving without rancor and without impugning ignoble motives to our comrades to whom we are bound in many cases by inseparable ties of common purpose and affection. In so far as we are radical Christians we must find a more solid ground for the combination of radicalism and Christianity than the creed of pacifism supplied. But we will always maintain our respect for the purity of purpose that animates the men who conceived the Fellowship of Reconciliation and will carry it on in spite of discouragement in these critical days. Perhaps the day will come when we will be grateful for their counsels.

Recognizing, as liberal Christianity does not, that the world of politics is full of demonic forces, we have chosen on the whole to support the devil of vengeance against the devil of hypocrisy. In the day in which we live, a dying social system commits the hypocrisy of hiding its injustices behind the forms of justice, and the victims of injustice express their politics in terms of resentment against this injustice. As Marxians we support this resentment against the hypocrisy. As Christians we know that there is a devil in the spirit of vengeance as well as in the spirit of hypocrisy. For that reason we respect those who try to have no traffic with devils at all. We cannot follow them because we believe that consistency would demand flight to the monastery if all the devils of man's collective life were to be avoided. But our traffic with devils may lead to corruption, and the day may come when we will be grateful for those who try to restrain all demons rather than choose between them.

A. A. MILNE

1882–1956

A. A. MILNE is best known to Americans, and even to the British public, as a writer of children's stories and poems, but his literary career as a novelist, dramatist, and journalist is generally overlooked. No less so are his activities as a pacifist between the two world wars, and his renunciation of that position when war broke out. His best-known book on the subject is *Peace with Honour*, published in 1934. From that work 'Onward, Christian Soldiers' is taken, displaying in defence of the pacifist position that combination of gravity and humour which characterized most of his writings. However, in 1940 he agreed to write a piece for the government which would explain to the public the reasons for his defection from the pacifist ranks. That short work he entitled *War with Honour*, even its title suggesting the road he had come; the position he took in that work is typical of the position taken by many other leading figures who found extenuating circumstances in the situation and who renounced their opposition to war upon the outbreak of actual fighting.

Onward, Christian Soldiers

I

Which is the truth about war: Ruskin's or Sydney Smith's? If Sydney Smith is right in saying 'God is forgotten in war – every principle of Christian charity trampled upon', it seems strange that Christianity has not yet had the faith or the courage to repudiate war. Right and Wrong are not just distinctions made for our children, so that the house can be kept quiet for Father to enjoy his sleep on a Sunday afternoon; nor are they high-sounding synonyms for Convenience and In-convenience. Whether he base his faith on the Ten Commandments or the Sermon on the Mount, the Christian is pledged to some ultimate standard of reference by which he conducts his life. If the conduct of his life is to include excursions into 'armed conflict', he must bring armed conflict to the measure of his own standard.

In this chapter, then, I propose to bring the war-convention to the measure of Christianity.

If, at times, I seem to be exhorting, cross-examining, reproaching the churches, and, more particularly, the Church of England; if, throughout, I seem to be assuming, both in my readers and myself, an acceptance of orthodox beliefs, it is only because, in the first case, the Church is the official exponent of Right and Wrong, and because, in the second case, a belief in Right and Wrong is, for my present purpose, the only orthodoxy which matters. When I speak of a Christian, I speak of anyone who finds in Christ's teaching his ideal of goodness.

The Churches have accepted war in just the way in which they have accepted epidemic disease. Nobody likes, or encourages, an outbreak of typhoid fever in his village, but, as the Vicar will point out in his next sermon, these trials are sent to us by God. In a particular case, of course, the trial may be attributed, more directly, to the neglect of a landlord or the wilful ignorance of the cottagers. If so, all good men will condemn the landlord or the cottagers. But although at times we are responsible for it, although at times we can prevent it, and always we can fight it, yet disease is an integral part of the world into which God has put us; and an outbreak of typhoid fever, however regrettable, is not necessarily a matter either for repentance or for remorse.

Just so do the Churches regard war. A particular war in which one's own country is engaged may be attributed to the wickedness of the enemy; a particular war in which two other countries are engaged may be attributed to the wickedness of both countries. Wicked things are done in war; by individuals (alas!) of all nations, and by the Governments of all nations but one's own. We should do our utmost, therefore, to prevent war. But an outbreak of war, however regrettable, is not *necessarily* a matter either for repentance or for remorse. War is an integral part of the world into which God has put us.

In short, whenever official Christianity has condemned a war, it has condemned *a* war. Not war.

In the first chapter of this book I described a war. Official Christianity condemned it unsparingly. English Christianity denounced the wickedness of Germany as fearlessly as German Christianity denounced the wickedness of England and the wickedness of Russia. Actually, the war would seem to have been started by Austria; but the Viennese are a gay people, their music is light and tuneful, and it was charitable to assume that they didn't quite know what they were up to. Even so, however, Servian Christianity spoke out finely on the subject. Let us, then, leave this particular war on which official Christianity has delivered its verdict, and consider a typical war. In fact, the war-convention.

Two nations are in dispute about something. One has it and the other claims it. Or neither has it and both claim it. It seems to be, and may in fact be to the material advantage of either to enforce possession of it. They talk; they threaten; but neither will give way. A 'state of war' is thereupon declared between them. From this moment a contest begins in which it is the aim of the nationals of one country to kill and mutilate, by certain agreed methods, as many as possible of the nationals of the other country, ignoring for this purpose any of God's commandments which seem to stand in the way. Incident to the contest, and accidental in the sense that a combatant, an explosive or a policy has gone further than was officially intended, are the rape, the blowing to pieces and the starvation of women and children in carefully unrecorded numbers. The contest (it is understood beforehand) is won by the nation whose Government accepts the slaughter of its men, women and children with the greater fortitude, and it is naturally a matter for constant prayer among the faithful that the slaughter of the opposing nationals shall be so intensified by God's help as to become beyond bearing. When, after a lapse of months or years, the fortitude of one Government gives way, the Government of the winning nation settles the original cause of dispute by taking as much of the loser's wealth or territory as it can profitably assimilate. . . .

This is War. No Church condemns it. Bishops approve heartily of it. Accredited Chaplains accompany the combatants to see that the religious side of their life is not neglected.

What does it all mean? Does one laugh or does one cry?

II

I said in an earlier chapter of this book that I wanted to make people think as I do about war. What I am really trying to make them do is to think again, *and from the beginning*, about war. So many of our beliefs are traditional beliefs which we have inherited without examination. The torture of prisoners until they confessed to a crime which they had not committed used to be accepted by Christians as natural, time-hallowed, approved of God. It seems now as if they were mistaken. If they have also been mistaken all these years about war, it need not be a matter for shocked surprise. The wisdom of our forefathers has proved again and again to be folly; their humanity, bestiality; their ideas of honour and justice things to weep over. To think as so many, perhaps unconsciously, think: 'War must be justifiable if the united opinion of mankind has accepted it for all these centuries' is to forget the abominations which mankind after 'all these centuries', has only just managed to reject. War has not lasted so very much longer than slavery and the rack and the burning of heretics.

I invite the Church, which has so recently lost its faith in the rack and the stake, to make an effort to lose its faith in war.

The Church, we may assume, regards murder as a sin against God. In most cases murder is an attempt by an individual to end a situation which can only be ended by the removal of some other individual. The sole reason for the murder is that the death of this other will preserve or increase the wealth, happiness or safety of the murderer.

War is an attempt by an organized group of people to end a situation which can be ended only by the removal of some other group's opposition. This opposition can be removed only by the killing of large numbers of the opposing group. The sole reason for the killing is that the deaths of these people will (it is assumed) preserve or increase the wealth, happiness or safety of the group to which the killers belong.

The motive for war, then, would seem to be identical with the motive for murder, the result to be the same, but multiplied a million times. It would seem that, if it be wrong to kill one other man who gets in the way, it must be wrong to kill a million other men who get in the way. Yet the Church says that it is not wrong. Let us ask somebody why.

M: Well?

C (*but whether the Archbishop of Canterbury or his humblest Curate; whether Canon, Clergyman or Christian, I cannot say*): To begin with, you are entirely ignoring the vital distinction between aggressive and defensive war.

M: Does the Church make this distinction?

C: Of course. Just as it makes the obvious distinction between the attempt to murder and the attempt to resist murder. If a man makes an unprovoked assault upon me with a knife, I am entitled to resist, and if I can only save myself by taking his life, both the Church and the Law will absolve me.

M: But they will not absolve the would-be murderer?

C: Of course not.

M: What you mean, then, is that, if a country wantonly attacks another country, the Church will absolve the defending country of the lives it takes in its own defence?

C: Precisely.

M: And denounce and condemn the attacking country?

C: Certainly.

M: Has the Church of England ever denounced England for this reason?

C: I am proud to think that it has never had occasion to.

M: Even the Boer War was a war of defence? An attempt to resist invasion – murder – attack – defeat – what?

C: I think it would be right to say that the Christian conscience was a little disturbed by some of the – er – undercurrents of the Boer War, but —

M: But the Church didn't actually denounce England?

C: No.

M: Has any national Church ever denounced its own country?

C: That I cannot say.

M: It would almost seem, wouldn't it, that the 'vital distinction' is not between aggression and defence, but between one's own country and the enemy's country?

C: There is nothing to prevent a Christian being a patriot.

M: The point is, which comes first in his mind? Patriotism or Christianity? Which gives way to the other?

C: Nothing can come before a man's duty to his God. But just as a devoted son will, without intention, judge his mother over-leniently, so a Christian may, without intention, judge his country over-leniently.

M: The Church of Rome, you say, is not a national Church?

C: No.

M: The Pope has no national prejudices?

C: I imagine not.

M: Since the last war cannot have been a completely defensive war on the part of all nations, one nation at least must have merited the condemnation of Christ. Did the Vicar of Christ condemn that nation? Did he threaten to excommunicate all Catholics who fought for that nation? Did he denounce them as murderers?

C: As head of an international Church the Pope is in a difficult position. I imagine that it his endeavour to avoid judging between nations.

M: Then since the Head of an international Church avoids judging between nations, and the Head of a national Church avoids condemning his own nation, it would seem that the vital distinction between the aggressive nation and the defensive nation is not only ignored by me, but also by the Churches.

C: I cannot admit that.

M: Very well, then. Let us assume that England, alone among nations, fights only wars that are defensive.

C: I cannot admit anything else.

M: And that all the clergy of all the other countries have continuously neglected their duty by failing to denounce her aggressors.

C: Well – er –

M: And that in resisting her aggressors England takes human lives in great numbers.

C: It is inevitable.

M: Generally speaking, the Church holds the view that human life is sacred?

C: Yes.

M: So sacred that a man may not even take his own life to end intolerable pain or unhappiness?

C: The Church condemns suicide, yes.

M: Because each of us is in God's hands, and it is for him to decide when death shall come?

C: Yes.

M: Then either war takes the decision out of God's hands, in which case it is a sin, or war is ordained by God, and we are not responsible for it. Which?

C: Of course we are responsible; but whatever the Churches have said or not said in the past, I am convinced that God Himself, who knows all hearts, will distinguish between those who deliberately make war, and those who merely repel it.

M: 'Repelling war' means, does it not, accepting the ordeal of battle? Even if this entails the loss of a million sacred lives, it is not a sin?

C: The mere fact of causing the death of a human being is not necessarily a sin. If it were so, then the execution of a murderer would be a sin.

M: Roughly speaking, you would compare murder and capital

punishment with (say) the invasion of a country and the repulsion of the invaders?

c: Roughly, yes.

m: But is not the sole moral justification of capital punishment the fact that it *saves* lives? Is not the argument that, if there were no executions, there would be many more murders? And is not this the only possible argument for the Church to admit?

c: Yes, I think perhaps that is true.

m: On the other hand, the acceptance of the ordeal of battle is certain to bring about thousands of deaths which would not otherwise have occurred. What is the moral justification of that?

c: Are you really suggesting that England should totally ignore a declaration of war, and make no defence whatever to an armed invasion?

m: I am suggesting that you should give me the views of a Christian Church, not of the Navy League.

c: To any Christian the idea of accepting passively such a wrong is intolerable.

m: In the sense that who can't suffer what?

c: Do you really mean that you are prepared for a German army to march through the streets of London, for Germany to dictate whatever humiliating terms she pleases, to exact indemnities, to make unlawful annexations, to —

m: Please, *please* pull yourself together! I am not prepared for, in the sense of being happily acquiescent in, any of these things. In fact, I should hate them. It would be easy to feel intensely humiliated by them. But then it is easy for an author to feel intensely humiliated whenever his play is rejected or his novel is a failure. It is easy for a clerk to hate being dictated to by a bullying employer. Even a clergyman can feel humiliated by the emptiness of his church or the reproof of his Bishop. But we don't go killing people in order to relieve, or prevent, our humiliation. Whence do you get this extraordinary Christian idea that, though Man must suffer all things rather than do wrong, a Nation can do all the wrong it likes rather than suffer anything?

c: I think you exaggerate.

m: For Heaven's sake, and the Church's sake, don't let me exaggerate. Let us get at the truth. If in 1940 a re-armed Germany, thirsting for revenge, declared war on England, you would approve of England taking up arms in defence?

c: She would be reluctantly forced to.

m: Which being so, you would approve?

c: Yes.

m: And approve of her killing as many Germans – men, women and children – as were necessary?

c: Yes, men; but certainly not women and children.

m: Please be honest about it. You know that aeroplanes are used in war; you know that a nation which accepts the ordeal of battle uses all the weapons of war; you know that, if aeroplanes are used, women and children are killed. You would approve, then, of your country killing as many Germans – men, women and children – as were necessary to break the enemy's spirit and end the war?

c: As many (alas!) as were inevitable, but no more, I hope, than were necessary.

m: And you would not call that sort of killing murder?

c: No.

m: Suppose that the war became general, new alliances were formed, and in the end our only hope of victory lay in the armed support of Russia. Suppose that Russia made it a condition of her support that the English people should renounce God – as, officially, she herself has done. Would the Church approve of a solemn renunciation of God by the Government on behalf of the people?

c: Are you deliberately trying to insult the Church?

m: Put it that I am deliberately trying to see if the Church *can* be insulted. Well?

c: The answer is No.

m: Suppose it were Turkey, and it was thought that the Turks would fight better if officially we became Mohammedans, and all shared the same religious enthusiasms? Would you approve?

c: The answer is No.

m: We could always change back after the war was over.

c: And add a lie to the sin on our soul?

m: But you don't object to lies, surely? You never have objected in any other war. Or did you really think that all the bulletins from the Front were true?

c: I admit sadly that in war —

m: May I take it as definite, then, that the Church would not approve of England renouncing Christianity or embracing Mohammedanism, even if these were the only ways of avoiding defeat?

c: You may.

m: And that, rather than consent to a recantation of your faith, you would be prepared for a German army to march through London, for Germany to dictate whatever humiliating terms she pleased, to exact indemnities, to make unlawful annexations, to —

c: Certainly.

m: You see what I am looking for, don't you? The point where Christianity ends and Patriotism begins. Let us go on looking for it. Suppose that in 1920 an inspired statesman had foreseen this war of 1940; had been convinced that it would be a war of attrition; and had realized that England's only hope lay in a *maximum* increase of population. Suppose that the Government had passed a law requiring immediate marriage and begetting of children from all adult males; and, since this would leave two million females still unmarried, had called for two million volunteers to commit adultery: Would the Church have approved?

c: Does that require an answer?

m: Most urgently. The Church has already said that it approves of murder on behalf of the State; I want to know if it approves of adultery.

c: I have already said that I do not call it murder.

m: But then you needn't call it adultery. You could call it 'Enlisting as a Temporary Husband'. *Pro Patria* . . . Well?

c: You know perfectly well what the answer is.

m: I assure you on my honour that I do not.

(And so, not knowing what the answer is, I shall not attempt to give it.)

But I hope that it was beginning to be clear whither the argument was leading us. It is difficult to see how a Church, which approves deliberate killing so long as it is *pro patria*, can afford to be horrified at deliberate adultery which is also *pro patria*. It is equally difficult at the moment, to imagine the Church of England giving its blessing to adultery, however patriotically conceived. If we try to reconcile these two difficulties, we shall come inevitably to the conclusion that the killing is approved because it is the conventional way of exhibiting patriotism, and that the adultery is only condemned because there is no tradition of patriotism behind it. For, logically, if a man puts his country before his God, he is bound to add acceptance of adultery and recantation to his acceptance of killing; and equally bound to reject all three if he puts his God first.

III

To a famous Churchman of an earlier day are attributed these words:

> Had I but served my God with half the zeal
> I served my King, he would not in mine age
> Have left me naked to mine enemies.

It is strange that he should have thought this. The Church today seems pledged to the belief that service to King and Country, whatever unlovely shape it takes, is, in some odd but inevitable way, service to God. A creed so startling demands Divine authority, and Divine authority is found in two texts from the gospels, recording the words of Christ. It is not suggested, of course, that Christ actually had the Great War in his mind when he spoke the words, but the words do show, as a Christian gentleman assured the world the other day, 'what Christ thought of Pacifists'.

1. 'When a strong man armed keepeth his palace, his goods are in peace.' Luke xi. 21.

The Christian apologist for war stops there, conveniently, hoping that the irreligious Pacifist doesn't read his Bible. For the next verse says: 'But when a stronger than he shall come upon him, and overcome him, he taketh from him all his armour wherein he trusted, and divideth his spoils'; which seems to show what Christ thought of Militarists. For the occasion of these words was the casting out of a devil; and, as will be remembered, some of the people said: 'He casteth out devils through Beelzebub the chief of the devils.' Whereupon Christ explained that Satan could not cast out Satan, and that devils could be cast out by only somebody stronger than themselves. So, in the parable which follows, the 'strong man armed' is Beelzebub, and the 'stronger than he' who takes from him 'all his armour wherein he trusted' is God. It is not altogether out of keeping with Christ's character as we know it to suppose that armour did not make any very powerful appeal to him; and it is not out of keeping with the situation to assume that the miracle of healing which he had just performed was not meant as a preliminary to the use of mustard gas.

However, Christ also said this:

2. 'Render unto Caesar the things which are Caesar's; and unto God the things that are God's.' Matthew xxii. 21.

This much-quoted text is generally held to justify the partition of one's soul. One cannot serve God and Mammon, no; but Caesar and God, yes, even when they seem to beckon in opposite directions.

Now the interesting thing about these words of Christ's is that they were not said to the Romans but to the Jews; and the Jews were a conquered race. Their conquerors were ruling in Jerusalem: just as (in the apprehension of the patriot) the Germans will be ruling in London, if we don't get some more aeroplanes. Now if we can imagine Christ coming to London at some future time when England has surrendered to Germany, and if we can imagine Mr Winston Churchill asking Him if we ought meekly to pay the indemnity exacted of us, and if Christ replied: 'Render unto Hitler the things which are Hitler's; and unto God the things that are God's,' we can see that Mr Churchill's patriotic spirit would not be greatly encouraged. What he would want to be told would be that the secret poison-gas factory at Gleneagles and the un-disclosed treaty with Switzerland justified an armed repudiation of the terms of Peace. And he has been told precisely the opposite.

For if Christ's answer is more than an escape from a dilemma, it is saying clearly: 'What matter if we are a conquered race, so long as we continue to serve God?'

It is doubtful, then, whether either of these texts really gives that Divine authority to war which the Christian must surely ask. Possibly the authority is given in some other words of Christ's which I have overlooked. (For instance: 'if thy right hand offend thee, cut it off' may have referred to the fact that Germany is on the right hand of France, looking towards the North Pole.) But even if I found the words, I should still be uncertain as to what interpretation I was meant to put on them. For there seem to be two possible theories which could be advanced in justification of Christianity's approval of war, and I do not know which of them my text should favour.

THEORY A: *Obedience to the State is God's first law, and takes precedence of all other laws which He has made.*

THEORY B: *What is called the Safety of the State is of such importance in God's sight that He holds a nation to be justified in using any means to achieve it.*

The difference between these two theories will be clear if we consider certain practical, though extravagant, applications of them.

Under Theory A:

A Government (either from sheer wilfulness or for the most patriotic reasons) orders, and obtains, a general indulgence in incest.

Then:

1. The members of the Government have to answer to God for their sin.

2. The people are absolved. (Unless they refuse to commit incest: in which case they have broken God's first law.)

Under Theory B:

A Government orders a general indulgence in incest.

Then:

1. If the order is made from sheer wilfulness, not only the members of the Government, but also the people, are answerable to God for their sin.

2. If the order is necessary for the salvation of the State, nobody is answerable to God, since His sanction is already assured.

[*Note:* As this still leaves it uncertain whether the responsibility of justifying the order is the Government's or the individual's we seem to want two Sub-theories. Under Sub-theory *a*: the individual may accept the Government's plea of necessity, and claim absolution. Under Sub-theory *B*: the individual must refer the plea of necessity to his own conscience.]

But even when we have decided to which of these theories we have found textual justification, there is still the difficulty of deciding at what point in the growth of a community the text begins to apply. It seems certain that, if two people declare war on each other, and throw bombs into each other's houses, the death or mutilation of their families has not the Divine Sanction. Is the sanction, then, given to any two *groups* of people: say, to twelve people on a desert island divided into two groups of six? If not, is it given only to communities; or to communities which have the standing of nations? And is the decision when a group becomes a community, or a community becomes a nation, in the hands of God, or in the hands of the latest Peace Conference? Does God wait for Lloyd George and Clemenceau to tell Him which new groups of people are to be allowed a free hand with the Ten Commandments, and are their names then duly registered in Heaven on a special White List?

Much of all this may sound frivolous or far-fetched; but I shall not mind, even if it is called 'facetious' and 'not in the best of taste'. It is designed to make people think again, *and from the beginning*, about war. Modern war means (among other things in this year of grace), quite definitely and without any mental escape, choking and poisoning and torturing to death thousands, probably hundreds of thousands, of women and children. Whether you are Christian or Jew, atheist or agnostic, you have got to fit acceptance of this into your philosophy of life. It is not enough to say: 'What else can nations do?' It is not enough, nor is it even true, to say: 'It has always been so.' Here is the fact now, and you have got to justify to yourself your acceptance of it; and the justification has got to be based on such ultimate truths as will always be sacred to you.

MARTIN BUBER

1878–1965

HAVING first begun his career as a political journalist, Martin Buber – after his 'conversion' to the intellectual and spiritual content of Hasidism – has become one of the great teachers of our time. Born in Vienna in 1878, his first studies at the universities of Vienna and Berlin were in art and philosophy. He was founder (and editor until 1924) of *Der Jude*, the most influential periodical for German-speaking Jews at that time.

In 1938 Buber left Nazi Germany and emigrated to Palestine, where he lived until his death. It was in these first years in the land that was to become Israel that he wrote the letter to Gandhi which is reprinted here. Gandhi had written in *Harijan* (26 November 1938) that the German Jews ought not to use violent resistance to the Nazi terror but ought instead to show their moral superiority by adopting nonviolence. Buber's reply criticized Gandhi for misunderstanding the situation, for making incorrect comparisons between the lot of the German Jews and that of the Indians earlier in South Africa, and for being inconsistent with his own views. It was published in Jerusalem in 1939 and collected in abridged form in *Pointing the Way* (1957), edited by Maurice Friedman.

Buber called for a 'philosophy of dialogue', a new and more open attitude which will mediate between opposing camps in a perilous age, a proposal that such communication between men replace the use of force. He spoke out again and again on this subject, most urgently perhaps in an address at Carnegie Hall in 1952, on one of his three visits to America. The address is also collected in *Pointing the Way* under the title 'Hope for this Hour'.

Letter to Mahatma Gandhi

Mahatma Gandhi,

He who is unhappy lends a deaf ear when idle tongues discuss his fate amongst themselves. But when a voice that he has long known and honoured, a great voice and an earnest one, pierces the vain clamour and calls him by his name, he is all attention. Here is a voice, he thinks, which can but give good counsel and genuine comfort: for he who speaks knows what suffering is: he knows that the sufferer is more in need of comfort than of counsel; and he has both the wisdom to counsel rightly and that simple union of faith and love which alone is the open-sesame to true comforting. But what he hears – containing though it does elements of a noble and most praiseworthy conception such as he expects from this speaker – is yet barren of all application to his peculiar circumstances. These words are in truth not applicable to him at all. They are inspired by most praiseworthy general principles; but the listener is aware that he, the speaker, has cast not a single glance at the situation of him whom he is addressing, that he sees him not nor does he know him and the straits under which he labours. Moreover, inter-mingled with the counsel and the comfort, a third voice makes itself heard drowning both the others, the voice of reproach. It is not that the sufferer disdains to accept reproach in this hour from the man he honours: on the contrary, if only there were mingled with the good counsel and the true comfort a word of just reproach giving to the former a meaning and a reason, he would recognize in the speaker the bearer of a message. But the accusation voiced is another altogether from that which he heard in the storm of events and in the hard beating of his own heart: it is almost the opposite of this. He weighs it and examines it – no, it is not a just one! and the armour of his silence is pierced. The friendly appeal achieves what the enemy's storming has failed to do: he must answer. He exclaims: Let the lords of the ice-inferno affix my name to a cunningly constructed scarecrow; this is the logical outcome of their own nature and the nature of their relations to me. But you, the man of good will, do you not know that you must see him whom you address, in his place and circumstance, in the throes of his destiny?

Jews are being persecuted, robbed, maltreated, tortured, murdered. And you, Mahatma Gandhi, say that their position in the country where they suffer all this is an exact parallel to the position of Indians in South Africa at the time when you inaugurated your famous 'Force of Truth' or 'Strength of the Soul' (Satyagraha) campaign. There the Indians occupied precisely the same place and the persecution there also had a religious tinge. There also the constitution denied equality of rights to the white and the black race including the Asiatics: there also the Indians were assigned to ghettos and the other disqualifications were, at all events, almost of the same type as those of the Jews in Germany. I read and reread these sentences in your article without being able to understand. Although I know them well, I reread your South African speeches and writings and called to mind, with all the attention and imagination at my command, every complaint which you made therein; and I did likewise with the accounts of your friends and pupils at that time; but all this did not help me to understand what you say about us. In the first of your speeches with which I am acquainted, that of 1896, you quoted two particular incidents to the accompaniment of the hisses of your audience: first, that a band of Europeans had set fire to an Indian village shop causing some damage; and second, that another band had thrown burning rockets into an urban shop. If I oppose to this the thousands on thousands of Jewish shops, destroyed and burnt-out, you will perhaps answer that the difference is only one of quantity and that the proceedings were almost of the same type. But, Mahatma, are you not aware of the burning of Synagogues and scrolls of the Law? Do you know nothing of all the sacred property of the community – in part of great antiquity, that has been destroyed in the flames? I am not aware that Boers and Englishmen in South Africa ever injured anything sacred to the Indians. I find further only one other concrete complaint quoted in that speech, namely, that three Indian school-teachers, who were found walking in the streets after 9 p.m. contrary to orders, were arrested and only acquitted later on. That is the only incident of the kind you bring forward. Now do you know or do you not know, Mahatma, what a concentration camp is like and what goes on there? Do you know of the torments in the concentration camp, of its methods of slow and quick slaughter? I cannot assume that you know of this; for then this tragi-comic utterance 'almost of the same type' could scarcely have crossed your lips. Indians were despised and despicably treated in South Africa: but they were not deprived of rights, they were not outlawed, they were not hostages for the coveted attitude of foreign powers. And do you think perhaps that a Jew in Germany could pronounce in public one single sentence of a speech such as yours without being knocked down? Of what significance is it to point to a certain something in common when such differences are overlooked? It does not seem to me convincing when you base your advice to us to observe Satyagraha in Germany on these similarities of circumstances. In the five years which I myself spent under the present régime, I observed many instances of genuine Satyagraha among the Jews, instances showing a strength of spirit wherein there was no question of bartering their rights or of being bowed down, and where neither force nor cunning was used to escape the consequences of their behaviour. Such actions, however, exerted apparently not the slightest influence on their opponents. All honour indeed to those who displayed such strength of soul! But I cannot recognize herein a parole for the general behaviour of German Jews which might seem suited to exert an influence on the oppressed or on the world. An effective stand may be taken in the form of non-violence against unfeeling human beings in the hope of gradually bringing them thereby to their senses; but a diabolic universal steam-roller cannot thus be withstood. There is a certain situation in which from the 'Satyagraha' of the strength of the spirit no 'Satyagraha' of the power of truth can result. The word 'Satyagraha' signifies testimony. Testimony without acknowledgement, ineffective, unobserved martyrdom, a martyrdom cast to the winds – that is the fate of innumerable Jews in Germany. God alone accepts their testimony, God 'seals' it, as is said in our prayers. But no maxim for suitable behaviour can be deduced therefrom. Such martyrdom is a deed – but who would venture to demand it?

But your comparing of the position of the Jews in Germany with that of the Indians in South Africa, compels me to draw your attention to a yet more essential difference. True, I can well believe that you were aware of this difference, great as it is, when you drew the exact parallel. It is obvious that when you think back to your time in South Africa it is a matter of course for you that then as now you always had this great Mother India. That fact was and still is so taken for granted that apparently you are entirely unaware of the fundamental differences existing between nations having such a mother (it need not necessarily be such a great Mother, it may be a tiny motherkin, but yet a mother, a mother's bosom and a mother's heart) and a nation that is orphaned, or to whom one says in speaking of his country: 'This is no more your mother!'

When you were in South Africa, Mahatma, there were living there

150,000 Indians. But in India there were far more than 200 millions! and this fact nourished the souls of the 150,000, whether they were conscious of it or not: they drew from this source their strength to live and their courage to live. Did you ask then as you ask the Jews now, whether they want a double home where they can remain at will? You say to the Jews: if Palestine is their home, they must accustom themselves to the idea of being forced to leave the other parts of the world in which they are settled. Did you also say to the Indians in South Africa that if India is their home, they must accustom themselves to the idea of being compelled to return to India? Or did you tell them that India was not their home? And if – though indeed it is inconceivable that such a thing could come to pass – the hundreds of millions of Indians were to be scattered tomorrow over the face of the earth; and if the day after tomorrow another nation were to establish itself in India and the Jews were to declare that there was yet room for the establishment of a national home for the Indians, thus giving to their diaspora a strong organic concentration and a living centre; should then a Jewish Gandhi – assuming there could be such – answer them, as you answered the Jews: this cry for the national home affords a colourable justification for your expulsion? Or should he teach them, as you teach the Jews: that the India of the Vedic conception is not a geographical tract, but that it is in your hearts? A land about which a sacred book speaks to the sons of the land is never merely in their hearts; a land can never become a mere symbol. It is in the hearts because it is the prophetic image of a promise to mankind: but it would be a vain metaphor if Mount Zion did not actually exist. This land is called 'Holy'; but this is not the holiness of an idea, it is the holiness of a piece of earth. That which is merely an idea and nothing more cannot become holy; but a piece of earth can become holy just as a mother's womb can become holy.

Dispersion is bearable: it can even be purposeful, if somewhere there is ingathering, a growing home centre, a piece of earth wherein one is in the midst of an ingathering and not in dispersion and from whence the spirit of ingathering may work its way out to all the places of the dispersion. When there is this, there is also a striving, common life, the life of a community which dares to live today because it hopes to live tomorrow. But when this growing centre, this increasing process of ingathering is lacking, dispersion becomes dismemberment. On this criterion the question of our Jewish destiny is indissolubly bound up with the possibility of ingathering and this in Palestine.

You ask : 'Why should they not, like other nations of the earth, make that country their home where they are born and where they earn their livelihood?' Because their destiny is different from that of all other nations of the earth : it is a destiny which in truth and justice should not be imposed on any nation on earth. For their destiny is dispersion, not the dispersion of a faction and the preservation of the main substance as in the case of other nations ; it is dispersion without the living heart and centre ; and every nation has a right to demand the possession of a living heart. It is different, because a hundred adopted homes without one original and natural one render a nation sick and miserable. It is different because although the well-being and the achievement of the individual may flourish on step-mother soil, the nation as such must languish. And just as you, Mahatma, wish that not only should all Indians be able to live and work, but that also Indian substance, Indian wisdom and Indian truth should prosper and be fruitful, so do we wish this for the Jews. For you there is no need to be aware, that the Indian substance could not prosper without the Indian's attachment to the mother-soil and without his ingathering therein. But we know what is the essential : we know it because it is just this that is denied us or was, at least, up to the generation which has just begun to work at the redemption of the mother-soil.

But this is not all : because for us, for the Jews who think as I do, painfully urgent as it is, it is indeed not the decisive factor. You say, Mahatma Gandhi, that to support the cry for a national home which 'does not make much appeal to you', a sanction is 'sought in the Bible'. No – this is not so. We do not open the Bible and seek therein sanction. The opposite is true : the promises of return, of re-establishment, which have nourished the yearning hope of hundreds of generations, give those of today an elementary stimulus, recognized by few in its full meaning but effective also in the lives of so many who do not believe in the message of the Bible. Still this too is not the determining factor for us who, although we do not see divine revelation in every sentence of Holy Scripture, yet trust in the spirit which inspired their speakers. Decisive for us is not the promise of the Land – but the command, the fulfilment of which is bound up with the land, with the existence of a free Jewish community in this country. For the Bible tells us and our inmost knowledge testifies to it, that once, more than 3,000 years ago, our entry into this land was in the consciousness of a mission from above to set up a just way of life through the generations of our people, such a way of life as can be realized not by individuals in the sphere of their private existence but only by a nation in the establishment of its society: communal ownership of the land,[1] regularly recurrent levelling of social distinc-tions,[2] guarantee of the independence of each individual,[3] mutual help,[4] a common Sabbath embracing serf and beast as beings with equal claim,[5] a Sabbatical year whereby, letting the soil rest, everybody is admitted to the free enjoyment of its fruits.[6] These are not practical laws thought out by wise men; they are measures which the leaders of the nation, apparently themselves taken by surprise and overpowered have found to be the set task and condition for taking possession of the land. No other nation has ever been faced at the beginning of its career with such a mission. Here is something which allows of no forgetting, and from which there is no release. At that time we did not carry out what was imposed upon us: we went into exile with our task unper-formed: but the command remained with us and it has become more urgent than ever. We need our own soil in order to fulfil it: we need the freedom of ordering our own life: no attempt can be made on foreign soil and under foreign statute. It may not be that the soil and the freedom for fulfilment be denied us. We are not covetous, Mahatma: our one desire is that at last we may obey.

Now you may well ask whether I speak for the Jewish people when I say 'we'. I speak only for those who feel themselves entrusted with the commission of fulfilling the command of justice delivered to Israel of the Bible. Were it but a handful – these constitute the pity of the nation and the future of the people depends on them; for the ancient mission of the nation lives on in them as the cotyledon in the core of the fruit. In this connexion I must tell you that you are mistaken when you assume that in general the Jews of today believe in God and derive from their faith guidance for their conduct. Jewry of today is in the throes of a serious crisis in the matter of faith. It seems to me that the lack of faith of present day humanity, its inability truly to believe in God, finds its concentrated expression in this crisis of Jewry: here all is darker, more fraught with danger, more fateful than anywhere else in the world. Neither is this crisis resolved here in Palestine; indeed we recognize its severity here even more than elsewhere among Jews. But at the same time we realize that here alone can it be resolved. There is no solution to be found in the life of isolated and abandoned individuals, although one may hope that

1. Lev. 25, 23.   4. Ex. 23, 4 ff.
2. Lev. 25, 13.   5. Ex. 23, 12.
3. Ex. 21, 24.   6. Lev. 25, 5-7.

the spark of faith will be kindled in their great need. The true solution can only issue from the life of a community which begins to carry out the will of God, often without being aware of doing so, without believing that God exists and this is His will. It may be found in this life of the community if believing people support it who neither direct nor demand, neither urge nor preach, but who share the life, who help, wait and are ready for the moment when it will be their turn to give the true answer to the inquirer. This is the innermost truth of the Jewish life in the Land; perhaps it may be of significance for the solution of this crisis of faith not only for Jewry but for all humanity. The contact of this people with this Land is not only a matter of sacred ancient history: we sense here a secret still more hidden.

You, Mahatma Gandhi, who know of the connexion between tradition and future, should not associate yourself with those who pass over our cause without understanding or sympathy.

But you say – and I consider it to be the most significant of all the things you tell us – that Palestine belongs to the Arabs and that it is therefore 'wrong and inhuman to impose the Jews on the Arabs'.

Here I must add a personal note in order to make clear to you on what premises I desire to consider this matter.

I belong to a group of people who, from the time when Britain conquered Palestine, have not ceased to strive for the concluding of genuine peace between Jew and Arab.

By a genuine peace we inferred and still infer that both peoples should together develop the Land without the one imposing his will on the other. In view of the international usages of our generation this appeared to us to be very difficult but not impossible. We were well aware and still are, that in this unusual – yea unexampled case, it is a question of seeking new ways of understanding and cordial agreement between the nations. Here again we stood and still stand under the sway of a commandment.

We considered it a fundamental point, that in this case two vital claims are opposed to each other, two claims of a different nature and a different origin, which cannot be pitted one against the other and between which no objective decision can be made as to which is just or unjust. We considered and still consider it our duty to understand and to honour the claim which is opposed to ours and to endeavour to reconcile both claims. We cannot renounce the Jewish claim; something even higher than the life of our people is bound up with the Land, namely the work which is their divine mission. But we have been and still are convinced that it must be possible to find some form of agreement between this claim and the other; for we love this land and we believe in its future; and, seeing that such love and such faith are surely present also on the other side, a union in the common service of the Land must be within the range of the possible. Where there is faith and love, a solution may be found even to what appears to be a tragic contradiction.

In order to carry out a task of such extreme difficulty – in the recognition of which we have to overcome an internal resistance on the Jewish side, as foolish as it is natural – we are in need of the support of well-meaning persons of all nations, and we had hope of such. But now you come and settle the whole existential dilemma with the simple formula: 'Palestine belongs to the Arabs.'

What do you mean by saying that a land belongs to a population? Evidently you do not intend only to describe a state of affairs by your formula, but to declare a certain right. You obviously mean to say that a people, being settled on the land, has such an absolute claim to the possession of this land that whoever settles in it without the permission of this people, has committed a robbery. But by what means did the Arabs attain to the right of ownership in Palestine? Surely by conquest and, in fact, a conquest by settlement. You therefore admit that this being so, it constitutes for them an exclusive right of possession; whereas the subsequent conquests of the Mamelukes and the Turks which were not conquests with a view to settlement, do not constitute such in your opinion, but leave the former conquering nation in rightful ownership. Thus settlement by force of conquest justifies for you a right of ownership of Palestine; whereas a settlement such as the Jewish one – the methods of which, it is true, though not always doing full justice to Arab ways of life, were, even in the most objectionable cases, far removed from those of conquest – do not justify in your opinion any participation in this right of possession. These are the consequences which result from your statement in the form of an axiom that a land belongs to its population. In an epoch of migration of nations you would first support the right of ownership of the nation that is threatened with dispossession or extermination; but were this once achieved, you would be compelled, not at once, but after the elapse of a suitable number of generations, to admit that the land belongs to the usurper.

Possibly the time is not far removed when – perhaps after a catastrophe the extent of which we cannot yet estimate – the representatives of humanity will have to come to some agreement on the re-establishment of relations between peoples, nations and countries, on the colonization of thinly populated territories as well as on a communal distribution of the necessary raw materials and on a logical intensification of the cultivation of the globe in order to prevent a new, enormously extended migration of nations which would threaten to destroy mankind. Is then the dogma of 'possession', of the inalienable right of ownership, of the sacred status quo to be held up against the men who dare to save the situation? For surely, we are witnesses of how the feeling, penetrating deep into the heart of national life, that this dogma must be opposed, is disastrously misused; but do not those representatives of the most powerful states share the guilt of this misuse, who consider every questioning of the dogma as a sacrilege?

And what if it is not the nations who migrate, but one nation? And what if this migrating nation should yearn towards its ancient home where there is still room for a considerable section of it, enough to form a centre side by side with the people to whom the land now 'belongs'? And what if this wandering nation, to whom the land once belonged, likewise on the basis of a settlement by force of conquest – and who were once driven out of it by mere force of domination, should now strive to occupy a free part of the land, or a part that might become free without encroaching on the living room of others, in order at last to acquire again for themselves a national home – a home where its people could live as a nation? Then you come, Mahatma Gandhi, and help to draw the barriers and to declare 'Hands off! This land does not belong to you!' Instead of helping to establish a genuine peace, giving us what we need without taking from the Arabs what they need, on the basis of a fair adjustment as to what they would really make use of and what might be admitted to satisfy our requirements!

Such an adjustment of the required living room for all is possible if it is brought into line with an all-embracing intensification of the cultivation of the whole soil in Palestine. In the present, helplessly primitive state of fellah agriculture the amount of land needed to produce nourishment for a family is ever so much larger than it otherwise would be. Is it right to cling to ancient forms of agriculture which have become meaningless, to neglect the potential productivity of the soil, in order to prevent the immigration of new settlers without prejudice to the old? I repeat: without prejudice. This should be the basis of the agreement for which we are striving.

You are only concerned, Mahatma, with the 'right of possession' on the one side: you do not consider the right to a piece of free land on the other side – for those who are hungering for it. But there is another of whom you do not inquire and who in justice, i.e. on the basis of the whole perceptible reality, would have to be asked: this other is the soil itself. Ask the soil what the Arabs have done for her in 1,300 years and what we have done for her in 50! Would her answer not be weighty testimony in a just discussion as to whom this land 'belongs'?

It seems to me that God does not give any one portion of the earth away so that the owner thereof may say as God does in the Holy Script: 'Mine is the Land.' Even to the conqueror who has settled on it, the conquered land is, in my opinion, only lent – and God waits to see what he will make of it.

I am told however, I should not respect the cultivated soil and despise the desert, I am told, the desert is willing to wait for the work of her children: we who are burdened with civilization are not recognized by her any more as her children. I have a veneration of the desert; but I do not believe in her absolute resistance, for I believe in the great marriage between man (Adam) and earth (Adama). This land recognizes us, for it is fruitful through us: and through its fruit-bearing for us it recognizes us. Our settlers do not come here as do the colonists from the Occident, with natives to do their work for them: they themselves set their shoulders to the plough, and they spend their strength and their blood to make the land fruitful. But it is not only for ourselves that we desire its fertility. The Jewish peasants have begun to teach their brothers, the Arab peasants, to cultivate the land more intensively; we desire to teach them further: together with them we want to cultivate the land – to 'serve' it as the Hebrew has it. The more fertile this soil becomes, the more space there will be for us and for them. We have no desire to dispossess them: we want to live with them. We do not want to rule, we want to serve with them.

You once said, Mahatma, that politics enmesh us nowadays as with serpent's coils from which there is no escape however hard one may try. You said you desired, therefore, to wrestle with the serpent. Here is the serpent in the fullness of its power! Jews and Arabs both have a claim to this land; but these claims are in fact reconcilable as long as they are

restricted to the measure which life itself allots, and as long as they are
limited by the desire for conciliation – that is, if they are translated into
the language of the needs of living people for themselves and their
children. But instead of this they are turned through the serpent's
influence into claims of principle and politics, and are represented with
all the ruthlessness which politics instils into those that are led by her.
Life with all its realities and possibilities disappears as does the desire for
truth and peace: nothing is known and sensed but the political parole
alone. The serpent conquers not only the spirit but also life. Who would
wrestle with her?

In the midst of your arguments, Mahatma, there is a fine word which
we gratefully accept. We should seek, you say, to convert the heart of
the Arab. Well then – help us to do so! Among us also there are many
foolish hearts to convert – hearts that have fallen a prey to that
nationalist egoism which only admits its own claims. We hope to
achieve this ourselves. But for the other task of conversion we need
your help. Instead, your admonition is only addressed to the Jews,
because they allow British bayonets to defend them against the bomb-
throwers. Your attitude to the latter is much more reserved: you say
you wish the Arabs had chosen the way of non-violence; but, according to the accepted canons of right and wrong there is nothing to be
said against their behaviour. How is it possible that in this case, you
should give credence – if only in a limited form – to the accepted canons,
whereas you have never done so before! You reproach us, that, having
no army of our own, we consent to the British army preventing an
occasional blind murder. But in view of the accepted canons you cast a
lenient eye on those who carry murder into our ranks every day without even noticing who is hit. Were you to look down on all, Mahatma,
on what is done and what is not done on both sides – on the just and the
unjust on both sides – would you not admit that we certainly are not
least in need of your help?

We began to settle on the land anew, thirty-five years before the
'shadow of the British gun' was cast upon it. We did not seek out this
shadow; it appeared and remained here to guard British interests and
not ours. We do not want force. But after the resolutions of Delhi, at
the beginning of March 1922, you yourself, Mahatma Gandhi, wrote:
'Have I not repeatedly said that I would have India become free even by
violence rather than that she should remain in bondage?' This was a
very important pronouncement on your part: you asserted thereby that

non-violence is for you a faith and not a political principle – and that the desire for freedom of India is even stronger in you than your faith. And for this, I love you. We do not want force. We have not proclaimed, as did Jesus, the son of our people, and as you do, the teaching of non-violence, because we believe that a man must sometimes use force to save himself or even more his children. But from time immemorial we have proclaimed the teaching of justice and peace: we have taught and we have learnt that peace is the aim of all the world and that justice is the way to attain it. Thus we cannot desire to use force. No one who counts himself in the ranks of Israel can desire to use force.

But, you say, our non-violence is that of the helpless and the weak. This is not in accordance with the true state of affairs. You do not know or you do not consider what strength of soul, what Satyagraha has been needed for us to restrain ourselves here after years of ceaseless deeds of blind violence perpetrated against us, our wives and our children, and not to answer with like deeds of blind violence. And on the other hand you, Mahatma, wrote in 1922 as follows: 'I see that our non-violence is skin-deep . . . This non-violence seems to be due merely to our helplessness . . . Can true voluntary non-violence come out of this seeming forced non-violence of the weak?' When I read those words at that time, my reverence for you took birth – a reverence so great that even your injustice toward us cannot destroy it.

You say it is a stigma against us that our ancestors crucified Jesus. I do not know whether that actually happened; but I consider it possible. I consider it just as possible as that the Indian people under different circumstances should condemn you to death – if your teachings were more strictly opposed to their own tendencies ('India,' you say, 'is by Nature non-violent'.) Not infrequently do nations swallow up the greatness to which they have given birth. How can one assert, without contradiction, that such action constitutes a stigma! I would not deny however, that although I should not have been among the crucifiers of Jesus, I should also not have been among his supporters. For I cannot help withstanding evil when I see that it is about to destroy the good. I am forced to withstand the evil in the world just as the evil within myself. I can only strive not to have to do so by force. I do not want force. But if there is no other way of preventing the evil destroying the good, I trust I shall use force and give myself up into God's hands.

'India,' you say, 'is by Nature non-violent.' It was not always so. The

Mahabharata is an epos of warlike, disciplined force. In the greatest of its poems, the Bhagavad Gitâ, it is told how Arjuna decides on the battlefield that he will not commit the sin of killing his relations who are opposed to him and he lets fall his bow and arrow. But the God reproaches him saying that such action is unmanly and shameful; there is nothing better for a knight in arms than a just fight.

Is that the truth? If I am to confess what is truth to me, I must say: There is nothing better for a man than to deal justly – unless it be to love; we should be able even to fight for justice – but to fight lovingly.

I have been very slow in writing this letter to you, Mahatma. I made repeated pauses – sometimes days elapsing between short paragraphs – in order to test my knowledge and my way of thinking. Day and night I took myself to task, searching whether I had not in any one point overstepped the measure of self-preservation allotted and even pre-scribed by God to a human community, and whether I had not fallen into the grievous error of collective egoism. Friends and my own conscience have helped to keep me straight whenever danger threatened. Weeks have now passed since then and the time has come, when negotiations are proceeding in the capital of the British Empire on the Jewish-Arab problem – and when, it is said, a decision is to be made. But the true decision in this matter can only come from within and not from without.

I take the liberty therefore of closing this letter without waiting for the result in London.

Martin Buber

Jerusalem, 24 February 1939.

VERA BRITTAIN

1896-

SINCE 1925 and her marriage to the American scholar George Catlin, novelist and essayist Vera Brittain has spent her time between England and America; she has been active in the peace movements of both countries. Born in Newcastle, she went up to Oxford in 1914, but left a year later to become a Red Cross nurse, serving four years in hospitals in London, Malta, and France. Of those years she has written, 'My work and experiences during the war turned me from an ordinary patriotic young woman into a convinced pacifist. . . .' It has been her unfailing conviction that even in the midst of war there is love between peoples, bonds of humanity which the most virulent propaganda can only temporarily submerge.

During the Second World War, which she spent in England, she wrote *Humiliation With Honour*, a collection of wartime letters to her son in the United States explaining to him the reasons for her pacifist faith and the complexities of her position; it is from this book, published in 1943, that this, the fifth letter, 'The Functions of a Minority', has been taken.

The Functions of a Minority

The many logical arguments put forward in support of war do not alter the fact that it is now the deadliest disease of our civilization, and must be overcome if that civilization is to continue. Mere victory over Hitler will not overcome it. It will only serve to aggravate the disease if the wrongs from which Hitlerism sprang – monopoly capitalism, imperialistic nationalism, poverty, hunger, unemployment, repression – continue unchecked into the post-war era. There is little evidence as yet that those who are conducting the war on behalf of the United Nations propose to check them.

Pacifists are people who want to fight the disease, instead of wasting life, time, and energy in attacking the symptoms. They have come by different roads – the best, perhaps, being actual experience of warfare – to the realization that modern war never achieves even the ends for which it is ostensibly waged, let alone a stable world and a peaceful society. Believing this, they would be false to themselves and their faith in man's capacity for redemption if they supported the present war and collaborated with its leaders.

Perhaps you will feel that those who share this conviction and act upon it ought to be specially enlightened people. A few indeed have been; it can justly be said of such men as H. R. L. Sheppard, George Lansbury, and Max Plowman that they were saints on earth. But unfortunately all three of them are dead; and we, their successors, have to struggle on as best we can without their special gifts of religious insight to help us. Often the words which St Paul wrote to the Corinthians in the early Church are only too true of modern pacifists: 'For ye are yet carnal: for whereas there is among you envying, and strife, and divisions, are ye not carnal and walk as men?'

Apart from such conflicts – which are, I fear, characteristic of all sinners who are trying to be saints with no better spiritual equipment than other people – there are one or two groups which do the cause of pacifism harm rather than good. I am not speaking here of the few actual shirkers who always manage to creep in war time under the pacifist umbrella. The movement itself objects to them at least as much as the general public, for they cannot be counted on either to carry conviction before a Tribunal, or to lend a hand in a 'Blitz'. They are as disadvantageous to true pacifism as those temporary adherents who wax eloquent in the cause of peace only during the intervals between wars. The two categories about which I meant to write you are the belligerent pacifists, and the self-righteous.

The 'pacifism' of the belligerents is nothing other than a form of inverted militarism. They are incurable minoritarians with a passion for unpopularity, who will make use of any movement which enables them to express their deep dislike of all majorities. Far from attempting to act as reconciling influences, their purpose is usually to challenge and provoke. If they do not succeed in getting themselves persecuted, suppressed, or imprisoned, they are disappointed. They feel that the sole test of their sincerity is the extent to which they can embarrass the government.

Pacifists of this type forget that embarrassing the government, necessary as it may be at times, is hardly a constructive occupation.

There are many important subjects, such as the state of the post-war world, which are vital to all persons of good will and intelligence but in which governments take little interest. You will find that the worse a government is, the less interest it takes.

Apparently it does not occur to these militant pacifists that the most effective method of war resistance is to increase the number of war resisters – who can be drawn only from the ranks of the war supporters, and are not attracted by provocation. The best method of making breaches in the solid wall of war acceptance is the joint consideration by pacifists and non-pacifists of problems in which the evil consequences of war are most apparent. It is clear, for instance, that in the bombing of civilians, and the food blockade of Europe, there is a departure from the standards of international law never equalled in previous wars.

The pacifist's contention that modern war, with its huge apparatus of propaganda, involves a process of spiritual deterioration which destroys such moral purpose as it ever had, is here supported by obvious facts which no reasonable person can deny. But belligerent pacifists regard the making of converts by an assemblage of facts and an appeal to reason as 'being respectable', or 'currying favour with the public'. They do infinite harm to pacifism by giving well-disposed people the impression that the movement is solely composed of irrational, obstinate, and irresponsible fanatics.

With the self-righteous we can have more sympathy, for it is always difficult to put a deep conviction into words without sounding 'smug'. I do not criticize them because they express themselves clumsily or priggishly; even a practised writer of many years' standing finds it hard to say precisely what he or she means on a matter of conscience. Where they fail is in their tendency to regard fighting men, and those who accept military methods, as thoughtless and ignorant, and to forget that the young soldiers, sailors, and airmen of today are as much victims of power politics as themselves.

Nobody could make this mistake who had once been part, even as a noncombatant, of an army at war, and had seen the sacrificial spirit in which young men, with their lives unfulfilled, endure their disabling wounds or go out to die. Ever since I watched the British soldiers at Étaples talking to my wounded German patients, I have realized that the fighting volunteer and the pacifist have far more in common than either has with the 'old men' who send the one to death and the other, to prison.[1] I know one young soldier, determined never to kill a fellow creature, who has become a volunteer member of a bomb-disposal unit because he suspects that in his case a 'conscientious objection' would be mainly a rationalization of fear and distaste. The test in each instance is the readiness to give up everything, including life itself, for the sake of a moral conviction.

We must recognize that, in the present state of opinion in this country and the United States, the decision to fight was inevitable for most of those who made it. A friend of the late Evelyn Underhill, Mrs Marjorie Vernon, emphasized this point in a letter sent to the Anglican Pacifist Fellowship. She wrote:

God, we are taught, judges us by our fundamental 'intention'. It seems to me that the average Englishman's 'intention' in taking part in this war is to vindicate freedom, truth, mercy, and justice. What would his 'intention' be if he kept out of it? Remember, England is not a truly Christian country. Ethically, perhaps she may lay claim to be – though even here there are gaps – but on the religious, the supernatural level, she certainly is not. . . . If all England were profoundly Christian her refusal to fight would not be a negative refusal, but would be vigorous and positive; not so much that she would not fight as that she *would* do something else. Realistically believing that 'to them that love God all things work together for good', she would be content to follow Christ's teaching, leaving the outcome – whatever it might be – in God's hands and fully accepting it. . . . At present, however, such an attitude and such behavior is practically unthinkable. Only a few people born out of due season see these truths which belong to the future rather than to 1941.

Despite the fairness of this judgement, I receive many letters from men and women in the armed forces who want to discuss the justification and purposes of the war. Later I shall have more to say about the bond of sympathy between the convinced pacifist, of whatever age, and the young generation which is again called upon to offer up its health, strength, and opportunities in a war made by elderly politicians whose aims and standards it does not share. But the development of that bond of sympathy depends upon our ability, as pacifists, to use rightly the type of sacrifice which we are called upon to make. It is nothing, in any

1. T. E. Lawrence bore witness to this resemblance in a famous passage from *Seven Pillars of Wisdom*: 'When we achieved and the new world dawned, the old men came out again and took from us our victory, and remade it in the likeness of the former world they knew. Youth could win, but had not learned to keep, and was pitiably weak against age. We stammered that we had worked for a new heaven and a new earth, and they thanked us kindly and made their peace.'

case, to the sacrifice demanded of the soldier. If he can face wounds and death, whether endured or inflicted, we can surely learn wisdom from criticism and degradation.

The essence of such wisdom is a clear understanding of pacifism and its function. Some people join the pacifist movement without examining either the ethics or the politics of their position, which explains the superficial escapism of inverted belligerency and government baiting. It is the pacifist's obligation to be both realist and idealist; to face existing facts while never losing sight of the world which he desires to create. His part, as a living leaven within the lump of popular traditions and assumptions, may seem trivial in itself, yet his task is nothing less than an attempt to change the thinking of his nation, and beyond that of a greater society.

He begins modestly by trying to enlarge – sometimes only one by one – the circle of those who endeavour to shape their lives in accordance with a particular set of values. By these 'values' I mean the conduct of that ideal community to which poets and prophets have given many names. Christ called it the Kingdom of Heaven. For Dante and Milton, it was Paradise; for Sir Thomas More, Utopia; for Blake a mystic 'Jerusalem' to be built by 'mental fight'.

The movement that seeks to create this community which knows neither force nor frontiers is inevitably a revolutionary movement. It is a society within society, a living force which depends neither on economic systems nor political machinery – though it may work through both – but upon the power of the spirit. Today it is the only movement which possesses this revolutionary character. The once progressive 'Left' has become reactionary; it is in alliance with those forces which applaud totalitarianism and war. It merely prefers one form of totalitarianism to another. Hence the paradox by which gatherings called to reaffirm the democratic principles of free speech and a free press are crowded by the supporters of a regime which suppresses both.

Perhaps you feel that a minority so small, surrounded by powerful forces so adverse to this growth, is unlikely ever to achieve its purpose of leavening the lump. But you must remember that nearly all the great revolutions of history not only started as minority movements, but seldom became anything else even when they had succeeded. In the words of John Wesley:

Give me one hundred men who fear nothing but God, hate nothing but sin, and have the love of Jesus in their hearts; and with them I can move the world.

I can think of few important movements for reform in which success was won by any method other than that of an energetic minority presenting the indifferent majority with a *fait accompli*, which was then accepted. The only exceptions are perhaps the great religious movements which, like Christianity, started from a tiny group, but went on to capture half of mankind. But even here, as I have tried to show you, there is a wide distinction between the genuine working believers and the vast bulk of lip-servers who make up the substantial majority of both religious bodies and political parties.

Shortly before this war, when we were driving together to a meeting George Lansbury told me that in his long life he had seen so many apparently hopeless causes succeed, that his faith in the ultimate rejection of war by civilized men and women remained unshaken. His life spanned a period which not only included such movements as slave emanicaption, the abolition of child labour, prison reform, trade unionism, socialism, and universal education, but saw social habits now universally accepted pass from the stage where they were regarded with horrified disapproval to one in which it was forgotten that their desirability had ever been questioned.

Once, on a public platform, I heard Dr Marie Stopes read aloud from a mid-Victorian newspaper a paragraph imputing recklessness and immorality to a certain group of 'advanced' persons. Was this a diatribe against free love, birth control, or companionate marriage? Not at all. The protest was directed against those who had adopted the habit of taking a regular bath.

One of the reforms most successfully carried through by a small minority was woman suffrage. There has been some confusion on this issue, since the First World War broke out before the effect of the suffragist propaganda was fully apparent. The gap between the demand for female suffrage, and the first partial acceptance of it in Britain in 1918, enabled the opponents of the feminist campaign to say that the vote was conceded to women as a reward for their part in winning the war. But in some countries, such as the United States, where woman suffrage was also granted at the end of the war, the amount of war service performed by women had been very small. The vote would never have been conceded had not a hard-working and articulate minority brought their claims, before the war, to a point where these appeared not only conceivable, but rational and just.

In the same way the movement to abolish war is likely not only to begin, but to end, as the achievement of a minority which ultimately persuades the majority to adopt its view. The elimination of war and the building of permanent peace differ from other great movements for the liberation of humanity from the evil within itself, only because the sphere of action is so much wider and the problems involved far more complicated.

The minority working for international peace has, as I see it, a four-fold function. Its members have first to fulfil the duty of self-conquest described in my last letter. This really involves a new conception of honour. It means understanding that we cannot exercise compassion until we have endured humiliation, nor effectively help the victims of society until we have been in the dock and the prison beside them. When a man has conquered his own bitterness and learned to wrest honour from shame, he has brought humanity's struggle to overcome war a little nearer to victory. He has also achieved a new kind of free-dom which compensates for his earlier frustration.

The respectable have so much to sacrifice: their prestige, their popu-larity with their neighbours, the good opinion of their friends, the approval of the government. Naturally they have to think carefully before associating with the oppressed or endorsing 'extreme' opinions, and we cannot be surprised that their decision regarding such association is frequently in the negative. Hence it is a great advantage to be so 'disrespectable' that one has nothing to lose. One can then quit the upperdogs and, joining the underdogs, begin to see their situation as they see it themselves. Charity born of shared experience is the only power which can finally vanquish evil; that is why those who believe in its authority must take the risks that it demands in a world which does not yet accept it. A Quaker friend once wrote to me of these risks:

Solid, dogged, unchanging love. Suffering and injustice lovingly endured. Force can restrain the evil man; only love can change him, and when Christ went to the Cross it was no mere acceptance of the inevitable, but his deliberate response to the hatred and selfishness of men, his final assault on the powers of evil. The battle continues now, in every individual life and in a world at war; the spiritual forces we cannot reckon, the human one is the scattered company of all who try to live that way.

Of the three other functions of our minority, I shall write you in my remaining letters. The first, which depends for its value upon the con-ception that I have called 'humiliation with honour', is to give what-ever assistance we can to those victims of power who endure more than ourselves – prisoners, refugees, the starving, the young, the bereaved. We must keep ourselves imaginatively conscious of the cost of war in human suffering; we must also investigate and expose that cost, and find, if we can, some form of redemptive consolation for those who have to pay it.

Second, I believe that we are called upon, humbly and without self-righteousness, to keep alive those civilized values of charity, compassion, and truth to which men return with relief and remorse as soon as war is over, wondering however their spiritual focus became so distorted. If this includes the duty of protest against hatred, cruelty, self-interest, and falsehood whenever we come across them, we must not shrink from the resulting unpopularity. It is quite different from the unpopularity-for-its-own-sake which the pacifist who would not be happy if he was not victimized sets out to incur. Our business is to keep our heads, and try to see the events of the war in the largest possible perspective against their background of history. We must endeavour to find out and tell the truth, facing facts as they are rather than as propaganda and wishful thinking desire them to be.

Finally, from our study of history and our careful watch on present developments, we must seize upon such evidence of the shape of the future as we are able to acquire. This does not mean constructing an Eldorado of gilt-edged 'Peace Aims' which have no relations to the facts as we know them. It does mean trying, within the limits of our knowledge, to plan for the post-war world as its dim outlines emerge through the stifling smoke clouds of war.

Our task is that of trying to change the course of history by acting as a revolutionary leaven within society. But we must know in what direction we wish to divert it before we can even begin. Idealists in general, and pacifists in particular, are apt to talk about 'the future' as if futurity were an end in itself. Obviously the future will be no better than the present unless we can learn from the mistakes of the past what its pattern should be.

SIMONE WEIL

1909–43

WHEN Simone Weil died in England in the summer of 1943, she was only thirty-four years old; she had not only established a reputation as a profound literary and social critic, but the events of a stormy life totally dedicated to others seemed to have woven a legend around her. A student of Alain, her learning extended from the sciences to the arts. She was involved in left-wing politics from her twentieth year, but her associations were more with workers and the trade-union movement than with professional political militants.

In *Reflections on War*, written when she was twenty-four, she bitterly denounced efforts to divert the attention of intellectuals and the working class to foreign involvements, even when they seemed to be anti-fascist wars. She wrote: 'The absurdity of an anti-fascist struggle which chooses war as its means of action thus appears quite clear. Not only would this mean to fight barbarous oppression by crushing peoples under the weight of even more barbarous massacre. It would actually mean spreading under another form the very regime that we want to suppress.' She was affirming the words of Karl Liebknecht that 'the main enemy is at home'.

However, she went to Spain when the civil war broke out and although she did not remain long, it was obvious that her views were changing. A Catholic 'outside the Church', as she put it, her Jewish background forced her to leave France in 1942. After a short stay in America, she returned to Europe, and went to England to make plans to parachute into occupied France. While in England, she refused to eat more than what she knew the French working man was eating; her constitution already much weakened by her way of life and the recent pattern of her wartime travels, she contracted tuberculosis and died in August of the following year.

'The Iliad, a Poem of Force', her great essay on war and violence, which connected the issues of the day with the classical literary tradition, was written in 1940 after the fall of France. It was originally published in two parts under the pseudonym 'Émile Novis' in *Cahiers du Sud*. In the United States it was published in the November 1945 issue of *Politics*, in a translation by Mary McCarthy.

The Iliad, a Poem of Force

The true hero, the true subject, the centre of the *Iliad* is force. Force employed by man, force that enslaves man, force before which man's flesh shrinks away. In this work, at all times, the human spirit is shown as modified by its relations with force, as swept away, blinded, by the very force it imagined it could handle, as deformed by the weight of the force it submits to. For those dreamers who considered that force, thanks to progress, would soon be a thing of the past, the *Iliad* could appear as an historical document; for others, whose powers of recognition are more acute and who perceive force, today as yesterday, at the very centre of human history, the *Iliad* is the purest and the loveliest of mirrors.

To define force – it is that *x* that turns anybody who is subjected to it into a *thing*. Exercised to the limit, it turns man into a thing in the most literal sense: it makes a corpse out of him. Somebody was here, and the next minute there is nobody here at all; this is a spectacle the *Iliad* never wearies of showing us:

> . . . the horses
> Rattled the empty chariots through the files of battle,
> Longing for their noble drivers. But they on the ground
> Lay, dearer to the vultures than to their wives.

The hero becomes a *thing* dragged behind a chariot in the dust:

> All around, his black hair
> Was spread; in the dust his whole head lay,
> That once-charming head; now Zeus had let his enemies
> Defile it on his native soil.

The bitterness of such a spectacle is offered us absolutely undiluted. No comforting fiction intervenes; no consoling prospect of immortality; and on the hero's head no washed-out halo of patriotism descends.

> His soul, fleeing his limbs, passed to Hades,
> Mourning its fate, forsaking its youth and its vigor.

Still more poignant – so painful is the contrast – is the sudden evocation, as quickly rubbed out, of another world: the far-away, precarious, touching world of peace, of the family, the world in which each man counts more than anything else to those about him.

> She ordered her bright-haired maids in the palace
> To place on the fire a large tripod, preparing
> A hot bath for Hector, returning from battle.
> Foolish woman! Already he lay, far from hot baths,
> Slain by grey-eyed Athena, who guided Achilles' arm.

Far from hot baths he was indeed, poor man. And not he alone. Nearly all the *Iliad* takes place far from hot baths. Nearly all of human life, then and now, takes place far from hot baths.

Here we see force in its grossest and most summary form – the force that kills. How much more varied in its processes, how much more surprising in its effects is the other force, the force that does *not* kill, i.e. that does not kill just yet. It will surely kill, it will possibly kill, or perhaps it merely hangs, poised and ready, over the head of the creature it *can* kill, at any moment, which is to say at every moment. In whatever aspect, its effect is the same: it turns a man into a stone. From its first property (the ability to turn a human being into a thing by the simple method of killing him) flows another, quite prodigious too in its own way, the ability to turn a human being into a thing while he is still alive. He is alive; he has a soul; and yet – he is a thing. An extraordinary entity this – a thing that has a soul. And as for the soul, what an extraordinary house it finds itself in! Who can say what it costs it, moment by moment, to accommodate itself to this residence, how much writhing and bending, folding and pleating are required of it? It was not made to live inside a thing; if it does so, under pressure of necessity, there's not a single element of its nature to which violence is not done.

A man stands disarmed and naked with a weapon pointing at him; this person becomes a corpse before anybody or anything touches him. Just a minute ago, he was thinking, acting, hoping:

> Motionless, he pondered. And the other drew near,
> Terrified, anxious to touch his knees, hoping in his heart
> To escape evil death and black destiny . . .
> With one hand he clasped, suppliant, his knees,
> While the other clung to the sharp spear, not letting go . . .

Soon, however, he grasps the fact that the weapon which is pointing at him will not be diverted; and now, still breathing, he is simply matter; still thinking, he can think no longer:

> Thus spoke the brilliant son of Priam
> In begging words. But he heard a harsh reply:
> He spoke. And the other's knees and heart failed him.

> Dropping his spear, he knelt down, holding out his arms.
> Achilles, drawing his sharp sword, struck
> Through the neck and breastbone. The two-edged sword
> Sunk home its full length. The other, face down,
> Lay still, and the black blood ran out, wetting the ground.

If a stranger, completely disabled, disarmed, strengthless, throws himself on the mercy of a warrior, he is not, by this very act, condemned to death; but a moment of impatience on the warrior's part will suffice to relieve him of his life. In any case, his flesh has lost that very important property which in the laboratory distinguishes living flesh from dead – the galvanic response. If you give a frog's leg an electric shock, it twitches. If you confront a human being with the touch or sight of something horrible or terrifying, this bundle of muscles, nerves, and flesh likewise twitches. Alone of all living things, the suppliant we have just described neither quivers nor trembles. He has lost the right to do so. As his lips advance to touch the object that is for him of all things most charged with horror, they do not draw back on his teeth – they cannot:

> No one saw great Priam enter. He stopped,
> Clasped the knees of Achilles, kissed his hands,
> Those terrible man-killing hands that had slaughtered so many of his sons.

The sight of a human being pushed to such an extreme of suffering chills us like the sight of a dead body:

> As when harsh misfortune strikes a man if in his own country
> He has killed a man, and arrives at last at someone else's door,
> The door of a rich man; a shudder seizes those who see him.
> So Achilles shuddered to see divine Priam;
> The others shuddered too, looking one at the other.

But this feeling lasts only a moment. Soon the very presence of the suffering creature is forgotten:

> He spoke. The other, remembering his own father, longed to weep;
> Taking the old man's arm, he pushed him away.
> Both were remembering. Thinking of Hector, killer of men,
> Priam wept, abased at the feet of Achilles.
> But Achilles wept, now for his father,
> Now for Patroclus. And their sobs resounded through the house.

It was not insensibility that made Achilles with a single movement of his hand push away the old man who had been clinging to his knees; Priam's words, recalling his own old father, had moved him to tears. It was merely a question of his being as free in his attitudes and movements as if, clasping his knees, there were not a suppliant but an inert object. Anybody who is in our vicinity exercises a certain power over us by his very presence, and a power that belongs to him alone, that is, the power of halting, repressing, modifying each movement that our body sketches out. If we step aside for a passer-by on the road, it is not the same thing as stepping aside to avoid a billboard; alone in our rooms, we get up, walk about, sit down again quite differently from the way we do when we have a visitor. But this indefinable influence that the presence of another human being has on us is not exercised by men whom a moment of impatience can deprive of life, who can die before even thought has a chance to pass sentence on them. In their presence, people move about as if they were not there; they, on their side, running the risk of being reduced to nothing in a single instant, imitate nothingness in their own persons. Pushed, they fall. Fallen, they lie where they are, unless chance gives somebody the idea of raising them up again. But supposing that at long last they have been picked up, honoured with cordial remarks, they still do not venture to take this resurrection seriously; they dare not express a wish lest an irritated voice return them forever to silence:

He spoke; the old man trembled and obeyed.

At least a suppliant, once his prayer is answered, becomes a human being again, like everybody else. But there are other, more unfortunate creatures who have become things for the rest of their lives. Their days hold no pastimes, no free spaces, no room in them for any impulse of their own. It is not that their life is harder than other men's nor that they occupy a lower place in the social hierarchy; no, they are another human species, a compromise between a man and a corpse. The idea of a person's being a thing is a logical contradiction. Yet what is impossible in logic becomes true in life, and the contradiction lodged within the soul tears it to shreds. This thing is constantly aspiring to be a man or a woman, and never achieving it – here, surely, is death but death strung out over a whole lifetime; here, surely is life, but life that death congeals before abolishing.

This strange fate awaits the virgin, the priest's daughter:

> I will not give her up. Sooner shall old age come upon her
> In our house in Argos, far from her native land,
> Tending the loom and sharing my bed.

It awaits the young wife, the young mother, the prince's bride:

> And perhaps one day, in Argos, you will weave cloth for another,
> And the Messeian or Hyperian water you will fetch,
> Much against your will, yielding to a harsh necessity.

It awaits the baby, heir to the royal sceptre:

> Soon they will be carried off in the hollow ships,
> I with them. And you, my child, will either go with me,
> To a land where you will work at wretched tasks,
> Labouring for a pitiless master. . . .

In the mother's eyes, such a fate is, for her child, as terrible as death; the husband would rather die than see his wife reduced to it; all the plagues of heaven are invoked by the father against the army that subjects his daughter to it. Yet the victims themselves are beyond all this. Curses, feelings of rebellion, comparisons, reflections on the future and the past, are obliterated from the mind of the captive; and the memory itself barely lingers on. Fidelity to his city and his dead is not the slave's privilege.

And what does it take to make the slave weep? The misfortune of his master, his oppressor, despoiler, pillager, of the man who laid waste his town and killed his dear ones under his very eyes. This man suffers or dies; *then* the slave's tears come. And really why not? This is for him the only occasion on which tears are permitted, are, indeed, required. A slave will always cry whenever he can do so with impunity – his situation keeps tears on tap for him.

> She spoke, weeping, and the women groaned,
> Using the pretext of Patroclus to bewail their own torments.

Since the slave has no licence to express anything except what is pleasing to his master, it follows that the only emotion that can touch or enliven him a little, that can reach him in the desolation of his life, is the emotion of love for his master. There is no place else to send the gift of love; all other outlets are barred, just as, with the horse in harness, bit, shafts, reins bar every way but one. And if, by some miracle, in the slave's breast a hope is born, the hope of becoming, some day, through somebody's influence, *someone* once again, how far won't these captives go to show love and thankfulness, even though these emotions are addressed to the very men who should, considering the very recent past, still reek with horror for them:

My husband, to whom my father and respected mother gave me,
I saw before the city transfixed by the sharp bronze.
My three brothers, children, with me, of a single mother,
So dear to me! They all met their fatal day.
But you did not allow me to weep, when swift Achilles
Slaughtered my husband and laid waste the city of Mynes.
You promised me that I would be taken by divine Achilles,
For his legitimate wife, that he would carry me away in his ships,
To Pythia, where our marriage would be celebrated among the Myrmidons,
So without respite I mourn for you, you who have always been gentle.

To lose more than the slave does is impossible, for he loses his whole inner life. A fragment of it he may get back if he sees the possibility of changing his fate, but this is his only hope. Such is the empire of force, as extensive as the empire of nature. Nature, too, when vital needs are at stake, can erase the whole inner life, even the grief of a mother:

But the thought of eating came to her, when she was tired of tears.

Force, in the hands of another, exercises over the soul the same tyranny that extreme hunger does; for it possesses, and *in perpetuo*, the power of life and death. Its rule, moreover, is as cold and hard as the rule of inert matter. The man who knows himself weaker than another is more alone in the heart of a city than a man lost in the desert.

Two casks are placed before Zeus's doorsill,
Containing the gifts he gives, the bad in one, the good in the other ...
The man to whom he gives baneful gifts, he exposes to outrage;
A frightful need drives across the divine earth;
He is a wanderer, and gets no respect from gods or men.

Force is as pitiless to the man who possesses it, or thinks he does, as it is to its victims; the second it crushes, the first it intoxicates. The truth is nobody really possesses it. The human race is not divided up, in the *Iliad*, into conquered persons, slaves, suppliants, on the one hand, and conquerors and chiefs on the other. In this poem there is not a single man who does not at one time or another have to bow his neck to force. The common soldier in the *Iliad* is free and has the right to bear arms; nevertheless he is subject to the indignity of orders and abuse:

> But whenever he came upon a commoner shouting out,
> He struck him with his sceptre and spoke sharply:
> 'Good for nothing! Be still and listen to your betters,
> You are weak and cowardly and unwarlike,
> You count for nothing, neither in battle nor in council.'

Thersites pays dear for the perfectly reasonable comments he makes, comments not at all different, moreover, from those made by Achilles:

> He hit him with his sceptre on back and shoulders,
> So that he doubled over, and a great tear welled up,
> And a bloody welt appeared on his back
> Under the golden sceptre. Frightened, he sat down,
> Wiping away his tears, bewildered and in pain.
> Troubled though they were, the others laughed long at him.

Achilles himself, that proud hero, the undefeated, is shown us at the outset of the poem, weeping with humiliation and helpless grief – the woman he wanted for his bride has been taken from under his nose, and he has not dared to oppose it:

> ... But Achilles
> Weeping, sat apart from his companions,
> By the white-capped waves, staring over the boundless ocean.

What has happened is that Agamemnon has deliberately humiliated Achilles, to show that he himself is the master:

> ... So you will learn
> That I am greater than you, and anyone else will hesitate
> To treat me as an equal and set himself against me.

But a few days pass and now the supreme commander is weeping in his turn. He must humble himself, he must plead, and have, moreover, the added misery of doing it all in vain.

In the same way, there is not a single one of the combatants who is spared the shameful experience of fear. The heroes quake like everybody else. It only needs a challenge from Hector to throw the whole Greek force into consternation – except for Achilles and his men, and they did not happen to be present:

> He spoke and all grew still and held their peace,
> Ashamed to refuse, afraid to accept.

But once Ajax comes forward and offers himself, fear quickly changes sides:

> A shudder of terror ran through the Trojans, making their limbs weak;
> And Hector himself felt his heart leap in his breast.
> But he no longer had the right to tremble, or to run away. . . .

Two days later, it is Ajax's turn to be terrified:

> Zeus the father on high, makes fear rise in Ajax.
> He stops, overcome, puts behind him his buckler made of seven hides,
> Trembles, looks at the crowd around, like a wild beast. . . .

Even to Achilles the moment comes; he too must shake and stammer with fear, though it is a river that has this effect on him, not a man. But, with the exception of Achilles, every man in the *Iliad* tastes a moment of defeat in battle. Victory is less a matter of valour than of blind destiny, which is symbolized in the poem by Zeus's golden scales:

> Then Zeus the father took his golden scales,
> In them he put the two fates of death that cuts down all men,
> One for the Trojans, tamers of horses, one for the bronze-sheathed Greeks.
> He seized the scales by the middle; it was the fatal day of Greece that sank.

By its very blindness, destiny establishes a kind of justice. Blind also is she who decrees to warriors punishment in kind. He that takes the sword, will perish by the sword. The *Iliad* formulated the principle long before the Gospels did, and in almost the same terms:

> Ares is just, and kills those who kill.

Perhaps all men, by the very act of being born, are destined to suffer violence; yet this is a truth to which circumstance shuts men's eyes. The strong are, as a matter of fact, never absolutely strong, nor are the weak absolutely weak, but neither is aware of this. They have in common a refusal to believe that they both belong to the same species: the weak see no relation between themselves and the strong, and vice versa. The man who is the possessor of force seems to walk through a non-resistant element; in the human substance that surrounds him nothing has the power to interpose, between the impulse and the act, the tiny interval that is reflection. Where there is no room for reflection, there is none either for justice or prudence. Hence we see men in arms behaving harshly and madly. We see their sword bury itself in the breast of a disarmed enemy who is in the very act of pleading at their knees. We see them triumph over a dying man by describing to him the outrages his corpse will endure. We see Achilles cut the throats of twelve Trojan boys on the funeral pyre of Patroclus as naturally as we cut flowers for a grave. These men, wielding power, have no suspicion of the fact that the consequences of their deeds will at length come home to them – they too will bow the neck in their turn. If you can make an old man fall silent, tremble, obey, with a single word of your own, why should it occur to you that the curses of this old man, who is after all a priest, will have their own importance in the gods' eyes? Why should you refrain from taking Achilles' girl away from him if you know that neither he nor she can do anything but obey you? Achilles rejoices over the sight of the Greeks fleeing in misery and confusion. What could possibly suggest to him that this rout, which will last exactly as long as he wants it to and end when his mood indicates it, that this very rout will be the cause of his friend's death, and, for that matter, of his own? Thus it happens that those who have force on loan from fate count on it too much and are destroyed.

But at the time their own destruction seems impossible to them. For they do not see that the force in their possession is only a limited quantity; nor do they see their relations with other human beings as a kind of balance between unequal amounts of force. Since other people do not impose on their movements that halt, that interval of hesitation, wherein lies all our consideration for our brothers in humanity, they conclude that destiny has given complete licence to them, and none at all to their inferiors. And at this point they exceed the measure of the force that is actually at their disposal. Inevitably they exceed it, since they are not aware that it is limited. And now we see them committed irretrievably to chance; suddenly things cease to obey them. Sometimes chance is kind to them, sometimes cruel. But in any case there they are, exposed, open to misfortune; gone is the armour of power that formerly protected their naked souls; nothing, no shield, stands between them and tears.

This retribution, which has a geometrical rigour, which operates automatically to penalize the abuse of force, was the main subject of Greek thought. It is the soul of the epic. Under the name of Nemesis, it functions as the mainspring of Aeschylus' tragedies. To the Pythagoreans, to Socrates and Plato, it was the jumping-off point of speculation upon the nature of man and the universe. Wherever Hellenism has penetrated, we find the idea of it familiar. In Oriental countries which are steeped in Buddhism, it is perhaps this Greek idea that has lived on under the name of Kharma. The Occident, however, has lost it, and no longer even has a word to express it in any of its languages: conceptions of limit, measure, equilibrium, which ought to determine the conduct of life are, in the West, restricted to a servile function in the vocabulary of technics. We are only geometricians of matter; the Greeks were, first of all, geometricians in their apprenticeship to virtue.

The progress of the war in the *Iliad* is simply a continual game of see-saw. The victor of the moment feels himself invincible, even though, only a few hours before, he may have experienced defeat: he forgets to treat victory as a transitory thing. At the end of the first day of combat described in the *Iliad*, the victorious Greeks were in a position to obtain the object of all their efforts, i.e. Helen and her riches – assuming of course, as Homer did, that the Greeks had reason to believe that Helen was in Troy. Actually, the Egyptian priests, who ought to have known, affirmed later on to Herodotus that she was in Egypt. In any case, that evening the Greeks are no longer interested in her or her possessions:

> 'For the present, let us not accept the riches of Paris;
> Nor Helen; everybody sees, even the most ignorant,
> That Troy stands on the verge of ruin.'
> He spoke, and all the Achaeans acclaimed him.

What they want is, in fact, everything. For booty, all the riches of Troy; for their bonfires, all the palaces, temples, houses; for slaves, all the women and children; for corpses, all the men. They forget one detail, that *everything* is not within their power, for they are not in Troy. Perhaps they will be there tomorrow; perhaps not. Hector, the same day, makes the same mistake:

> For I know well in my entrails and in my hearts,
> A day will come when Holy Troy will perish,
> And Priam, and the nation of Priam of the good lance.
> But I think less of the grief that is in store for the Trojans,
> And of Hecuba herself, and of Priam the king,
> And of my brothers, so numerous and so brave,
> Who will fall in the dust under the blows of the enemy,
> Than of you that day when a Greek in his bronze breastplate
> Will drag you away weeping and deprive you of your liberty.
>
> But as for me, may I be dead, and may the earth have covered me
> Before I hear you cry out or see you dragged away!

At this moment what would he not give to turn aside those horrors which he believes to be inevitable? But at this moment nothing he *could* give would be of any use. The next day but one, however, the Greeks have run away miserably, and Agamemnon himself is in favour of putting to the sea again. And now Hector, by making a very few concessions, could readily secure the enemy's departure; yet now he is even unwilling to let them go empty-handed:

> Set fires everywhere and let the brightness mount the skies
> Lest in the night the long-haired Greeks,
> Escaping, sail over the broad back of ocean . . .
> Let each of them take home a wound to heal
>   . . . thus others will fear
> To bring dolorous war to the Trojans, tamers of horses.

His wish is granted; the Greeks stay; and the next day they reduce Hector and his men to a pitiable condition:

> As for them – they fled across the plain like cattle
> Whom a lion hunts before him in the dark midnight . . .
> Thus the mighty Agamemnon, son of Atreus, pursued them,
> Steadily killing the hindmost; and still they fled.

In the course of the afternoon, Hector regains the ascendancy, withdraws again, then puts the Greeks to flight, then is repulsed by Patroclus who has come in with his fresh troops. Patroclus, pressing his advantage, ends by finding himself exposed, wounded and without armour, to the sword of Hector. And finally that evening the victorious Hector hears the prudent counsel of Polydamas and repudiates it sharply:

> Now that wily Kronos's son has given me
> Glory at the ships; now that I have driven the Greeks to the sea,
> Do not offer, fool, such counsels to the people.
> No Trojan will listen to you; nor would I permit it . .
> So Hector spoke, and the Trojans acclaimed him. . . .

The next day Hector is lost. Achilles has harried him across the field and is about to kill him. He has always been the stronger of the two in combat; how much the more so now, after several weeks of rest, ardent for vengeance and victory, against an exhausted enemy? And Hector stands alone, before the walls of Troy, absolutely alone, alone to wait for death and to steady his soul to face it:

> Alas, were I to slip through the gate, behind the rampart,
> Polydamas at once would heap dishonour on me . . .
> And now that through my recklessness I have destroyed my people,
> I fear the Trojans and the long-robed Trojan women,
> I fear to hear from some one far less brave than I:
> 'Hector, trusting his own strength too far, has ruined his people. . . .'
> Suppose I were to down my bossed shield,
> My massive helmet, and, leaning my spear against the wall,
> Should go to meet renowned Achilles? . . .
> But why spin out these fancies? Why such dreams?
> I would not reach him, nor would he pity me,
> Or respect me. He would kill me like a woman
> If I came naked thus . . .

Not a jot of the grief and ignominy that fall to the unfortunate is Hector spared. Alone, stripped of the prestige of force, he discovers that the courage that kept him from taking to the shelter of the walls is not enough to save him from flight:

> Seeing him, Hector began to tremble. He had not the heart
> To stay . . .
> . . . It is not for a ewe nor the skin of an ox,
> That they are striving, not these ordinary rewards of the race;
> It is for a life that they run, the life of Hector, tamer of horses.

Wounded to death, he enhances his conqueror's triumph by vain supplications:

> I implore you, by your soul, by your knees, by your parents. . . .

But the auditors of the *Iliad* knew that the death of Hector would be but a brief joy to Achilles, and the death of Achilles but a brief joy to the Trojans, and the destruction of Troy but a brief joy to the Achaeans.

Thus violence obliterates anybody who feels its touch. It comes to seem just as external to its employer as to its victim. And from this springs the idea of a destiny before which executioner and victim stand equally innocent, before which conquered and conqueror are brothers in the same distress. The conquered brings misfortune to the conqueror, and vice versa:

> A single son, short-lived, was born to him.
> Neglected by me, he grows old – for far from home
> I camp before Troy, injuring you and your sons.

A moderate use of force, which alone would enable man to escape being enmeshed in its machinery, would require superhuman virtue, which is as rare as dignity in weakness. Moreover, moderation itself is not without its perils, since prestige, from which force derives at least three quarters of its strength, rests principally upon that marvellous indifference that the strong feel toward the weak, an indifference so contagious that it infects the very people who are the objects of it. Yet ordinarily excess is not arrived at through prudence or politic considerations. On the contrary, man dashes to it as to an irresistible temptation. The voice of reason is occasionally heard in the mouths of the characters in the *Iliad*. Thersites' speeches are reasonable to the highest degree; so are the speeches of the angry Achilles:

> Nothing is worth my life, not all the goods
> They say the well-built city of Ilium contains. . . .
> A man can capture steers and fatted sheep
> But, once gone, the soul cannot be captured back.

But words of reason drop into the void. If they come from an inferior, he is punished and shuts up; if from a chief, his actions betray them. And failing everything else, there is always a god handy to advise him to be unreasonable. In the end, the very idea of wanting to escape the role fate has allotted one – the business of killing and dying – disappears from the mind:

> We to whom Zeus
> Has assigned suffering, from youth to old age,
> Suffering in grievous wars, till we perish to the last man.

Already these warriors, like Craonne's so much later, felt themselves to be 'condemned men'.

It was the simplest trap that pitched them into this situation. At the outset, at the embarkation, their hearts are light, as hearts always are if you have a large force on your side and nothing but space to oppose you. Their weapons are in their hands; the enemy is absent. Unless your spirit has been conquered in advance by the reputation of the enemy, you always feel yourself to be much stronger than anybody who is not there. An absent man does not impose the yoke of necessity. To the spirits of those embarking no necessity yet presents itself; consequently they go off as though to a game, as though on holiday from the confinement of daily life.

> Where have they gone, those braggadocio boasts
> We proudly flung upon the air at Lemnos,
> Stuffing ourselves with flesh of horned steers,
> Drinking from cups brimming over with wine?
> As for Trojans – a hundred or two each man of us
> Could handle in battle. And now one is too much for us.

But the first contact of war does not immediately destroy the illusion that war is a game. War's necessity is terrible, altogether different in kind from the necessity of peace. So terrible is it that the human spirit will not submit to it so long as it can possibly escape; and whenever it can escape it takes refuge in long days empty of necessity, days of play, of reverie, days arbitrary and unreal. Danger then becomes an abstraction; the lives you destroy are like toys broken by a child, and quite as incapable of feeling; heroism is but a theatrical gesture and smirched with boastfulness. This becomes doubly true if a momentary access of vitality comes to reinforce the divine hand that wards off defeat and death. Then war is easy and basely, coarsely loved.

But with the majority of the combatants this state of mind does not persist. Soon there comes a day when fear, or defeat, or the death of beloved comrades touches the warrior's spirit, and it crumbles in the hand of necessity. At that moment war is no more a game or a dream; now at last the warrior cannot doubt the reality of its existence. And this reality, which he perceives, is hard, much too hard to be borne, for it enfolds death. Once you acknowledge death to be a practical possibility, the thought of it becomes unendurable, except in flashes. True enough, all men are fated to die; true enough also, a soldier may grow old in battles; yet for those whose spirits have bent under the yoke of war, the relation between death and the future is different than for other men. For other men death appears as a limit set in advance on the future; for the soldier death *is* the future, the future his profession assigns him. Yet the idea of man's having death for a future is abhorrent to nature. Once the experience of war makes visible the possibility of death that lies locked up in each moment, our thoughts cannot travel from one day to the next without meeting death's face. The mind is then strung up to a pitch it can stand for only a short time; but each new dawn reintroduces the same necessity; and days piled on days make years. On each one of these days the soul suffers violence. Regularly, every morning, the soul castrates itself of aspiration, for thought cannot journey through time without meeting death on the way. Thus war effaces all conceptions of purpose or goal, including even its own 'war aims'. It effaces the very notion of war's being brought to an end. To be outside a situation so violent as this is to find it inconceivable; to be inside it is to be unable to conceive its end. Consequently, nobody does anything to bring this end about. In the presence of an armed enemy, what hand can relinquish its weapon? The mind ought to find a way out, but the mind has lost all capacity to so much as look outward. The mind is completely absorbed in doing itself violence. Always in human life, whether war or slavery is in question, intolerable sufferings continue, as it were, by the force of their own specific gravity, and so look to the outsider as though they were easy to bear; actually, they continue because they have deprived the sufferer of the resources which might serve to extricate him.

Nevertheless, the soul that is enslaved to war cries out for deliverance, but deliverance itself appears to it in an extreme and tragic aspect, the aspect of destruction. Any other solution, more moderate, more reasonable in character, would expose the mind to suffering so naked, so violent that it could not be borne, even as memory. Terror, grief, exhaustion, slaughter, the annihilation of comrades – is it credible that these things should not continually tear at the soul, if the intoxication of force had not intervened to drown them? The idea that an unlimited effort should bring in only a limited profit or no profit at all is terribly painful.

> What? Will we let Priam and the Trojans boast
> Of Argive Helen, she for whom so many Greeks
> Died before Troy, far from their native land?
> What? Do you want us to leave the city, wide-streeted Troy,
> Standing, when we have suffered so much for it?

But actually what is Helen to Ulysses? What indeed is Troy, full of riches that will not compensate him for Ithaca's ruin? For the Greeks, Troy and Helen are in reality mere sources of blood and tears; to master them is to master frightful memories. If the existence of an enemy has made a soul destroy in itself the thing nature put there, then the only remedy the soul can imagine is the destruction of the enemy. At the same time the death of dearly loved comrades arouses a spirit of sombre emulation, a rivalry in death:

> May I die, then, at once! Since fate has not let me
> Protect my dead friend, who far from home
> Perished, longing for me to defend him from death.

> So now I go to seek the murderer of my friend,
> Hector. And death shall I find at the moment
> Zeus wills it – Zeus and the other immortal.

It is the same despair that drives him on toward death, on the one hand, and slaughter on the other:

> I know it well, my fate is to perish here,
> Far from father and dearly loved mother; but meanwhile
> I shall not stop till the Trojans have had their fill of war.

The man possessed by this twofold need for death belongs, so long as he has not become something still different, to a different race from the race of the living.

What echo can the timid hopes of life strike in such a heart? How can it hear the defeated begging for another sight of the light of day? The threatened life has already been relieved of nearly all its consequence by a single, simple distinction: it is now unarmed; its adversary possesses a weapon. Furthermore, how can a man who has rooted out of himself the notion that the light of day is sweet to the eyes respect such a notion when it makes its appearance in some futile and humble lament?

> I clasp tight your knees, Achilles. Have a thought, have pity for me.
> I stand here, O son of Zeus, a suppliant, to be respected.
> In your house it was I first tasted Demeter's bread,
> That day in my well-pruned vineyard you caught me
> And sold me, sending me far from father and friends,
> To holy Lemnos; a hundred oxen was my price.
> And now I will pay you three hundred for ransom.
> This dawn is for me my twelfth day in Troy,
> After so many sorrows. See me here, in your hands,
> Through some evil fate. Zeus surely must hate me
> Who again puts me into your hands. Alas, my poor mother, Laothoe,
> Daughter of the old man, Altes – a short-lived son you have borne.

What a reception this feeble hope gets!

> Come, friend, you too must die. Why make a fuss about it?
> Patroclus, he too has died – a far better man than you are.
> Don't you see how handsome I am, how mighty?
> A noble father begat me, and I have a goddess for mother.
> Yet even I, like you, must some day encounter my fate,
> Whether the hour strikes at noon, or evening, or sunrise,
> The hour that comes when some arms-bearing warrior will kill me.

To respect life in somebody else when you have had to castrate yourself of all yearning for it demands a truly heart-breaking exertion of the powers of generosity. It is impossible to imagine any of Homer's warriors being capable of such an exertion, unless it is that warrior who dwells, in a peculiar way, at the very centre of the poem – I mean Patroclus, who 'knew how to be sweet to everybody', and who throughout the *Iliad* commits no cruel or brutal act. But then how many men do we know, in several thousand years of human history, who would have displayed such god-like generosity? Two or three? – even this is doubtful. Lacking this generosity, the conquering soldier is like a scourge of nature. Possessed by war, he, like the slave, becomes a thing, though his manner of doing so is different – over him too, words are as powerless as over matter itself. And both, at the touch of force, experience its inevitable effects: they become deaf and dumb.

Such is the nature of force. Its power of converting a man into a thing is a double one, and in its application double-edged. To the same degree, though in different fashions, those who use it and those who endure it are turned to stone. This property of force achieves its maximum effectiveness during the clash of arms, in battle, when the tide of the day has turned, and everything is rushing toward a decision. It is not the planning man, the man of strategy, the man acting on the resolution taken, who wins or loses a battle; battles are fought and decided by men deprived of these faculties, men who have undergone a transformation, who have dropped either to the level of inert matter, which is pure passivity, or to the level of blind force, which is pure momentum. Herein lies the last secret of war, a secret revealed by the *Iliad* in its similes, which liken the warriors either to fire, flood, wind, wild beasts, or God knows what blind cause of disaster, or else to frightened animals, trees, water, sand, to anything in nature that is set into motion by the violence of external forces. Greeks and Trojans, from one day to the next, sometimes even from one hour to the next, experience, turn and turn about, one or the other of these transmutations:

> As when a lion, murderous, springs among the cattle
> Which by thousands are grazing over some vast marshy field. . . .
> And their flanks heave with terror; even so the Achaeians
> Scattered in panic before Hector and Zeus, the great father.

> As when a ravening fire breaks out deep in a bushy wood
> And the wheeling wind scatters sparks far and wide,
> And trees, root and branch, topple over in flames;
> So Atreus' son, Agamemnon, roared through the ranks
> Of the Trojans in flight. . . .

The art of war is simply the art of producing such transformations, and its equipment, its processes, even the casualties it inflicts on the enemy, are only means directed toward this end – its true object is the warrior's soul. Yet these transformations are always a mystery; the gods are their authors, the gods who kindle men's imagination. But however caused, this petrifactive quality of force, twofold always, is essential to its nature; and a soul which has entered the province of force will not escape this except by a miracle. Such miracles are rare and of brief duration.

The wantonness of the conqueror that knows no respect for any creature or thing that is at its mercy or is imagined to be so, the despair of the soldier that drives him on to destruction, the obliteration of the slave or the conquered man, the wholesale slaughter – all these elements combine in the *Iliad* to make a picture of uniform horror, of which force is the sole hero. A monotonous desolation would result were it not for those few luminous moments, scattered here and there throughout the poem, those brief, celestial moments in which man possesses his soul. The soul that awakes then, to live for an instant only and be lost almost at once in force's vast kingdom, awakes pure and whole; it contains no ambiguities, nothing complicated or turbid; it has no room for anything but courage and love. Sometimes it is in the course of inner deliberations that a man finds his soul: he meets it, like Hector before Troy, as he tries to face destiny on his own terms, without the help of gods or men. At other times, it is in a moment of love that men discover their souls – and there is hardly any form of pure love known to humanity of which the *Iliad* does not treat. The tradition of hospitality persists, even though several generations, to dispel the blindness of combat.

> Thus I am for you a beloved guest in the breast of Argos . . .
> Let us turn our lances away from each other, even in battle.

The love of the son for the parents, of father for son, of mother for son, is continually described, in a manner as touching as it is curt:

> Thetis answered, shedding tears,
> 'You were born to me for a short life, my child, as you say . . .'

Even brotherly love:

> My three brothers whom the same mother bore for me,
> So dear. . . .

Conjugal love, condemned to sorrow, is of an astonishing purity. Imagining the humiliations of slavery which await a beloved wife, the husband passes over the one indignity which even in anticipation would stain their tenderness. What could be simpler than the words spoken by his wife to the man about to die?

> . . . . Better for me
> Losing you, to go under the earth. No other comfort
> Will remain, when you have encountered your death-heavy fate,
> Only grief, only sorrow. . . .

Not less touching are the words expressed to a dead husband:

> Dear husband, you died young, and left me your widow
> Alone in the palace. Our child is still tiny,
> The child you and I, crossed by fate, had together.
> I think he will never grow up . . .
> For not in your bed did you die, holding my hand
> And speaking to me prudent words which forever
> Night and day, as I weep, might live in my memory.

The most beautiful friendship of all, the friendship between comrades-at-arms, is the final theme of The Epic:

> . . . But Achilles
> Wept, dreaming of the beloved comrade; sleep, all-prevailing,
> Would not take him; he turned over again and again.

But the purest triumph of love, the drowning grace of war, is the friendship that floods the hearts of mortal enemies. Before it a murdered son or a murdered friend no longer cries out for vengeance. Before it – even more miraculous – the distance between benefactor and suppliant, between victor and vanquished, shrinks to nothing:

> But when thirst and hunger had been appeased,
> Then Dardanian Priam fell to admiring Achilles.
> How tall he was, and handsome; he had the face of a god;
> And in his turn Dardanian Priam was admired by Achilles,
> Who watched his handsome face and listened to his words.
> And when they were satisfied with contemplation of each other . . .

These moments of grace are rare in the *Iliad*, but they are enough to make us feel with sharp regret what it is that violence has killed and will kill again.

However, such a heaping-up of violent deeds would have a frigid effect, were it not for the note of incurable bitterness that continually makes itself heard, though often only a single word marks its presence, often a mere stroke of the verse, or a run-on line. It is in this that the *Iliad* is absolutely unique, in this bitterness that proceeds from tenderness and that spreads over the whole human race, impartial as sunlight. Never does the tone lose its colouring of bitterness; yet never does the bitterness drop into lamentation. Justice and love, which have hardly any place in this study of extremes and of unjust acts of violence, nevertheless bathe the work in their light without ever becoming noticeable themselves, except as a kind of accent. Nothing precious is scorned, whether or not death is its destiny; everyone's unhappiness is laid bare without dissimulation or disdain; no man is set above or below the condition common to all men; whatever is destroyed is regretted. Victors and vanquished are brought equally near us; under the same head, both are seen as counterparts of the poet, and the listener as well. If there is any difference, it is that the enemy's misfortunes are possibly more sharply felt.

> So he fell there, put to sleep in the sleep of bronze,
> Unhappy man, far from his wife, defending his own people. . . .

And what accents echo the fate of the lad Achilles sold at Lemnos!

> Eleven days he rejoiced his heart among those he loved,
> Returning from Lemnos; the twelfth day, once more,
> God delivered him into the hands of Achilles,
> To him who had to send him, unwilling, to Hades.

And the fate of Euphorbus, who saw only a single day of war.

> Blood soaked his hair, the hair like to the Graces' . . .

When Hector is lamented:

> . . . guardian of chaste wives and little children. . . .

In these few words, chastity appears, dirtied by force, and childhood delivered to the sword. The fountain at the gates of Troy becomes an object of poignant nostalgia when Hector runs by, seeking to elude his doom:

> Close by there stood the great stone tanks,
> Handsomely built, where silk-gleaming garments
> Were washed clean by Troy's lovely daughters and housewives
> In the old days of peace, long ago, when the Greeks had not come.
> Past these did they run their race, pursued and pursuer.

The whole of the *Iliad* lies under the shadow of the greatest calamity the human race can experience – the destruction of a city. This calamity could not tear more at the heart had the poet been born in Troy. But the tone is not different when the Achaeans are dying, far from home.

Insofar as this other life, the life of the living, seems calm and full, the brief evocations of the world of peace are felt as pain:

> With the break of dawn and the rising of the day,
> On both sides arrows flew, men fell.
> But at the very hour that the woodcutter goes home to fix his meal
> In the mountain valleys when his arms have had enough
> Of hacking great trees, and disgust rises in his heart,
> At that hour, by their valour, the Danaans broke the front.

Whatever is not war, whatever war destroys or threatens, the *Iliad* wraps in poetry; the realities of war, never. No reticence veils the step from life to death:

> Then his teeth flew out; from two sides,
> Blood came to his eyes; the blood that from lips and nostrils
> He was spilling, open-mouthed; death enveloped him in its black cloud.

The cold brutality of the deeds of war is left undisguised; neither victors nor vanquished are admired, scorned, or hated. Almost always, fate and the gods decide the changing lot of battle. Within the limits fixed by fate, the gods determine with sovereign authority victory and defeat. It is always they who provoke those fits of madness, those treacheries, which are forever blocking peace; war is their true business; their only motives, caprice and malice. As for the warriors, victors or vanquished, those comparisons which liken them to beasts or things can inspire neither admiration nor contempt, but only regret that men are capable of being so transformed.

There may be, unknown to us, other expressions of the extraordinary sense of equity which breathes through the *Iliad*; certainly it has not been imitated. One is barely aware that the poet is a Greek and not a Trojan. The tone of the poem furnishes a direct clue to the origin of its oldest portions; history perhaps will never be able to tell us more. If one believes with Thucydides that eighty years after the fall of Troy, the Achaeans in their turn were conquered, one may ask whether these songs, with their rare references to iron are not the songs of a conquered people, of whom a few went into exile. Obliged to live and die, 'very far from the homeland', like the Greeks who fell before Troy, having lost their cities like the Trojans, they saw their own image both in the conquerors, who had been their fathers, and in the conquered, whose misery was like their own. They could still see the Trojan war over that brief span of years in its true light, unglossed by pride or shame. They could look at it as conquered and as conquerors simultaneously, and so perceive what neither conqueror nor conquered ever saw, for both were blinded. Of course, this is mere fancy; one can see such distant times only in fancy's light.

In any case, this poem is a miracle. Its bitterness is the only justifiable bitterness, for it springs from the subjections of the human spirit to force, that is, in the last analysis, to matter. This subjection is the common lot, although each spirit will bear it differently, in proportion to its own virtue. No one in the *Iliad* is spared by it, as no one on earth is. No one who succumbs to it is by virtue of this fact regarded with contempt. Whoever, within his own soul and in human relations, escapes the dominion of force is loved but loved sorrowfully because of the threat of destruction that constantly hangs over him.

Such is the spirit of the only true epic the Occident possesses. The *Odyssey* seems merely a good imitation, now of the *Iliad*, now of Oriental poems; the *Aeneid* is an imitation which, however brilliant, is disfigured by frigidity, bombast, and bad taste. The *chansons de geste*, lacking the sense of equity, could not attain greatness: in the *Chanson de Roland*, the death of an enemy does not come home to either author or reader in the same way as does the death of Roland.

Attic tragedy, or at any rate the tragedy of Aeschylus and Sophocles, is the true continuation of the epic. The conception of justice enlightens it, without ever directly intervening in it; here force appears in its coldness and hardness, always attended by effects from whose fatality neither those who use it nor those who suffer it can escape; here the shame of the coerced spirit is neither disguised, nor enveloped in facile pity, nor held up to scorn; here more than one spirit bruised and degraded by misfortune is offered for our admiration. The Gospels are the last marvellous expression of the Greek genius, as the *Iliad* is the first: here the Greek spirit reveals itself not only in the injunction given mankind to seek above all other goods, 'the kingdom and justice of our Heavenly Father', but also in the fact that human suffering is laid bare, and we see it in a being who is at once divine and human. The accounts of the Passion show that a divine spirit, incarnate, is changed by misfortune, trembles before suffering and death, feels itself, in the depths of its agony, to be cut off from man and God. The sense of human misery gives the Gospels that accent of simplicity that is the mark of the Greek genius, and that endows Greek tragedy and the *Iliad* with all their value. Certain phrases have a ring strangely reminiscent of the epic, and it is the Trojan lad dispatched to Hades, though he does not wish to go, who comes to mind when Christ says to Peter: 'Another shall gird thee and carry thee whither thou wouldst not.' This accent cannot be separated from the idea that inspired the Gospels, for the sense of human misery is a pre-condition of justice and love. He who does not realize to what extent shifting fortune and necessity hold in subjection every human spirit, cannot regard as fellow-creatures nor love as he loves himself those whom chance separated from him by an abyss. The variety of constraints pressing upon man give rise to the illusion of several distinct species that cannot communicate. Only he who has measured the dominion of force, and knows how not to respect it, is capable of love and justice.

The relations between destiny and the human soul, the extent to which each soul creates its own destiny, the question of what elements in the soul are transformed by merciless necessity as it tailors the soul to fit the requirements of shifting fate, and of what elements can on the other hand be preserved, through the exercise of virtue and through grace – this whole question is fraught with temptations to falsehood, temptations that are positively enhanced by pride, by shame, by hatred, contempt, indifference, by the will to oblivion or to ignorance. Moreover, nothing is so rare as to see misfortune fairly portrayed; the tendency is either to treat the unfortunate person as though catastrophe were his natural vocation, or to ignore the effects of misfortune on the soul, to assume, that is, that the soul can suffer and remain unmarked by it, can fail, in fact, to be recast in misfortune's image. The Greeks, generally speaking, were endowed with spiritual force that allowed them to avoid self-deception. The rewards of this were great; they discovered how to achieve in all their acts the greatest lucidity, purity, and simplicity. But the spirit that was transmitted from the *Iliad* to the Gospels by way of the tragic poets never jumped the borders of Greek civilization; once Greece was destroyed, nothing remained of this spirit but pale reflections.

Both the Romans and the Hebrews believed themselves to be exempt from the misery that is the common human lot. The Romans saw their country as the nation chosen by destiny to be mistress of the world; with the Hebrews, it was their God who exalted them and they retained their superior position just as long as they obeyed Him. Strangers, enemies, conquered peoples, subjects, slaves, were objects of contempt to the Romans; and the Romans had no epics, no tragedies. In Rome gladiatorial fights took the place of tragedy. With the Hebrews, misfortune was a sure indication of sin and hence a legitimate object of contempt; to them a vanquished enemy was abhorrent to God himself and condemned to expiate all sorts of crimes – this is a view that makes cruelty permissible and indeed indispensable. And no text of the Old Testament strikes a note comparable to the note heard in the Greek epic, unless it be certain parts of the book of Job. Throughout twenty centuries of Christianity, the Romans and the Hebrews have been admired, read, imitated, both in deed and word; their masterpieces have yielded an appropriate quotation every time anybody had a crime he wanted to justify.

Furthermore, the spirit of the Gospels was not handed down in a pure state from one Christian generation to the next. To undergo suffering and death joyfully was from the very beginning considered a sign of grace in the Christian martyrs – as though grace could do more for a human being than it could for Christ. Those who believe that God himself, once he became man, could not face the harshness of destiny without a long tremor of anguish, should have understood that the only people who can give the impression of having risen to a higher plane, who seem superior to ordinary human misery, are the people who resort to the aids of illusion, exaltation, fanaticism, to conceal the harshness of destiny from their own eyes. The man who does not wear the armour of the lie cannot experience force without being touched by it to the very soul. Grace can prevent this touch from corrupting him, but it cannot spare him the wound. Having forgotten it too well, Christian tradition can only rarely recover that simplicity that renders so poignant every sentence in the story of the Passion. On the other hand, the practice of forcible proselytization threw a veil over the effects of force on the souls of those who used it.

In spite of the brief intoxication induced at the time of the Renaissance by the discovery of Greek literature, there has been, during the course of twenty centuries, no revival of the Greek genius. Something of it was seen in Villon, in Shakespeare, Cervantes, Molière, and – just once – in Racine. The bones of human suffering are exposed in *L'École des Femmes* and in *Phèdre*, love being the context – a strange century indeed, which took the opposite view from that of the epic period, and would only acknowledge human suffering in the context of love, while it insisted on swathing with glory the effects of force in war and in politics. To the list of writers given above, a few other names might be added. But nothing the peoples of Europe have produced is worth the first known poem that appeared among them. Perhaps they will yet rediscover the epic genius, when they learn that there is no refuge from fate, learn not to admire force, not to hate the enemy, nor to scorn the unfortunate. How soon this will happen is another question.

BERTRAND RUSSELL

1872-

It would be hard to imagine any public figure in the last century who has contributed more than Bertrand Russell to the defence of individual liberties against the demands of organized society. From his participation in the No Conscription movement in England during the First World War to his present advocacy of unilateral disarmament – activities interspersed by imprisonment and public censure – he has sought to apply the logic of philosophy to contemporary needs.

He maintains that at no time was he ever a 'complete' pacifist; in *War and Non-Resistance* (1915) he stated that

> The principle that it is always wrong to employ force against another human being has been held in its extreme form by Quakers and by Tolstoy, but has always been rejected by the great majority of mankind as inconsistent with the existence of civilized society. In this, no doubt, the majority of mankind are in the right. But I think that the occasions where forcible resistance is the best course are much fewer than is generally believed, and that some very great and important advances in civilization might be made if this were more widely recognized. The so-called 'right of self-defence', in particular, seems to have only a very limited sphere of application, and to be often supported by arguments involving both mistakes as to political questions and a wrong conception of the best type of character.

His great concern has been with the preservation of civilization, and it is in this light that one must see his efforts to defend the rights and liberties of the individual. In his preface to *Justice in War-time* (1916), he expressed the wish that the publication of the articles collected in that volume 'might make the English people aware of the crimes that have been committed in its name, to recall it to the temper in which peace can be made and preserved, and to point the way to a better national pride than that of dominion'. He did not overlook the sins of Germany, but insisted that responsibility for the war was not one-sided. Therefore, 'because I prize civilization. . . but above all because I love England . . .' he would reveal what he felt was the truth of matter, regardless of how unpopular such a publication would be at the time. He has recently called for Britain's unilateral disarmament, as a step worthy of English history, as an example to other nations in the midst of the most perilous armaments race in the world's history.

The two selections taken from Bertrand Russell's work are 'Man's Peril' taken from *Portraits from Memory* (1956) and 'Inconsistency?' from *Common Sense and Nuclear Warfare* (1959).

Man's Peril

I am speaking on this occasion not as a Briton, not as a European, not as a member of a Western democracy, but as a human being, a member of the species Man, whose continued existence is in doubt. The world is full of conflicts: Jews and Arabs; Indians and Pakistanis; white men and Negroes in Africa; and, over-shadowing all minor conflicts, the titanic struggle between Communism and anti-Communism.

Almost everybody who is politically conscious has strong feelings about one or more of these issues; but I want you, if you can, to set aside such feelings for the moment and consider yourself only as a member of a biological species which has had a remarkable history and whose disappearance none of us can desire. I shall try to say no single word which should appeal to one group rather than to another. All, equally, are in peril, and, if the peril is understood, there is hope that they may collectively avert it. We have to learn to think in a new way. We have to learn to ask ourselves not what steps can be taken to give military victory to whatever group we prefer, for there no longer are such steps. The question we have to ask ourselves is: What steps can be taken to prevent a military contest of which the issue must be disastrous to all sides?

The general public, and even many men in positions of authority, have not realized what would be involved in a war with hydrogen bombs. The general public still thinks in terms of the obliteration of cities. It is understood that the new bombs are more powerful than the old and that, while one atomic bomb could obliterate Hiroshima, one hydrogen bomb could obliterate the largest cities such as London, New York, and Moscow. No doubt in a hydrogen-bomb war great cities would be obliterated. But this is one of the minor disasters that would have to be faced. If everybody in London, New York, and Moscow were exterminated, the world might, in the course of a few centuries, recover from the blow. But we now know, especially since the Bikini test, that hydrogen bombs can gradually spread destruction over a much wider area than had been supposed. It is stated on very good authority that a bomb can now be manufactured which will be 25,000 times as powerful as that which destroyed Hiroshima. Such a bomb, if exploded near the ground or under water, sends radio-active particles into the upper air. They sink gradually and reach the surface of the earth in the form of a deadly dust or rain. It was this dust which infected the Japanese fishermen and their catch of fish although they were outside what American experts believed to be the danger zone. No one knows how widely such lethal radio-active particles might be diffused, but the best authorities are unanimous in saying that a war with hydrogen bombs is quite likely to put an end to the human race. It is feared that if many hydrogen bombs are used there will be universal death – sudden only for a fortunate minority, but for the majority a slow torture of disease and disintegration.

I will give a few instances out of many. Sir John Slessor, who can speak with unrivalled authority from his experiences of air warfare, has said: 'A world war in this day and age would be general suicide'; and has gone on to state: 'It never has and never will make any sense trying to abolish any particular *weapon* of war. What we have got to abolish is *war*.' Lord Adrian, who is the leading English authority on nerve physiology, recently emphasized the same point in his address as President of the British Association. He said: 'We must face the possibility that repeated atomic explosions will lead to a degree of general radio-activity which no one can tolerate or escape'; and he added: 'Unless we are ready to give up some of our old loyalties, we may be forced into a fight which might end the human race,' Air Chief Marshal Sir Philip Joubert says: 'With the advent of the hydrogen bomb, it would appear that the human race has arrived at a point where it must abandon war as a continuation of policy or accept the possibility of total destruction.' I could prolong such quotations indefinitely.

Many warnings have been uttered by eminent men of science and by authorities in military strategy. None of them will say that the worst results are certain. What they do say is that these results are possible and no one can be sure that they will not be realized. I have not found that the views of experts on this question depend in any degree upon their politics or prejudices. They depend only, so far as my researches have revealed, upon the extent of the particular expert's knowledge. I have found that the men who know most are most gloomy.

STARK, INESCAPABLE PROBLEM

Here, then, is the problem which I present to you, stark and dreadful and inescapable: Shall we put an end to the human race; or shall mankind renounce war? People will not face this alternative because it is so difficult to abolish war. The abolition of war will demand distasteful limitations of national sovereignty. But what perhaps impedes understanding of the situation more than anything else is that the term 'mankind' feels vague and abstract. People scarcely realize in imagination that the danger is to themselves and their children and their grandchildren, and not only to a dimly apprehended humanity. And so they hope that perhaps war may be allowed to continue provided modern weapons are prohibited. I am afraid this hope is illusory. Whatever agreements not to use hydrogen bombs had been reached in time of peace, they would no longer be considered binding in time of war, and both sides would set to work to manufacture hydrogen bombs as soon as war broke out, for if one side manufactured the bombs and the other did not, the side that manufactured them would inevitably be victorious.

On both sides of the Iron Curtain there are political obstacles to emphasis on the destructive character of future war. If either side were to announce that it would on no account resort to war, it would be diplomatically at the mercy of the other side. Each side, for the sake of self-preservation, must continue to say that there are provocations that it will not endure. Each side may long for an accommodation, but neither side dare express this longing convincingly. The position is analogous to that of duellists in former times. No doubt it frequently happened that each of the duellists feared death and desired an accommodation, but neither could say so, since, if he did, he would be thought a coward. The only hope in such cases was intervention by friends of both parties suggesting an accommodation to which both could agree at the same moment. This is an exact analogy to the present position of the protagonists on either side of the Iron Curtain. If an agreement making war improbable is to be reached, it will have to be by the friendly offices of neutrals, who can speak of the disastrousness of war without being accused of advocating a policy of 'appeasement'. The neutrals have every right, even from the narrowest consideration of self-interest, to do whatever lies in their power to prevent the outbreak of a world war, for if such a war does break out, it is highly probable that all the inhabitants of neutral countries, along with the rest of mankind, will perish. If I were in control of a neutral government, I should certainly consider it my paramount duty to see to it that my country would continue to have inhabitants, and the only way by which I could make this probable would be to promote some kind of accommodation between the powers on opposite sides of the Iron Curtain.

I, personally, am of course, not neutral in my feeling and I should not wish to see the danger of war averted by an abject submission of the West. But, as a human being, I have to remember that, if the issues between East and West are to be decided in any manner that can give any possible satisfaction to anybody, whether Communist or anti-Communist, whether Asian or European or American, whether white or black, then these issues must not be decided by war. I should wish this to be understood on both sides of the Iron Curtain. It is emphatically not enough to have it understood on one side only. I think the neutrals, since they are not caught in our tragic dilemma, can, if they will, bring about this realization on both sides. I should like to see one or more neutral powers appoint a commission of experts, who should all be neutrals, to draw up a report on the destructive effects to be expected in a war with hydrogen bombs, not only among the belligerents but also among neutrals. I should wish this report presented to the governments of all the Great Powers with an invitation to express their agreement or disagreement with its findings. I think it possible that in this way all the Great Powers could be led to agree that a world war can no longer serve the purposes of any of them, since it is likely to exterminate friend and foe equally and neutrals likewise.

As geological time is reckoned, Man has so far existed only for a very short period – 1,000,000 years at the most. What he has achieved, especially during the last 6,000 years, is something utterly new in the history of the Cosmos, so far at least as we are acquainted with it. For countless ages the sun rose and set, the moon waxed and waned, the stars shone in the night, but it was only with the coming of Man that these things were understood. In the great world of astronomy and in the little world of the atom, Man has unveiled secrets which might have been thought undiscoverable. In art and literature and religion, some men have shown a sublimity of feeling which makes the species worth preserving. Is all this to end in trivial horror because so few are able to think of Man rather than of this or that group of men? Is our race so destitute of wisdom, so incapable of impartial love, so blind even to the simplest dictates of self-preservation, that the last proof of its silly cleverness is to be the extermination of all life on our planet? – for it will be not only men who will perish, but also the animals, whom no one can accuse of Communism or anti-Communism.

I cannot believe that this is to be the end. I would have men forget their quarrels for a moment and reflect that, if they will allow themselves to survive, there is every reason to expect the triumphs of the future to exceed immeasurably the triumphs of the past. There lies before us, if we choose, continual progress in happiness, knowledge, and wisdom. Shall we, instead, choose death, because we cannot forget our quarrels? I appeal, as a human being to human beings: remember your humanity, and forget the rest. If you can do so, the way lies open to a new Paradise; if you cannot, nothing lies before you but universal death.

Inconsistency?

Opponents of my recent activities in the campaign against H-bomb warfare have brought up what they consider to be an inconsistency on my part and have used statements that I made ten years ago to impair the force of the statements that I have made more recently. I should like to clear up this matter once for all.

At a time when America alone possessed the atom bomb and when the American Government was advocating what was known as the Baruch Proposal, the aim of which was to internationalize all the uses of atomic energy, I thought the American proposal both wise and generous. It seemed to me that the Baruch scheme, if adopted, would prevent an atomic arms race, the appalling dangers of which were evident to all informed opinion in the Western World. For a time it seemed possible that the U.S.S.R. would agree to this scheme, since Russia had everything to gain by agreeing and nothing to lose. Unfortunately, Stalin's suspicious nature made him think that there was some trap, and Russia decided to produce her own atomic weapons. I thought, at that time, that it would be worth while to bring pressure to bear upon Russia and even, if necessary, to go so far as to threaten war on the sole issue of the internationalizing of atomic weapons. My aim, then as now, was to prevent a war in which both sides possessed the power of producing world-wide disaster. Western statesmen, however, confident of the supposed technical superiority of the West, believed that there was no danger of Russia achieving equality with the non-Communist world in the field of nuclear warfare. Their confidence in this respect has turned out to have been mistaken. It follows that, if nuclear war is now to be prevented, it must be by new methods and not by those which could have been employed ten years ago.

My critics seem to think that, if you have once advocated a certain policy, you should continue to advocate it after all the circumstances have changed. This is quite absurd. If a man gets into a train with a view to reaching a certain destination and on the way the train breaks down, you will not consider the man guilty of an inconsistency if he gets out of the train and employs other means of reaching his destination. In like manner, a person who advocates a certain policy in certain circumstances will advocate a quite different policy in different circumstances.

I have never been a complete pacifist and have at no time maintained that all who wage war are to be condemned. I have held the view, which I should have thought was that of common sense, that some wars have been justified and others not. What makes the peculiarity of the present situation is that, if a great war should break out, the belligerents on either side and the neutrals would be all, equally, defeated. This is a new situation and means that war cannot still be used as an instrument of policy. It is true that the threat of war can still be used, but only by a lunatic. Unfortunately, some people *are* lunatics, and, not long ago, there were such lunatics in command of a powerful State. We cannot be sure this will not happen again and, if it does, it will produce a disaster compared with which the horrors achieved by Hitler were a flea-bite. The world at present is balanced in unstable equilibrium upon a sharp edge. To achieve stability, new methods are required, and it is these new methods that those who think as I do are attempting to urge upon the East and upon the West.

I do not deny that the policy that I have advocated has changed from time to time. It has changed as circumstances have changed. To achieve a single purpose, sane men adapt their policies to the circumstances. Those who do not are insane.

Though I do not admit inconsistency, I would not be wholly sincere if I did not admit that my mood and feelings have undergone a change somewhat deeper than that resulting from strategic considerations alone. The awful prospect of the extermination of the human race, if not in the next war, then in the next but one or the next but two, is so sobering to any imagination which has seriously contemplated it as to demand very fundamental fresh thought on the whole subject not only of international relations but of human life and its capabilities. If you were quarrelling with a man about some issue that both you and he had thought important just at the moment when a sudden hurricane threatened to destroy you both and the whole neighbourhood, you would probably forget the quarrel. I think what is important at present is to make mankind aware of the hurricane and forgetful of the issue which had been producing strife. I know it is difficult after spending many years and much eloquence on the evils of Communism or Capitalism, as the case may be, to see this issue as one of relative un-importance. But, although this is difficult, it is what both the Communist Rulers and the men who shape the policy of the West will have to achieve if mankind is to survive. To make such a realization possible is the purpose of the policy which I now advocate.

CONSCIENTIOUS
OBJECTION

CONSCIENTIOUS objection, the passive resistance of an individual to the demands of a social group to coerce him to act contrary to his scruples, generally takes the form of the refusal by an individual to serve in the armed forces at the demand of the State. It is, naturally, a pacifist's most striking act of faith, although conscientious objection is by no means confined to pacifists; the attention of the governments and public in the First World War, for example, was focused on the conscientious objection of many socialists who scrupled to enter a war for which they held capitalism responsible. Some socialists, however, expressed no hesitation about participating on the side of the proletariat in a class war against capitalist interests.

The religious objector in both world wars in England and America was in most cases able to defend his position within the context of the law, some by doing alternative service of one form or another. But conscientious objectors who absolutely refused to cooperate with the government received, with hardly an exception, prison sentences. In Germany in the First World War, those refusing non-combative service were judged insane; in France they were shot as deserters.

While the number of conscientious objectors has increased with each war, so have the numbers of men conscripted. There were approximately 4,000 American conscientious objectors in the First World War and 50,000 in the Second, but the number of men conscripted rose from just under 3,000,000 to 13,000,000. On the whole, there is increasing willingness on the part of governments in non-Communist countries to accord status to conscientious objection, but the laws under which individual cases are judged remain archaic.

The early history of conscientious objection is largely associated with the Christian Church which, in its first three centuries, was absolute in its opposition to warfare. Readers further interested in the subject, on which there is a large literature, should consult Clarence Marsh Case's *Non-Violent Coercion* (1923) and Hi Doty's *Bibliography of Conscientious Objection to War*.

The four selections printed below range in time from 295 to the Second World War. The trial of Maximilianus is quoted from *Acta*

Martyrum (Ratisbon, 1859). *Questions to a Conscientious Objector* (1679), an account of a Quaker on trial, is taken from an article of the same title by Henry J. Cadbury in *Fellowship*, May 1960. Howard Schoenfeld's 'The Danbury Story', first appeared in an anthology of the Second World War conscientious objectors' prison experiences under the title *Prison Etiquette*. 'The Nature of Conscription' is taken from A. J. Muste's *Of Holy Disobedience*, published in 1952.

The Trial of Maximilianus

A conscription meeting which was held on 12 March 295, in the town of Thevesta in North Africa. Commission consisted of the proconsul Dion, the fiscal counsel, the imperial agent, and the tax collector, who in case of exemption from military service had to take over the money paid in lieu of it. Other persons concerned were the conscript Maximilianus, the father who accompanied him and the beadle.

THE PROCONSUL: The conscript Maximilianus is fit for military service. Consequently he has to be put under the foot rule. [To Maximilianus] What is your name?

MAXIMILIANUS: Why do you want to know my name? I am forbidden to become a soldier, as I am a Christian.

THE PROCONSUL: All right. Officer, put this man under the foot rule.

MAXIMILIANUS: As you please. [He places himself under the foot rule.] But I cannot become a soldier, I cannot do evil. I am a Christian.

THE PROCONSUL: Measure him!

THE OFFICER: He is five feet ten.

THE PROCONSUL: Let him have the badge.

MAXIMILIANUS: I do not want the badge. I cannot be a soldier.

THE PROCONSUL: You will be a soldier or you will be killed.

MAXIMILIANUS: I will not be a soldier. You may cut off my head if you like. I cannot be a soldier for the world, I am a soldier for my God.

THE PROCONSUL [to Victor, the father of the conscript]: Advise your son.

THE FATHER: My son knows his duty.

THE PROCONSUL: In the sacred surroundings of our masters Diocletian and Maximian, Constantius and Maximus, there are Christian soldiers who fulfil their military duty.

MAXIMILIANUS: They know what they are doing. I, as a Christian, cannot commit an evil deed.

THE PROCONSUL: What evil do those commit who fulfil their military duty?

MAXIMILIANUS: You know very well.

THE PROCONSUL: Be a soldier. Remember that your refusal of service may be the cause of a cruel death.

MAXIMILIANUS: I shall not die. If it happens that I leave this world my soul will live with Jesus Christ, my Lord.

THE PROCONSUL [to the officer]: Cancel the name of Maximilianus upon the muster role. [To Maximilianus] As you wickedly refuse to fulfil your military duty, receive the sentence which you deserve, and which will be an example to others. [Reads from a tablet.] Since Maximilianus refuses to take his oath as a soldier he is sentenced to die by the sword.

MAXIMILIANUS: God be praised!

Questions to a Conscientious Objector (1679)

The Account of Philip Ford's being summoned to appear before the Lieutenancy at Guildhall, London in the 1st mo. 1678/0 where Sir Thomas Davies was chairman, with queries proposed and answers thereto with a copy of their warrant and particular[s] of goods distrained.

Q. Complaint is made that you appeared not with your arms according to summons.

A. Here's a summons dated the 7th of February last which I received.

Q. Received you not one before?

A. Yes.

Q. Wherefore did you not then appear?

A. Before the first summons came I received a summons from the Prince of Peace to march under his banner, which is love, who came not to destroy men's lives but to save them. And being [en]listed under this banner I dare not desert my colours to march under the banner – shop – of the kings of the earth.

Q. Prince of Peace, Prince of Peace, who is that, the Pope?

A. No, the Pope is the Prince of plotters and murderers.

Q. Do you not pay taxes to the King?

A. Yes, and that with a ready mind. I pay tribute to Caesar, that so I may live a peaceable and godly life under his government, and rather than Caesar should want his tribute should search the fish's mouth.

Q. The King builds ships and buys guns and powder with it.

A. When Christ bid Peter pay the tribute for them two, he did not bid inquire what use Caesar would put it to. And as not his concern, so not mine.

Q. Caesar maintained his armies and navies with it.

A. It may be so.

Q. Do not you pay to the city watch?

A. Yes, and that freely.

Q. Do not you believe a man may be killed with an halbert?

A. I believe a man may be killed with a knife that is made intentionally to cut his victuals with.

Q. But do not you believe a man may be killed with an halbert?

A. I make a distinction betwixt the military power and the civil. The military power's command is, Go, fire, kill and destroy. The civil power's command is, Go, keep the peace.

Q. The military power is not so.

A. Be pleased to read your commission. (It was read, the substance being to exercise the soldiers and be subject to superior officers, and they to the King, etc.) Be pleased to take notice, you are first to exercise the soldiers and make them expert to kill one another. Then when the word of command is given, Go charge, horse, foot, cannon, fire, kill and destroy, you must be subject to superior officers, and so fall on and deface the workmanship of God.

Q. What precept in Scripture can you show for this your practice, if all men were of your mind?

A. The children of Israel were required once a year to go up to Jerusalem to worship, and them that did not, several plagues were pronounced against them. At which time when they went, though at war with their neighbour nations round about, at that time when gone, God turned the hearts of their enemies that no inroad was made upon them in all their borders. And that temple worship, which if all were come to the same Lord, God would take care of all that put their trust in him.

Q. Did not the Christians in former ages assist the Emperors in their wars?

A. Yes, they did, and please to peruse Tertullian. There you may find the product of their enterprises when their faith in God began to fail them, and they took carnal weapons, there the apostasy entered, and the Pope got over most called Christians.

Q. You must be subject to the King's laws.

A. I am so. All laws being fulfilled by active or passive obedience. And that which for conscience' sake I cannot comply with I shall endeavour patiently to undergo the penalty.

Q. Then fine him five pounds a time.

A. As to that use your pleasure, for if I were sure you would take all I have, I could not give one farthing to prevent it.

Q. You say you can pay tribute to Caesar. This is a tribute to appear with your arms at the King's command.

A. Christ Jesus the Prince of Peace who paid tribute to Caesar gives the word of command to his followers to love their enemies, do good to those that hate them and despitefully use them and persecute them. And your command to your followers is to kill your enemies. So that I choose rather to obey the captain of my salvation than you, whatever he may suffer you to inflict upon me for so doing.

Withdraw. Call him in.

Q. The Court being informed upon oath, that you have been absent from your duty two and twenty times, have fined you only a mark a time, which if you will tender here to the Court you will see how the Court will be to you.

A. I dare not tender one farthing in consideration thereof. But this please to take notice of that when David came before King Saul going to battle he required his armour to be put on him. Which David rejected and would not use it, which to me seems a greater contempt of authority than my refusing to bear my own arms, yet for all that Saul did not mark[1] David as you have marked me.

Q. You mistake the point. David did not refuse to wear the armour because it was King Saul's. He refused it because it was not easy for him.

A. If my musket were easy for me, neither should I [refuse it].

The warrant authorizing distraint then follows:

1. to mark = to fine a mark, i.e. 13s. 4d.

Whereas the several persons undernamed duly charged by his Majesty's Lieutenancy of the said city to find arms in the company of the Trained Bands of the said city and were also by order of the said lieutenancy to appear in their arms at several duties performed of the Blue Regiment in the said city upon the several days last past in that company whereof the Honorable Sir William Pritchard, Knight, is Captain, have refused and neglected to appear in arms upon the said duty in contempt of Acts of Parliament in this behalf made. His Majesty's said Lieutenancy have and do hereby inflict upon the said parties the several sums of money to their names here respectively set down mentioned. These are therefore in his Majesty's name to will and require you forthwith upon sight hereof to levy upon the goods and chattels of the said several persons the said several sums of money according to the said Acts of Parliament, and hereof fail you not at your peril, viz.

Philip Ford for defaults 13s. 4d a default, £14 13s. 4d.

The Danbury Story

The Warden adjusted his glasses.

'Men,' he said, 'This is my last appeal to you. Your group is conspiring to buck the authority of the bureau of prisons. If you persist in your foolhardy conspiracy not only your lives, but the lives of the 600 other men in this institution will be adversely affected. So will the lives of the thousands that will follow them. If you won't think of yourselves, think of them. Do you want them to be punished for your actions?'

The Warden paused. His future in the prison system was bound up in his ability to meet such situations as this, and he was doing his best to reason with us. He was a man of about fifty, with a clean cut, intelligent face.

His position was both delicate and difficult. If word of our impending strike reached the public there would, undoubtedly, be a terrific reaction to it, and he was certain to be made the scapegoat. On the other hand if word failed to reach the public he would probably be accused of suppressing the news, and meanwhile his authority within the prison seemed sure to be undermined.

The Warden was a man with a comparatively advanced outlook. There were adequate recreational facilities in his prison, smoking was permitted in the mess hall, movies were shown once a week, inmates were allowed to put on shows, the yard period was long, the institution's soft ball team was given ample time to practice, and the prison generally was run along what are considered liberal lines.

The Warden was a good natured man with a sense of humor and a keen feeling of sympathy for the underdog. Ironically, he requested the prison bureau to send us to his prison; and, to be perfectly honest, the worst we suffered under his administration was solitary confinement, whereas wardens at other prisons allowed guards to beat and torture inmates of our type.

The Warden was a sports enthusiast of the first order. No broadcast of a fight or an important game passed without the inmates hearing it. He had been known to rouse the whole prison after lights out to show a new fight film, even going so far as to let the men in solitary out to see it. And no inmate was happier than he over the fact that the prison soft ball team was undefeated in a really excellent league, and was scheduled to play the other undefeated team, a group of college men, in a few weeks, for the championship of that area.

The prison team's high standing was due to the good pitching of a convict in our group of strikers, and it was this, coupled with the Warden's love of sports, that was partially responsible for the extraordinary event which occurred in the prison later.

The Warden was a liberal with a position of authority in an evil system. On the whole he attempted to use his authority to alleviate the evil. The attempt was foredoomed and futile. Despite everything he had done, his prison was still a hell on earth.

Negroes were segregated, teen-aged convicts were thrown into solitary, foul food was served frequently, the lunacy ward was used to coerce the sane, reading matter was censored unmercifully, stool pigeons plied their rotten trade, men 'blew their tops', and the constant surveillance and grinding monotony of confinement took its inevitable toll.

The reforms instituted by the Warden seemed to us to be of a piddling nature when placed alongside the general horror of everyday prison life, though we weren't striking against the prison system at that time. Many of us had clashed with the system and would continue to do so, but on this occasion our strike was of a more fundamental nature.

Inescapably, the Warden was forced to oppose us, and uphold his authority; and, with it, the authority of the evil system that gave him his power. For a kind man, which he seemed to me to be, it was a tragic situation.

A good impulse prompted him to ask the prison bureau to send us to his prison. His fate was to discover us unmanageable. We were a proud, stiff-necked lot who openly boasted we were the most radical men in the country. We lined up that way, radical versus liberal, and began our struggle.

The Warden continued to speak.

'If you carry through with this strike, not only will your lives be affected, but liberalism itself may be wiped out in the prison bureau. All of you know how hard some of us in the bureau have struggled to better the lot of the inmate. We've made progress lately, and we expect to make more, but the forces against us are powerful, and the balance delicate. A strike at this time may upset the balance and throw the prison bureau backwards to the conditions of 20 years ago. None of you men want that.'

'But we aren't striking against the prison bureau,' someone said.

'It doesn't make any difference why you're striking. The question is can any group in a federal prison call a strike at any time. The issue here is whether your group of twenty or thirty men has the authority in this prison or whether the people of the United States through the Federal Bureau of Prisons and the Warden have it.'

The Warden was good humored and even friendly despite the forcefulness of his words.

'I want to be fair to you men,' he said. 'In many ways the circumstances behind this strike are unusual, and therefore I'm willing to make concessions. For example I might allow your group to cease work on the designated day and turn the chapel over to you, provided you give your word not to ask the rest of the inmate body to join you. You'll have to make it clear, however, that you're not protesting against the prison bureau and that the nature of the services are religious, rather than a strike.'

The fairness of this proposal struck me at once and I was genuinely sorry we couldn't agree with the Warden on it. Unfortunately, any arrangement other than a strike would have destroyed the meaning and effect of our protest.

'Any inmate who wants to join us has been invited to do so,' a convict said.

The Warden shook his head.

334

'Impossible. Supposing everybody joins you. Who will man the hospitals and take care of the sick? Who will take care of the kitchen and other chores?'

'We'll leave skeleton crews on duty,' another convict said.

'None of the other inmates are going to join us, anyway,' someone else said.

Others chipped in with similar comments.

The Warden raised his hand for silence.

'I've made my offer,' he said. 'It's up to you to decide whether you'll take it or not. If not, you'll have to take the consequences.'

We decided to take the consequences.

The other inmates, though they failed to join the strike, kept us informed and/or misinformed via the grapevine of the Prison Bureau's moves the following day.

The Bureau, thoroughly aroused, acted swiftly.

Apparently fearing a general strike of riot proportions, carloads of Department of Justice men, armed with machine guns and tear gas, were unloaded at the prison gates, according to the grapevine. Other Department of Justice men, it seemed, were released in the prison disguised as inmates. Guards, on their own hook, and probably without official knowledge, went their rounds letting the inmates know they'd be safe in starting fights with any in our group of conscientious objectors, if they wanted to do so. Our case as pacifists would be less clear in the public eye if we fought back, thereby making it possible for the Bureau to get tougher with us.

Early in the afternoon stool pigeons began circulating among the men in an effort to bring inmate pressure to bear on us. The prison would be punished as a whole if the strike took place, they explained. Smoking, letter writing, and visiting privileges would be withdrawn from all. Other punitive measures would be taken.

The six or seven hundred bootleggers, counterfeiters, embezzlers, smugglers, pimps, white slavers, con men, dope peddlers, robbers, murderers, and what have you, comprising the so-called criminal population of the prison stood to lose considerably by our strike; yet not one of them put the slightest pressure on us to change our stand.

During the few months we had been in prison the inmates had grown to love and respect us – as we had them. They were a patient, forebearing body, daily putting up with the most degrading and despicable treatment by the prison bureau. We cast our lot in with theirs from the beginning, and all of our group of ministers, divinity students, and socialists had been in solitary or restrictions at one time or another for protesting against the evil conditions under which they lived.

Furthermore, in our group of absolutists, were many spiritually developed men of almost saintly stature. Even the judges who sentenced them recognized it. One judge, after hearing the Union Theological Seminary students in our group, wept and apologized as he passed sentence on them. Another judge, sentencing Arle Brooks, after reviewing his life of service to others in a probationary report, remarked that he felt like Pontius Pilate.

These men and the others seemed to me, a socialist, to be the first truly religious men I had ever met, and I have known rabbis, ministers, priests, and church goers all my life. Under their influence many an inmate, who had never known kindness or even decent treatment before, discovered his own spiritual potential.

The guards and prison officials were also aware of the unusual situation in the prison, and more than one commented on it. There was less swearing, fighting and sex talk; more studying, discussion and quiet re-appraisement. A general restoration of self respect seemed to be taking place among the men.

Our strike was one in which they had no apparent stake; yet they were as zealous of our welfare as if they had been blood relatives.

By late afternoon the prison was in a state of nervous apprehension. When the supper whistle blew that evening the men poured out of their cell blocks and surged across the prison yard toward the mess hall, carrying us along with them. Midway, they came to a sudden halt.

The Warden was standing on a small box in the center of the yard. Guards quickly rounded the men up and herded them into a bunched mass in front of him. Other convicts continued to pour out into the mob. I moved toward the rear and two guards detached themselves and moved in behind me. Other guards stationed themselves wherever there were conscientious objectors. The men stirred restlessly, anxious to get to their suppers. Night was falling and a high wind was whipping through the yard.

The Warden began to speak.

As everyone knew, he said, a general strike was being called the next morning by a small group of inmates. The nature of the strike as he saw it did not concern the rest of the inmates and he expressed the belief that they wouldn't join us. We were not striking against the Prison Bureau or the administration of the prison, he pointed out, but against the government of the U.S.

The patriotism of the group calling the strike, though we were not yet at war, was of a questionable nature. We had deliberately disobeyed the law of the land and that was why we were in prison. We had been trouble makers from the beginning and now we were wilfully calling a strike against the best interests of the nation.

Everybody was against war, including himself, and he had gone along with us as long as he could, offering to allow us the use of the chapel for prayer and meditation on the designated day, but we had rejected the offer, preferring to flout the authority of the prison bureau and the government.

The selfishness of our course was apparent. A strike in the prison bureau at this time might prove disastrous. The Bureau was more liberal than at any time in its history. He dwelt on the gains that had been made recently and emphasized the benefits accruing to the inmates. Our strike would be a blow to those gains, giving the reactionary opposition an opportunity to criticize, and halt them, possibly destroy them altogether. The inmates would see the wisdom of steering clear of our strike, and the selfishness of it. He expressed his confidence in the men, and knew he could count on them for support. He paused for applause.

Silence met him.

Hastily, he continued his speech. He emphasized again the gains that had been made in the bureau, the threat to them, the selfishness of our group of men. We had so little consideration for the inmates we were going to deprive them of their food, if we had our way, by calling the kitchen help out on strike. We were going to deprive the hospital of help, leaving the sick and dying to shift for themselves. The Warden was interrupted by a clear, but respectful voice.

'That's not quite true, Warden.'

The speaker was Arle Brooks, a minister of the Disciples of Christ, known among the men for his meek character and spiritual humility.

The Warden focused his attention on Arle.

'Seize that man,' he said, pointing at him.

Guards quickly surrounded Arle, locking their arms together around him.

The inmates, knowing Arle's character, broke into spontaneous laughter at the unnecessary precaution. The laughter died instantly when the Warden ordered Arle taken away and thrown into solitary.

A wave of angry muttering swept through the crowd.

The Warden demanded silence and went on with his speech. The muttering continued ominously. The Warden quickly ended on a patriotic note, got off his box, and staying close to his guards disappeared into one of the buildings. Guards shoved the men across the yard toward the mess hall. The muttering continued.

After supper we circulated among the men as much as possible, attempting to quiet them. By lights out, the prison was somewhat calmer. I was quartered in an inside steel wire enclosed space, called a medium custody dormitory by the prison officials. The floors were concrete and the small area was enclosed by concrete walls. In it were eight or nine crowded rows of steel cots on which the men slept. Between the steel wire and the back wall was a small walk along which guards made their nightly rounds. In the dead of night I was aroused by a guard carrying a flashlight. He shook me awake.

'Get your clothes and follow me.'

I picked my way through the mass of sleeping men and followed him into an adjoining room where I was allowed to dress. Speech was forbidden. After a long wait a guard came down the cat walk leading two other conscientious objectors. We followed them silently down the corridor through the maze of the prison. I had no idea what was in store for us, but knowing the prison bureau, I had no doubt that it was going to be unpleasant. We emerged in front of a large waiting room. Inside were the other men of our group, sitting silently. We went in and took our places with them. I lit a cigarette. A guard took it from me. The clock on the wall ticked.

A Lieutenant of guards entered and checked our names against the list he was carrying. He disappeared down the corridor, suddenly; and, as suddenly, reappeared. He read a name.

'David Dollinger.'

Dave arose and followed him. David was a divinity student whose first act in prison had been against the segregation of Negroes. Walking into the mess hall he had deliberately stepped out of the white men's line and sat at a Negro table. The mess hall is the most heavily guarded spot in a prison and the simple action took extreme courage. His punishment was swift and ruthless; yet afterwards, he had consistently opposed the Bureau's racist policy along with the rest of us. Outside, he had done settlement work in slums, while still attending Theological Seminary. Previously, he had held an English exchange scholarship which, in the religious world, parallels the Rhodes Scholarship. He failed to return.

We waited. The guards watched. The silence was heavy, broken only by the ticking of the clock. The sound of footsteps, coming from the distant end of the corridor, reached us. The Lieutenant arrived at the door, entered, and looked at his list.

'Sturge Steinert,' he said.

Steinert arose and followed him. We listened as the echo of dual footsteps receded in the corridor and faded out. Steinert was a socialist who had been a student at Temple University. The American Legion had awarded him a scholarship for winning an essay contest on Americanism. The scholarship, I believe, was withdrawn when he carried his ideals into practice. He also failed to return.

The Lieutenant entered and read another name.

'Gordon Goley.'

Goley was a religious man who had renounced all things material, and devoted his full time to a study of the Bible. Independently, through prayer and meditation, he had attained a spiritual stature as yet unachieved by most western religionists. His unaffected simplicity and truly holy character were a source of inspiring strength, and his mere presence in any group was a powerful agent for good. In the ancient meaning of the term, he was, and is, probably the only living holy man in the United States.

He too, failed to return.

The Lieutenant called for us, one by one. The wait, for those of us who were not at the top of the list, seemed interminable. I became extremely nervous. I looked around the room at the men waiting with me, for reassurance.

They were the finest people I had ever known. Gathered up from everywhere they seemed to me to embody the conscience of America. Each could have obtained his release from prison instantly by registering in the draft, and nearly all, being ministers and divinity students, would have been automatically exempted from service. The rest, for one reason or another, would also have been free at that time. Each in his own way had led an exemplary life, and I was proud to be associated with them.

Eventually, the Lieutenant entered and called my name. I arose and followed him. Walking down the corridor, I remember being amused by the situation, and for the moment, enjoying the sensation of participating in a comic opera. The reality of the waiting Lord High Executioner destroyed the brief pleasantry.

At the end of the corridor I was frisked before being led through the steel barred door that opened into a section of the prison that was devoted to administration offices. The Lieutenant opened the door to the Warden's office, and motioned me to enter.

I had had the sensation of being in comic opera, but the sensation now on entering the Warden's office, was that of stepping into an Arabian Night's adventure.

For months we had seen nothing in the way of furniture or decoration except steel cots, metal chairs, and concrete walls. The Warden's office, by contrast, seemed luxurious. Furnished with thick rugs, modern furniture, invitingly deep chairs, and an abundance of wall pictures, the comparative splendor of the room momentarily dazzled me.

Incongruously, the Warden completed the picture. Apparently having left a social function to return to the prison, he was still wearing full dress evening clothes, the coat of which he had discarded in favor of a smoking jacket. He was sitting at his desk, a volume of poetry in one hand, while, with the other, he tuned a station in on his desk radio. The luxury of his office coupled with his, for a prison, bizarre dress had the effect of sharply emphasizing the differences in our positions.

The Warden invited me to be seated and, to my astonishment asked me had I read Walt Whitman's 'Leaves of Grass', which he had in his hand. His manner was friendly and disarming though he continued to manipulate the dial of the radio nervously throughout the interview. He expressed his regret that he hadn't had the opportunity to discuss my viewpoint with me previously and hoped when I was released we could meet on more social terms over a glass of beer. I returned the polite sentiment. He went on to show his interest in my reasons for joining in the present strike, and I showed him a copy of a note I had given earlier to the Captain of guards, stating my motives. He read the short note, which, as I remember it, went something like this:

'As an expression of solidarity with the student peace strike outside, the majority of the people of the United States, and countless millions throughout the world, I intend to refuse to work on 23 April 1941. I am not striking against the U.S. government or the Bureau of Prisons, but against war, which I believe to be the greatest evil known to man.'

The Warden brought the interview to a close a few minutes later and called the Lieutenant of guards who led me away, and threw me into solitary confinement.

A friendly guard explained to me later that a dictaphone was concealed in the Warden's office, connected with his radio, and that transcripts of his interviews with each of us were made and sent to Washington. What the purpose was, I cannot imagine.

Solitary confinement was referred to as 'constructive meditation' by the prison authorities. It differed in no way, insofar as I know, from solitary confinement anywhere. Men went in, endured the terrifying ordeal, and came out weakened, sometimes dulled and apathetic for months or years afterwards, and sometimes broken altogether. During my stay in prison at least one man attempted suicide in solitary preferring death to the barbaric torture.

My cell measured five of my paces long and two wide. The walls and floor were bare concrete. The door was metal with a small glass square built in it. Guards spied in on me from time to time. Owing to our number, a new cell block, not ordinarily used for solitary purposes had to be opened up, and the advantage was that light seeped in to us through glass apertures. Strict silence was maintained, though I soon discovered I could get a response from George Houser, who was in the next cell, by pounding on the wall.

The first day dragged uneventfully, the second monotonously, the third worse. I paced my cell for hours on end, throwing myself on my cot exhausted, and losing myself in daydreams. Insatiable sexual desires overwhelmed me, and I lost count of the days in the interminable silence, which was broken only by the dull voice of the guard during count. I began to look forward to mealtimes when an inmate, prevented from talking to me by the presence of a guard, deposited a tray inside the cell. One evening I found a cigarette and match neatly taped on the underside of the tray. Delighted, I smoked it to the end, burning my fingers, becoming dizzy and nauseated on the smoke.

The days passed. I made up songs and listened to the words in my head. I wrote mental essays, novels, plays and short stories. I scratched my growing beard and braided my hair to while away the time. I reviewed my life, picking out the incidents I liked best and dwelling on them endlessly. I thought about god and prayed. I pounded the wall and paced the cell. One day I began screaming mad parodies of patriotic music at the top of my lungs, and brought a guard scurrying down the corridor to my cell. I told him I'd been bit by a patriot and had caught patriotic fever. He grinned at me and told me to shut up. I fell on my cot and laughed at my own joke.

More than anything I longed to hear a voice, not dully counting but saying something with feeling in it, a speech, a polite conversation, a political discussion, or even a poetry recitation.

I got my wish on the calmest and quietest day of all, a Sunday when not a sound of any kind was audible in the cell block. Unexpectedly, Ernest Kirkjian, an ascetic of Armenian descent, began to sing the Latin version of Ave Maria. The holy music sounded incredibly beautiful after the awful days of silence, and it seemed to me I was hearing, really hearing and feeling, the human voice in its true splendor for the first time. The saintliness and purity of angels seemed to me to be in Kirkjian's song, and something profound and hitherto untouched inside me, went out and mingled with it.

The song ended, and down the corridor, Bill Lovell began to intone the Lord's prayer. The other Christians joined in and recited it, and Al Herling, Stan Rappaport and myself joined together and recited an ancient Hebrew prayer.

It was a good day.

Weeks passed.

One day a guard entered the cell block, walked down the corridor and opened the door to Benedict's cell. Benedict, like most of the pacifists in our group, was a fine athlete. Outside, his physical prowess was a legend in amateur athletic circles, and, in particular, he excelled as a soft ball pitcher. Big muscled, strong and agile, his speed ball was so swift only one man in the prison could catch him. The prison team, built around his pitching, was tied for first place in its league, and his ability to hold the opposition scoreless had placed it there. The inmates, probably for the first time in the history of prison ball, were solidly behind their team, which originally entered the league expecting to serve as a scrub practise team for the other amateurs in that area.

The Warden, a sports lover, was delighted with the unusual situation, and it did not surprise us to hear the guard offer Benedict his freedom if he would pitch the championship play-off games, which were scheduled for that day. Benedict pointed out he was in no condition to pitch after his long confinement, and wasn't sure he could make it. The guard explained he would be given time to limber up and mentioned how disappointed the inmates would be if the championship was lost. Benedict thereupon said he would do it. He added, however, only on condition that all the men in solitary, including the inmates not in the pacifist group, were released. The guard said he would speak to the Warden about it, and we heard him trudge down the corridor.

We waited in silence till he came back. The Warden could not agree to Benedict's terms, but he offered a compromise. He would release all the conscientious objectors for the game, and Benedict permanently. Benedict refused. The guard disappeared, returning shortly thereafter with another offer. The Warden would release everybody for the game, and Benedict permanently. Benedict refused. The Guard disappeared.

About a half hour later a Lieutenant of guards entered and told Benedict the men were warming up for the first game. The inmates, he said, were aware of his refusal to pitch, and were resentful toward him and the rest of us. He then said he thought he could prevail on the Warden to release all the conscientious objectors permanently, and the other men in solitary for the game, if Benedict would do it. Benedict refused.

Fully an hour passed before the Captain of guards entered and released us. The prison team had lost the first game of the series, and the Warden, unable to endure further losses, had agreed to Benedict's terms.

Grinning hugely, we left our cells, and laughing at each other's pasty complexions, bearded faces, and unkempt hair, hurried out into the prison yard. A wave of applause went through the inmate stands as Benedict rushed down the field and began warming up.

Benedict, in true Frank Merriwell fashion, summoned his strength after the long weeks of demoralized living, and, in a superhuman and prodigious performance, pitched batter after batter out, enabling the prison team to rally and score, and win the series.

Word of the remarkable feat reached the neighboring cities through the sports pages of their newspapers, and later, when Benedict was released, over 20,000 people paid fancy admission prices to see him in action at a benefit game.

Morale broke down completely in the prison after the games, when we were rounded up, including Benedict, and thrown back into solitary. The guard on duty was so disgusted he did not even bother to lock our cells.

The next day at noon the Warden reversed his stand and released us. The midday whistle had blown and the men were already in the mess hall, eating. We straggled across the empty yard, basking in the sun, enjoying our freedom. A spontaneous wave of applause broke out among the men as the first of our group entered the hall. Surging across the hall the wave became a crescendo. Six hundred pairs of hands joined in and the crescendo became pandemonium. Guards ran up and down the aisles; they were ignored. The pandemonium increased when Benedict entered the hall, maintaining itself at an incredible pitch. A volcano of thunderous and deafening applause burst out when Arle Brooks entered, but when the so-called criminals who had been in solitary came in, the convicts literally went wild, beating their metal cups on the tables, and stamping their feet.

We stood in the center of the hall, astounded at the demonstration. It became clear to me that although they were applauding Benedict, Brooks, and all of us who had been in solitary, they were doing something more. A mass catharsis of human misery was taking place before our eyes. Some of the men were weeping, others were laughing like madmen. It was like nothing I had ever seen before, and nothing I ever expect to see again.

A. E. J. MUSTE

1895–

BORN in Holland in 1895 and brought to the United States in 1901, A. E. J. Muste is considered today the outstanding spokesman in the United States for the Christian pacifist position. He was ordained to the ministry of the Reformed Church in America in 1909, and first came to the public's notice in connexion with his role in organizing the Lawrence, Massachusetts, textile mills strike of 1919, a strike the police beat down with brutality not unaccustomed for the period. His active espousal of principles and methods of nonviolence date to this time, and since then he has participated in virtually every pacifist movement of national and international scope. He has been associated with such organizations as the Fellowship of Reconciliation, the War Resisters' League, and the Church Peace Mission. Today he is the F.O.R.'s Secretary Emeritus and an editor of *Liberation* magazine.

For a brief period in the thirties he was one of the outstanding leaders of the Trotskyite section of the Communist movement in the United States, but resigned from it in 1936. After spending the summer of that year in Europe, Mr Muste again became convinced of the self-defeating character of the resort to violence. He takes a thoroughgoing religious pacifist position, believing that only the dynamic of religion will enable man to abolish wars and build a better social order by means which do not constantly defeat the ends sought.

Such books as *Non-violence In An Aggressive World* (1938) and *Not By Might* (1947), as well as numerous articles and pamphlets, have displayed a continuing interest in the acts of nations. But his emphasis has remained resolutely on the acts of individuals. In 'War is the Enemy' (1942) he said 'If God's peaceable Kingdom is ever to come on earth, it must, as Isaac Pennington wrote in 1661, "have a beginning before it can grow and be perfected. And where should it begin but in some particulars (individuals) in a nation and so spread by degrees. Therefore whoever desires to see this lovely state brought forth in the general must cherish it in the particular".'

The following extract from Mr Muste's *Of Holy Disobedience* (1952) has been chosen because of its emphasis on personal statement and action.

The Individual Conscience

THE NATURE OF CONSCRIPTION

Participation in alternative service is quite often defended on the ground that our opposition is to war rather than conscription; except in the matter of war we are as ready to serve the nation as anybody; therefore, as long as we are not drafted for combat or forced against our will into the armed services, we are ready to render whatever service of a civilian character may be imposed upon us.

Is this a sound position? Let me emphasize that it is conscription for war under the conditions of the second half of the twentieth century that we are talking about. The question as to whether sometime and under some circumstances we might accept conscription for some conceivable purpose not related to war, is not here at stake. It is academic and irrelevant. The question with which we are dealing is that of conscripting youth in and for modern war.

As pacifists we are opposed to all war. Even if recruitment were entirely on a voluntary basis, we would be opposed. It seems to me we might infer from this that we should be *a fortiori* opposed to military conscription, for here in addition to the factor of war itself, the element of coercion by government enters in, coercion which places young boys in a military regime where they are deprived of freedom of choice in virtually all essential matters. They may not have the slightest interest in the war, yet they are made to kill by order. This is surely a fundamental violation of the human spirit which must cause the pacifist to shudder.

The reply is sometimes made that pacifists are *not* being conscripted for military purposes and therefore – presumably – *they* are not faced with the issue of the nature of military conscription. I shall later contend that it is not really possible to separate conscription and war, as I think this argument does. Here I wish to suggest that even if the question is the conscription of non-pacifist youth, it is a fundamental mistake for pacifists ever to relent in their opposition to this evil, ever to devote their energies primarily to securing provisions for cos in a draft law or to lapse into a feeling that conscription has somehow become more palatable if such provisions are made by the State. It is not our own children if we are pacifist parents, our fellow-pacifist Christians if we are churchmen, about whom we should be most deeply concerned. In the first place, that is a narrow and perhaps self-centered attitude. In the second place, pacifist youths have some inner resources for meeting the issue under discussion. The terrible thing which we should never lose sight of, to which we should never reconcile our spirits, is that the great mass of 18-year olds are drafted for war. They are given no choice. Few are at the stage of development where they are capable of making fully rational and responsible choice. Thus the fathers immolate the sons, the older generation immolates the younger, on the altar of Moloch. What God centuries ago forbade Abraham to do even to his own son – 'Lay not thy hand upon the lad, neither do thou anything unto him' – this we do by decree to the entire youth of a nation.

We need to ask ourselves whether such conscription is in any real sense a lesser evil. As we have already said, the pacifist is opposed to war and we have all sensed the danger of arguing against conscription *on the ground that* the nation could raise all the troops it needed by voluntary enlistment. Nevertheless, there is a point to an impassioned argument which George Bernanos makes in the book we mentioned at the outset, *Tradition of Freedom.* He states that the man created by western or Christian civilization 'disappeared in the day conscription became law ... the principle is a totalitarian principle if ever there was one – so much so that you could deduce the whole system from it, as you can deduce the whole of geometry from the propositions of Euclid'.

To the question as to whether France, the Fatherland, should not be defended if in peril, he has the Fatherland answer: 'I very much doubt whether my salvation requires such monstrous behavior' as defense by modern war methods. If men wanted to die on behalf of the Fatherland, moreover, that would be one thing but 'making a clean sweep, with one scoop of the hand of an entire male population' is another matter altogether: 'You tell me that, in saving me, they save themselves. Yes, if they can remain free; no, if they allow you to destroy, by this un-heard of measure, the national covenant. For as soon as you have, by simple decree, created millions of French soldiers, it will be held as proven that you have sovereign rights over the persons and the goods of every Frenchman, that there are no rights higher than yours and where, then will your usurpations stop? Won't you presently presume to decide what is just and what is unjust, what is Evil and what is Good?'

It is pretty certainly an oversimplification to suggest, as Bernanos here does, that the entire totalitarian, mechanized 'system' under which men today live or into which they are increasingly drawn even in countries where a semblance of freedom and spontaneity remains, can be traced to its source in the military conscription which was instituted by the French Revolution in the eighteenth century. But what cannot, it seems to me, be successfully denied is that today totalitarianism, depersonalization, conscription, war, and the conscripting, war-making power-state are inextricably linked together. They constitute a whole, a 'system'. It is a disease, a creeping paralysis, which affects all nations, on both sides of the global conflict. Revolution and counter-revolution, 'peoples' democracies' and 'western democracies', the 'peace-loving' nations on both sides in the war, are cast in this mold of conformity, mechanization and violence. This is the Beast which, in the language of the Apocalypse, is seeking to usurp the place of the Lamb.

We know that 'war will stop at nothing' and we are clear that as pacifists we can have nothing to do with it. But I do not think that it is possible to distinguish between war and conscription, to say that the former is and the latter is not an instrument or mark of the Beast.

DISOBEDIENCE BECOMES IMPERATIVE

Non-conformity, Holy Disobedience, becomes a virtue and indeed a necessary and indispensable measure of spiritual self-preservation, in a day when the impulse to conform, to acquiesce, to go along, is the instrument which is used to subject men to totalitarian rule and involve them in permanent war. To create the impression at least of outward unanimity, the impression that there is no 'real' opposition, is something for which all dictators and military leaders strive assiduously. The more it seems that there is no opposition, the less worthwhile it seems to an ever larger number of people to cherish even the thought of opposition. Surely, in such a situation it is important not to place the pinch of incense before Caesar's image, not to make the gesture of conformity which is involved, let us say, in registering under a military conscription law. When the object is so plainly to create a situation where the individual no longer has a choice except total conformity or else the concentration camp or death; when reliable people tell us seriously that experiments are being conducted with drugs which will paralyze the wills of opponents within a nation or in an enemy country, it is surely neither right nor wise to wait until the 'system' has driven us into a corner where we cannot retain a vestige of self-respect unless we can say No. It does not seem wise or right to wait until this evil catches up with us, but rather to go out to meet it – to *resist* – before it has gone any further.

As Bernanos reminds us, 'things are moving fast, dear reader, they are moving very fast'. He recalls that he 'lived at a time when passport formalities seemed to have vanished forever'. A man could 'travel around the world with nothing in his wallet but his visiting card'. He recalls that 'twenty years ago, Frenchmen of the middle class refused to have their fingerprints taken; fingerprints were the concern of convicts'. But the word 'criminal' has 'swollen to such prodigious proportions that it now includes every citizen who dislikes the Régime, the Party, or the man who represents them. . . . The moment, perhaps, is not far off when it will seem natural for us to leave the front-door key in the lock at night so that the police may enter at any hour of the day or night, *as it is to open our pocket-books to every official demand*. And when the State decides that it would be a practical measure . . . to put some outward sign on us, why should we hesitate to have ourselves branded on the cheek or on the buttock, with a hot iron, like cattle? The purges of "wrong-thinkers", so dear to the totalitarian regimes, would thus become infinitely easier.'

To me it seems that submitting to conscription even for civilian service is permitting oneself thus to be branded by the State. It makes the work of the State in preparing for war and in securing the desired impression of unanimity much easier. It seems, therefore, that pacifists should refuse to be thus branded.

In the introductory chapter to Kay Boyle's volume of short stories about occupied Germany, *The Smoking Mountain*, there is an episode which seems to me to emphasize the need of Resistance and of not waiting until it is indeed too late. She tells about a woman, professor of philology in a Hessian university who said of the German experience with Nazism: 'It was a gradual process.' When the first *Jews Not Wanted* signs went up, 'there was never any protest made about them, and, after a few months, not only we, but even the Jews who lived in that town, walked past without noticing any more that they were there. Does it seem impossible to you that this should have happened to civilized people anywhere?'

The philology professor went on to say that after a while she put up a picture of Hitler in her class-room. After twice refusing to take the oath of allegiance to Hitler, she was persuaded by her students to take it. 'They argued that in taking this oath, which so many anti-Nazis had taken before me, *I was committing myself to nothing, and that I could exert more influence as a professor than as an outcast in the town.*'

She concluded by saying that she now had a picture of a Jew, Spinoza, where Hitler's picture used to hang, and added: 'Perhaps you will think that I did this ten years too late, and perhaps you are right in thinking this. *Perhaps there was something else we could all of us have done, but we never seemed to find a way to do it, either as individuals or as a group, we never seemed to find a way.*' A decision by the pacifist movement in this country to break completely with conscription, to give up the idea that we can 'exert more influence' if we conform in some measure, do not resist to the uttermost – this might awaken our countrymen to a realization of the precipice on the edge of which we stand. It might be the making of our movement.

THE RECONCILING RESISTANCE

Thus to embrace Holy Disobedience is not to substitute Resistance for Reconciliation. It is to practice both Reconciliation and Resistance. In so far as we help to build up or smooth the way for American militarism and the regimentation which accompanies it, we are certainly not practising reconciliation toward the millions of people in the Communist bloc countries against whom American war preparations, including conscription, are directed. Nor are we practising reconciliation toward the hundreds of millions in Asia and Africa whom we condemn to poverty and drive into the arms of Communism by our addiction to military 'defense'. Nor are we practising love toward our own fellow-citizens, including also the multitude of youths in the armed services, if, against our deepest insight, we help to fasten the chains of conscription and war upon them.

Our works of mercy, healing and reconstruction will have a deeper and more genuinely reconciling effect when they are not entangled with conscript service for 'the health, safety and interest' of the United States or any other war-making State. It is highly doubtful whether Christian mission boards can permit any of their projects in the Orient to be manned by men supposed to be working for 'the health, safety and interest' of the United States. The Gospel of reconciliation will be preached with a new freedom and power when the preachers have broken decisively with American militarism. It can surely not be preached at all in Communist lands by those who have not made that break. It will be when we have gotten off the back of what someone has called the wild elephant of militarism and conscription on to the solid ground of freedom, and only then, that we shall be able to live and work constructively. Like Abraham we shall have to depart from the City-which-is in order that we may help to build the City-which-is-to-be whose true builder and maker is God.

It is, of course, possible, perhaps even likely, that if we set ourselves apart as those who will have no dealings whatever with conscription, will not place the pinch of incense before Caesar's image, our fellow-citizens will stone us, as Stephen was stoned when he reminded his people that it was they who had 'received the law as it was ordained by angels, and kept it not'. So may we be stoned for reminding our people of a tradition of freedom and peace which was also, in a real sense, 'ordained by angels' and which we no longer keep. But, it will thus become possible for them, as for Paul, even amidst the search for new victims to persecute, suddenly to see again the face of Christ and the vision of a new Jerusalem.

Some one may at this point reflect that earlier in this paper I counseled against people too readily leaving the normal path of life and that I am now counseling a policy which is certain to create disturbance in individual lives, families and communities. That is so. But to depart from the common way in response or reaction to a conscription law, in the attempt to adapt oneself to an abnormal state of society, is one thing. To leave father, mother, wife, child, yea and one's own life also, at the behest of Christ or conscience is quite another. Our generation will not return to a condition under which every man may sit under his own vine and fig tree, with none to make him afraid, unless there are those who are willing to pay the high cost of redemption and deliverance from a regime of regimentation, terror and war.

Finally, it is of crucial importance that we should understand that for the individual to pit himself in Holy Disobedience against the war-making and conscripting State, wherever it or he be located, is not an act of despair or defeatism. Rather, I think we may say that precisely this individual refusal to 'go along' is now the beginning and the core of any realistic and practical movement against war and for a more peaceful and brotherly world. For it becomes daily clearer that political and military leaders pay virtually no attention to protests against current foreign policy and pleas for peace when they know perfectly well that when it comes to a showdown, all but a handful of the millions of protesters will 'go along' with the war to which the policy leads. All but a handful will submit to conscription. Few of the protesters will so much as risk their jobs in the cause of 'peace'. The failure of the policy-makers to change their course does not, save perhaps in very rare instances, mean that they are evil men who want war. They feel, as indeed they so often declare in crucial moments, that the issues are so complicated, the forces arrayed against them so strong, that they 'have no choice' but to add another score of billions to the military budget, and so on and on. Why should they think there is any reality, hope or salvation in 'peace advocates' who when the moment of decision comes also act on the assumption that they 'have no choice' but to conform?

Precisely in a day when the individual appears to be utterly helpless, to 'have no choice', when the aim of the 'system' is to convince him that he is helpless as an individual and that the only way to meet regimentation is by regimentation, there is absolutely no hope save in going back to the beginning. The human being, the child of God, must assert his humanity and his sonship again. He must exercise the choice which he no longer has as something accorded him by society, which he 'naked, weaponless, armourless, without shield or spear, but only with naked hands and open eyes' must create again. He must understand that this naked human being is the one *real* thing in the face of the mechanics and the mechanized institutions of our age. He, by the grace of God, is the seed of all the human life there will be on earth in the future, though he may have to die to make that harvest possible. As *Life* magazine stated in its unexpectedly profound and stirring editorial of 20 August 1945, its first issue after the atom bombing of Hiroshima: 'Our sole safeguard against the very real danger of a reversion to barbarism is the kind of morality which compels the individual conscience, be the group right or wrong. The individual conscience against the atomic bomb? Yes. There is no other way.'

CHRISTIAN PACIFISM
AND NONVIOLENCE
TODAY

M

DIDERICH H. LUND

1888–

FOR four years Diderich Lund, a member of the Norwegian Section of the War Resisters' International, was active in the resistance movement inside Norway during the Nazi occupation of his country, but in 1944, on good advice, he escaped to Sweden. He spent several weeks in England during the war and returned in 1945 to Norway to help in reconstruction. Before the war ended, he wrote the pamphlet *Resistance in Norway*. The selection here presented is adapted from a paper read at the first post-war conference of the War Resisters' International at Shrewsbury, England in 1948, and reprinted from *Peace News*, 14 January 1949.

Pacifism Under the Occupation

World War II is past, and the bitter challenge which we in Norway faced in the occupation remains only in our memories. But it would be both dangerous and unrealistic to dismiss the possibility of another war, however much we would like to persuade ourselves that such a war is impossible. Pacifists who live in countries that may risk the threat of invasion (and which of us can say that he does not?) must consider how they will meet a foreign army of occupation.

We discovered early in the occupation of Norway that a great deal depended on how we had prepared ourselves before the outbreak of war. The calm and detached exchange of views becomes almost impossible after war breaks out, and in most countries only a small minority think of any alternative to military warfare when it comes to fighting for the values they wish to defend. It is, therefore, of the highest importance to pacifists to make the best use of the time, however short, which is now at our disposal, to increase this minority and spread this knowledge.

First and foremost, pacifists must educate themselves and others to a full recognition of the supreme value of fundamental democratic principles, being aware of the fact that the life of the individual can be most fully and deeply developed in a democratic society.

We must fight principles which we abhor, but must never direct our hatred against persons. To avoid this error we must make ours the conception of the image of God in every human being.

We must never be misled into believing that the end justifies the means, but realize that with evil means the best intentions will come to nothing. By adopting such a rule of life each of us may succeed in making himself an unconquerable fortress.

Before the outbreak of the war I believed that pacifists were obligated to struggle for what they considered right and good, and not content themselves simply with refusing to take part in preparations for war, and in fighting. Under the German occupation we found that most of us might live comparatively comfortably and undisturbed, if we could only force our eyes not to see, and our ears not to hear. But the urge to help when you see someone in distress is very strong, and just as strong will be the demand to fight for the values that make life worth living.

Faced with this demand, most people think only of seizing a gun and meeting violence with violence. But here the pacifist line of action stands out very clearly, as taught by Mahatma Gandhi. 'Where there is only a choice between cowardice and violence, I would advise violence. But I believe that non-violence is infinitely superior to violence, that forgiveness is more manly than punishment'.

And for such non-violent resistance conditions in Norway under German occupation were so ideal that the overwhelming majority of the people took to it almost spontaneously and practised it with skill and vigour.

One important reservation must be made, however. A great many people took the way of non-violent resistance because they felt it was the only effective way for a small nation to fight against overwhelming force. Our non-violence was not the voluntary relinquishment by a strong nation of the use of violence against a weaker one.

As in most of the occupied countries, a strong resistance movement grew up in Norway. Unlike them, however, was its non-violent nature. It is true that there was also a secret military organization, the Milorg, partly consisting of soldiers trained in Great Britain during the last years of the war and brought secretly into Norway. But it was the unarmed resistance of the civilians that sustained the nation and kept it united during the occupation.

Like any movement, the non-violent resistance movement calls for adequate leadership, and it was interesting to see how the struggle itself brought leaders forth. The first were those who had, before the war, taken a clear stand for democracy and against Nazism, and who now openly and courageously stood up for their beliefs. Most of these first leaders were silenced, but they had been inspiring examples of the utmost importance to those who stood ready to take their places.

In the economic field our resistance broke down completely, although it soon became clear that every economic activity authorized by the Germans was intended to aid their war effort, even so humble and innocent an activity as growing potatoes. Norwegian men of business, contractors and workmen offered their services to the invader, and continued to do so throughout the war, in spite of strong agitation directed against it by the resistance leaders.

Moreover, where social conditions were bad and feelings of envy or hatred prevailed between different social groups, Nazism made a certain amount of progress. Fortunately there were not many such groups, for in Norway, where the Labour Party had been in power since 1936, we had gone far toward peaceful cooperation between trade unions and employers, between labour and capital.

After the resistance became organized an underground press was established to publish the facts and counteract the bewildering propaganda, and to print for broadcast distribution among the people 'paroles' advising them when to obey and when to refuse to obey a German order. The paroles were valuable as well in giving a feeling to the population that in some way justice and order still reigned, and as a rule were obeyed by practically everyone concerned. The Germans could do nothing but accept the situation, and in spite of their strenuous efforts to wipe out the secret presses, and the many thousands of Norwegians who lost their lives or were imprisoned and tortured, nothing could silence the voice of the press. New helpers were ready at any moment to fill the empty places, and new printing presses were always available.

Perhaps the most dangerous underground activity was the propaganda among the German troops. Not much of this work was done by the Norwegians, but we saw instances of excellent and daring propaganda by the German soldiers themselves, done at tremendous risk.

Service in and around the concentration camps set up by the Germans opened a new field of activity to daring youth. Contact had to be made between prisoners and the outside world, to tell prisoners which of their comrades, safely out of reach, they could name to the Gestapo if torture became unbearable, or to find out which had been named and were in danger. Now and then a prisoner threatened with torture and death had to be taken out of prison by some stratagem. The stories of these incidents are full of fantastic and thrilling details of cunning and daring and sacrifice, and they have filled our hearts with joy and pride as the facts became known.

Hiding places were arranged for those hunted by the Gestapo. The homes of elderly ladies were much preferred for this, and many of them sheltered fugitives constantly throughout the war years. But the solidarity was so general and widespread that one had the feeling one might enter any door and ask for protection. It was necessary also to give financial support to those who had lost their income as a result of engaging in resistance work, or those left behind by people who had escaped, or who had been imprisoned or executed; but everyone contributed, and it was never difficult to get the money.

Although the non-violent resistance movement did not make use of sabotage in its military form, as did the Milorg, sabotage in factories or in administration that impeded German activities was accepted. However, this form of sabotage proved to be much less effective than was generally believed, and it would have been better to have refused entirely to do questionable work. Sabotage is fundamentally a secondary weapon, but if you have not the moral force to carry through open opposition, or if circumstances make it impossible, sabotage can be a last resort.

All of these activities, however, including occasionally the necessary destruction of the Germans' records and documents by fire or explosion, were carried out without violence to the Germans – only Norwegian lives were at stake.

But *secret* warfare is not always the most advisable. One of the most inspiring features of the unarmed resistance in Norway, and the one which appeared most strongly to the whole nation, was its open and uncompromising nature, expressed from the first moment by so many, and by individuals as well as by groups, at the risk of liberty and of life.

The first resistance came, perhaps somewhat unexpectedly, from the hundreds of thousands of youth in the athletic clubs. The Nazis tried to take over control of the clubs, probably to use them eventually for military ends. Immediately all organized athletic activity ceased, and remained in abeyance for the five years of the occupation.

The next to resist was the Supreme Court of Justice, whose members resigned their offices when the Germans tried to reshape the fundamental principles of justice in the image of the Nazi system.

But the men who most of all became the prototypes of our spiritual resistance and unarmed struggle were our teachers and our clergy. All along the line the teachers refused to follow Nazi orders to alter their teaching to accord with Nazi principles, and the teachers took the consequences of their resistance. Hundreds were sent to prison or to compulsory labour in the Arctic, and schools were closed, though to some extent teaching went on secretly in the homes of the pupils. After half a year of privation and suffering in the frigid climate of Finnmark the teachers won, and the Germans sent them home and allowed them to resume their work. These men became important centres of resistance activity, and their example greatly strengthened our self-reliance and our faith.

Just as important was the undaunted and unflinching resistance of the Church. It was directed, with fine discrimination, not against the occupying power as such, but against the anti-Christian measures of the occupying power, and it tried to keep away from nationalistic resistance in its vulgar sense. In the best of its statements you could hear the authentic voice of primitive Christianity, challenging not the secular order, which in itself may be ethically neutral, but the perversion of that order to false ideals. The Church fought its combat openly and fearlessly, with an ability and a moral strength against which Quisling and the Germans stood powerless.

The clergymen and the bishops resigned their offices as civil servants and the salaries attached to them. But they went on with their work as preachers and the spiritual leaders of their parishioners, until they were forcibly transferred to places where the Germans hoped that they would be harmless. The leaders were sent to prison or to concentration camps; but the seed they had sown bore fruit many times over, and in one way or another most of those who were left continued their activity. The dissenting churches joined the State Church in its resistance with the same courage and ability.

Many more instances of open resistance could be enumerated, such as the open letter signed with the names and addresses of several hundred thousand parents protesting against the Nazis' efforts to win the children to their creed. These open demonstrations were the essence of the unarmed resistance, and its signal feature. They made it a struggle of the whole people, a struggle in which everybody felt he was playing an important part, and in which there was a place for young and old, for women as well as for men.

You cannot carry through a successful unarmed resistance without the secret machinery, of which I spoke earlier, to do its task. This secret activity is necessary and dangerous and full of dramatic incidents, and it is possible to carry it on, as it was carried on in Norway, according to high moral principles and without violence. But it was the open resistance that gave to the struggle, more than anything else, its glamour and its glow.

Our attitude toward the Germans was determined on the one hand by our hatred of the brutality and the inhuman cruelty which the Gestapo constantly practised and the soldiers defended, a hatred of their whole political and ideological system. It was tempered, however, by our understanding that we had no right to hold the individual responsible for all the acts done in the name of the system.

Now and then I tried to speak in a friendly way to a German soldier, but we very soon came to the point where I had to tell him how I looked on the Nazi system and the dirty work he was engaged on. At that point the friendly intercourse was at an end, and I was lucky if I was not reported to the Gestapo. Hardly a German would admit to a feeling of guilt in coming as a soldier to Norway, and without that admission intercourse was impossible. On the other hand, however, it was obvious to everyone that there were thousands of German soldiers who were opposed to the system. One might blame them for not having expressed their opposition (an expression which would almost certainly have meant death), but when one saw the unhappy and hopeless faces among them one understood that they felt powerless in the grip of demonic forces over which they had no control.

Most of them were terribly afraid of the Gestapo, even more than we were. For Norwegians, to resist was to feel ourselves one with the struggle of the whole nation, and to lean on the moral and material support of our own people and of our friends. The Germans had all of these factors ranged against them, and the few who dared to resist were shot as traitors. We could not therefore demand from them without qualification the same resistance against Nazism which we expected from our own people. It was for this reason also that our judgement of our own quislings was much harder than that of the average German.

I should like to be able to impress upon you all that strange feeling of quiet happiness that filled most of us even under hard and difficult conditions.

The unshakable conviction of fighting in a good cause has always been the strongest incitement to the making of fanatical soldiers, and perhaps we also need fanatics. But above all we need efficiency and wisdom, courage and readiness to self-sacrifice. If we possess to some degree these qualities, non-violent resistance will give us the sure and joyful knowledge of fighting in the cause of justice and of love.

And we shall also know that our fight is the only one leading to *lasting* victory.

C.O.R.E.

THE Congress of Racial Equality (1942 – its history is described on pages 24–5) grew up within the F.O.R.; the directorships of both groups overlapped for years and the original impetus for C.O.R.E. came from two memoranda which James Farmer sent A. J. Muste. Farmer was an F.O.R. worker then and is National Director of C.O.R.E. now; A. J. Muste was at that time Executive Secretary of the F.O.R. The memoranda, reprinted for the first time here in their entirety, proposed plans for 'Brotherhood Mobilization'. They stressed that, while the membership should be open to anyone actively interested in improving race relations, all members would be obliged to make a commitment to nonviolence. The role of pacifists in such an organization, Farmer correctly predicted, would necessarily be great from the outset, but C.O.R.E. did not want to be dragged into an extended argument over 'larger' issues when its own goals were so clear. Its commitment to nonviolence was and remains essentially one of method in a particular situation, in spite of the religious orientation of many of its founding members.

C.O.R.E. achieved national prominence during the period leading up to the massive March on Washington of August 1963 and the Civil Rights Act of 1964. For years C.O.R.E. has worked with the National Association for the Advancement of Colored People, the Southern Christian Leadership Conference, the Student Nonviolent Coordinating Committee and other groups in activities largely aimed at breaking down patterns of racial segregation in transportation, eating facilities, educational institutions, and residential housing.

The 'freedom rides', generally considered a phenomenon of the early sixties, were in fact initiated several years earlier. The first one took place between 9–23 April 1947 and was then called a 'Journey of Reconciliation'. Bayard Rustin and George Houser, who took part in that 'ride', wrote an account of their experiences; it is reprinted here for the first time. Its original title was *We Challenged Jim Crow!*

The Beginning

19 February, 1942

MEMORANDUM TO A. J. MUSTE ON PROVISIONAL
PLANS FOR BROTHERHOOD MOBILIZATION

The plans herein suggested are but preliminary formulations to provide a basis for further discussion. Obviously, before any such program is put into operation, it must be discussed in detail by the National Council, or some committee which N.C. may designate, and should have much more elaborate and expert planning than went into this brief statement. Hence, any disagreement with certain points of the statement should by no means prevent a consideration of the general idea.

From its inception, the Fellowship has thought in terms of developing definite, positive, and effective, alternatives to violence as a technique for resolving conflict. It has sought to translate love of God and man, on one hand, and hatred of injustice on the other, into specific action. Leading naturally into a study of the Gandhian movement, this quest has been served mightily by the clear analysis in Shridharani's *War Without Violence* and by the work of J. Holmes Smith, New Vistas have been opened, new horizons revealed. In general terms, we have spoken of the new technique as 'non-violent direct action'.

There are two great fields in which our contemplations have rested: the industrial and the racial. For obvious reasons the former has been temporarily canceled as a field for great activity along these lines. But the latter remains, probably more urgent today than ever before since slavery. Several contemporary approaches to the problem, such as the N.A.A.C.P. and the Urban League, have proved their value, from specialized angles, and must therefore be encouraged and supported. But they have also demonstrated their inadequacy in dealing effectively with the total aspects of a problem as comprehensive as that of race in America. Hence, the need for a virile and comprehensive program such as our study and experimentation in non-violence should logically lead into.

Regarding such a movement, we may venture a few general observations:

1. Certain societal and cultural differences between the United States

and India, and certain basic differences between the problems to be dealt with in the two countries, militate strongly against an uncritical duplication of the Gandhian steps in organization and execution. The American race problem is in many ways distinctive, and must to that extent be dealt with in a distinctive manner. Using Gandhi-ism as a base, our approach must be creative in order to be effectual.

2. If any such movement is to amount to more than a gesture of protest, however valuable such a gesture may be, it must seek to draw *mass* following. Therefore, the movement cannot be limited to pacifists, but must try to 'mobilize' all persons who want to see an end to racial discrimination in America, and are willing to commit themselves to a disciplined non-violence in working toward that goal.

3. If such an endeavor is not to degenerate into violence and chaos, pacifists must serve as its nucleus, its moving force.

4. Such a program must be on a religious base if it is to possess genuine motive power and is to appeal to masses of people, black and white, Jewish and Gentile.

5. The difficulty in developing and utilizing mass discipline in unified action is so great that we would probably not attempt vital mass non-violent direct action, except on an experimental scale, until discipline and training was perfected. There should be no hesitancy, however, in carrying out education and 'moral suasion' projects from the very beginning. This, of course, is following the Gandhian and common-sense procedure of launching vital campaigns only when satisfactory discipline and unity is arrived at.

In light of the foregoing observations, I urge that the Fellowship of Reconciliation (in collaboration with the A.F.S.C. if such collaboration is deemed feasible and can be worked out) immediately lay plans for launching a nation-wide Brotherhood Mobilization, concerning which I offer the following specific suggestions:

Time Plan

There ought to be a time goal on the mobilization and preparation for effective mass action. I, therefore, suggest that the Brotherhood Mobilization be placed on a Five-Year or even a Ten-Year Plan, after which, it is to be hoped, relentless non-cooperation, economic boycott, civil disobedience, etcetera, will be thrown into swing wherever and whenever necessary.

Naturally, such a 'time plan' would be outlined in successive stages, each of which would be given to a specific emphasis. For example: (1) Securing necessary initial finances and endorsements by strategic individuals and groups capable of supplying mass audience; (2) a vast enlistment drive; (3) Systematic organization for action, etc.

Organization and Membership

Such a venture, it seems to me, ought to be considered, in its early stages at least, as a semi-autonomous project of the F.O.R. (and of the A.F.S.C. if possible). After a period of time – probably at the end of the five- or ten-year period – it may be wise to make the set-up of the movement thoroughly democratic. At such time, the F.O.R. will doubtless to some degree find it necessary to 'wean' the movement. Long before that time, however, it should become largely self-supporting.

ADDITIONAL MEMORANDUM FROM JAMES FARMER
9 MARCH 1942
I

An extremely critical question in the effective execution of any such project as that suggested in the preceding memo lies in the vastly different inclinations to participation in various brands of non-violent action, found among different groups in American society. A great number of people will doubtless be willing to work in a quiet manner to broaden the human fellowship and abolish all forms of racial discrimination, and will agree to utilize organized, persistent, and concerted *educational* and *moral suasion* methods toward effecting that end. Many others will go even further and participate in a thorough-going, nation-wide, cooperative community, sharing cooperatively the burdens of the movement and the mutual destiny of its participants. Still others will be willing to engage in all-out-non-violent direct action (economic boycott, non-cooperation, pickets, demonstrations, civil disobedience, etcetera) whenever and wherever such action is necessary and strategic. How can the energies and talents of all those people most effectively be harnessed in the mobilization for brotherhood without eliminating any who agree thoroughly with the aims and objectives but are not inclined to participate in the more aggressive and demanding phases of the program, and without frustrating those inclined to the most direct forms of non-violent action?

The most likely answer to that question seems to me to be provided by establishing different *levels* of membership or participation in the movement. Probably *three levels* are required. The first should be of the greatest possible mass constituency, including all persons who are opposed to every form of racial discrimination and desire to see it ended, and are willing to dedicate themselves to non-violent methods in effecting that end. The second level, drawn from members of the first, should be composed of those persons who will participate in a carefully planned cooperative community which will provide the economic base for the movement, and will effectively apply some principle of mutual aid in providing for such persons as will be thrown out of jobs by virtue of their participation in the movement. The third level, recruited from the lower ones, should be composed of those persons who will take part in aggressive and relentless non-violent direct action.

Obviously, the first level will be the largest of the three; the second, next in size, and the third, the smallest, most selective group. It should also be understood that in this suggestion the members of the third level would also be participants in the second level, and members of the second level would also be included in activities of the first level. It should be hoped and expected that many members of lower levels could be induced eventually to enter higher levels. Thus, the lower levels would continually feed the higher ones with members – the ideal, however impossible, being that all members be participants of the third level, participating in all phases of the work of the movement. The three levels should work in a coordinated fashion, like the fingers on the hand or like three functional divisions of a military force.

By following such a pattern of membership, we should be enabled to exercise a wide membership appeal, to allow to devotees of direct action a maximum freedom of operation, and to avoid a perpetual wrangling over the validity or relative validity of various brands of actions.

Another critical matter deserving a great deal of special thought is the matter of a cooperative community to which I have referred in passing. This cooperative arrangement should be so planned, I think, as to serve the following four basic objectives:

1. To supply the social and spiritual comradeship which can be achieved only through true *community*.
2. To free participants in the movement, as far as possible, from dependence upon the capitalistic system.

3. To supply the basic financial needs of the movement, thus, as far as possible, rendering the movement as self-sufficient and serving as economic base.
4. To apply *mutual aid* in meeting the needs and sharing the misfortunes of participants in the movement.

Towards the building of such a cooperative community, I offer the following preliminary suggestions:

1. That *second level* members impose upon themselves a voluntary *income tax* consistent with each person's ability to help bear the financial burdens of the project.
2. That a network of interracial consumers' cooperatives (and wherever possible producers' cooperatives) be developed on a nation-wide scale among the *second level* members, turning a certain percentage of the dividends over to the *Brotherhood Mobilization*.
3. That interracial housing cooperatives, interracial cooperative farms, and interracial eating cooperatives be likewise developed, with the co-op houses and farms serving as strategic local or regional headquarters for the total movement, and the eating co-ops, like the producers and consumers co-ops, turning a certain percentage of their savings over to the movement.
4. That plans be developed for the cooperative production and cooperative marketing of *folk craft* and *art,* by Negroes and Whites alike. Flax can be grown, spun, and woven. Wool craft, pottery, glass work, sculpturing, coal carving, gourd work, wood carving, straw work, etc., will find a prominent place in such a project. Contrary to the usual opinion, silk can be grown in America, and thus silk culture might well enter in the plan. Fine folk metal-ware is also a possibility. Such development of *folk craft* and *art* would supply to participants a tremendous spiritual value, by virtue of their working with their hands to produce useful objects. It could become a tremendous public relations and educational implement for the movement by providing an avenue for utilitarian and artistic expression. It might ultimately supplement industrialization by utilizing the labor of many *marginal persons*[1] in our industrial society, and the spare time labor of others,

1. By 'marginal persons' I mean those great masses of unsettled persons who are not established in our industrial society. It is not at all impossible that their numbers will consistently increase as industrialization becomes more complete.

in developing utilitarian and artistic objects of finer quality than those which can be produced by industrial mass production. It will enable many Negroes and poor White people to solve their unemployment problem through folk craft.

Obviously, to develop a meaningful cooperative community, we shall have to place great emphasis upon drawing in persons from lower classes; black and white. Far too many movements for racial justice have virtually confined their activities to the middle classes.

It is obvious that in order to develop such a community, we must work closely with, and secure the counsel of the Cooperative League of America.

Membership Pattern

A. The audience and membership of such a movement will, of course be far wider and more heterogeneous than that of the sponsoring groups. The members will be united by devotion to the cause and commitment to non-violence in working toward the desired end. There are literally hundreds of thousands of persons over the country who are opposed to racial discrimination, and many more who have no conviction in favor of it. Our task should be to persuade those without positive conviction to join the ranks of those opposed to discrimination, to mobilize and unite those people while persistently striving to enlarge their ranks and to provide them with dynamic program and method. The membership therefore ought to proceed along the following lines:

1. It ought to be recruited from all sections of the country and from all ages, races, classes, and religions. In general, we can appeal to labor groups, church groups, schools, and social and civic organizations in addition to the unorganized and unaffiliated. I am certain that many church groups and labor groups can be tied up solidly behind it. Reaching the Negroes, however – and they will naturally comprise the preponderance of the membership in southern sections – is a unique and even more difficult problem. Aside from those which will be reached in appeals to the above mentioned groups, the masses of Negroes can be reached only through the three following specifically 'Negro' channels:

(a) *The Negro Church*, which is the only institution channelizing the *hoi polloi.* I am now convinced that, if managed well, great support can be received from certain sections of the Negro church.

(b) *Negro Fraternal Organizations* (fraternities, sororities, lodges, etc.), in which tremendous numbers of civic minded persons can be found.

(c) *Negro Schools,* through which the present and potential intelligentsia can be reached.

2. Members should be asked to contribute a small minimum fee of perhaps 25c. annually. Eventually, it is hoped a cooperative arrangement can be perfected whereby members automatically bear the financial burden of the movement according to ability.

B. Regarding organization, I should think the Cell idea ought to be considered basic, with F.O.R. cells, wherever possible, serving as nuclei. The movement may well follow the pattern set by the F.O.R.: regional, local, and cell. Much of the grass-roots organizing can be done by a large number of volunteer organizers working in their own localities.

We might also consider the practicability of utilizing a technique similar to that employed by the A.F.S.C. in the past years. We might send out a nation-wide call for volunteer workers with certain qualifications, or we might get key college professors to select one, two, or three good persons from the graduating class who would be willing to give the 'after-graduation year' of their life to service in Mobilization for Brotherhood. (I am confident, after my November tour of southern Negro colleges, that the response to such a call in Negro colleges would be overwhelming.) The volunteers could be given a three-month cooperative training for their task at a centralized point in the summer, and could then be sent out in teams or caravans for nine months of organizing and educational work in many parts of the nation. A large percentage of their expenses for the nine months may well be cared for by church groups and others in return for part-time work of some nature. It is indispensable that a movement as ambitious as this have some organ of expression. A page in *Fellowship* and a periodical mimeographed news-bulletin may serve temporarily. But I think we should look toward the day when a small paper can be printed, and perhaps a quarterly journal providing the theoretical and critical approach.

Aim

Above all, the Brotherhood Mobilization must present a distinctive and radical approach. It must strive, for example, not to make housing in ghettos more tolerable, but to destroy residential segregation : Not to make Jim Crow facilities the equal of others, but to abolish Jim Crow; not to make racial discrimination more bearable, but to wipe it out. In the words of the Twenty-Sixth Annual Conference of the F.O.R., we must 'effectively repudiate every form of racism . . .', we must forget the instrumentalities through which that nation-wide repudiation can be effected. We must not stop until racial brotherhood is established in the United States as a fact as well as an ideal. Ironically enough, the present unfortunate circumstances brought on by the war afford an excellent setting for immediate spade-work in this direction.

James Farmer

The First Freedom Ride

On 3 June 1946, the Supreme Court of the United States announced its decision in the case of Irene Morgan versus the Commonwealth of Virginia. State laws demanding segregation of interstate passengers on motor carriers are now unconstitutional, for segregation of passengers crossing state lines was declared an 'undue burden on interstate commerce'. Thus it was decided that state Jim Crow laws do not affect interstate travelers. In a later decision in the Court of Appeals for the District of Columbia, the Morgan decision was interpreted to apply to interstate train travel as well as bus travel.

The Executive Committee of the Congress of Racial Equality and the Racial-Industrial Committee of the Fellowship of Reconciliation decided that they should jointly sponsor a 'Journey of Reconciliation' through the upper South in order to determine to how great an extent bus and train companies were recognizing the Morgan decision. They also wished to learn the reaction of bus drivers, passengers, and police to those who non-violently and persistently challenge Jim Crow in interstate travel.

During the two-week period from 9–23 April, an interracial group of men, traveling as a deputation team, visited fifteen cities in Virginia, North Carolina, Tennessee, and Kentucky. More than thirty speaking engagements were met before church, N.A.A.C.P., and college groups. The Morgan decision was explained and reports made on what was happening on the buses and trains in the light of this decision. The response was most enthusiastic.

To clarify the incidents described below, it will be necessary to list the sixteen participants by race.

Negro: Bayard Rustin, of the Fellowship of Reconciliation and part-time worker with the American Friends Service Committee; Wallace Nelson, free-lance lecturer; Conrad Lynn, New York attorney; Andrew Johnson, Cincinnati student; Dennis Banks, Chicago musician; William Worthy, of the New York Council for a Permanent F.E.P.C.; Eugene Stanley, of A. and T. College, Greensboro, North Carolina; Nathan Wright, church social worker from Cincinnati.

White: George Houser, of the F.O.R. and Executive Secretary of the Congress of Racial Equality; Ernest Bromley, Methodist minister from North Carolina; James Peck, editor of the Workers Defense League *News Bulletin*; Igal Roodenko, New York horticulturist; Worth Randle, Cincinnati biologist; Joseph Felmet, of the Southern Workers Defense League; Homer Jack, Executive Secretary of the Chicago Council Against Racial and Religious Discrimination; Louis Adams, Methodist minister from North Carolina.

During the two weeks of the trip, twenty-six tests of company policies were made. Arrests occurred on six occasions, with a total of twelve men arrested.

AN ACCOUNT OF THE TEST TRIPS

The report of what happened on the test trips should be much more complete than is here possible. For purposes of brevity, many important comments and psychological reactions have had to be omitted.

Between eight and ten men participated in simultaneous tests. This made it possible to split the group into two parts – either for two separate tests on the same bus line, or for testing both Greyhound and Trailways buses when both companies had buses to the next point on the itinerary.

Washington, D.C., to Richmond, Va., 9 April

No difficulties were encountered. On both the Trailways and Greyhound buses the Negroes in the group sat up front, and the white in the rear. Other passengers tended to cross the color line too. A white couple sat on the back seat of the Greyhound with two Negroes. A Negro woman sat beside a young white man in the center of the bus when she could have taken a vacant seat by a Negro man. Rustin gave his seat, third from front, to an elderly Negro woman, and then sat by a white lad directly behind the driver. Nothing was said.

Richmond, Va., to Petersburg, Va., 10 April

Because there have been so many cases in the Richmond courts testing segregation in interstate travel, no more arrests are made there. Both the Greyhound and Trailways group reached Petersburg without incident. The Trailways bus taken was local, running only between the two cities. The tickets used were interstate, of course. The Greyhound bus was a crowded, through bus, but no attempt was made to force Rustin and Johnson to move from the front. Nelson and Lynn rode in front of the Trailways. A Negro man in the rear spoke to Houser and Roodenko, saying a Negro might be able to get away with riding up front here, but some bus drivers are crazy, 'and the farther South you go, the crazier they get'. Two Negro women talking about Peck, sitting in the rear of the Greyhound reading his *New York Times*, said: 'He wouldn't know what it was all about if he was asked to move.' Then they laughed.

Petersburg, Va., to Raleigh, N.C., 11 April

Lynn was arrested on the Trailways before the bus left the station for sitting in the second seat from the front. The bus driver was courteous, but insistent. Lynn explained the Morgan decision quietly. The driver countered that he was in the employ of the bus company, not the Supreme Court, and that he followed company rules about segregation. He said aloud, so all passengers could hear: 'Personally, I don't care where you sit, but I have my orders. Are you going to move?' Lynn said that he could not. The driver got the police. There were no threats, nor abusive language. It took about an hour and a half to get a warrant for Lynn's arrest. The magistrate in Petersburg would not sign the warrant until the bus company attorney in Richmond had been called, and dictated the statement of the warrant over the telephone. The warrant read that Lynn was guilty of disorderly conduct for not obeying the reasonable request of the bus driver to move to the rear in compliance with the company rules. The bus operator apologized for having to arrest Lynn. A policeman, referring to equality for Negroes said, 'I'm just not Christian enough.' Passengers on the bus were patient, and relatively neutral, while they waited almost two hours. A Negro porter made the only fuss when he boarded the bus, and, looking at Lynn, said, 'What's the matter with him? He's crazy. Where does he think he is? We know how to deal with him. We ought to drag him off.' Lynn was released on $25 bond.

Petersburg, Va., to Durham, N.C., 11 April

On the Greyhound to Durham there were no arrests. Peck and Rustin sat up front. About ten miles out of Petersburg the driver told Rustin to move. When Rustin refused, the driver said he would 'attend to that at Blackstone'. However, at the bus station in Blackstone, after consultation with other drivers, the bus went on to Clarksville. There the group changed buses. At Oxford, N.C., the driver sent for the police, who refused to make an arrest. Persons waiting to get on at Oxford were delayed for forty-five minutes. A middle-aged Negro school teacher was permitted to board, to plead with Rustin to move: 'Please move. Don't do this. You'll reach your destination either in front or in back. What difference does it make?' Rustin explained his reason for not moving. Other Negro passengers were strong in their support of Rustin, one of them threatening to sue the bus company for the delay. When Durham was reached without arrest, the Negro school teacher begged Peck not to use his name in connection with the incident at Oxford: 'It will hurt me in the community. I'll never do that again.'

Raleigh, N.C., to Chapel Hill, N.C., 12 April

Lynn and Nelson rode together on the double seat next to the very rear of the Trailways bus, and Houser and Roodenko in front of them. The bus was very crowded. The one other Negro passenger, a woman, seated across from Nelson, moved to the very rear voluntarily when a white woman got on the bus and there were no seats in front. When two white college men got on, the driver told Nelson and Lynn to move to the rear seat. When they refused on the basis of their interstate passage, he said the matter would be handled in Durham. A white passenger asked the driver if he wanted any help. The driver replied, 'No, we don't want to handle it that way.' By the time the group reached Durham, the seating arrangement had changed and the driver did not press the matter.

Durham, N.C., to Chapel Hill, N.C., 12 April

Johnson and Rustin were in the second seat from the front on a Trailways bus. The driver asked them to move to the rear as soon as he saw them. A station superintendent was called to repeat the order. Five minutes later the police arrived and Johnson and Rustin were arrested for refusing to move when ordered to do so. Peck, who was seated in about the middle of the bus, got up after the arrest, saying to the police, 'If you arrest them you'll have to arrest me, too, for I'm going to sit in the rear.' The three men were held at the police station for half an hour. They were released without charge when an attorney arrived on their behalf. A suit will be pressed against the company and the police for false arrest. The conversation with the Trailways official indicated that the company knew there was an interracial group making a test. The official said to the police: 'We know all about this. Greyhound is letting them ride. But we're not.'

Chapel Hill, N.C., to Greensboro, N.C., 12 April

Johnson and Felmet were seated in front. The driver asked them to move as soon as he boarded. They were arrested quickly, for the police station was just across the street from the bus station. Felmet did not get up to accompany the police until the officer specifically told him he was under arrest. Because he delayed rising from his seat, he was pulled up bodily, and shoved out of the bus. The bus driver distributed witness cards to occupants of the bus. One white girl said: 'You don't want me to sign one of those. I'm a damn Yankee and I think this is an outrage.' Rustin and Roodenko, sensing the favorable reaction on the bus, decided they would move to the seat in the front vacated by Johnson and Felmet. Their moving forward caused much discussion by passengers. The driver returned soon, and when Rustin and Roodenko refused to move, they were arrested also. A white woman at the front of the bus, a Southerner, gave her name and address to Rustin as he walked by her. They were arrested on charges of disorderly conduct for refusing to obey the order of the bus driver, and, in the case of the whites, interfering with arrest. The men were released on $50 bonds.

The bus was delayed nearly two hours. Taxi drivers standing around the bus station were becoming aroused by the events. One hit Peck a hard blow on the head, saying, 'Coming down here to stir up the niggers.' Peck stood quietly looking at them for several moments, but said nothing. Two persons standing by, one Negro and one white, reprimanded the cab driver for his violence. The Negro was told, 'You keep out of this.' In the police station, some of the men standing around could be heard saying, 'They'll never get a bus out of here tonight.'

After the bond was placed, Rev. Charles Jones, local white Presbyterian minister, speedily drove the men to his home. They were pursued by two cabs filled with taxi men. As the interracial group got on the front porch of the Jones home, the two cabs pulled up at the curb, and men jumped, out two of them with sticks for weapons, and others picked up sizeable rocks. They started toward the house, but were called back by one of their number. In a few moments the phone rang, and an anonymous voice said to Jones, 'Get those damn niggers out of town or we'll burn your house down. We'll be around to see that they go.' The police were notified and they arrived in about twenty minutes. The interracial group felt it wise to leave town before nightfall. Two cars were obtained and the group was driven to Greensboro by way of Durham for an evening engagement.

Greensboro, N.C., to Winston-Salem, N.C., 14 April

Two tests were made on Greyhound. In the first test Lynn sat in front; in the second, Nelson. A South Carolinian seated by Bromley on the first bus said, 'In my state he would either move or be killed.' He was calm as Bromley talked with him about the Morgan decision.

Winston-Salem, N.C., to Asheville, N.C., 15 April

From Winston-Salem to Statesville the group traveled by Greyhound. Nelson was seated with Bromley in the second seat from the front. Nothing was said. At Statesville the group transferred to the Trailways, with Nelson still in front. In a small town about ten miles from Statesville the driver approached Nelson and told him he would have to move to the rear. When Nelson said that he was an interstate passenger, the driver said that the bus was not interstate. When Nelson explained that his ticket was interstate the driver returned to his seat and drove on. The rest of the trip to Asheville was through mountainous country, and the bus stopped at many small towns. A soldier asked the driver why Nelson was not forced to move. The driver explained that there was a Supreme Court decision and that he could do nothing about it. He said, 'If you want to do something about this, don't blame this man [Nelson]: kill those bastards up in Washington.' The soldier explained to a rather large, vociferous man why Nelson was allowed to sit up in front. The large man commented, 'I wish I was the bus driver.' Near Asheville the bus became very crowded, and there were women standing up. Two women spoke to the bus driver, asking him why Nelson was not moved. In each case the driver explained that the Supreme Court decision was responsible. Several white women took seats in the Jim Crow section in the rear.

Asheville, N.C., to Knoxville, Tenn., 17 April

Banks and Peck were in the second seat on the Trailways. A white passenger asked the bus driver to tell Banks to move while the bus was still in the station. Banks replied, 'I'm sorry, I can't,' and explained that he was an interstate passenger. The police were called and the order repeated. A twenty-minute consultation took place before the arrest was made. When Peck was not arrested, he said, 'We're traveling together, and you will have to arrest me too.' He was arrested for sitting in the rear. The two men were released from the city jail on $100 bond each. On 18 April the case came up for trial in the police court before Judge Sam Cathay. Mr Curtis Todd of Winston-Salem was the attorney for Banks and Peck. (There were no Negro attorneys in Asheville, and this was the first time a Negro attorney had appeared in this court.) The indictment was that the men had violated the Jim Crow law. The two witnesses for the state – the bus driver and the policeman – testified so accurately that it was not necessary to call defense witnesses. They both said there was no disorder on the part of the arrested men. Neither the judge nor the state's attorney knew about the Morgan decision, and they had to borrow Attorney Todd's copy. When the judge learned the maximum sentence was thirty days, he gave thirty day sentences, to be under the supervision of the highway commissioner. Pending appeal, the men were released on $250 bonds.

Knoxville, Tenn., to Nashville, Tenn., 17 April

Wright and Jack sat at the front of a Greyhound bus. Before the driver boarded, a red-headed soldier asked him if he was going to move Wright. The driver approached Wright and asked him politely: 'Would you like to move?' Wright said he would not. The driver disappeared for fifteen minutes. Two Negroes in the rear of the bus discussed the situation audibly, saying, 'They are going to get the police, and they'll probably hit him.' The other said, 'When in Rome, I believe in doing as the Romans do.' When the bus driver returned, he drove off without raising any more questions. This bus trip was at night.

Knoxville, Tenn., to Louisville, Ky., 18 April

Worthy and Roodenko sat in the front of a Greyhound bus. The bus reached Corbin, Tennessee, some hundred miles from Knoxville, before Worthy was asked to move. The driver hinted that there would be violence from the crowd if Worthy did not move. A white woman from Tennessee talked with the officials in the bus station and to the bus driver, protesting threatened arrests. The bus driver received orders to drive on.

Nashville, Tenn., to Louisville, Ky., 19 April

Wright and Jack had reserved seats on an all-coach reserved train of the Louisville and Nashville. There was no difficulty in getting on the train. Two conductors approached to collect the tickets. One asked Jack if Wright were his prisoner. Learning they were friends, he told Wright that company rules meant he would have to move to the Jim Crow car. 'That is the way it is done down here,' he concluded. When Wright refused to move, he said he would be back later. When he came back he said: 'If we were in Alabama, we would throw you out of the window.' He threatened to have Wright arrested in Bowling Green, Kentucky, but no arrest took place. A woman sitting the second seat behind the men approached them after the conductor left, giving them her name and address, and saying that they could call on her for help.

Weaversville, N.C., to Bristol, Va., 19 April

No test was made. Banks was the only Negro on the bus, and he was on the rear seat. The bus was extremely crowded. The driver asked Banks to move from the rear seat to the double seat in front of the rear seat so that only one white person, and not four, would have to sit beside him. Banks complied. He had a friendly conversation with a young white farmer who sat beside him.

Bristol, Va., to Roanoke, Va., 19 April

Banks and Peck rode together on a Greyhound. The driver approached them twice, but on neither occasion insisted that they move.

Cincinnati, Ohio, to Roanoke, Va., 19 April

Worthy and Houser had coach reservations on the Norfolk and

Western. At the gate the railroad man expressed consternation that Worthy had a seat in a white coach, but no attempt was made to keep him from taking it.

Roanoke, Va., to Washington, D.C., 20 April

Worthy and Bromley sat together in a white coach on the Norfolk and Western. No questions of any kind were raised. Bromley got off at Charlottesville, Virginia. For the last part of the trip to Washington, a white girl sat beside Worthy rather than sit on her suitcase in the aisle.

Roanoke, Va., to Lynchburg, Va., 21 April

Banks and Houser sat together in the front of a Greyhound bus. No incident occurred.

Lynchburg, Va., to Washington, D.C., 22 April

Nelson and Houser were seated at the front of the Trailways bus. The driver did not see Nelson until he was about five miles out of the station. When he stopped at a service station, he asked Nelson to move to the rear. Nelson refused on the ground that he was an interstate passenger. Houser explained that they were traveling together. The driver said they could ride in the rear. Houser asked whether that too would not be breaking the Jim Crow rules of the company by which the driver said he was guided. The driver then said that Houser would have to sit one seat in front of Nelson in the rear. It took more than an hour to get a warrant for Nelson's arrest. State police took Nelson to the small town of Amherst, where he was held for $50 bail. The bus driver apologized profusely for his action when Houser got off at Amherst to put up the bond for Nelson. The passengers were very patient, rather neutral in attitude.

Amherst, Va., to Washington, D.C., 22 April

Nelson and Houser took a train on the Southern Railway at Amherst. They asked the conductor where they could ride together. He asked if Nelson were Houser's prisoner. Upon learning that they were friends, he said it was against the rules for them to ride together on that train. He said, 'I'll turn you over to the officials at Charlottesville if you sit together.' They sat together in the Jim Crow car, where the conductor asked Houser if he refused to move. Again he threatened arrest in Charlottesville, but no arrest was made.

Charlottesville, Va., to Washington, D.C., 23 April

Banks rode alone in the front of the Trailways. Peck and Randle were riding on the rear seat. For two hours out of Charlottesville there was no incident. In the small town of Culpeper, Va., the driver told Banks to move to the rear. It took about an hour and a half to get a warrant issued for Banks' arrest. A Negro woman who had a concession on selling bus tickets in town came on board the bus and offered to help Banks in any way she could. The warrant read that Banks was guilty of not obeying the order of the driver. Nothing was said to Peck or Randle, sitting in the rear, in spite of the fact that the rules of the company state that white persons shall not sit in the rear. Banks was released on a $25 bond.

ACCOUNT OF THE TRIALS

As of July 6, 1947, four trials have been held. In Petersburg, Va., Conrad Lynn received a $10 fine. In Chapel Hill, N.C., Bayard Rustin and Igai Roodenko were found guilty of violating the state Jim Crow law. Rustin was given a fine only to cover court costs, while Roodenko was sentenced to thirty days on the road gang. The judge said he purposely discriminated against the white person involved. Likewise, when Andrew Johnson and Joe Felmet were tried on June 24, Felmet was given the maximum sentence of thirty days on the road gang, while Johnson received a $25 fine. The judge tried to give Felmet six months only to discover this was beyond the maximum permitted. The indictment for the four arrested in Chapel Hill was changed from disorderly conduct and interfering with arrest to a violation of state Jim Crow law on the ground that since the men were planning stop-overs in three cities within the state, they were not interstate passengers.

The Asheville case against Peck and Banks has been outlined in the body of this report. The cases in Amherst and Culpeper, Va., will be scheduled for trial pending the outcome of another case involving the same legal principles.

All convictions are being appealed. Persons interested in receiving reports on trials as they occur should write to George Houser and Bayard Rustin, 2929 Broadway, asking to be placed on the appropriate mailing list. Contributions to help cover costs of trials will be gratefully received.

GENERAL OBSERVATIONS

Confusion

The one word which most universally describes the attitude of police, of passengers, and of the Negro and white bus riders is 'confusion'. Persons taking part in the psychological struggle in the buses and trains either did not know of the Morgan decision or, if they did, possessed no clear understanding of it. Thus when police officers and bus drivers in authority took a stand, they tended to act on the basis of what they knew – the state Jim Crow law. In the South, where the caste system is rigidly defined, this confusion is extremely dangerous, leading to frustration, usually followed by aggression in some form.

Apathy and Neutrality

The great majority of the passengers were apathetic and did not register their feelings even in situations where it was apparent from facial expressions that they were for or against the action which the group was taking.

Bus Company Directives

It was generally apparent that the bus companies were attempting to circumvent the intentions of the Supreme Court in the Irene Morgan decision by reliance on state Jim Crow laws, by company regulations, and by subtle pressures.

Negro Reaction

Negroes generally tend to follow the dominant reaction of the bus. There were exceptions to this, of course, but generally there was at first fear, followed by caution. Where cautious Negroes saw resistant Negroes sitting in the front unmolested, they tended to move from the rear forward, too.

Absence of Violence in Bus

There were no acts of violence on the part of anyone in the buses. The most extreme negative reactions were verbal, but without profanity. Typical was the young Marine who said, 'The k.k.k. is coming up again and I guess I'll join up.' The one act of violence against a member of the group was on the part of a taxi cab driver outside the bus station at Chapel Hill. This act – a single but hard blow to the head – was directed against a white man.

'Uncle Tom' Reaction

On three occasions when Negro testers protested discrimination by sitting in the front, other Negroes – a porter, a school teacher, and a day laborer – urged the resisters in very emotional terms to comply with the law. Their request was in part the result of fear, or as in the case of the Negro porter, an attempt to ingratiate themselves with white authorities. Such reactions are to be expected in a caste system and represent the kind of personal degradation which ought to spur us on to eliminate caste.

The Responsibility of Authority

Policemen and bus drivers have a great responsibility in social change of this kind. Success or failure, violence or peaceful change, is in large part determined by the position they take. White persons generally ignored Negroes in the front of buses or in the non-Jim Crow cars on trains, until the bus drivers or train conductors raised an issue. We are of the opinion that if the bus drivers had not taken action, the passengers in most cases would have continued to ignore the Negroes sitting in the front or in white coaches. Between Statesville and Asheville, N.C., a clear statement from the driver explaining the Morgan decision quieted protesting white passengers. It is our belief that when those in authority take a clear stand, passengers who might resent a Negro's presence in a non-traditional position will accept the situation with a typical shrug of the shoulder – 'Well, this is the law. What can you do?'

Police Attitude

In no case of arrest was there a single example of police inconsideration. The police were polite and calm, and if there were police who were anti-Negro there was no indication of it. In fact, one officer, when pressed for a reason for his unwillingness to sit beside a Negro himself, said, 'I'm just not Christian enough, I guess.' This would not necessarily be true in the lower South.

Non-Violence

Without exception those arrested behaved in a non-violent fashion. They acted without fear, spoke quietly and firmly, showing great consideration for the police and bus drivers, and repeatedly pointed to the fact that they expected the police to do their duty as they saw it. We cannot over-emphasize the necessity for this courteous and intelligent manner while breaking with the caste system. It is our belief that the reason the police behaved politely stems from the fact that there was not the slightest provocation in the attitude of the resisters. On the contrary, we tried at all times to understand their attitude and position first.

Interracial Group a Necessity

Another reason for the lack of tension was the interracial character of the group. We did not allow a single situation to develop so that the struggle appeared to be between white and Negro persons, but rather that progressives and democrats, white and black, were working by peaceful means to overcome a system which they felt to be wrong.

Need for Southerners

The more Southern people refuse to accept Jim Crow, the better. If even a small portion of the white population refused Jim Crow as now practiced, it could not survive. Resentment against Northerners, who are considered plants and imports, would have greatly reduced the effectiveness of our trip had there not been a number of people in our group who were born in the South and some who are now living there.

Taking the Initiative

Much was gained when someone within our group took the lead in discussion when bus drivers, or train conductors, and police appeared. Those who seemed certain of their facts and who spoke clearly and assuredly set the tone. Attitudes were greatly accelerated in the proper direction whenever a person of liberal sentiments spoke up first.

Learning About the Morgan Decision

As the trip progressed it became evident that the police and bus drivers were learning about the Irene Morgan decision as word was passed from city to city and from driver to driver about the 'test cases'. We see here again the need for incidents as 'teaching techniques'. The following paragraph from a letter written by a student at Chapel Hill, supports this contention: 'I don't know whether all the stir has been in vain or not. Everyone on this campus now knows about the Fellowship of Reconciliation, the Congress of Racial Equality, and the Supreme Court decision. What is more important, many people, including my two very conservative roommates, are thinking seriously about the whole non-violent approach to social problems.'

Chief Danger

The incident at Chapel Hill indicates that one of the chief dangers of violence is from crowds which gather outside buses. Such persons are unable to hear the discussion or to know and debate the facts given within. They merely pick up bits of hearsay and false rumors. It is also true that many taxi drivers, pool room fellows, and idlers are apt to be in the groups which hang around bus terminals. Many men in these groups depend on Jim Crow for personal status. No matter how poor they are, they can 'feel better than the niggers'.

Direct Action

It is our belief that without direct action on the part of groups and individuals, the Jim Crow pattern in the South can not be broken down. We are equally certain that such direct action must be non-violent.

The Importance of Women

It appeared that women were more intellectually inquisitive, open for discussion, and liberal in their sentiments than men. On several occasions women not only defended those who broke with Jim Crow, but gave their names and addresses in offering to act as witnesses. In appealing for aid in the psychological struggle within the bus one might do well to concentrate on winning over women.

Greyhound Failed to Arrest

All the arrests occurred on the Trailways Buses. It is difficult to account for this. One might suppose that the fact that Trailways services largely Southern states and is not used so universally in interstate travel as the Greyhound lines, may in part account for the difference.

Southern Reactionary Position

If the attitude of those Southerners who did speak up could be put in a nutshell, it is in the words of one Southerner who said, 'The South is the South and will always be this way. We don't care about the Supreme Court decision.' This is not so much an attitude of resistance to change as it is one of despair and cynicism.

People Prepared for Change

We believe that the great majority of the people in the upper South are prepared to accept the Irene Morgan decision and to ride on buses and trains with Negroes. One white woman, reluctantly taking a seat beside a Negro man, said to her sister who was about to protest, 'I'm tired. Anything for a seat.'

Aggression Against Whites

Persons who did not wish to see change, particularly the bus drivers, became more angry with the white participants than with the Negroes. This is an important observation, since, except in extreme cases, the white resisters may have to bear the brunt of hostility.

Flux

The situation in the upper South is in a great state of flux. Where numerous cases have been before the courts recently, as in northern Virginia, the barriers are already down, and Negroes can, in large part, ride without fear of arrest. Repeated arrests have occurred in other parts of Virginia. This is in part true of North Carolina, eastern Tennessee and Kentucky.

DOROTHY DAY

1897–

IN 1933, six years after having formally embraced Roman Catholicism, and in the depths of the Depression, Dorothy Day, together with Peter Maurin, founded *The Catholic Worker*. In that same year the first 'house of hospitality' – a shelter providing direct relief to the unemployed – was opened and the views of the new movement became clear. Since then *The Catholic Worker*, still selling for its original penny, has consistently protested mass production in factory and field and has supported a 'back to the land' movement based on subsistance farming. Vows of voluntary poverty and pacifism have been part of the discipline which the movement has made integral with its social philosophy.

Positions unpopular with the large body of the Roman Catholic Church have cost Miss Day much support, but she has often said that if it came to a choice between silence or leaving the Church, she would choose silence. A strong supporter of conscientious objection during the war, *The Catholic Worker* continues to oppose those aid programmes which are politically inspired (almost all of them, according to the paper) or work in factories producing armaments. Since 1955, Miss Day and others have repeatedly been arrested in non-cooperation demonstrations against compulsory civil defence drills.

'The Pope and Peace' is taken from the February 1954 issue of *The Catholic Worker*.

The Pope and Peace

On New Year's day I began to read the Pope's Christmas message which was printed partly in the *New York Times*, and noticed that directly under his message, on page one, column one, the Soviet wishes the world a merry Christmas. Christmas, the broadcast said, always conveys the finest cherished hopes of plain people and their deep-rooted faith in the possibility of a peaceful happy life, but no time in the past few years has the conversion of that possibility into reality been so close and so real as at the present time. The broadcast added that certain 'governments of the West have been forced to pay heed to the popular demand that the spirit of negotiation prevail over decisions based on force'.

More than half the Pope's message of 5,000 words was discussion of the materialism that results from technological progress and particularly from the 'spirit which finds what is to be most highly prized in human life is the advantages that can be derived from the forces and elements of nature.'

The *Times* went on to say, that the Pope's message was one of the gloomiest of modern times. He is not satisfied with the progress towards peace and regards what peace we have as a very fragile affair. 'Many people were astonished that the Pope did not speak of Catholics who suffer persecution behind the iron curtain except for a brief reference to them in the blessing which concluded the messages.' Perhaps the Holy Father thought the persecuted ones were in a better spiritual way than those who were living under the materialism of the West.

There were two columns of excerpts of the message and they were most provocative of thought. They were about work and leisure, the nature of man, the need for and the blessings of technological advance but also the futility in placing our hopes in these, and the dangers of men becoming spiritual pygmies, the need to do away with the inequalities in living standards and the fallacy of hoping to gain peace by raising the standard of living and increasing productivity.

Pope Pius said many of the things we have been saying over and over again in *The Catholic Worker*, but the concluding paragraphs of *the Times* two columns, dealing as it does with Utopias, authority and State, might seem to be especially for our meditation. As we are told by St Peter to be ready to give reason for the faith that is in us, I must in all humility, as publisher of *The Catholic Worker*, try to comment on it and explain again what anarchism and pacifism means to me, and what I think it meant to Peter Maurin. Bob Ludlow and Ammon Hennacy can speak for themselves.

We have often enough been accused of taking quotes out of context, or taking what words appeal to us, or agree with us. Here are the Pope's words which seem not to agree with us.

'The Christian statesman does not serve the cause of national or international peace when he abandons the solid basis of objective experience and clear cut principles and transforms himself, as it were, into a divinely inspired herald of a new social world, helping to confuse even more minds already uncertain. He is guilty of this fault who thinks he can experiment with the social order, and especially he who is not resolved to make the authority of the state and the observance of its laws prevail among all classes of society. It is perhaps necessary to demonstrate that weakness in authority more than any other weakness undermines the strength of a nation, and that the weakness of one nation brings with it the weakness of Europe and imperils the general peace.'

Observation is made in the *New York Times* that it thought attention is being called to the unrest of France and her opposition to a united Europe. But my comment will be in reference to our own attitudes to the State and its laws.

Our Lord said, 'He who will be the leader among you, let him be the servant', and on washing the feet of his disciples, 'As I have done, so do ye also.' 'Christ became obedient unto death, even to the death of the Cross.' Be ye subject to every living thing, St Paul says.

To be a follower of Jesus, one would certainly not seek after authority, or look for political office. It is thrust upon one by ability and recognition of that ability by others, as it was in the case of St Peter, St Ambrose, Pius XII and so on.

In Christian statesmen, where there are such, then it would seem necessary to cultivate humility, courage, holy indifference, holy poverty, in order to fulfil one's high office. And perhaps one would not stay in that office long. To lead by example rather than by law seems to have always been the Christian way. St Francis, humblest, poorest of men, was pushed into a position of authority. In the present day, Don Luigi Sturzo, in the past and the present Mayor of Florence, in the present from all account of him, was pushed into office.

The problem of authority and freedom is one of the greatest problems of the day. Russia certainly cannot be accused of lack of authoritarianism. Though they may be said to be 'experimenting with the social order', they are certainly resolved to make the authority of State and observance of the law prevail among all classes of society. The Soviet Union is no longer a classless society when they admit to a middle classs. There is a good society, however, where classes are functional rather than acquisitive, as Tawney said.

How obey the laws of a state when they run counter to man's conscience? 'Thou shalt not kill,' Divine law states. 'A new precept I give unto you that you love your brother as I have loved you.' St Peter disobeyed the law of men and stated that he had to obey God rather than man. Wars today involve total destruction, obliteration bombing, killing of the innocent, the stockpiling of atom and hydrogen bombs. When one is drafted for such war, when one registers for the draft for such a war, when one pays income tax, eighty per cent of which goes to support such war, or works where armaments are made, one is participating in this war. We are all involved in war these days. War means hatred and fear. Love casts out fear.

The social order which depends on profits, which does not consider the nature of man's needs, as to living space, food and work, is a bad social order, and we must work to make that kind of an order in which 'it is easier for man to be good'.

The modern States which built up a Hitler, which did not depopulate concentration camps and gas chambers by providing living space, giving asylum or by imposing economic sanctions, are monstrosities. When they are driven to force finally, they fail to accomplish that peace which they set out for. It is a greater blood bath than ever, with threat of more to come.

We need to look back to the city states of Italy (all of their good aspects, as Kropotkin did) and to the guilds; to our own early American principles, 'he governs best who governs least', we need to study such a teacher as Don Luigi Sturzo who held political office and founded a party which worked toward credit unions, cooperatives, labor unions, land for the people, as the beginning of an order in which men could be conscious of their dignity, and responsibility; we need to consider the principle of subsidiarity when we talk of authority and freedom.

Everything needs to be broken down into smaller units to be workable and according to man's nature, whether it is States, cities, factories. A union, a cooperative, is no better than the men in it, than the locals or cells which make it up.

Man must be responsible, in other words, to exercise his freedom which is God's greatest gift to him. The greatest message which Peter Maurin had for us was this reminder of man's freedom. That is why he never used the word pacifist or anarchist. Privately he admitted to both positions and letters from his brother in France, tell us that he always considered himself a pacifist.

Tom Sullivan and Jack English went to see Peter once in the hospital during the last years of his life when he was not able to think, as he used to put it, and could not elaborate on what he said.

They asked him then, 'Was he a pacifist?' He said, 'No.'

A year or so later, I asked him what he would do about conscription, and he answered then, 'I would resist.'

How to square these two answers, which we both are sure that we heard correctly. I have thought about it a good deal these last few years, and now again since reading Brendan O'Grady's thesis on Peter Maurin, where the text of Peter's brother's letters occur.

Going over Peter's essays again I have thought that greater even than Peter's message of poverty, manual labor and the works of mercy, was his message of man's freedom and personal responsibility. It was a timeless problem he was dealing with. It was a problem which a better social order would make easier to solve, and it is a problem which will always remain with us 'until the day dawn and the shadows flee and the Desire of the everlasting hills shall come'.

Peter did not want to be fragmented, if we can use that word, by being called a pacifist or an anarchist, both of which words would serve to set him apart from men by their very extreme position.

First of all we are Catholics, children of our holy Father Pope Pius XII. And first of all we are Catholics, before we are Americans, Russians, Germans, Italians, French or Chinese. We are members of the body of Christ, or potential members. We are sons of God.

A great and terrible thought, setting us free, and also making us realize our responsibility.

Ammon Hennacy is an individual anarchist and a well ordered and peaceful man, subjecting himself in all things to others around him, whether it is his army Captain boss, or his daughter's needs, or the duties of his Church which he has voluntarily chosen in a true metanoia.

In thinking of Peter and Ammon I am thinking of men meek and humble of heart, desiring no power over others, no position of authority, yet forced to speak out by the exigencies of the times, with authority. They are lovers of poverty, content with little, stripping themselves.

I remember Peter when we picketed the German consulate back in 1935 down at the Battery, picking up the leaflets we were handing out and which had been strewn around by bystanders who had not yet been taught by the radio and press that Hitler was an enemy to man. They thought we were communists.

Peter was obeying authority in the shape of a policeman who told us we were littering the street. Peter thought of authority and law in relation to the Thomistic doctrine of the common good which he was always talking about. He had a book on the subject which he was always trying to get us to read. Have we read half the books on his list?

I think of Ammon removing boulders and fallen trees from the roads as he walks along, not because he uses a car but to give evidence to his conviction of man's responsibility which goes with his freedom.

These are men so responsible, so conscious of the common good that perhaps their use of the word Anarchist may provoke a study of Statism and authority as well as of Man's freedom and responsibility.

In the Soviet's Christmas message they speak of the plain people. On the other hand, the Pope, surveying the materialism of the faithful, is sorrowful and warns us – 'Above all, man needs a religious formation . . . a Christian concept of work . . . Sunday and its unique dignity as the day devoted to the worship of God . . . a mutual agreement to oppose the cause of division reigning among nations in the discrepancy of the standard of living and of productivity.' He urges too 'a continental union of peoples, different indeed, but geographically and historically bound together'. Away with doubts, suspicions, fears.

'If anyone asks in advance for an absolute guarantee of success, the answer is that there is a risk, but a necessary one; a risk, but in keeping with present possibilities, a reasonable risk. The supreme incitement to action is the gravity of the moment.'

So in 1954 we continue to work towards the brotherhood of man and the Fatherland of God.

DANILO DOLCI

1924–

In 1952, Danilo Dolci, an Italian architect, settled in Trappeto, near Palermo in Sicily. On earlier visits he had been appalled by the sub-marginal living conditions of the large majority of people; this time he established a kindergarten, a 'people's university', and finally had a social survey made of the area to draw attention to Sicily's extreme poverty. When little attention was paid the statistics, he began a fast and finally got promises of governmental aid.

Heavily indebted to Gandhian techniques, Dolci and one thousand others undertook a fast to protest against unemployment in January 1956 – since in the intervening time the government had done little to relieve the desperate situation. When the authorities did not provide work, he and the workers went on the now-famous 'strike-in-reverse' by repairing, on a voluntary basis, a long-neglected road. The group claimed 'the right to work' as provided for in the Italian constitution. For his efforts, he and twenty-two others were arrested, tried, and imprisoned, although the court noted 'the high moral value of Dolci's action'.

Three of Dolci's books have been published in England and the United States, and this extract from the trial itself is taken from the second of these, *Outlaws* (1961). The translation is by R. Munroe. In January 1958, Dolci was awarded the Lenin Peace Prize which he accepted in a non-partisan spirit. The proceeds were used to set up five 'Study and Planning Centres for Full Employment' in western Sicily.

Trial Statement

Palermo County Court Hearing of 24 March 1956, 9.00 a.m.

Presiding Judge: Dr Rosario Trainito.
Associate Judges: Deputy Attorney General, Dr Pasquale Lo Torto.
Clerk of the Court: Dr Viviani.

The accused, Dolci, Zanini, Termini, Speciale, Abbate are brought into court between *carabinieri*, handcuffed and in chains.

As soon as the court is declared open, Avv. Battaglia, for the defence, rises to speak.

AVV. BATTAGLIA: I wish to point out to the court in the name of all defending counsel that the accused are still handcuffed and in chains . . .

PUBLIC PROSECUTOR: This was considered necessary for the maintenance of public order.

AVV. BATTAGLIA [*continuing*] : . . . in open violation of Article 427 of the Code of Penal Procedure, which lays down that the prisoner shall be present in court 'unfettered in his person'. I request, therefore, that the law be duly observed.

PUBLIC PROSECUTOR: I agree to the request if the Presiding Judge has no objection.

PRESIDING JUDGE: Prisoners' Escort! Remove the handcuffs!

The charges are then read aloud.

PRESIDING JUDGE: Will the prisoner Dolci rise and step forward into the court.

Dolci leaves the dock and advances almost to the judges' table.

PRESIDING JUDGE: Tell the court what you have to say in answer to the charges laid against you.

D. DOLCI: One day last November, in the vicinity of our house in the Spine Sante quarter of Partinico, a five-month-old girl, weighing only four pounds, fourteen ounces, died in convulsions, vomiting up her intestines.

She died because her parents had not had the means to give her the necessary treatment and she was not taken to a hospital in time. The child's mother had sent an older girl to us for help, but the child had stopped on the way to play and had forgotten to come on to us. By the time we arrived, we found that, once again, we had come too late.

This is not an isolated episode, a single incident. In Partinico such things happen frequently. The official figures issued by the Home for Children and Expectant Mothers in Partinico show that the infant mortality rate reaches 8.7 per cent. This event made a new and profound impression on me: we were no longer able to save the individual cases, to help all those who turned to us singly for assistance. We had managed to do something, but not nearly enough. And it was certainly not enough simply to provide the authorities with evidence of the appalling conditions in which the people of Partinico lived. We had already pointed out that the 350 'outlaws' had only received from the Italian State a total of 650 years of schooling between them as against a total of 3,000 years in prison. I need only give three other facts to illustrate my point: only one out of the 350 'outlaws' had both father and mother who had attended the fourth elementary class at school; in Trappeto, during 1954–5, ten elementary classes had forty-three different teachers; while trawlers have continued to fish within the three-mile limit for the past eleven years and every effort on our part to get the abuse stopped has been met with derision by the Customs Police themselves.

In Montelepre, public works for training craftsmen have been opened by the Ministry of Works. In Partinico the situation has not changed. We have appealed several times to the President of the Republic, to the Prime Minister, to all the Deputies and Senators. We have even appealed to the Regional authorities to provide, in particular, work, schools for the children, and assistance for the families of those in prison.

We knew that the situation was becoming increasingly dangerous: in the last two years, sixteen crimes of violence, between murders and suicides, have been committed in the Partinico area.[1] In view of this, we sent appeals and documentary evidence to the press and to the responsible authorities in the certainty that something would be done. But it never was.

In the meantime, however, a new spirit had been born in the people of Partinico. They had begun to take part in the life of the community; to turn, for example, to the trade unions. This was exactly what we wanted; we wanted to see people, whatever their opinions, making a move to establish a more civilized state of mind, more in keeping with the world of today.

1. 9 April 1956. Another young man has been stabbed through the heart in Partinico tonight. He was only seventeen. An old woman, who saw it happen, died on the spot from fright.

23 April 1956. Another woman was murdered in Via della Madonna; she was only nineteen.

5 May, 1956. Another man has been murdered, the fourth in a month; this makes a total of twenty.

29 May 1956. The body of a youth has been found in an advanced state of decomposition in the water-tank of the house.

7 June 1956. Someone has been shot in the head, but it looks as if he has escaped serious injury.

At the end of last November the situation was tense. The number of robberies had increased; even our next-door neighbours went out stealing lemons. A man was accused of murdering his brother for three thousand lire. The people came to us for help, not one by one but by the dozens. And these were not just single isolated cases.

There were too many of them for us to handle. Once again we telegraphed the authorities. It was December and you know what winter means to the poor. We didn't want to see people go out to steal or to commit crimes. But what could we do? We were being pressed by the population to find some solution, some remedy.

And so it was that we went out for the first time on to the old 'dirt road' of Valguarnera, as it is called locally, about a mile outside the town. The path was in a hopeless state of disrepair: loose stones and deep ruts prevented carts from passing over it and the people wanted it repaired. I am not an anarchist; we were not anarchists intent on destroying the road. We wanted to see it repaired and it was within our power to repair it. The Superintendent of Police ordered us home with the promise that work would be found. That time, we obeyed. We could not afford to act imprudently. It was too grave a risk to act without witnesses in the middle of the countryside when, on the one side, were men with families and, on the other, members of the police force who are not used to strikes or, I believe, to reading and observing the Constitution. Besides, I had been asked to speak on television about our problems; and so that time we went quietly home and, after consulting with the unemployed and their families, I wrote the text of my talk for the programme.

I left for Turin. In Rome I met Mauro Gobbini, Carlo Levi, Valerio Volpini, Leone Bertone, Maria Sacchetti Fermi, Guido Calogero, Alberto Carocci and Benjamino Segre.

In Pisa I met Aldo Capitini and Walter Binni.

In Florence I met Enzo Enriques Agnoletti, Maria Chiappelli, Romano Bilenchi, Ettore Bernabei, Signora Rosselli, Giovanni Michelucci and others; in Milan, Elio Vittorini, Franco Alasia, Riccardo Bauer, Piero Malvezzi, Adriano Alloisio and his friends; in Turin, Franco and Gigliola Venturi, Norberto Bobbio, Giulio Einaudi, Luigi Barale, Umberto Facca and others.

I explained our plans and needs to all these friends. I told them that we could not abandon the population to its own devices, that we had to make common cause with it by returning to work, for instance, on the old path. We had no intention of making trouble but we knew what we had to do: return to work in an orderly but determined manner, repair the path and bring it back into use again, do a real job of good work. To make it quite clear, in fact, that there exists, even in Partinico, a vast source of riches, work, and that there is no shortage of strong arms capable of bringing about a miracle and changing the face of that corner of the earth.

I explained our plan to work on the old road in my talk on television without raising any objections from the political editors of the R.A.I. beyond some slight 'toning down', more of form than of substance.

I was worried, nevertheless. We could not act with a clear conscience as long as there was the least danger of the same thing happening as had happened at Venosa and in other places before. I spoke of my doubts and asked the advice of various groups of people so as to make doubly sure of what we were doing. Then I returned to Partinico. During my return journey I met Ignazio Silone, Mario Alicata, Vittorio Gorresio, Corrado Cagli, Raniero Panzieri and Cesare Zavattini in Rome.

When I got back, we sent yet another appeal to the authorities and to the Press in which we stated that we could not sit back idly any longer, and that it was a crime against our families and against society not to work. Men cannot be left to hang about the streets in idleness, as if they were beggars or children.

Let the authorities tell us what work there is to be done and we'll do it. We have always asserted that the only way of escaping from our difficulties is by working and indeed this is borne out by Article IV of the Constitution in which it is clearly stated that work is not only a right but a duty. We believe sincerely that the Constitution is something to be taken seriously. Didn't Giovanni Gronchi, President of the Republic, say so in his inaugural message? Didn't the fallen heroes of the Resistance Movement who died for the Constitution say so with their blood?

The Constitution is the only law in Italy of which no one need be ashamed.

So then we planned a one-day fast, but it was forbidden by the police and we were formally warned, in the name of everyone, not to go and work on the path.

It was decided to fast for one whole day to show, by fasting in common, that the things of this world cannot be changed for the better without meditation, purity of heart and sacrifice. It was our intention to gather together to meditate in silence on what had to be done to change this small world of ours. The police sent for me and informed me that the demonstration was illegal.

I replied that I couldn't see that it was a crime to fast, particularly in so isolated a spot, sitting by the sea on the beach at San Cataldo. The *carabinieri* lieutenant doubted very much whether it was lawful for so many people to assemble on a beach. When I explained to him that every summer, as a child, I went to bathe on the crowded beaches at Rimini and on the Ligurian Riviera without having to have permission from the police, the lieutenant expressed grave doubts as to my veracity. 'Perhaps there were police among the bathers,' he said.

'If you insist on our keeping a certain distance from each other,' I replied, 'just tell us and we'll bring a tape measure with us and stick to whatever distance you say, a yard, a yard and a half, two yards – anything you like. We have no intention of violating the law: we are in favour of law and order.' And when I taxed the officer with the guarantee of work given in Article IV of the Constitution, he replied, not without a trace of affection in his voice: 'My good Dolci, my good Dolci, all that's just a Utopia.'

On the Monday of the fast . . .

PRESIDING JUDGE: You are not charged with fasting.

DOLCI: I'm coming on to the rest in a minute. On the Monday of the fast, it was raining hard in the morning. During the night we heard that, late the previous evening, the *carabinieri* had forbidden the captains of the fishing boats to tie up at San Cataldo. The people took this order as an insult. Since the fast itself was more important to us than the place where it was held, it was decided, at four in the morning, that the Trappeto fishermen (non-political) should stay in the Fishermen's Home in Trappeto, that the Balestrate fishermen (non-political) should stay in their Home in Balestrate and that the unemployed of Partinico should fast in the Camera del Lavoro and at the U.I.L.,[1] both of which organizations, more than anyone else, had supported the plan. It was decided that this was the best arrangement because a quick reconnaissance, in which we were accompanied by journalists, photographers and later on by a reporter from the television, showed us that there were about two hundred police officers with cars, trucks, etc., in the area of Trappeto alone. Apart from getting wet uselessly all day, we would have only risked an encounter with the police by going to San Cataldo. Besides, we did not want to do anything underhand. We wanted each

1. Italian Workers' Union. The Social-Democrat trade union.

one of us to be able to show the world and ourselves in particular that we had nothing to be ashamed of and that we wanted to behave like gentlemen.

Only a few, who were not warned in time, went to the beach of Ciammarita despite the intermittent rain. But we sent word to them to return and no pressure had to be exerted by the police. During the morning we sent off telegrams to the authorities and there was a meeting at the Town Hall in Partinico. I arrived late and only went in, in passing, as I heard it was intended to distribute soup and I did not consider that this was the right way to solve the problem of unemployment and work. This was on the Monday. On Wednesday, a meeting was held at the Camera del Lavoro in Partinico (the U.I.L. withdrew at the last moment and the other groups which had been invited, had decided not to take part officially; nevertheless, people of every political tendency, including the uncommitted, were present) and it was carefully explained that those who worked on the old road would be doing so for nothing. Professor Lucio Lombardo-Radice was also present and addressed the meeting. We made it clear to everyone that, if the work was to be done in a true spirit of generosity, no one could come forward afterwards and say: 'I want to be paid for my work on the old road.'[1] There were to be no ulterior motives behind the work. If, as it was hoped, the Council later agreed to give official approval for the work, no one, equally, was to say: 'I took part in the strike so I'm entitled to a job.' The first to be employed would be those most in need.

Your Honour, let us put our cards on the table. If they prevented us from working, we still intended to stay there for the full eight hours, sitting on the ground with our arms crossed. It was our intention, in fact, to turn the work on the road into a sort of effective Labour Exchange.

PRESIDING JUDGE: But if your plan was not to be paid and the object of the demonstration was purely symbolic, why did you refuse to disperse and insist that you wanted to work for the full eight hours? Wouldn't a symbolic half-hour's work have done as well?

DOLCI: I never said that the plan was symbolic. We wanted to do a proper job of work.

In order not to break the law we went out to the old road in scattered parties taking only our work tools with us. I would like to point out that no one took so much as a penknife with him to cut his bread.

1. Under Italian law, a workman is entitled to be paid for any work carried out. (*Translator's note.*)

PRESIDING JUDGE: No one is accusing you of being in improper possession of arms.

AVV. TAORMINA: It can be inferred from the charges laid against the accused that the police considered work-tools to be weapons.

DOLCI: May I repeat that we took no weapons with us, not even a knife to cut the bread, and that this was meant to be a symbol of a new spirit. The people understood its meaning – that the days of the machine gun were finished and that true revolutions were born from within. There was to be an end of shooting.

About ten minutes after we had started work on the old road, a *carabinieri* lieutenant arrived with some police officers and ordered us to stop work. Everyone had not yet arrived and there were not many of us there. We went on working. 'What's all this?' asked the lieutenant. 'You refuse to obey the orders of the police?'

Let me explain my state of mind at that moment. If you were to order me, Your Honour, to kill my father, or you yourself, or the Public Prosecutor, or anyone else, I would not obey you because my conscience would not let me; because it is a crime. For me, it is just as much a crime against the land and against mankind to stop work – for the very reason that it is our duty to work, not only for ourselves but for the good of all. And besides, too many promises had been made, year after year, and then never kept.

Being ordered off and believing myself to be under arrest, I left the track accompanied by three policemen. It was then that I met Superintendent La Corte. I held out my hand to him as a gesture intended to underline the pacific nature of the demonstration, but he turned away and refused to shake hands. It was then also that, a moment or two later, I met the other policemen who were advancing on the old track with sticks and, I think, tear bombs. I said to one of the police officers: 'I hope you won't do these poor people any harm.'

A mile farther on, I met Abbate with another group coming from the town. Chief Superintendent Di Giorgi was also nearby and he ordered the policemen who were accompanying me to let me free. On this, I informed them that I would return to work with the others and, taking the longest route so that they would not stop me, I ran with Ciccio Abbate, partly by the road and partly across the fields, until we came to where the others were working.

When I arrived I was told to go away again and I asked whether they wanted me to go away or to arrest me. Chief Superintendent Di Giorgi had already arrived and was telling the people not to listen to us as we were trying to suborn them. I wanted to see the law respected and I quoted Article IV to show that, according to the spirit of the Constitution, to deny a man his right to work was equal to murdering him. At the sound of the word 'murderer', I saw the superintendent stiffen as if he'd been struck by lightning. The attitude of the police was roughly speaking as follows. 'We are the representatives of the law, the law is always right, so we are always right.' The superintendent ordered the police to arrest me. I sat down on the ground, in imitation of Gandhi. They lifted me up bodily and four or five of them carried me face downwards by my feet and wrists. When they saw that, in this way, they might break a bone, they turned me over onto my back and carried me like that instead.

PRESIDING JUDGE: How much do you weigh?

DOLCI: Ninety-five kilos [approx. 210 pounds] and I am one metre eighty-two centimetres tall [approx. 5 foot 11 inches].

Every now and then, when the police were tired, they dropped me on the ground, into the mud. I urged the people to go on working but not to resist the police. I told them to sit down on the ground if they were prevented from working. I had told Guido Calogero in Rome that this was how we intended to behave and we had made it clear that it was to be a typical act of non-violence, on the Indian model.

I admit that I continued to urge the people to go on working, from the police car. 'Go on working,' I shouted. 'Go on digging.'

That is all I have to say. But before I stop I would like to know first whether the court intends to discuss the accusations launched against me by the superintendent and by Senator Santi Savarino in an article published in the *Giornale d'Italia*.

PRESIDING JUDGE: No. The court will only hear such facts as are relevant to the charges before the court.

AVV. BATTAGLIA: I would like to ask the accused two questions. First question: Did you hear the blasts on the trumpet?

DOLCI: I am not deaf. I can hear perfectly well. I saw a police officer with a trumpet but I heard no sound from it. I must point out, however, that I had left the spot more than half an hour before.

AVV. BATTAGLIA: Did the police tear your trousers?

DOLCI: When I was lifted up my trousers split from top to bottom but I am certain that the police did not tear them on purpose.

Hearing of 27 March 1956. 8.20 a.m.
T. Di Giorgi, Chief Superintendent of Police, gives evidence for the prosecution.

DI GIORGI: I confirm my evidence given before the Examining Magistrate.

I repeat my statement that Dolci did not kick or hit out. I wish to point out, however, that he did wave his arms about in an attempt to shake off the police officers who were carrying him.

As already stated, Dolci made a forward movement as if to sit down on the ground, then straightened up again. It was just after Dolci straightened up that the police officers reached him and seized him. I was able to observe that both Abbate and Speciale also waved their arms about wildly in an attempt to shake off the police officers who held them.

I repeat my assertion that, on being instructed either to leave the spot or be taken into custody, Dolci uttered the following words in my direction: 'Arrest me if you can.' And immediately afterwards: 'Whoever goes against us is a murderer.' At the same time, Dolci asserted that he was exercising his right to work under the Constitution, to which I replied: 'It's Police Regulations that I have to obey and I must therefore order you home.'

The words, 'whoever goes against us is a murderer', were taken up by Speciale, Abbate and two others, who were later identified as Ferrante and Macaluso. I also heard the words repeated quite clearly by Zanini and Termini who were standing some thirty to forty yards away on the other side of the stream.

DOLCI: They were at least fifty yards away. You couldn't possibly have heard them from where you were.

DI GIORGI: At that moment I was standing where the path curves slightly upwards. When I caught the words to which I am referring, and saw Dolci, Abbate and Speciale trying to throw off the police officers holding them, Police Superintendent La Corte, *carabinieri*, Lieutenant Petralito and several other police officers and *carabinieri*, whose names I do not know, were standing near me. When I moved to the spot just mentioned, where the path curves upwards, I had left the *carabinieri* truck about two hundred yards away; after that I didn't see it any more because I couldn't. I cannot say, therefore, where the truck was standing when Dolci was seized and taken towards it.

I met Dolci and Speciale where the old road begins, accompanied by two police officers. A short time before, I had come across Abbate who was making his way towards the old road. I asked him for his identity card as, although he was carrying no tools, I had the impression that he was making for the old road.

Abbate was wearing a red tie.

In other words, the first person I saw was Abbate coming from the town in the direction of the old road. About ten minutes later I saw Dolci and Speciale, accompanied by two police officers. When I met Dolci and Speciale, I noted that Abbate, whom, as already stated, I had seen ten minutes before, was also with them. As stated to the Examining Magistrate, when I first saw Dolci and Speciale with Abbate on the old road, I advised all the above-named not to return to the place where the work was taking place, at which they replied that they would make no promises. In fact, Dolci, Speciale and Abbate returned to the main body of the demonstrators. I also proceeded towards the demonstrators and came up to them where the path rises and comes to a corner. Dolci, Abbate and Speciale, on the other hand, returned by another route on my right – or rather on my left – down a road which leads towards the countryside and along which they hurried. When I reached the point where the path curves, I halted because the demonstrators were coming towards me, waving their tools. I noted immediately that Dolci, Abbate and Speciale were among them.

DOLCI: I would like to explain that the words used by me, 'Not to ensure work for all in accordance with the spirit of the Constitution is to commit murder', were spoken on purpose. These words were not uttered on the spur of the moment but represented a state of mind reached after a long examination of the problem of unemployment in general, and the best means of solving it. This is confirmed by certain manifestoes which were put up in Partinico at my suggestion by the Camera del Lavoro and the U.I.L. These contained nothing but the text of Article IV of the Constitution and an extract from my writings.

MARTIN LUTHER KING, Jr

1929–

MARTIN LUTHER KING, JR, achieved world-wide prominence at the time (1956–7) when he and others organized and led the nonviolent Negro bus boycott in Montgomery, Alabama, in protest against discriminatory seating practices. The story of the events leading up to the fourteen-month-long boycott and the eventual backdown on the part of the white operators of the transit system is told in his book *Stride Toward Freedom* (1958).

When his home was dynamited by anguished whites who saw their 'supremacy' challenged, he spoke calmly from the shattered front porch to an enraged crowd of Negro supporters: 'Our use of passive resistance in Montgomery is not based on resistance to get rights for ourselves, but to achieve friendship with the men who are denying us our rights, and change them through friendship and a bond of Christian understanding before God.'

He has consistently advocated meeting violence with love and emphasized that his influences are biblical and Gandhian. 'Even now, in reading Gandhi's words again, I am given inspiration. The spirit of passive resistance came to me from the Bible and the teaching of Jesus. The techniques of execution came from Gandhi.'

He is president of the Southern Christian Leadership Conference which, together with C.O.R.E., S.N.C.C., and the N.A.A.C.P., continues to spearhead the nonviolent struggle of Negroes for equal rights.

Dr King was awarded the 1964 Nobel Peace Prize for his work in this field.

'Pilgrimage to Nonviolence' is reprinted from *The Christian Century* of 13 April 1960, and offers the most complete statement of his progress to his present views. 'Suffering and Faith' appeared in *The Christian Century* 27 April 1960.

Pilgrimage to Nonviolence

Ten years ago I was just entering my senior year in theological seminary. Like most theological students I was engaged in the exciting job of studying various theories. Having been raised in a rather strict fundamentalistic tradition, I was occasionally shocked as my intellectual journey carried me through new and sometimes complex doctrinal lands. But despite the shock the pilgrimage was always stimulating, and it gave me a new appreciation for objective appraisal and critical analysis. My early theological training did the same for me as the reading of Hume did for Kant: it knocked me out of my dogmatic slumber.

At this stage of my development I was a thoroughgoing liberal. Liberalism provided me with an intellectual satisfaction that I could never find in fundamentalism. I became so enamored of the insights of liberalism that I almost fell into the trap of accepting uncritically everything that came under its name. I was absolutely convinced of the natural goodness of man and the natural power of human reason.

I

The basic change in my thinking came when I began to question some of the theories that had been associated with so-called liberal theology. Of course there is one phase of liberalism that I hope to cherish always: its devotion to the search for truth, its insistence on an open and analytical mind, its refusal to abandon the best light of reason. Liberalism's contribution to the philological-historical criticism of biblical literature has been of immeasurable value and should be defended with religious and scientific passion.

It was mainly the liberal doctrine of man that I began to question. The more I observed the tragedies of history and man's shameful inclination to choose the low road, the more I came to see the depths and strength of sin. My reading of the works of Reinhold Niebuhr made me aware of the complexity of human motives and the reality of sin on every level of man's existence. Moreover, I came to recognize the complexity of man's social involvement and the glaring reality of collective evil. I came to feel that liberalism had been all too sentimental concerning human nature and that it leaned toward a false idealism.

I also came to see that liberalism's superficial optimism concerning human nature caused it to overlook the fact that reason is darkened by sin. The more I thought about human nature the more I saw how tragic inclination for sin causes us to use our minds to rationalize our actions. Liberalism failed to see that reason by itself is little more than an instrument to justify man's defensive ways of thinking. Reason, devoid of the purifying power of faith, can never free itself from distortions and rationalizations.

In spite of the fact that I had to reject some aspects of liberalism, I never came to an all-out acceptance of neo-orthodoxy. While I saw neo-orthodoxy as a helpful corrective for a liberalism that had become all too sentimental, I never felt that it provided an adequate answer to the basic questions. If liberalism was too optimistic concerning human nature, neo-orthodoxy was too pessimistic. Not only on the question of man but also on other vital issues neo-orthodoxy went too far in its revolt. In its attempt to preserve the transcendence of God, which had been neglected by liberalism's overstress of his immanence, neo-orthodoxy went to the extreme of stressing a God who was hidden, unknown and 'wholly other'. In its revolt against liberalism's overemphasis on the power of reason, neo-orthodoxy fell into a mood of antirationalism and semifundamentalism, stressing a narrow, uncritical biblicism. This approach, I felt, was inadequate both for the church and for personal life.

So although liberalism left me unsatisfied on the question of the nature of man, I found no refuge in neo-orthodoxy. I am now convinced that the truth about man is found neither in liberalism nor in neo-orthodoxy. Each represents a partial truth. A large segment of Protestant liberalism defined man only in terms of his essential nature, his capacity for good. Neo-orthodoxy tended to define man only in terms of his existential nature, his capacity for evil. An adequate understanding of man is found neither in the thesis of liberalism nor in the antithesis of neo-orthodoxy, but in a synthesis which reconciles the truths of both.

During the past decade I also gained a new appreciation for the philosophy of existentialism. My first contact with this philosophy came through my reading of Kierkegaard and Nietzsche. Later I turned to a study of Jaspers, Heidegger and Sartre. All of these thinkers stimulated my thinking; while finding things to question in each, I nevertheless learned a great deal from study of them. When I finally turned to a serious study of the works of Paul Tillich I became convinced that existentialism, in spite of the fact that it had become all too fashionable, had grasped certain basic truths about man and his condition that could not be permanently overlooked.

Its understanding of the 'finite freedom' of man is one of existentialism's most lasting contributions, and its perception of the anxiety and conflict produced in man's personal and social life as a result of the perilous and ambiguous structure of existence is especially meaningful for our time. The common point in all existentialism, whether it is atheistic or theistic, is that man's existential situation is a state of estrangement from his essential nature. In their revolt against Hegel's essentialism, all existentialists contend that the world is fragmented. History is a series of unreconciled conflicts and man's existence is filled with anxiety and threatened with meaninglessness. While the ultimate Christian answer is not found in any of these existential assertions, there is much here that the theologian can use to describe the true state of man's existence.

Although most of my formal study during this decade has been in systematic theology and philosophy, I have become more and more interested in social ethics. Of course my concern for social problems was already substantial before the beginning of this decade. From my early teens in Atlanta I was deeply concerned about the problem of racial injustice. I grew up abhorring segregation, considering it both rationally inexplicable and morally unjustifiable. I could never accept the fact of having to go to the back of a bus or sit in the segregated section of a train. The first time that I was seated behind a curtain in a dining car I felt as if the curtain had been dropped on my selfhood. I had also learned that the inseparable twin of racial injustice is economic injustice. I saw how the systems of segregation ended up in the exploitation of the Negro as well as the poor whites. Through these early experiences I grew up deeply conscious of the varieties of injustice in our society.

II

Not until I entered theological seminary, however, did I begin a serious intellectual quest for a method to eliminate social evil. I was immediately influenced by the social gospel. In the early fifties I read Rauschenbusch's *Christianity and the Social Crisis*, a book which left an indelible imprint on my thinking. Of course there were points at which I differed with Rauschenbusch. I felt that he had fallen victim to the 19th-century 'cult of inevitable progress', which led him to an unwarranted optimism concerning human nature. Moreover, he came perilously close to identifying the kingdom of God with a particular social and economic system – a temptation which the church should never give in to. But in spite of these shortcomings Rauschenbusch gave to American Protestantism a sense of social responsibility that it should never lose. The gospel at its best deals with the whole man, not only his soul but his body, not only his spiritual well-being, but his material well-being. Any religion that professes to be concerned about the souls of men and is not concerned about the slums that damn them, the economic conditions that strangle them and the social conditions that cripple them is a spiritually moribund religion awaiting burial.

After reading Rauschenbusch I turned to a serious study of the social and ethical theories of the great philosophers. During this period I had almost despaired of the power of love in solving social problems. The 'turn the other cheek' philosophy and the 'love your enemies' philosophy are only valid, I felt, when individuals are in conflict with other individuals; when racial groups and nations are in conflict a more realistic approach is necessary. Then I came upon the life and teachings of Mahatma Gandhi. As I read his works I became deeply fascinated by his campaigns of nonviolent resistance. The whole Gandhian concept of satyagraha (satya is truth which equals love, and graha is force; satyagraha thus means truth-force or love-force) was profoundly significant to me. As I delved deeper into the philosophy of Gandhi my skepticism concerning the power of love gradually diminished, and I came to see for the first time that the Christian doctrine of love operating through the Gandhian method of nonviolence was one of the most potent weapons available to oppressed people in their struggle for freedom. At this time, however, I had a merely intellectual understanding and appreciation of the position, with no firm determination to organize it in a socially effective situation.

When I went to Montgomery, Alabama, as a pastor in 1954, I had not the slightest idea that I would later become involved in a crisis in which nonviolent resistance would be applicable. After I had lived in the community about a year, the bus boycott began. The Negro people of Montgomery, exhausted by the humiliating experiences that they had constantly faced on the buses, expressed in a massive act of non-cooperation their determination to be free. They came to see that it was ultimately more honorable to walk the streets in dignity than to ride the buses in humiliation. At the beginning of the protest the people called on me to serve as their spokesman. In accepting this responsibility my mind, consciously or unconsciously, was driven back to the Sermon on the Mount and the Gandhian method of nonviolent resistance. This principle became the guiding light of our movement. Christ furnished the spirit and motivation while Gandhi furnished the method.

The experience in Montgomery did more to clarify my thinking on the question of nonviolence than all of the books that I had read. As the days unfolded I became more and more convinced of the power of nonviolence. Living through the actual experience of the protest, non-violence became more than a method to which I gave intellectual assent; it became a commitment to a way of life. Many issues I had not cleared up intellectually concerning nonviolence were now solved in the sphere of practical action.

A few months ago I had the privilege of traveling to India. The trip had a great impact on me personally and left me even more convinced of the power of nonviolence. It was a marvelous thing to see the amazing results of a nonviolent struggle. India won her independence, but without violence on the part of Indians. The aftermath of hatred and bitterness that usually follows a violent campaign is found nowhere in India. Today a mutual friendship based on complete equality exists between the Indian and British people within the commonwealth.

I do not want to give the impression that nonviolence will work miracles overnight. Men are not easily moved from their mental ruts or purged of their prejudiced and irrational feelings. When the under-privileged demand freedom, the privileged first react with bitterness and resistance. Even when the demands are couched in nonviolent terms, the initial response is the same. I am sure that many of our white brothers in Montgomery and across the south are still bitter toward Negro leaders, even though these leaders have sought to follow a way of love and nonviolence. So the nonviolent approach does not imme-diately change the heart of the oppressor. It first does something to the hearts and souls of those committed to it. It gives them new self-respect; it calls up resources of strength and courage that they did not know they had. Finally, it reaches the opponent and so stirs his conscience that reconciliation becomes a reality.

III

During recent months I have come to see more and more the need for the method of nonviolence in international relations. While I was con-vinced during my student days of the power of nonviolence in group conflicts within nations, I was not yet convinced of its efficacy in con-flicts between nations. I felt that while war could never be a positive or absolute good, it could serve as a negative good in the sense of pre-venting the spread and growth of an evil force. War, I felt, horrible as it is, might be preferable to surrender to a totalitarian system. But more and more I have come to the conclusion that the potential destructiveness of modern weapons of war totally rules out the possibility of war ever serving again as a negative good. If we assume that mankind has a right to survive then we must find an alternative to war and destruction. In a day when sputniks dash through outer space and guided ballistic missiles are carving highways of death through the stratosphere, nobody can win a war. The choice today is no longer between violence and nonviolence. It is either nonviolence or nonexistence.

I am no doctrinaire pacifist. I have tried to embrace a realistic pacifism. Moreover, I see the pacifist position not as sinless but as the lesser evil in the circumstances. Therefore I do not claim to be free from the moral dilemmas that the Christian nonpacifist confronts. But I am convinced that the church cannot remain silent while mankind faces the threat of being plunged into the abyss of nuclear annihilation. If the church is true to its mission it must call for an end to the arms race.

In recent months I have also become more and more convinced of the reality of a personal God. True, I have always believed in the personality of God. But in past years the idea of a personal God was little more than a metaphysical category which I found theologically and philosophically satisfying. Now it is a living reality that has been validated in the experiences of everyday life. Perhaps the suffering, frustration and agonizing moments which I have had to undergo occasionally as a result of my involvement in a difficult struggle have drawn me closer to God. Whatever the cause, God has been profoundly real to me in recent months. In the midst of outer dangers I have felt an inner calm and known resources of strength that only God could give. In many instances I have felt the power of God transforming the fatigue of despair into the buoyancy of hope. I am convinced that the universe is under the control of a loving purpose and that in the struggle for righteousness man has cosmic companionship. Behind the harsh appearances of the world there is a benign power. To say God is personal is not to make him an object among other objects or attribute to him the finiteness and limitations of human personality; it is to take what is finest and noblest in our consciousness and affirm its perfect existence in him. It is certainly true that human personality is limited, but personality as such involves no necessary limitations. It simply means self-consciousness and self-direction. So in the truest sense of the word, God is a living God. In him there is feeling and will, responsive to the deepest yearnings of the human heart: this God both evokes and answers prayers.

The past decade has been a most exciting one. In spite of the tensions and uncertainties of our age something profoundly meaningful has begun. Old systems of exploitation and oppression are passing away and new systems of justice and equality are being born. In a real sense ours is a great time in which to be alive. Therefore I am not yet discouraged about the future. Granted that the easygoing optimism of yesterday is impossible. Granted that we face a world crisis which often leaves us standing amid the surging murmur of life's restless sea. But every crisis has both its dangers and its opportunities. Each can spell either salvation or doom. In a dark, confused world the spirit of God may yet reign supreme.

Suffering and Faith

Some of my personal sufferings over the last few years have also served to shape my thinking. I always hesitate to mention these experiences for fear of conveying the wrong impression. A person who constantly calls attention to his trials and sufferings is in danger of developing a martyr complex and of making others feel that he is consciously seeking sympathy. It is possible for one to be self-centered in his self-denial and self-righteous in his self-sacrifice. So I am always reluctant to refer to my personal sacrifices. But I feel somewhat justified in mentioning them in this article because of the influence they have had in shaping my thinking.

Due to my involvement in the struggle for the freedom of my people, I have known very few quiet days in the last few years. I have been arrested five times and put in Alabama jails. My home has been bombed twice. A day seldom passes that my family and I are not the recipients of threats of death. I have been the victim of a near-fatal stabbing. So in a real sense I have been battered by the storms of persecution. I must admit that at times I have felt that I could no longer bear such a heavy burden, and have been tempted to retreat to a more quiet and serene life. But every time such a temptation appeared, something came to strengthen and sustain my determination. I have learned now that the Master's burden is light precisely when we take his yoke upon us.

My personal trials have also taught me the value of unmerited suffering. As my sufferings mounted I soon realized that there were two ways that I could respond to my situation: either to react with bitterness or seek to transform the suffering into a creative force. I decided to follow the latter course. Recognizing the necessity for suffering I have tried to make of it a virtue. If only to save myself from bitterness, I have attempted to see my personal ordeals as an opportunity to transform myself and heal the people involved in the tragic situation which now obtains. I have lived these last few years with the conviction that unearned suffering is redemptive.

There are some who still find the cross a stumbling block, and others consider it foolishness, but I am more convinced than ever before that it is the power of God unto social and individual salvation. So like the Apostle Paul I can now humbly yet proudly say, 'I bear in my body the marks of the Lord Jesus.' The suffering and agonizing moments through which I have passed over the last few years have also drawn me closer to God. More than ever before I am convinced of the reality of a personal God.

C. WRIGHT MILLS

1916–1962

WITH the publication of *White Collar* in 1951, the sociologist C. Wright Mills became widely known as a keen observer of the American scene, a writer at once scholarly and popular. Deeply interested since his student days in Texas in the structure of power in the State, such incisive analyses of aspects of American life as *White Collar* and *The Power Elite* (1956) made his work controversial to an enlarging public. In the last years of his life, he turned increasing attention to the problems and politics of war and peace. In this period he wrote 'A Program for Peace', and 'A Pagan Sermon to the Christian Clergy', both for *The Nation*, and a full-length study entitled *The Causes of World War Three*.

His last work to be published before his death, *Listen Yankee: The Revolution in Cuba*, brought a storm of protest, not only from quarters opposed to the book's 'views', but also from scholarly circles which felt that Mills had become a writer of polemic journalism. His argument, however, was that the only true objectivity lay in an honest depiction of the views of the other side.

In 1945 Mills received a John Simon Guggenheim Fellowship and was appointed to the faculty at Columbia University. He was Professor of Sociology at the time of his death. 'A Pagan Sermon to the Christian Clergy', from the 8 March 1958 issue of *The Nation* is reprinted below.

A Pagan Sermon to the Christian Clergy

To say that war has become total is to say that the reach of modern weaponry now makes every soul on earth a quite possible victim of sudden hell. It is to say that weapons have become absolute, and that every calculation from on high now includes a military calculation. It is to say that the decision-makers of every nation, in particular those of the United States, are now possessed by the crackpot metaphysics of militarism. But more than that: it is to say that the morality of war now dominates the curious spiritual life of the fortunate peoples of Christendom.

World War III is already so total that most of its causes are accepted as 'necessity'; most of its meaning as 'realism'. In our world 'necessity' and 'realism' have become ways to hide lack of moral imagination. In the cold war of the politicians and journalists, intellectuals and generals, businessmen and preachers, it is above all else moral imagination that is most obviously lacking. One reason for this lack, I am going to argue, is what must surely be called the moral default of the Christians.

The ethos of war is now the ethos of virtually all public thought and sensibility. But I must limit this article to the fact of moral insensibility in the Western world and to the religious failure that supports it.

By moral insensibility I refer to the mute acceptance – or even the unawareness – of moral atrocity. I mean the lack of indignation when confronted with moral horror. I mean the turning of this atrocity and this horror into morally approved conventions of feeling. I mean, in short, the incapacity for *moral* reaction to event and character, to high decision and the drift of human circumstance.

Such moral insensibility has its roots in World War I; it became full-blown during World War II. The 'saturation bombing' of that war was an indiscriminate bombing of civilians on a mass scale; the atomic bombing of the peoples of Hiroshima and Nagasaki was an act committed without warning and without ultimatum. By the time of Korea, the strategy of obliteration had become totally accepted as part of our moral universe.

The pivotal decision, made by the United States and by the Soviet Union, is the monstrous one, as Lewis Mumford has put it, of trying 'to solve the problem of absolute power, presented by nuclear weapons, by concentrating their national resources upon instruments of genocide'. The spokesmen of each side say they know that war is obsolete as a means of any policy save mutual annihilation, yet they search for peace by military means and in doing so, they succeed in accumulating ever new perils. Moreover, they have obscured this fact by their dogmatic adherence to violence as the only way of doing away with violence. There has not before been an arms race of this sort – a scientific arms race dominated by the strategy of obliteration. And at every turn of this hideous competition, each side becomes more edgy, and the chance becomes greater that accidents of character or of technology will trigger the sudden hell.

The key moral fact about this situation is the virtual absence within ourselves of absolute opposition to these assumptions of our ruling elites, to their strategy, and to the policies by which they are carrying it out. And the key public result is the absence of any truly debated alternatives. In some part the absence both of opposition and of alternatives rests upon, or at least is supported by, the fact of moral insensibility.

Between catastrophic event and everyday interest there is a vast moral gulf. Who in North America experienced, as human beings, World War II? Men fought; women waited; both worked. About the war they all said the same kinds of things. Nobody rebelled, nobody knew public grief. In the emotional economy, there was efficiency without purpose. It was a curiously unreal business. A sort of numbness seemed to prohibit any real awareness of what was happening. It was without dream and so without nightmare, and if there were anger and fear and hatred – and there were – still no mainsprings of feeling and conviction and compassion were let loose in despair or furor; no human complaint was focused rebelliously upon the political and moral meanings of the universal brutality. People sat in the movies between production shifts watching with aloofness and even visible indifference, as children were 'saturation bombed' in the narrow cellars of European cities. Man had become an object; and in so far as those for whom he was an object felt about the spectacle at all, they felt powerless, in the grip of larger forces, having no part in those affairs that lay beyond their immediate areas of daily demand and gratification. It was a time of moral somnambulance. And worst of all, from the religious point of view, the people of this continent were often brightly hopeful – while what used to be called the deepest convictions were as fluid as water.

It is as if the ear had become a sensitive soundtrack, the eye a precision camera, experience an exactly-timed collaboration between microphone and lens. And in this expanded world of mechanically vivified communications, the capacity for experience is alienated, and the individual becomes the spectator of everything but the human witness of nothing.

In all the emotional and spiritual realms of life, facts now outrun sensibility, and these facts, emptied of their human meanings, are readily gotten used to. There is no more human shock in official man; there is no more sense of moral issue in his unofficial follower. There is only the unopposed supremacy of technique for impersonal, calculated, wholesale murder. This lack of response I am trying to sum up by the altogether inadequate phrase 'moral insensibility', and I am suggesting that the level of moral sensibility, as part of public and private life, has in our time sunk below human sight.

Religion today is part of this sorry moral condition; to understand the crucial decisions of our pivotal times, it is not necessary to consider religious institutions or personnel or doctrine. Neither preachers nor laity matter; what they do and what they say can be readily agreed with, and safely ignored. I am aware that there are exceptions, but the average output is correctly heard as a parade of worn-out phrases. In the West, religion has become a subordinate part of the overdeveloped society.

If there is one safe prediction about religion in this society, it would seem to be that if tomorrow official spokesmen were to proclaim XYZ-ism, next week 90 per cent of religious declaration would be XYZ-ist. At least in their conforming rhetoric, religious spokesmen would reveal that the new doctrine did not violate those of the church. As a social and as a personal force, religion has become a dependent variable. It does not originate; it reacts. It does not denounce; it adapts. It does not set forth new models of conduct and sensibility; it imitates. Its rhetoric is without deep appeal; the worship it organizes is without piety. It has become less a revitalization of the spirit in permanent tension with the world than a respectable distraction from the sourness of life. In a quite direct sense, religion has generally become part of the false consciousness of the world and of the self.

Among the cheerful robots of the mass society, not human virtue but human shortcomings, attractively packaged, lead to popularity and success. They are men and women without publicly relevant consciousness, without awareness of shocking human evil, and their religion is the religion of good cheer and glad tidings. That it is a religion without dreary religious content is less important than that it is socially brisk and that it is not spiritually unsettling. It is a getting chummy with God, as a means to quite secular good feelings.

With such religion, ours is indeed a world in which the idea of God is dead. But what is important is that this fact itself is of no felt consequence. Men and women, in brief, are religiously indifferent; they find no religious meanings in their lives and in their world.

The verbal Christian belief in the sanctity of human life has not of course been affected by the impersonal barbarism of twentieth-century war. But this belief does not itself enter decisively into the plans now being readied for World War III. A savage politician once asked how many divisions the Pope had – and it was a relevant question. No one need ask how many chaplains any army that wants them has. The answer is: as many as the generals and their other satraps feel the need of. Religion has become a willing spiritual means and a psychiatric aide of the nation-state.

Total war must indeed be difficult for the Christian conscience to confront, but the current Christian way out makes it easy; war is defended morally and Christians easily fall into line – as they are led to justify it – in each nation in terms of 'Christian faith' itself. Men of religious congregations do evil; ministers of God make them feel good about doing it. Rather than guide them in the moral cultivation of their conscience, ministers, with moral nimbleness, blunt that conscience, covering it up with peace of mind.

The moral death of religion in North America is inherent neither in religion nor specifically in Christianity. At times this religion has been insurgent; at other times, complacent; and it has been characterized by repeated revivals. Just now it is neither revolutionary nor reactionary, and it makes no real effort to revive itself in order to examine great public issues and the troubles of individuals from a fresh religious perspective. It does not count in the big political balance of life and death.

This is not surprising. In their struggle for success, religious institutions have come into competition with two great contemporary forces: amusement and politics. Each of these has been winning over religion; and when religion has seemingly won over them, it has failed as religion.

The most obvious competition is with the world of industrialized entertainment. Competing with these mass means of distraction, churches have themselves become minor institutions among the mass media of communications. They have imitated and borrowed the strident techniques of the insistent publicity machines, and in terms of the pitch-man (with both the hard and the soft sell), they have quite thoroughly banalized the teachings, and indeed the very image, of Christ.

I do not believe that anything recognizably Christian can be put over in this way. I suggest that this religious malarkey *diseducates* congregations; that it kills off any real influence religious leaders might have. Even if the crowds come, they come only for the show and if it is the nature of crowds to come, it is also their nature soon to go away. And in all truth, are not the television Christians in reality armchair atheists? In value and in reality they live without the God they profess; despite ten million Bibles sold each year in the United States alone, they are religiously illiterate. 'If Christ had been put on television to preach the Sermon on the Mount,' Malcolm Muggeridge has recently remarked, 'viewers would either have switched on to another channel, or contented themselves with remarking that the speaker had an interesting face. Christ might have become a television personality, but there would have been no Christianity.'

If you, as Christian ministers, accept the entertainment terms of success, you cannot succeed. The very means of your 'success' make for your failure as witnesses, for you must appeal to such diverse moral appetites that your message will necessarily be generalized to the point of moral emptiness. If you do not specify and confront real issues, what you say will surely obscure them. If you do not alarm anyone morally, you will yourself remain morally asleep. If you do not *embody* controversy, what you say will inevitably be an acceptance of the drift to the coming hell. And in all this you will continue well the characteristic history of Christianity, for the Christian record *is* rather clear: from the time of Constantine to the time of global radiation and the uninterceptible missile, Christians have killed Christians and been blessed for doing so by other Christians.

Politics, like religion, has of course also come into competition with and been deeply influenced by the world of entertainment and its means of attraction and distraction. But the realities of politics and of economics are nowadays very difficult to ignore; they just won't down, for they are part of the insistent military lie that now dominates official civilized endeavor.

Religion cannot compete with this political peril. What vision of hell compares with the realities we have and do now confront? And the point is that ministers of God are not foremost among those few men who would define and expose the morality of the political decisions and lack of decisions that lie back of these morally atrocious events and preparations. For a church whose congregations contains all political views and which is out for statistical success feels it must prosperously balance 'above' politics – which means that it serves whatever moral default the affairs of mankind reveal.

As a mass medium, religion has become a religiously ineffective part of the show that fills up certain time slots in the weekly routine of cheerful robots. The minister goes his curious way, bringing glad tidings into each and every home.

Believe me, I do not wish to be rude, but I am among those pagans who take declarations seriously, and so I must ask you, as declared Christians, certain questions:

What does it mean to preach? Does it not mean, first of all, to be religiously conscious? I do not see how you can preach unless as a man you are the opposite to the religiously indifferent. To be religiously conscious, I suppose, is to find some sort of religious meaning in one's own insecurities and desires, to know oneself as a creature in some kind of relation with God which increases your hope that your expectations and prayers and actions will come off. I must ask: for you today, what is that religious meaning?

To preach, secondly, means to serve as a moral conscience, and to articulate that conscience, I do not see how you can do that by joining the publicity fraternity and the week-end crusaders. You cannot do it by 'staying out of politics'. I think there is only one way in which you can compete as religious men with religious effect: you must be yourself in such a way that your views emanate unmistakably from you as a moral center. From that center of yourself, you must speak. So I must ask: why do you not make of yourself the pivot, and of your congregation the forum, of a public that is morally led and that is morally standing up? The Christian ethic cannot be incorporated without compromise; it can live only in a series of individuals who are capable of morally incorporating themselves.

Do not these times demand a little Puritan defiance? Do not they demand the realization of how close hell is to being a sudden and violent reality of man's world today? Should not those who still have access to the peoples of Christendom stand up and denounce with all the righteousness and pity and anger and charity and love and humility their faith may place at their command the political and the militarist assumptions now followed by the leaders of the nations of Christendom? Should they not denounce the pseudo-religiosity of men of high office who would steal religious phrases to decorate crackpot policies and immoral lack of policies? Should they not refuse to allow immorality to find support in religion? Should they not refuse to repeat the official, un-Christian slogans of dull diplomats who do not believe in negotiation, who mouth slogans which are at most ineffective masks for lack of policy? Should they not realize that the positive moral meaning of what is called 'neutralism' lies in the resolve that the fate of mankind shall not be determined by the idiotically-conducted rivalry of the United States and the Soviet Union?

I do not wish to be politically dogmatic, but merely brief and, as you gentlemen surely have recognized, I am religiously illiterate and unfeeling. But truly I do not see how you can claim to be Christians and yet not speak out totally and dogmatically against the preparations and testing now under way for World War III. As I read it, Christian doctrine in contact with the realities of today cannot lead to any other position. It cannot condone the murder of millions of people by clean-cut young men flying intricate machinery over Euro-Asia, zeroed in on cities full of human beings – young men who two years before were begging the fathers of your congregations for the use of the family car for a Saturday night date.

There is no necessity for more military emphasis on missiles. There is no need for more 'science' in education; it is not 'realism' to spend more money on arms. Necessity and need and realism are the desperate slogans of the morally crippled. The necessity is for moral imagination. The need is for political new beginnings. Realism means to stop at once and if need be unilaterally all preparations for World War III. There is no other realism, no other necessity, no other need.

You will not find in moral principles the solution to the problems of war, but without moral principles men are neither motivated nor directed to solve them. But nowadays we pagans see that Christian morals are more often used as moral cloaks of expedient interests than ways of morally uncloaking such interests.

War is not today inevitable; it is, immediately, the result of nationalist definitions of world reality, of dogmatic reliance upon the military as the major or even the only means of solving the explosive problems of this epoch of despair and of terror. And because this is now so, to lift up and to make knowledgeable the level of moral sensibility is the strategic task of those who would be at peace. Your role in the making of peace is less the debating of short-run and immediate policies than the confrontation of the whole attitude toward war and the teaching of new views of it by using them in criticism of current policies and decisions. And in the end, I believe the decisive test of Christianity lies in your witness of the refusal by individuals and by groups to engage in war. Pacifism, I believe, is the test of your Christianity – and of you. At the very least, it ought to be *the* debate within Christendom.

The brotherhood of man is now less a goal than an obvious condition of biological survival. Before the world is made safe again for American capitalism or Soviet communism or anything else, it had better be made safe for human life.

But you may say: 'Don't let's get the church into politics.' If you do say that, you are saying: 'Don't let's get the church into the world; let's be another distraction from reality.' This world *is* political. Politics, understood for what it really is today, has to do with the decisions men make which determine how they shall live and how they shall die. They are not living very well, and they are not going to die very well, either. Politics is now the locale of morality; it is the locale both of evil and of good. If you do not get the church into the moral issues of politics, you cannot confront evil and you cannot work for good. You will be a subordinate amusement and a political satrap of whatever is going. You will be the great Christian joke.

Men and ideas, the will and the spirit, are now being tested, perhaps in all truth for the final time; and in this testing so far, you Christians are standing in default. The key sign of this is the fact of your general lack of effective opposition, of your participation in the fact of moral insensibility. That, of course, is a world fact about publics and masses and elites, but it is all the more grievous among Christians, if only because of the expectations that they have aroused about themselves. Yet who among you has come out clearly on the issues of internecine war and the real problems of peace? Who among you is considering what it means for Christians to kill men and women and children in ever more efficient and impersonal ways? Who among you uses his own religious imagination to envision another kind of basis for policies governing how men should treat with one another? Who among you, claiming even vague contact with what Christians call 'The Holy Spirit', is calling upon it to redeem the day because you know the times are evil?

If you are not today concerned with this – the moral condition of those in your spiritual care – then, gentlemen, what is your concern? As a pagan who is waiting for your answer, I merely say: you claim to be Christian. And I ask: what does that mean as a biographical and as a public fact?

In moral affairs you are supposed to be among the first of men. No moral affair today compares with the morality of warfare and the preparation for it, for in these preparations men usurp – as you might say – the prerogatives of God. By sitting down and by keeping quiet, by all too often echoing the claptrap of the higher immorality that now passes for political leadership – you are helping to enfeeble further in this time of cruel troubles the ideals of your Founder. Christianity is part of the moral defeat of man today. Perhaps it is no longer important enough to be considered a cause of it; perhaps it is only among the passive doctrines of the spectators of man's moral defeat.

I hope you do not demand of *me* gospels and answers and doctrines and programs. According to your belief, my kind of man – secular, prideful, agnostic and all the rest of it – is among the damned. I'm on my own; you've got your God. It is up to you to proclaim gospel, to declare justice, to apply your love of man – the sons of God, all of them, you say – meaningfully, each and every day, to the affairs and troubles of men. It is up to you to find answers that are rooted in ultimate moral decision and to say them out so that they are compelling.

I hope your Christian conscience is neither at ease nor at attention, because if it is I must conclude that it is a curiously expedient and ineffective apparatus. I hope you do not believe that in what you do and in how you live, you are denouncing evil, because if you do, then I must conclude that you know nothing of evil and so nothing of good. I hope you do not imagine yourselves to be the bearer of compassion, because if you do, you cannot yet know that today compassion without bitterness and terror is mere girlish sentiment, not worthy of any fullgrown man. I hope you do not speak from the moral center of yourself, because if you do, then in the dark nights of your soul, in fear and in trembling, you must be cruelly aware of your moral peril in this time of total war, and – given what you, a Christian, say and believe – I, a pagan, pity you.

CONCLUSION

ALBERT CAMUS

1913–1960

ALTHOUGH Camus fought during the Second World War in the Resistance and would not have considered himself a pacifist, all his writing displays a concern with the problem of killing – suicide and murder, different aspects of the same 'encounter between human inquiry and the silence of the universe'. In his essays, novels, and plays he grappled with the problem of the individual caught in history's illogical web, and it was man and humanity that he affirmed. The world had seen enough of men and women dying for causes; it was time to live for one. 'Neither Victims nor Executioners' appeared serially in the autumn of 1946 in *Combat*, the daily newspaper of the Resistance, which Camus helped edit during the Nazi occupation and for a short time after the war. It was published in English in the July–August 1947 issue of *Politics*. Camus was awarded the Nobel Prize for literature in 1957, the second youngest writer to receive this honour. He died three years later in an automobile accident. The translation is by Dwight Macdonald.

Neither Victims Nor Executioners

THE CENTURY OF FEAR

The seventeenth century was the century of mathematics, the eighteenth that of the physical sciences, and the nineteenth that of biology. Our twentieth century is the century of fear. I will be told that fear is not a science. But science must be somewhat involved since its latest theoretical advances have brought it to the point of negating itself while its perfected technology threatens the globe itself with destruction. Moreover, although fear itself cannot be considered a science, it is certainly a technique.

The most striking feature of the world we live in is that most of its inhabitants – with the exception of pietists of various kinds – are cut off from the future. Life has no validity unless it can project itself toward the future, can ripen and progress. Living against a wall is a dog's life.

True – and the men of my generation, those who are going into the factories and the colleges, have lived and are living more and more like dogs.

This is not the first time, of course, that men have confronted a future materially closed to them. But hitherto they have been able to transcend the dilemma by words, by protests, by appealing to other values which lent them hope. Today no one speaks any more (except those who repeat themselves) because history seems to be in the grip of blind and deaf forces which will heed neither cries of warning, nor advice, nor entreaties. The years we have just gone through have killed something in us. And that something is simply the old confidence man had in himself, which led him to believe that he could always elicit human reactions from another man if he spoke to him in the language of a common humanity. We have seen men lie, degrade, kill, deport, torture – and each time it was not possible to persuade them not to do these things because they were sure of themselves and because one cannot appeal to an abstraction, i.e. the representative of an ideology.

Mankind's dialogue has just come to an end. And naturally a man with whom one cannot reason is a man to be feared. The result is that – besides those who have not spoken out because they thought it useless – a vast conspiracy of silence has spread all about us, a conspiracy accepted by those who are frightened and who rationalize their fears in order to hide them from themselves, a conspiracy fostered by those whose interest it is to do so. 'You shouldn't talk about the Russian culture purge – it helps reaction.' 'Don't mention the Anglo-American support of Franco – it encourages communism.' Fear is certainly a technique.

What with the general fear of a war now being prepared by all nations and the specific fear of murderous ideologies, who can deny that we live in a state of terror? We live in terror because persuasion is no longer possible; because man has been wholly submerged in History; because he can no longer tap that part of his nature, as real as the historical part, which he recaptures in contemplating the beauty of nature and of human faces; because we live in a world of abstractions, of bureaus and machines, of absolute ideas and of crude messianism. We suffocate among people who think they are absolutely right, whether in their machines or in their ideas. And for all who can live only in an atmosphere of human dialogue and sociability, this silence is the end of the world.

To emerge from this terror, we must be able to reflect and to act accordingly. But an atmosphere of terror hardly encourages reflection. I believe, however, that instead of simply blaming everything on this fear, we should consider it as one of the basic factors in the situation, and try to do something about it. No task is more important. For it involves the fate of a considerable number of Europeans who, fed up with the lies and violence, deceived in their dearest hopes and repelled by the idea of killing their fellow men in order to convince them, likewise repudiate the idea of themselves being convinced that way. And yet such is the alternative that at present confronts so many of us in Europe who are not of any party – or ill at ease in the party we have chosen – who doubt socialism has been realized in Russia or liberalism in America, who grant to each side the right to affirm its truth but refuse it the right to impose it by murder, individual or collective. Among the powerful of today, these are the men without a kingdom. Their view-point will not be recognized (and I say 'recognized', not 'triumph'), nor will they recover their kingdom until they come to know precisely what they want and proclaim it directly and boldly enough to make their words a stimulus to action. And if an atmosphere of fear does not encourage accurate thinking, then they must first of all come to terms with fear.

To come to terms, one must understand what fear means: what it implies and what it rejects. It implies and rejects the same fact: a world where murder is legitimate, and where human life is considered trifling. This is the great political question of our times, and before dealing with other issues, one must take a position on it. Before anything can be done, two questions must be put: 'Do you, or do you not, directly or indirectly, want to be killed or assaulted? Do you or do you not, directly or indirectly, want to kill or assault?' All who say No to both these questions are automatically committed to a series of consequences which must modify their way of posing the problem. My aim here is to clarify two or three of these consequences.

SAVING OUR SKINS

I once said that, after the experiences of the last two years, I could no longer hold to any truth which might oblige me, directly or indirectly to demand a man's life. Certain friends whom I respected retorted that I was living in Utopia, that there was no political truth which could not one day reduce us to such an extremity, and that we must therefore either run the risk of this extremity or else simply put up with the world as it is.

They argued the point most forcefully. But I think they were able to put such force into it only because they were unable to really *imagine* other people's death. It is a freak of the times. We make love by telephone, we work not on matter but on machines, and we kill and are killed by proxy. We gain in cleanliness, but lose in understanding.

But the argument has another, indirect meaning: it poses the question of Utopia. People like myself want not a world in which murder no longer exists (we are not so crazy as that!) but rather one in which murder is not legitimate. Here indeed we are Utopian – and contradictory. For we do live, it is true, in a world where murder is legitimate, and we ought to change it if we do not like it. But it appears that we cannot change it without risking murder. Murder thus throws us back on murder, and we will continue to live in terror whether we accept the fact with resignation or wish to abolish it by means which merely replace one terror with another.

It seems to me every one should think this over. For what strikes me, in the midst of polemics, threats and outbursts of violence, is the fundamental good will of every one. From Right to Left, every one, with the exception of a few swindlers, believes that his particular truth is the one to make men happy. And yet the combination of all these good intentions has produced the present infernal world, where men are killed, threatened and deported, where war is prepared, where one cannot speak freely without being insulted or betrayed. Thus if people like ourselves live in a state of contradiction, we are not the only ones, and those who accuse us of Utopianism are possibly themselves also living in a Utopia, a different one but perhaps a more costly one in the end.

Let us, then, admit that our refusal to legitimize murder forces us to reconsider our whole idea of Utopia. This much seems clear: Utopia is whatever is in contradiction with reality. From this standpoint, it would be completely Utopian to wish that men should no longer kill each other. That would be absolute Utopia. But a much sounder Utopia is that which insists that murder be no longer legitimized. Indeed, the Marxian and the capitalist ideologies, both based on the idea of progress, both certain that the application of their principles must inevitably bring about a harmonious society, are Utopian to a much greater degree. Furthermore, they are both at the moment costing us dearly.

426

We may therefore conclude, practically, that in the next few years the struggle will be not between the forces of Utopia and the forces of reality, but between different Utopias which are attempting to be born into reality. It will be simply a matter of choosing the least costly among them. I am convinced that we can no longer reasonably hope to save everything, but that we can at least propose to save our skins, so that *a* future, if not *the* future, remains a possibility.

Thus (1) to refuse to sanction murder is no more Utopian than the 'realistic' ideologies of our day, and (2) the whole point is whether these latter are more or less costly. It may, therefore, be useful to try to define, in Utopian terms, the conditions which are needed to bring about the pacification of men and nations. This line of thought, assuming it is carried on without fear and without pretensions, may help to create the preconditions for clear thinking and a provisional agreement between men who want to be neither victims nor executioners. In what follows, the attempt will be not to work out a complete position, but simply to correct some current misconceptions and to pose the question of Utopia as accurately as possible. The attempt, in short, will be to define the conditions for a political position that is modest – i.e. free of messianism and disencumbered of nostalgia for an earthly paradise.

THE SELF-DECEPTION OF THE SOCIALISTS

If we agree that we have lived for ten years in a state of terror and still so live, and that this terror is our chief source of anxiety, then we must see what we can oppose to this terror. Which brings up the question of Socialism. For terror is legitimized only if we assent to the principle: 'the end justifies the means'. And this principle in turn may be accepted only if the effectiveness of an action is posed as an absolute end, as in nihilistic ideologies (anything goes, success is the only thing worth talking about), or in those philosophies which make History an absolute end (Hegel, followed by Marx: the end being a classless society, everything is good that leads to it).

Such is the problem confronting French Socialists, for example. They are bothered by scruples. Violence and oppression, of which they had hitherto only a theoretical idea, they have now seen at first hand. And they have had to ask themselves whether, as their philosophy requires, they would consent to use that violence themselves, even as a temporary expedient and for a quite different end. The author of a recent preface to Saint-Just, speaking of men of an earlier age who had similar scruples, wrote contemptuously: 'They recoiled in the face of horrors.' True enough. And so they deserved to be despised by strong, superior spirits who could live among horrors without flinching. But all the same, they gave a voice to the agonized appeal of commonplace spirits like ourselves, the millions who constitute the raw material of History and who must some day be taken into account, despite all contempt.

A more important task, I think, is to try to understand the state of contradiction and confusion in which our Socialists now exist. We have not thought enough about the moral crisis of French Socialism, as expressed, for example in a recent party congress. It is clear that our Socialists, under the influence of Léon Blum and even more under the pressure of events, have preoccupied themselves much more with moral questions (the end does not justify all means) than in the past. Quite properly, they wanted to base themselves on principles which rise superior to murder. It is also clear that these same Socialists want to preserve Marxian doctrine, some because they think one cannot be revolutionary without being Marxist, others, by fidelity to party tradition, which tells them that one cannot be socialist without being Marxist. The chief task of the last party congress was to reconcile the desire for a morality superior to murder with the determination to remain faithful to Marxism. But one cannot reconcile what is irreconcilable.

For if it is clear that Marxism is true and there is logic in History, then political realism is legitimate. It is equally clear that if the moral values extolled by the Socialist Party are legitimate, then Marxism is absolutely false since it claims to be absolutely true. From this point of view, the famous 'going beyond' Marxism in an idealistic and humanitarian direction is a joke and an idle dream. It is impossible to 'go beyond' Marx, for he himself carried his thought to its extreme logical consequences. The Communists have a solid logical basis for using the lies and the violence which the Socialists reject, and the basis is that very dialectic which the Socialists want to preserve. It is therefore hardly surprising that the Socialist congress ended by simply putting forward simultaneously two contradictory positions – a conclusion whose sterility appears in the results of the recent elections.

This way, confusion will never end. A choice was necessary, and the Socialists would not or could not choose.

I have chosen this example not to score off the Socialists but to illustrate the paradoxes among which we live. To score off the Socialists, one would have to be superior to them. This is not yet the case. On the contrary, I think this contradiction is common to all those of whom I speak, those who want a society which we can both enjoy and respect; those who want men to be both free and just, but who hesitate between a freedom in which they know justice is finally betrayed and a justice in which they see freedom suppressed from the first. Those who know What Is To Be Done or What Is To Be Thought make fun of this intolerable anguish. But I think it would be better, instead of jeering at it, to try to understand and clarify this anguish, see what it means, interpret its quasi-total rejection of a world which provokes it, and trace out the feeble hope that suffuses it.

A hope that is grounded precisely in this contradiction, since it forces – or will force – the Socialists to make a choice. They will either admit that the end justifies the means, in which case murder can be legitimized; or else, they will reject Marxism as an absolute philosophy, confining themselves to its critical aspect, which is often valuable. If they choose the first, their moral crisis will be ended, and their position will be unambiguous. If the second, they will exemplify the way our period marks the end of ideologies, that is, of absolute Utopias which destroy themselves, in history, by the price they ultimately exact. It will then be necessary to choose a most modest and less costly Utopia. At least it is in these terms that the refusal to legitimize murder forces us to pose the problem. Yes, that is the question we must put, and no one, I think, will venture to answer it lightly.

PARODY OF REVOLUTION

Since August 1944, everybody talks about revolution, and quite sincerely too. But sincerity is not in itself a virtue: some kinds are so confused that they are worse than lies. Not the language of the heart but merely that of clear thinking is what we need today. Ideally, a revolution is a change in political and economic institutions in order to introduce more freedom and justice; practically, it is a complex of historical events, often undesirable ones, which brings about this happy transformation.

Can one say that we use this word today in its classical sense? When people nowadays hear the word, 'revolution', they think of a change in property relations (generally collectivization) which may be brought about either by majority legislation or by a minority coup.

This concept obviously lacks meaning in present historical circumstances. For one thing, the violent seizure of power is a romantic idea which the perfection of armaments has made illusory. Since the repressive apparatus of a modern State commands tanks and airplanes, tanks and airplanes are needed to counter it. 1789 and 1917 are still historic dates, but they are no longer historic examples.

And even assuming this conquest of power were possible, by violence or by law, it would be effective only if France (or Italy or Czechoslovakia) could be put into parentheses and isolated from the rest of the world. For, in the actual historical situation of 1946, a change in our own property system would involve, to give only one example, such consequences to our American credits that our economy would be threatened with ruin. A right-wing coup would be no more successful, because of Russia with her millions of French Communist voters and her position as the dominant continental power. The truth is – excuse me for stating openly what every one knows and no one says – the truth is that we French are not free to make a revolution. Or at least that we can be no longer revolutionary all by ourselves, since there no longer exists any policy, conservative or socialist, which can operate exclusively with a national framework.

Thus we can only speak of world revolution. The revolution will be made on a world scale or it will not be made at all. But what meaning does this expression still retain? There was a time when it was thought that international reform would be brought about by the conjunction or the synchronization of a number of national revolutions – a kind of totting-up of miracles. But today one can conceive only the extension of a revolution that has already succeeded. This is something Stalin has very well understood, and it is the kindest explanation of his policies (the other being to refuse Russia the right to speak in the name of revolution).

This viewpoint boils down to conceiving of Europe and the West as a single nation in which a powerful and well-armed minority is struggling to take power. But if the conservative forces – in this case, the U.S.A. – are equally well armed, clearly the idea of revolution is replaced by that of ideological warfare. More precisely, world revolution today involves a very great danger of war. Every future revolution will be a foreign revolution. It will begin with a military occupation – or, what comes to the same thing, the blackmail threat of one. And it will become significant only when the occupying power has conquered the rest of the world.

Inside national boundaries, revolutions have already been costly enough – a cost that has been accepted because of the progress they are assumed to bring. Today, the costs of a world war must be weighed against the progress that may be hoped for from either Russia or America gaining world power. And I think it of first importance that such a balance be struck, and that for once we use a little imagination about what this globe, where already thirty million fresh corpses lie, will be like after a cataclysm which will cost us ten times as many.

Note that this is a truly objective approach, taking account only of reality without bringing in ideological or sentimental considerations. It should give pause to those who talk lightly of revolution. The *present day* content of this word must be accepted or rejected as a whole. If it be accepted, then one must recognize a conscious responsibility for the coming war. If rejected, then one must either come out for the *status quo* – which is a mood of absolute Utopia in so far as it assumes the 'freezing' of history – or else give a new content to the word 'revolution', which means assenting to what might be called relative Utopia. Those who want to change the world must, it seems to me, now choose between the charnel-house threatened by the impossible dream of history suddenly struck motionless, and the acceptance of a relative Utopia which gives some leeway to action and to mankind. Relative Utopia is the only realistic choice; it is our last frail hope of saving our skins.

INTERNATIONAL DEMOCRACY AND DICTATORSHIP

We know today that there are no more islands, that frontiers are just lines on a map. We know that in a steadily accelerating world, where the Atlantic is crossed in less than a day and Moscow speaks to Washington in a few minutes, we are forced into fraternity – or complicity. The forties have taught us that an injury done a student in Prague strikes down simultaneously a worker in Clichy, that blood shed on the banks of a Central European river brings a Texas farmer to spill his own blood in the Ardennes, which he sees for the first time. There is no suffering, no torture anywhere in the world which does not affect our everyday lives.

Many Americans would like to go on living closed off in their own society, which they find good. Many Russians perhaps would like to carry on their Statist experiment holding aloof from the capitalist world. They cannot do so, nor will they ever again be able to do so. Likewise, no economic problem, however minor it appears, can be solved outside the comity of nations. Europe's bread is in Buenos Aires, Siberian machine-tools are made in Detroit. Today, tragedy is collective.

We know, then, without shadow of a doubt, that the new order we seek cannot be merely national, or even continental; certainly not occidental nor oriental. It must be universal. No longer can we hope for anything from partial solutions or concessions. We are living in a state of compromise, i.e. anguish today and murder tomorrow. And all the while the pace of history and the world is accelerating. The twenty-one deaf men, the war crimininals of tomorrow, who today negotiate the peace carry on their monotonous conversations placidly seated in an express train which bears them toward the abyss at a thousand miles an hour.

What are the methods by which this world unity may be achieved, this international revolution realized in which the resources of men, of raw materials, of commercial markets and cultural riches may be better distributed? I see only two, and these two between them define our ultimate alternative.

The world can be united from above, by a single State more power-ful than the others. The U.S.S.R. or the U.S.A. could do it. I have nothing to say to the claim that they could rule and remodel the world in the image of their own society. As a Frenchman, and still more as a Mediterranean, I find the idea repellent. But I do not insist on this senti-mental argument. My only objection is, as stated in the last section, that this unification could not be accomplished without war – or at least without serious risk of war. I will even grant what I do not believe: that it would not be an atomic war. The fact remains, nevertheless, that the coming war will leave humanity so mutilated and impoverished that the very idea of law and order will become anachronistic. Marx could justify, as he did, the war of 1870 for it was a provincial war fought with Chassepot rifles. In the Marxian perspective, a hundred thousand corpses are nothing if they are the price of the happiness of hundreds of millions of men. But the sure death of millions of men for the hypo-thetical happiness of the survivors seems too high a price to pay. The dizzy rate at which weapons have evolved, a historical fact ignored by Marx, forces us to raise anew the whole question of means and ends. And in this instance, the means can leave us little doubt about the end. Whatever the desired end, however lofty and necessary, whether happiness or justice or liberty – the means employed to attain it represent so enormous a risk and are so disproportionate to the slender hopes of success, that, in all sober objectivity, we must refuse to run this risk.

This leaves us only the alternative method of achieving a world order: the mutual agreement of all parties. This agreement has a name: international democracy. Of course every one talks about the U.N. But what is international democracy? It is a democracy which is international. (The truism will perhaps be excused, since the most self-evident truths are also the ones most frequently distorted.) International – or national – democracy is a form of society in which law has authority over those governed, law being the expression of the common will as expressed in a legislative body. An international legal code is indeed now being prepared. But this code is made and broken by governments, that is by the executive power. We are thus faced with a regime of international dictatorship. The only way of extricating ourselves is to create a world parliament through elections in which all peoples will participate, which will enact legislation which will exercise authority over national governments. Since we do not have such a parliament, all we can do now is to resist international dictatorship; to resist on a world scale; and to resist by means which are not in contradiction with the end we seek.

THE WORLD SPEEDS UP

As every one knows, political thought today lags more and more behind events. Thus the French fought the 1914 war with 1870 methods, and the 1939 war with 1918 methods. Antiquated thinking is not, however, a French speciality. We need only recall that the future of the world is being shaped by liberal-capitalist principles, developed in the eighteenth century and by 'scientific socialist' principles developed in the nineteenth. Systems of thought which, in the former case, date from the early years of modern industrialism, and, in the latter, from the age of Darwinism and the Renanian optimism, now propose to master the age of the atomic bomb, of sudden mutations, and of nihilism.

It is true that consciousness is always lagging behind reality: History rushes onward while thought reflects. But this inevitable backwardness becomes more pronounced the faster History speeds up. The world has changed more in the past fifty years than it did in the previous two hundred years. Thus we see nations quarrelling over frontiers when every one knows that today frontiers are mere abstractions. Nationalism was, to all appearances, the dominant note at the Conference of the Twenty-one.

Today we concentrate our political thinking on the German problem, which is a secondary problem compared to the clash of empires which threatens us. But if tomorrow we resolve the Russo-American conflict, we may see ourselves once more outdistanced. Already the clash of empires is in process of becoming secondary to the clash of civilizations. Everywhere the colonial peoples are asserting themselves. Perhaps in ten years, perhaps in fifty, the dominance of Western civilization itself will be called into question. We might as well recognize this now, and admit these civilizations into the world parliament, so that its code of law may become truly universal, and a universal order be established.

The veto issue in the U.N. today is a false issue because the conflicting majorities and minorities are false. The U.S.S.R. will always have the right to reject majority rule so long as it is a majority of ministers and not a majority of peoples, all peoples, represented by their delegates. Once such a majority comes into being, then each nation must obey it or else reject its law – that is, openly proclaim its will to dominate. . . .

To reply once more and finally to the accusation of Utopia: for us, the choice is simple – Utopia or the war now being prepared by antiquated modes of thought. . . . Sceptical though we are (and as I am), realism forces us to this Utopian alternative. When our Utopia has become part of history, as with many others of like kind, men will find themselves unable to conceive reality without it. For History is simply man's desperate effort to give body to his most clairvoyant dreams.

A NEW SOCIAL CONTRACT

All contemporary political thinking which refuses to justify lies and murder is led to the following conclusions: (1) domestic policy is in itself a secondary matter; (2) the only problem is the creation of a world order which will bring about those lasting reforms which are the distinguishing mark of a revolution; (3) within any given nation there exist now only administrative problems, to be solved provisionally after a fashion, until a solution is worked out which will be more effective because more general.

For example, the French Constitution can only be evaluated in terms of the support it gives or fails to give to a world order based on justice and the free exchange of ideas. From this viewpoint, we must criticize the indifference of our Constitution to the simplest human liberties. And we must also recognize that the problem of restoring the food supply is ten times more important than such issues as nationalization or election figures. Nationalization will not work in a single country. And although the food supply cannot be assured either within a single country, it is a more pressing problem and calls for expedients, provisional though they may be.

And so this viewpoint gives us a hitherto lacking criterion by which to judge domestic policy. Thirty editorials in *Aube* may range themselves every month against thirty in *Humanité*, but they will not cause us to forget that both newspapers, together with the parties they represent, have acquiesced in the annexation without a referendum of Briga and Tenda, and that they are thus accomplices in the destruction of international democracy. Regardless of their good or bad intentions, M. Bidault and M. Thorez are both in favour of international dictatorship. From this aspect, whatever other opinion one may have of them, they represent in our politics not realism but the most disastrous kind of Utopianism.

Yes, we must minimize domestic politics. A crisis which tears the whole world apart must be met on a world scale. A social system for everybody which will somewhat allay each one's misery and fear is today our logical objective. But that calls for action and for sacrifices, that is, for men. And if there are many today who, in their secret hearts, detest violence and killing, there are not many who care to recognize that this forces them to reconsider their actions and thoughts. Those who want to make such an effort, however, will find in such a social system a rational hope and a guide to action.

They will admit that little is to be expected from present-day governments, since these live and act according to a murderous code. Hope remains only in the most difficult task of all: to reconsider everything from the ground up, so as to shape a living society inside a dying society. Men must therefore, as individuals, draw up among themselves, within frontiers and across them, a new social contract which will unite them according to more reasonable principles.

The peace movement I speak of could base itself, inside nations, on work-communities and, internationally, on intellectual communities; the former, organized cooperatively, would help as many individuals as possible to solve their material problems, while the latter would try to define the values by which this international community would live, and would also plead its cause on every occasion.

More precisely, the latter's task would be to speak out clearly against the confusions of the Terror and at the same time to define the values by which a peaceful world may live. The first objectives might be the drawing up of an international code of justice whose Article No. 1 would be the abolition of the death penalty, and an exposition of the basic principles of a sociable culture ('*civilisation du dialogue*'). Such an undertaking would answer the needs of an era which has found no philosophical justification for that thirst for fraternity which today burns in Western man. There is no idea, naturally, of constructing a new ideology, but rather of discovering a style of life.

Let us suppose that certain individuals resolve that they will consistently oppose to power the force of example; to authority, exhortation; to insult, friendly reasoning; to trickery, simple honour. Let us suppose they refuse all the advantages of present-day society and accept only the duties and obligations which bind them to other men. Let us suppose they devote themselves to orienting education, the press and public opinion toward the principles outlined here. Then I say that such men would be acting not as Utopians but as honest realists. They would be preparing the future and at the same time knocking down a few of the walls which imprison us today. If realism be the art of taking into account both the present and the future, of gaining the most while sacrificing the least, then who can fail to see the positively dazzling realism of such behaviour?

Whether these men will arise or not I do not know. It is probable that most of them are even now thinking things over, and that is good. But one thing is sure: their efforts will be effective only to the degree they have the courage to give up, for the present, some of their dreams, so as to grasp the more firmly the essential point on which our very lives depend. Once there, it will perhaps turn out to be necessary, before they are done, to raise their voices.

TOWARDS SOCIABILITY

Yes, we must raise our voices. Up to this point, I have refrained from appealing to emotion. We are being torn apart by a logic of History which we have elaborated in every detail – a net which threatens to strangle us. It is not emotion which can cut through the web of a logic which has gone to irrational lengths, but only reason which can meet logic on its own ground. But I should not want to leave the impression, in concluding, that any programme for the future can get along without our powers of love and indignation. I am well aware that it takes a powerful prime mover to get men into motion and that it is hard to throw one's self into a struggle whose objectives are so modest and where hope has only a rational basis – and hardly even that. But the problem is not how to carry men away; it is essential, on the contrary, that they not be carried away but rather that they be made to understand clearly what they are doing.

To save what can be saved so as to open up some kind of future – that is the prime mover, the passion and the sacrifice that is required. It demands only that we reflect and then decide, clearly, whether humanity's lot must be made still more miserable in order to achieve far-off and shadowy ends, whether we should accept a world bristling with arms where brother kills brother; or whether, on the contrary, we should avoid bloodshed and misery as much as possible so that we give a chance for survival to later generations better equipped than we are.

For my part, I am fairly sure that I have made the choice. And, having chosen, I think that I must speak out, that I must state that I will never again be one of those, whoever they be, who compromise with murder, and that I must take the consequences of such a decision. The thing is done, and that is as far as I can go at present. Before concluding, however, I want to make clear the spirit in which this article is written.

We are asked to love or to hate such and such a country and such and such a people. But some of us feel too strongly our common humanity to make such a choice. Those who really love the Russian people, in gratitude for what they have never ceased to be – that world leaven which Tolstoy and Gorky speak of – do not wish for them success in power-politics, but rather want to spare them, after the ordeals of the past, a new and even more terrible bloodletting. So, too, with the American people, and with the peoples of unhappy Europe. This is the kind of elementary truth we are liable to forget amidst the furious passions of our time.

Yes, it is fear and silence and the spiritual isolation they cause that must be fought today. And it is sociability ('*le dialogue*') and the universal intercommunication of men that must be defended. Slavery, injustice and lies destroy this intercourse and forbid this sociability; and so we must reject them. But these evils are today the very stuff of History, so that many consider them necessary evils. It is true that we cannot 'escape History', since we are in it up to our necks. But one may propose to fight within History to preserve from History that part of man which is not its proper province. That is all I have to say here. The 'point' of this article may be summed up as follows:

Modern nations are driven by powerful forces along the roads of power and domination. I will not say that these forces should be furthered or that they should be obstructed. They hardly need our help and, for the moment, they laugh at attempts to hinder them. They will then, continue. But I will ask only this simple question: what if these forces wind up in a dead end, what if that logic of History on which so many now rely turns out to be a will o' the wisp? What if, despite two or three world wars, despite the sacrifice of several generations and a whole system of values, our grandchildren – supposing they survive – find themselves no closer to a world society? It may well be that the survivors of such an experience will be too weak to understand their own sufferings. Since these forces are working themselves out and since it is inevitable that they continue to do so, there is no reason why some of us should not take on the job of keeping alive, through the apocalyptic historical vista that stretches before us, a modest thoughtfulness which, without pretending to solve everything, will constantly be prepared to give some human meaning to everyday life. The essential thing is that people should carefully weigh the price they must pay.

To conclude: all I ask is that, in the midst of a murderous world, we agree to reflect on murder and to make a choice. After that, we can distinguish those who accept the consequences of being murderers themselves or the accomplices of murderers, and those who refuse to do so with all their force and being. Since this terrible dividing line does actually exist, it will be a gain if it be clearly marked. Over the expanse of five continents throughout the coming years an endless struggle is going to be pursued between violence and friendly persuasion, a struggle in which, granted, the former has a thousand times the chances of success than that of the latter. But I have always held that, if he who bases his hopes on human nature is a fool, he who gives up in the face of circumstances is a coward. And henceforth, the only honourable course will be to stake everything on a formidable gamble: that words are more powerful than munitions.

BIBLIOGRAPHY

THIS bibliography has been prepared in consultation with the International Fellowship of Reconciliation and is based on the *Select List* from the *Bibliography of Books on War, Pacifism, Non-violence and Related Studies* compiled by William Robert Miller and published by the American Fellowship of Reconciliation in 1960. It has been supplemented and adapted for British readers by Daniel Bowles.

THE LIVING OF THE PACIFIST LIFE

Brittain, Vera. *Humiliation With Honour*. London: Andrew Dakers, 1942. A British mother's wartime letters to her son in the United States, reaffirming her pacifist faith in terms understandable to a fifteen-year-old.

—— *The Rebel Passion*. London: Allen & Unwin, 1964. A history of the International Fellowship of Reconciliation.

Fox, George. *Journal*. London: Pitman, 1905. The autobiography of the founder of the Religious Society of Friends (Quakers).

Gandhi, Mohandas K. *The Story of My Experiments with Truth: An Autobiography*. Ahmedabad: Navajivan, 1956. A self-portrait of the Indian leader which reveals the relationship between personal commitment and social action in his life.

Gillett, Nicolas (ed.). *Men Against War*. London: Gollancz, 1965. Accounts of Asoka, Bright, Ceresole, Gandhi, Hammarskjoeld, Penn, Smuts and Tolstoy.

Hassler, Alfred. *Diary of a Self-Made Convict*. London: Gollancz, 1955. The day-by-day account of a pacifist editor's imprisonment as a conscientious objector in World War II.

Jack, Homer A. (ed.). *The Gandhi Reader*. Bloomington, Ind.: Indiana University Press, 1956. A compact chronicle of the life and teachings of Gandhi, comprising articles by many writers including Bhave, Holmes, Nehru, Rolland, Tagore, and Gandhi himself.

Pickett, Clarence E. *For More Than Bread*. Boston: Little, Brown, 1953. A history of the American Friends Service Committee and its redemptive work, written by its Executive Secretary Emeritus.

Woolman, John. *Journal and Other Writings*. New York: Dutton, 1952. Spiritual depth and active social concern are closely related in the writings of this Quaker saint who was a progenitor of the anti-slavery movement in colonial America.

THE PSYCHOLOGY AND SOCIOLOGY OF ACTIVE LOVE

Fromm, Erich. *The Art of Loving*. London: Allen & Unwin, 1957. A psychoanalytic study of parental, fraternal, sexual and divine love. The author sees in mature, self-affirming and self-giving love 'the only satisfactory answer to the problem of human existence'.

Menninger, Karl and Jeanetta L. *Love Against Hate*. New York: Harcourt, Brace, 1959. A psychological study of man's basic conflicts.

Sorokin, Pitirim A. *Altruistic Love*. Boston: Beacon, 1950. A sociological study of types, factors, and techniques of moral transformation.

PRACTICAL PACIFISM AND NONVIOLENCE

American Friends Service Committee (publ.). *Speak Truth to Power*. Philadelphia: A.F.S.C., 1955. A Quaker analysis of power and international tensions, proposing nonviolent policies to meet these and examining the implications of such alternatives to military reliance.

Bondurant, Joan V. *Conquest of Violence*. London: Oxford University Press, 1958. An analysis of the theory and practice of Gandhian *satyagraha* as a means of conducting social and political conflict.

Case, Clarence Marsh. *Non-Violent Coercion*. London: Allen & Unwin, 1923. A pioneer study of religious non-resistance and nonviolent direct action by a capable and objective sociologist. Includes discussion of peace sects and conscientious objectors as well as of the early Gandhi.

Diwakar, R. R. *Satyagraha*. Chicago: Regnery, 1948. A concise, systematic outline of the origin, practice and prospects of nonviolence, by a disciple of Gandhi.

Gandhi, Mohandas K. *Satyagraha: Nonviolent Resistance*. Ahmedabad: Navajivan, 1958. A collection of Gandhi's writings on nonviolence.

Gregg, Richard B. *The Power of Nonviolence*. London: Clarke, 1959. A study and exposition of the method of nonviolent resistance, emphasizing psychological factors. Includes instructions for training and examples of the use of nonviolent techniques in recent history in Europe, Asia and the U.S.A.

Huxley, Aldous. *An Encyclopedia of Pacifism*. London: Chatto & Windus, 1937. A series of brief essays on aspects of war, militarism, munitions, and the pacifist answer. While much of the material is tied to issues that are now dead, much else remains that is pertinent today.

James, William. *The Moral Equivalent of War*. London: Peace News, 1963 (pamphlet). A proposal to harness men's aggressive impulses to constructive, peaceful purposes.

King, Martin Luther. *Stride Toward Freedom*. London: Gollancz, 1959. An authoritative account of the Christian nonviolent campaign by which Negroes in Montgomery, Alabama, ended segregated seating on buses in 1957.

King-Hall, Stephen. *Defence in the Nuclear Age*. London: Gollancz, 1958. From a non-pacifist perspective, a British naval officer discusses the relation of warfare and politics and, in the light of the nuclear-weapons stalemate, proposes nonviolent resistance as a substitute for these weapons.

Lonsdale, Kathleen. *Is Peace Possible?* Harmondsworth: Penguin, 1957. A scientist discusses problems of peace, freedom and justice in an era of expanding world population and technical development.

Miller, William Robert. *Nonviolence: A Christian Interpretation*. London: Allen & Unwin, 1964. An analysis of the philosophy and mechanics of nonviolence, with accounts of a wide range of examples of the use of nonviolence in past conflicts.

Muste, A. J. *Nonviolence in an Aggressive World*. New York: Harper, 1940. A discussion of the relevance of nonviolence to the political and economic situation of the United States before World War II.

Niebuhr, Reinhold. *Moral Man and Immoral Society*. London: Scribner's, 1933. A discussion of the dilemma of an absolute Christian ethic of love in a world of relativities, written when the author was a leading figure in the American Fellowship of Reconciliation.

Roberts, Adam, *et al. Civilian Defence*. London: Peace News, 1964 (pamphlet). A symposium on nonviolent methods of defence as alternatives to war, containing articles by Jerome Frank, Arne Naess and Gene Sharp.

Shidharani, Krishnalal. *War Without Violence*. New York: Harcourt, Brace, 1939. A participant in Gandhi's *satyagraha* campaigns describes and discusses these and other Gandhian programmes.

Sibley, Mulford Q. (ed.). *The Quiet Battle*. New York and London: Doubleday, 1963. Extracts concerning the theory and practice of nonviolent action from de la Boétie, Gandhi, de Ligt, Crook, Sharp, Luthuli, King, Hughan, etc.

Weaver, Anthony. *War Outmoded*. London: Housmans, 1960 (pamphlet). An introductory survey of the social mechanisms of war and the alternatives offered by nonviolence.

Weinberg, Arthur and Lila (eds.). *Instead of Violence*. New York: Grossman, 1963. An anti-war anthology containing extracts from 125 sources throughout history.

For further references

Peace News (publ.). *A Select Bibliography on Nonviolence*. London: Peace News, 1965 (pamphlet). A list, with annotations and cross-references, of 200 works on nonviolence and its applications.

RESOURCES IN PHILOSOPHY AND PSYCHOLOGY

Fromm, Erich. *The Sane Society*. London: Routledge & Kegan Paul, 1956. A psychoanalyst diagnoses the 'cultural neuroses' of our times and points the way to a society in which human love and creativity can flourish.

Huxley, Aldous. *Ends and Means*. London: Chatto & Windus, 1937. A discussion of contemporary and ideal societies in which war and violence are shown as the fundamental obstruction to progress from one to the other, since 'the means employed determine the nature of the ends produced'.

Thoreau, Henry David. *On the Duty of Civil Disobedience*. London: Peace News, 1963 (pamphlet). An essay that was influential in Gandhi's thought and action, avowing the primacy of moral judgement – and action based on it – over the prerogatives of the state.

THE RELIGIOUS WELLSPRINGS OF CHRISTIAN PACIFISM

Ferré, Nels F. S. *Christ and the Christian*. London: Collins, 1958. A Christology rooted in the Nicene Creed which, with its stress on the incarnation of divine love in the human Jesus, has potent pacifist implications.

Heard, Henry Fitzgerald. *The Code of Christ*. London: Cassell, 1943. A study of the Beatitudes as a Christian code of action directed toward the vision of God, in which peacemaking is seen as a culmination of the six preceding beatitudes which leads into the last two crucial ones.

Kagawa, Toyohiko. *Love, the Law of Life*. London: S.C.M. Press, 1930. A systematic presentation of the mysticism of a great Japanese Christian, dealing with the application of love in the major areas of human activity. Absolute pacifism emerges as an integral part of this way of life.

Kelly, Thomas R. *A Testament of Devotion*. London: Hodder & Stoughton, 1957. A spiritual guidebook that combines the mystical and the practical in religion.

Lassere, Jean. *War and the Gospel*. London: Clarke, 1962. A scholarly study, using resources in New Testament theology, by a pacifist minister of the French Reformed Church.

Macgregor, G. H. C. *The New Testament Basis of Pacifism*. London: Fellowship of Reconciliation, 1953. A textual study of the New Testament ethic and its bearing on the problem of war. The essay 'The Relevance of an Impossible Ideal' is included in this edition; this is Dr Macgregor's reply to Reinhold Niebuhr's critique of pacifism.

Raven, Charles E. *The Theological Basis of Christian Pacifism*. London: Fellowship of Reconciliation, 1952. Lectures on the relationship of belief to practice, in terms of the grace of Christ, the love of God and the fellowship of the Holy Spirit.

Rutenber, Culbert G. *The Dagger and the Cross*. New York: Fellowship, 1958. An exposition of Christian pacifism from the perspective of neo-Reformation theology.

Tolstoy, Leo. *The Kingdom of God and Peace Essays*. New York: Oxford University Press, 1936. A collection of writings reflecting Tolstoy's conversion to a life based on non-cooperation with evil and violence.

—— *The Law of Violence and the Law of Love*. London: Unicorn Press, 1959. Written shortly before his death, this is Tolstoy's spiritual 'last testament', expounding the need for individual commitment to Christ and criticizing the widespread superficiality of nominal Christianity.

CHRISTIAN PACIFISM AND THE CHURCHES

Bainton, Ronald H. *Christian Attitudes Toward War and Peace*. London: Hodder & Stoughton, 1960. A comprehensive historical survey of pacifism, the crusades, and the just war from pre-Christian antiquity to the nuclear age, by a distinguished church historian.

Cadoux, C. J. *The Early Church and the World*. Edinburgh: Clark, 1925. A scholarly examination of the Gospel and the writings of the Church fathers, showing how the pacifism of the early Church finally yielded to the demands of the state.

Heering, G. J. *The Fall of Christianity*. London: Allen & Unwin, 1930. An historical study of the Church, the state and war, with emphasis on the period from Constantine to the modern era.

Jones, Rufus M. (ed.). *The Church, the Gospel and War*. New York: Harper, 1948. A symposium of articles by famous English and American churchmen.

Muste, A. J. *Not by Might*. New York and London: Harper, 1947. An appraisal of the post-war international scene, with a proposal for the adoption of Christian principles as a radically new foreign policy for the United States.

Nuttall, Geoffrey F. *Christian Pacifism in History*. Oxford: Blackwell, 1958. Brief, documented studies of pacifism in the early Church, in the Middle Ages, in the sixteenth and seventeenth centuries, and in present-day England.

Windass, Stanley. *Christianity Versus Violence*. London: Sheed & Ward, 1964. A critical examination of the policies of the Church concerning war in the light of their historical development and the present international situation.

THE CONSCIENTIOUS OBJECTOR IN WARTIME

Brock, Hugh. *The Century of Total War*. London: Peace News, 1962 (pamphlet). A brief history of conscientious objection in Britain during World War I, and other anti-war civil disobedience, 1915–58.

Gray, Harold S. *Character 'Bad': The Story of a Conscientious Objector*. New York: Harper, 1934. Letters from prison giving an intimate account of why men became conscientious objectors in World War I, and how they stood up to the cruelties meted out to them.

Sibley, Mulford, and Jacob, Philip E. *Conscription of Conscience*. London: Oxford University Press, 1952. A comprehensive, informative, and objective study of American conscientious objectors during the period from 1940 to 1947.

Fay, Sidney B. *The Origins of the World War*. New York: Macmillan, 1930. A history of the real causes of World War I, showing the falseness of wartime propaganda.

Hamlin, C. H. *The War Myth in United States History*. New York: Fellowship, 1946. A minority report on the wars fought by the U.S. from 1776 to 1945, examining their causes and exploding the myth of the 'sole guilt' of the enemy in each case.

Nef, John U. *War and Human Progress*. London: Routledge & Kegan Paul, 1950. A comprehensive study of the debilitating effects of war on culture in all its aspects.

Simmons, Clifford (ed.). *The Objectors*. London: Gibbs & Phillips, 1965. A symposium on five conscientious objectors in World War II.

Toynbee, Arnold J. *War and Civilisation*. London: Oxford University Press, 1950. A compilation of extracts from Toynbee's *A Study of History,* showing that war has been the 'proximate cause of the breakdown of every civilisation which is known for certain to have broken down'.

MISCELLANEOUS

Myrdal, Gunnar. *An American Dilemma*. New York and London: Harper, 1944. An exhaustive, intelligently interpreted analysis of the cultural, social and economic situation of the Negro in the United States.

Paton, Alan. *Cry, the Beloved Country*. Harmondsworth: Penguin, 1958. A novel of the tragedy of racial friction in contemporary South Africa, valuable for its insight in depicting this type of human conflict.

SOURCES FOR BOOKS

Books can be borrowed in person or by post from:

The Commonwealth Collection, Llwyn-y-Gwcw, Merthyr Tydfil, Glamorgan. Duplicated list available.

Library of the Society of Friends, Friends House, Euston Road, London N.W.1.

Reconciliation Library, 3 Hendon Avenue, London N.3. Printed catalogue, 5s.

Housmans, Publishers and Booksellers, 5 Caledonian Road, London N.1, have a comprehensive stock of publications on all aspects of pacifism, nonviolence and peacemaking, and a reference collection of pamphlets published since 1914.

SOME CURRENT PERIODICALS

The Catholic Worker (39 Spring Street, New York City). A monthly newspaper that presents a Roman Catholic anarchist viewpoint which embraces pacifism.

Challenge (29 Great James Street, London W.C.1). Monthly newsletter of the Anglican Pacifist Fellowship.

Christian Action Newsletter (2 Amen Court, London E.C.4). A quarterly magazine emphasizing the campaign for nuclear disarmament and the struggle for human freedom in Africa.

Fellowship (Box 271, Nyack, New York). Published in two editions: a 36-page bimonthly issue containing articles, reviews, poetry, etc., ranging in content from theology to social analysis and factual studies on current issues; and a four-page semi-monthly Peace Information edition containing news and comment.

Gandhi Marg (Rajghat, New Delhi 1). A quarterly journal of Gandhian thought, featuring articles by writers from many countries as well as India.

Liberation (110 Christopher Street, New York 14, N.Y.). An independent monthly that frequently features articles on pacifism and its related concerns, such as nonviolence in racial conflict, experiments in community, political issues, etc., from a radical and secular viewpoint.

New Zealand Christian Pacifist (Box 2400, Wellington). Organ of the Christian Pacifist Society of New Zealand.

Our Generation Against Nuclear War (3510 rue Ste. Famille, Montreal 18, Quebec). An international quarterly journal containing articles on all aspects of the arms race, nuclear weapons, and opposition and alternatives to them.

The Pacifist (Dick Sheppard House, 6 Endsleigh Street, London W.C.1). Monthly journal of the Peace Pledge Union.

Pax Bulletin (37 Northiam, London N.12). Thrice-yearly comment from the Roman Catholic association, Pax.

The Peacemaker (10a Mount Ida Avenue, Melbourne E.3, Victoria). Published by the Federal Pacifist Council of Australia.

Peace News (5 Caledonian Road, London N.1). The international pacifist weekly newspaper, containing news, comment, articles, reviews, etc., reflecting a radical, chiefly secular outlook. Particularly features discussion on non-violence, peace action, military activities, international affairs, racial problems, education, films and the arts.

Peace Press (3 Hendon Avenue, London N.3). A twice-monthly international information service published by the International Confederation for Disarmament and Peace.

Reconciliation (9 Coombe Road, New Malden, Surrey). Monthly magazine of the Fellowship of Reconciliation which stresses religious questions and contains reviews of books of interest to pacifists.

Reconciliation Quarterly (3 Hendon Avenue, London, N.3). Published by the International Fellowship of Reconciliation; contains serious contributions to theological thought, assessment of political situations, examples of practical peace work and news of the Fellowship.

War Resistance (88 Park Avenue, Enfield, Middlesex). Quarterly organ of the War Resisters' International.

Two important new Penguin reference books

THE PENGUIN ENGLISH DICTIONARY

Containing more than 45,000 entries and specially prepared for Penguins by a team led by Professor G. N. Garmonsway of London University, this new dictionary places particular emphasis on current usage. Definitions, which include hundreds of post-war words and senses, are as direct and simple as possible, and a new and immediately understandable system is introduced as a guide to pronunciation. In all *The Penguin English Dictionary* makes an unrivalled catalogue of English words as used today in print and speech.

THE PENGUIN ENCYCLOPEDIA

This concise and authoritative new encyclopedia has been geared deliberately for use in the second half of the twentieth century. Articles by specialists, under more than 6,000 main headings, pay particular attention to the rapidly advancing areas of science and technology; but the arts and humanities have not been neglected. These simple, accurate, and intelligent explanations are likely to prove equally handy for the schoolboy, the student, and the family bookshelf. Specially commissioned for Penguins, this up-to-date work is remarkably comprehensive and fully cross-referenced. It will be followed by a gazetteer and a dictionary of biography.